Solidarity in Europe

D1322353

Solidarity in Europe is a comprehensive study of the idea of solidarity from the early nineteenth century to the present day. It covers social and political theory, Protestant and Catholic social ethics and the development of the concept of solidarity in eight European nations – Germany, United Kingdom, France, Italy, Spain, Sweden, Norway and Denmark. Steinar Stjernø examines how solidarity has been defined, and how this definition has changed since the early nineteenth century. He analyses different aspects of solidarity: what is the foundation of solidarity? Is it personal or common interest, 'sameness', altruism, religion, empathy or cognition? What is the goal of solidarity? How inclusive should it be? The book also compares the different concepts of solidarity in social democratic, Christian democratic, communist and fascist parties.

STEINAR STJERNØ is Professor of Social Work and Social Policy at Oslo University College. He has published a range of books on poverty, social welfare agencies and social policy.

Solidarity in Europe

The History of an Idea

Steinar Stjernø

CAMBRIDGE
UNIVERSITY PRESS

CAMBRIDGE UNIVERSITY PRESS
Cambridge, New York, Melbourne, Madrid, Cape Town, Singapore,
São Paulo, Delhi, Dubai, Tokyo

Cambridge University Press
The Edinburgh Building, Cambridge CB2 8RU, UK

Published in the United States of America by Cambridge University Press, New York

www.cambridge.org
Information on this title: www.cambridge.org/9780521605113

© Steinar Stjernø 2004

This publication is in copyright. Subject to statutory exception
and to the provisions of relevant collective licensing agreements,
no reproduction of any part may take place without the written
permission of Cambridge University Press.

First published 2005
This digitally printed version 2009

A catalogue record for this publication is available from the British Library

Library of Congress Cataloguing in Publication data
Stjernø, Steinar.
Solidarity in Europe : the history of an idea / Steinar Stjernø.
    p.   cm.
Includes bibliographical references and index.
ISBN 0 521 84394 4
1. Solidarity – History.   2. Solidarity – Europe – History.   3. Solidarity – Political
aspects – Europe.   4. Europe – Politics and government.   I. Title.
HM717.S85   2004
302′.14′094 – dc22   2004052680

ISBN 978-0-521-84394-2 Hardback
ISBN 978-0-521-60511-3 Paperback

Cambridge University Press has no responsibility for the persistence or
accuracy of URLs for external or third-party internet websites referred to in
this publication, and does not guarantee that any content on such websites is,
or will remain, accurate or appropriate.

Contents

Tables

Acknowledgements

This book grew out of a personal and professional interest in solidarity. I was twenty years old when in 1965 a friend, Tore Linné Eriksen, later a prominent Scandinavian scholar and activist concerned with African affairs, involved me in the campaign against the apartheid system in South Africa. Studies in political science brought me to educational training of those who were to work with the poor, the students of social work, and to research on poverty and social assistance. Parallel political commitment entailed both personal commitment to the development of the welfare state and strong interests in Third World issues. Thus, when in 2000 I finished my second electoral term as rector/president of Oslo University College and was entitled to a two-year sabbatical, I had the opportunity to pursue a project that combined research in social policy with my political commitment – to study the idea of solidarity.

I thank Oslo University College for the opportunity to pursue a topic with which I have been so long preoccupied, the School of Social Welfare, University of California, Berkeley, for receiving me as a visiting scholar and giving me excellent working conditions, and Universitá per Stranieri, Perugia for a grant that enabled me to improve my Italian.

This project would not have been possible without the assistance and professional service of the following libraries and archives: Labour Movement Archives and Library of Copenhagen, Stockholm and Oslo; UC Berkeley Library; Istituto di Gramsci, Istituto Lelio e Lisli Basso and Istituto Don Sturzo in Rome; The National Library of France; and first and foremost the Library of the Faculty of Business, Public Administration and Social Work, Oslo University College. I am also grateful to Professor Ana Guillen, University of Oviedo, Spain, for having provided the programmes of the Spanish socialist party. The Eurobarometer data have been provided by Norwegian Social Science Data Services (NSD), but the NSD has no responsibility for the analysis or interpretations of the data. The Research Council of Norway has given financial support to expert linguistic assistance.

I could not list all those who have given helpful comments and criticism, but some should be mentioned: Jonathan Bradshaw, Berge Furre, Bente Puntervold Bø, Nils Finn Christiansen, Erik Oddvar Eriksen, Tore Linné Eriksen, Valeria Fargion, Neil Gilbert, Geir Høgnsæs, Kåre Hagen, Aksel Hatland, Knut Halvorsen, Bjørn Hvinden, Asbjørn Johannessen, Knut Kjeldstadli, Dennis Lindbergh, Håkon Lorentzen, Wolfgang Merkel, James Midgley, Wim van Oorschot, Rolf Rønning, Josef Schmid, Sissel Seim, Mike Seltzer, Rune Slagstad, Reiulf Steen, Gunnar Stålsett, Stefan Svallfors, Lars Inge Terum, Dieter Rauch, Reimut Zohlnhöfer, Einar Øverbye, Klas Åmark. Tore Linné Eriksen and Mike Seltzer have both commented on content and corrected my English. Lawrence Young has generously improved my English, and John Taylor and Sheila Kane have done great work in the final linguistic corrections and copyediting. Thanks to all – and thanks to all those who contributed to the book as participants in discussions in seminars and conferences.

Abbreviations

ATTAC	The International movement for democratic control of financial markets and their institutions
CCD	Italian Christian Democratic Centre
CDU	German Christian Democratic Party
CDU	Italian United Christian Democrats
CPSU	Communist Party of the Soviet Union
CSU	German Christian Social Union (associated with the CDU)
DC	Italian Christian Democrats
DNA	Norwegian Labour Party
DS	Democrats of the Left (previously PCI and PDS)
FDP	German Free Democratic Party
FI	Forza Italia (Onward Italy)
ICFTU	International Confederation of Free Trade Unions
KrF	Christian People's Party
LO	Trade Union Congress (Norway and Sweden)
MRP	French Republican People's Movement
NATO	North Atlantic Treaty Organisation
NGO	Non-governmental organisations
NKP	Norwegian Communist Party
NPM	New Public Management
OECD	Organisation for Economic Development and Cooperation
PCE	Spanish Communist Party
PCF	French Communist Party
PCI	Italian Communist Party
PDS	Italian Party of the Democratic Left (previously PCI)
PP	Spanish People's Party
PPI	Italian People's Party
PS	French Socialist Party
PSI	Italian Socialist Party
PSOE	Spanish Socialist Workers' Party

SAP	Swedish Labour Party
SFIO	The French Section of the International Labour (later French Socialist Party)
SPD	German Social Democratic Party
SPÖ	Austrian Social Democratic Party
SV	Norwegian Socialist Left Party
UNICEF	United Nations International Children's Fund
US	United States
USPD	German Socialist Unity Party
WHO	World Health Organization
WTO	World Trade Organization

Introduction: to study the idea of solidarity

There are many reasons for studying the idea of solidarity. Early social philosophers and sociologists in the nineteenth century observed that traditional feelings of togetherness and social bonds were torn apart in the process that gave birth to modern society, and they saw solidarity as a means for social cohesion and integration. The international labour movement made class solidarity a slogan and a weapon against social and political adversaries. The welfare state is often seen as the result of a struggle for solidarity and the institutional expression of solidarity. In Catholic social teaching and Protestant social ethics, solidarity gradually became more important than charity. Thus, solidarity is a key concept in the social theory and in the modern political discourse of two of the main political traditions within European politics – social democracy and Christian democracy. The key position of solidarity in social theory and modern political discourse is a compelling reason to make the concept an object of study.

In addition, solidarity is a key concept in social policy research. Predominant classifications of welfare states make the degree of solidarity in social benefits and structure a distinguishing criterion. In his path-breaking book *The Three Worlds of Welfare Capitalism* Gösta Esping-Andersen links universalism to the socialist idea of solidarity (1990). The two kinds of parties studied in this book – social democratic and Christian democratic – were the political protagonists in the development of generous welfare states. Esping-Andersen's thesis is supported by Evelyne Huber and John D. Stephens in their book *Development and Crisis of the Welfare State* (Huber and Stephens 2001). In *The Politics of Social Solidarity*, Peter Baldwin investigates how solidarity between the working class and farmers was conducive to the introduction of a universal pension system, and how the willingness to share risks was crucial for this expression of solidarity (Baldwin 1990). However, as this study will show, it is one thing to establish the fact that a social alliance developed that led to a universal welfare state, with institutions that we today might see as an expression of solidarity; it is another to establish the fact that

1

actors and parties saw this social alliance as an expression of solidarity. This book asks the question *to what extent did actors and parties formulate their politics in the language of solidarity?*

Third, we shall see that the concept of solidarity is applied in both social theory and politics with different meanings and connotations. This book concludes that solidarity can most fruitfully be defined as the preparedness to share resources with others by personal contribution to those in struggle or in need and through taxation and redistribution organised by the state. It is not an attitude that is narrowly based upon self-interest. The self and its identifications have expanded significantly here, and political altruism finds expression. Solidarity implies a readiness for collective action and a will to institutionalise that collective action through the establishment of rights and citizenship. However, this definition is only one of many possible definitions. *Solidarity* is sometimes used as a nebulous concept that is not defined at all. Its use may be a subterfuge in political rhetoric to hide the fact that the *phenomenon* of solidarity is missing or on the decline in the real world. This tendency and the central position of the concept in social theory and in political discourse make it imperative to explicate different views, definitions and implications. The unclear and sometimes deceptive use of the term solidarity in political rhetoric makes communication complicated, and often creates misunderstandings, unfounded agreement and disagreement in political discourse and in everyday language. One of the tasks of social science should be to assist citizens and politicians, by improving communication and the possibility for improved reciprocal understanding. A study of the idea of solidarity might make communication and critical understanding easier to foster.

Finally, in an age of individualism, the idea of solidarity seems to be threatened and on the defensive. The triumph of capitalism and the expansion of markets and market ideology make collective arrangements and the ideas on which they are founded more precarious. The discussion about the welfare state can be understood as an attempt to answer the question – to what extent and in what way should society impose institutions and arrangements built upon solidarity? The growing ethnic plurality of Western Europe, the increase in xenophobic attitudes and the huge gap between the rich and the poor nations makes solidarity a burning global issue. Increased individualism and, in particular, the emphasis placed on the personal freedom to choose and mould one's own way in the world, challenge the traditional value of solidarity. Globalisation of the world economy directs our attention to the lack of corresponding political and legal institutions that might ensure some kind of solidarity. These challenges to the practice of solidarity in modern society are good reasons, in themselves, to make the concept of solidarity an object of closer inspection. Some might object that the implicit premise of this book is that solidarity is good. This is partly, but only partly, true. Although Leninist and fascist solidarity are briefly discussed, I do not discuss solidarity in deviant social groups, such as criminals and terrorists. Solidarity is not morally good *per se* – it is good only to the extent that its inclusiveness, goal and implications for the individual are morally acceptable.

The study of ideas

The study of political ideas has long been seen as old-fashioned in modern political science. Neighbouring disciplines, such as philosophy, history and – to some extent – literature, have expanded to fill the resulting gap. The history of ideas, an offshoot of the history of philosophy, with Aristotle as the founding father, took the lead in this endeavour.[1] In the past decades, the field was renewed by Foucault's contributions within modern discourse analysis, by Anglo-Saxon analytical philosophy of language, and by German conceptual history in the hermeneutic tradition. The study of political ideology, in the second part of this book, is inspired by the last two approaches.

The German historian Reinhart Koselleck is inspired by the hermeneutic tradition from Dilthey to Hans-Georg Gadamer. He has reached beyond this tradition as a historian preoccupied with social and political history and the analysis of conceptual change in political language. Koselleck, and his colleagues Ernst Brunner and Walter Conze, published an impressive seven-volume encyclopaedia, *Geschichtliche Grundbegriffe. Historisches Lexikon zur politisch-sozialen Sprache in Deutschland* in 1972 (Brunner, Conze and Koselleck 1972).

Koselleck argues that a profound change within classic themes took place from the middle of the eighteenth century. Old words began to acquire new meanings, and, with the passing of time, no longer needed to be explained (Koselleck 1972). The question is how best to understand the dissolution of the old world and the birth of the new modern world, and the conceptual changes that this transition brought about. How did old words change their meaning? The *Begriffsgeschichte* – conceptual

---

[1] Arthur Lovejoy's *The Great Chain of Being* in 1936 had for a long time a strong influence on the study of ideas (Wilson 1987). Lovejoy suggested that particular unit-ideas should be the focus of study. Individual authors, particular texts, classic or canonised, about ideas, doctrines or '-ism' were to be highlighted, without any need for a contextual approach. The next decades were dominated by the study of the texts of great writers, key ideas, doctrines, theories and '-isms'. For a history of the history of ideas, see Kelley (1990).

history – of Koselleck, and his colleagues, includes concepts that grasp the process of change that accompanied the political and industrial revolution. The transformation of society, during the period from 1750 to 1850, brings forth numerous examples of words and concepts that fall out of usage or change their meaning in usage. New concepts emerge as well, establishing a new way of talking about politics and society (Koselleck 1996). Many concepts were *democratised* in the sense that new classes and social groups began using them. Concepts were *temporalised* and given meanings that were associated with the time in which they were applied. Old concepts lost their general meaning and acquired a meaning coined by the present. New concepts and *-isms* appeared, to characterise new phenomena or to describe society in a new way. Expressions were *ideologised*, became more abstract, and aggregates were expressed in the singular, what Koselleck calls *Kollektivsingulare*, i.e. the concept of freedom instead of many freedoms, progress instead of progresses, etc. Finally, concepts were *politicised*. Concepts such as *democracy, citizen, equality, society* and *progress* acquired a new meaning that is more in accordance with the usage today. *Solidarity* was among these concepts, but it is not included in the 115 extensive analyses of basic concepts in the encyclopaedia, even if we do find an exposition of the concept of *Brüderlichkeit* – brotherhood or fraternity.

The British historian and philosopher Quentin Skinner is a representative of the Anglo–Saxon analytical philosophy of language tradition and the so-called Cambridge School. Skinner published his path-breaking study *The Foundations of Modern Political Thought* in 1980, but presented his methodological approach eleven years earlier, in the polemic article *Meaning and Understanding in the History of Ideas* (Skinner 1969; 1980). Another protagonist of the Cambridge School is J. G. A. Pocock. Skinner and Pocock have been inspired by one another, and both take John Austin's theory of speech-acts as their point of departure. Pocock has been preoccupied with the study of linguistics – how stable language structures and speech acts are repeated and modified in such a way that languages and vocabularies succeed one another. His objective is to study political language as a distinctive discourse, not in the Foucaultian sense, but as dynamic structures that are modified and changed. Words are given new meanings, taken out of one context and put into another (Pocock 1985; Richter 1995).

Four aspects of the debate about the study of concepts or ideas in the texts of Koselleck and Skinner are of interest for the study presented in this book. What should be the object of study? How should we conceive of the relationship between text and context? What should be the role (or possibility) of causal analysis? What is the relationship between the analysis of ideas and concepts and the analysis of discourses?

For Koselleck, the objects of study are basic concepts and their workings in history. These concepts are *indicators* and *factors*. They refer to (or indicate) specific historical phenomena, and they are factors in shaping and changing society. Examples of these basic concepts are central constitutional terms, key terms in the political and economic organisation of society, key concepts of political movements and their slogans, theoretical and other ambitious core concepts, and ideologies that constitute the space of action and the world of work (Koselleck 1996). Although it is necessary to distinguish between words and concepts, Koselleck sees the difference between them as a pragmatic one and the transition from word (or term) to concept operates on a sliding scale. Words and concepts are ambiguous, he argues. Words may become unambiguous, but concepts always remain ambiguous. 'A word becomes a concept when it implies the entire political and social context in which it is applied', he says. The materials used for the conceptual studies by Koselleck, and his colleagues, are encyclopaedias, dictionaries, handbooks and works of the language written during the period of time being studied.

Skinner, in his article *Meaning and Understanding in the History of Ideas*, argued that it is not possible to write about ideas without focusing upon the various agents who use the idea. Their various situations and their intentions are important elements for our understanding (Skinner 1969). Skinner seems to deny the utility of studying concepts over long time spans, as Koselleck has done and this study attempts to do. What should be studied is the political language of a defined and limited period, and to do this, it is necessary to analyse a range of political texts from that same period, he argues.

These different views about what should be the object of study seem less important when we come to the relationship between text and context. Skinner argues, that if we are to understand an idea, it will be necessary to understand the society in which the agent formulates that idea. The context is insufficiently understood when political, economic and other societal characteristics are not made clear. To speak (or write) is to perform a speech-act. We also need to understand what an agent is doing when he or she utters a statement. We need to know the intention of the agent when performing a speech-act and the force of that performance. We must distinguish between the *locutionary* aspect of a speech-act – which refers to the meaning of words and sentences – and the *illocutionary* aspect, which refers to the force of the statement. The illocutionary aspect determines whether or not the statement is meant to be a threat, an assertion, a challenge, etc. Finally, the *perlocutionary* aspect is the effect of the statement upon the person who listens or reads the statement or text. In practice, this means studying political ideas in light of their background in every relevant text that constitutes the linguistic context of an author, the texts to which the author relates, and the relevant social and political aspects of the society in which the author lives. This is an enormous ambition and makes it, as Skinner himself asserts, impossible to write the history of a concept in this strict sense. To take heed of this would mean to be restricted to in-depth studies of a limited time-period with few actors and make impossible comparative studies of long periods with many actors such as this study.

Koselleck argues in a similar but more careful way, that conceptual history should deal with the use of specific language in specific situations, within which concepts are developed and used by specific speakers. He insists that his main emphasis is more a history of the social structure than of linguistics. Concepts, of course, may be used and reused in varying ways. Variations in their use may be more or less frequent and more or less divergent from earlier meanings. Although these variations may be marginal or profound, linguistic recycling ensures a minimum degree of continuity. Conceptual history may resemble the history of ideas. Any assertion about continuity must be supported by evidence based upon concrete and repeated usage of the vocabulary (Koselleck 1989; 1996). Koselleck's project takes the middle ground *between* a history of words and a history of phenomena: it is neither one nor the other. 'Conceptual history has the convergence of concept and history as its theme', he says. The method includes an analysis of the different meanings of a concept (semasiological), a study of the different concepts that are used for the same phenomena (onomasiological), as well as a discussion of questions related to social and political phenomena and the human arts. His project avoids both seeing the history of ideas as an idealistic *Geistesgeschichte* and seeing it as merely a reflection of material processes. Here, Skinner and Koselleck seem to be close to each other.

Another issue to be discussed is the nature of explanation in the study of ideas. Koselleck is clearly more preoccupied with hermeneutic interpretation than with causal analysis and does not explicitly discuss causal explanation contra interpretive understanding. He emphasises that his method oscillates between semasiological and onomasiological questions and issues related to social and political phenomena and the human arts (Koselleck 1972). Skinner's preoccupation with the relationship between text and context does not imply a causal or determinative role for context. The social context is relevant only insofar as it conditions the interpreter's understanding of what constitutes the range of 'conventionally recognisable meanings' in that society. Thus, Skinner, too, shares a hermeneutic or interpretative stance rather than one professing causal explanation (Janssen 1985).

It should be clear from the discussion above that Skinner differs fundamentally from Foucault and his version of discourse analysis in asserting that individual authors of texts *do* matter. He does not – like Foucault – adopt an approach without subjects or agents, and he does not accept the view that individuals are prisoners within a discourse or language. Although Skinner recognises that we are all limited by the concepts available to us when we wish to communicate, he maintains that language constitutes a resource as well as a constraint (Skinner 1988). How else are we able to account for conceptual change? Conventions are challenged and concepts are either undermined or enriched and acquire new meanings, and subjects or agents *do* count in this process. The idea of discourse, in a more generic sense, is a necessary implication of Skinner's approach. The historian should primarily study languages of discourse and only secondarily the relationship between the individual contributions to those languages of discourse. Koselleck, too, sees his conceptual analysis as being compatible with discourse analysis in the generic sense. Each depends inescapably upon the other, he asserts. A discourse requires basic concepts in order to give expression to the content that is to be communicated. An analysis of concepts requires an understanding of linguistic and extralinguistic contexts, including those provided by discourses. Only by such knowledge of context can the analyst determine the multiple meanings of a concept, its content, importance and the extent to which it is contested (Koselleck 1996).

Michael Freeden, professor of politics at Oxford, has sought to integrate Anglo-Saxon analytical rigour with hermeneutics and *Begriffsgeschichte* and postmodern insights. He criticises Skinner for his 'individualist bias' and argues that insofar as tradition affects the formation of human, and political, ideas, the role of tradition cannot be rejected. Ideas as units do not need to be studied only in an idealistic way, as units living their own lives, Freeden argues. What matters is the way unit ideas are studied (Freeden 1996) – a view that this author endorses.

Freeden proposes an approach that he describes as eclectic and suggests a set of analytical concepts for the study of political ideology. *Main*, or *key* political concepts, as the one denoted here, are terms such as liberty, rights, equality, justice, power and democracy. *Ideologies* are distinctive configurations of such political concepts, but these concepts can be combined in indeterminate and unlimited configurations. *Morphology* denotes the internal ideational arrangements of an ideology. Freeden prefers morphology to *structure* because morphology is more apt to denote the flexible and pliant aspects of ideology and because he wants to evade the connotations of structure in modern social theory. Thus, morphology implies that there are no absolute boundaries between many ideologies so that ideologies may to a larger or lesser extent overlap one another.

Ideologies are three-tier formations: they consist of the components of a concept, a concept and a system of concepts. The building blocks of political ideologies are political concepts, and those consist of an ineliminable core and other variable components that are associated with the core in a limited number of recognisable patterns. Concepts may be *core*, *adjacent* or *peripheral* concepts. Marginal concepts are those that have little significance and are intellectually emotionally marginal to the core concept. Concepts may move from the core to the margin and vice versa. Concepts at the perimeter are additional ideas that link ideology, core and adjacent concepts to the external reality and make them relevant for social and political practice.

Freeden's emphasis on the fluidity, flexibility and potential hybrid character of any ideology is closely associated with his ambition to learn from hermeneutics and postmodernism. Concepts, language and meaning are socially constructed, he argues, but he seeks to escape from strong relativism by insisting that empirical analysis and data set some limits for how concepts, language and ideologies may be understood.

The contribution of this book

What, then, is the relevance of the discussion above for the study of the concept of solidarity in this book? First, I presuppose the necessity of discussing the social and political context within which change takes place when studying the change of a basic political concept such as solidarity. According to Skinner, such a study, ideally, should include the intention of the agent, the meaning of statements, their force and their effects upon listeners and readers. Second, I recognise that my own approach does not meet Skinner's methodological demands. His requirements are too strict for a comparative study addressing changes over a longer time-span. Conducting a study of many nations over more than one hundred years requires me to resign myself to a less than complete study of contextual factors. The intentions of authors and the force of their statements – not to mention the effects upon others of different statements made at different times and places – are requirements far beyond what is possible in a comparative project that covers more than one hundred years. On this matter, my study more closely resembles those of Koselleck and Freeden than those of Skinner. Besides that, I simply do not agree with Skinner that it is impossible to trace the development and change of basic ideas over long time-spans. To assert this is certainly not to imply that concepts or ideas are immutable units that can be studied without reference to their linguistic, social and political context, as Skinner maintains. However, I do agree that attempting to do so is an ambition that is not without its own risks. It will be necessary to limit the data to be studied and this will naturally entail the danger of misinterpretation. My defence for doing this is a pragmatic one. An exploratory approach, like my own, may be fruitful enough to yield something that others might criticise, revise or build upon.

Third, my ambition, but only to a limited extent, is that of Pocock; to study the full political language used by many political parties of the periods covered would represent too many actors over too long a period of time. Although I will comment on the different conceptual contexts of solidarity, my intention is not to analyse the conceptual changes of the other concepts within each context. My comments on the differing conceptual contexts of *solidarity* are made only to the extent necessary to understand the meaning of the different ideas of solidarity in the parties studied. In principle, it is necessary to study the existence or non-existence of languages that compete with or rival the language of solidarity in all periods. Again, because of the need to limit this work, this will be done solely for the last period under study in this book.

Fourth, this study might fill a lacuna in the work of Skinner, and those of his colleagues using a similar approach. Generally, as Melvin Richter has noted, they have concentrated on the ideas of individual theorists and have lacked interest in the political language of movements and parties, which is the focus of this study (Richter 1995). Besides that, most of their works have concentrated on periods before the nineteenth century, whereas my work seeks to map the development of the idea of solidarity and its relation to other key political concepts into our own time.

Fifth, as previously mentioned, the main source for what I consider to be the empirical part of this book – Part II – are party programmes, supported by party resolutions and articles and texts from party leaders and party theorists. The ambition is to identify semasiological and onomasiological aspects of the concept of solidarity in this material. Both Skinner and Koselleck have analysed a broader range of sources, although usually in a more restricted geographical area than the eight nations studied here. In the article in *Geschichtliche Grundbegriffe* about fraternity, and elsewhere in that work, Koselleck and his colleagues apply a wide range of texts, but it is not easy to determine their criteria for selecting those texts. The advantage of the specific and delimited criteria used in this study is that we may be more confident that what is studied is the establishment and change of specific *institutionalised* political concepts of solidarity.

Finally, my study is limited to the two types of parties that have declared solidarity to be a basic value. Some would argue that a study of solidarity should include conservatism and liberalism as well as parties who have declared themselves as respectively conservative and liberal. Conservatism has naturally entailed ideas about community, sometimes based on the family, an organic conception of society, or the nation, or constituted by the adherence to common religion or culture. Even some versions of liberalism, the ideology that has most strongly emphasised the value of individual autonomy, have introduced concepts that are related to solidarity. Michael Freeden has demonstrated that John Stuart Mill was preoccupied with concepts such as *sense of unity with mankind* and *feeling for the general good* (Freeden 1996). Even so, liberal and conservative parties have generally developed other political concepts and languages, and the need to delimit this work has made it impossible to include conservatism and liberalism as well.

In the first part of this book, I try to map the different concepts of solidarity that are found in the classic texts of sociology, in Marxist theory and in Christian religious doctrine. My intention here is to establish the structure of differing concepts of solidarity, as a heuristic device for the empirical study presented in Part II. References to contexts and intentions are few, and the danger of misinterpretation is greater here than in the second part. The authors selected are those who are generally considered to be protagonists within classic sociology, Marxist theory and Catholic and Protestant social ethics, in so far as they have contributed to the development of the concept of solidarity.

In the second part of this book, I trace the change in the ideas of solidarity in political parties in Western Europe. I try to better understand the changes that have occurred by discussing social and political contextual factors that may have contributed to such change. I seek to identify critical junctures in the process of change and contextual factors that influenced change. In the third part of this book, references to contexts are again few, except for general references to the shared political and social situation from the 1970s until today. My discussion here is concentrated upon the contributions made by established social theorists that have participated in the discussion about the concept of solidarity in the last few decades.

Method and material: parties and programmes

The study is about the history of an idea and not about the (perlocutionary) effects this idea has had on the political practice of these parties. Yet, the underlying and implicit premise for the choice of this research question is that *ideas count* – especially key concepts in parties where ideology has been important, as in the labour movement and, to a somewhat lesser degree, the Christian democratic movement. Of course, some general references to the effects of the idea of solidarity in politics are unavoidable. However, my approach will not provide any kind of picture of the role of the *phenomenon* of solidarity in those parties, nor of the use of the concept in daily political struggle. The relationship between language and ideology, on the one hand, and political practice, on the other, is a topic for research in itself (Skinner 1988). The language used in a party's programme and its political practice might be strongly correlated, positively or negatively, or not associated at all, although some research studies indicate that a large share of promises in programmes are kept (Rallings 1987). Strong use of *solidarity* in the rhetoric of a party might be associated with a politics based upon the phenomenon of solidarity, or it might compensate for the absence of that phenomenon in the party's political practice. Even so, when a political actor uses the concept of solidarity primarily to legitimate his or her own actions, that political actor's freedom of action will become restricted. He or she will find it far more difficult to act in a way that is obviously in conflict with language used to justify past actions.

There are three important elements that must be distinguished whenever a concept such as solidarity is to be studied. The first element is the *idea*, notion or concept of solidarity itself, which for the purposes of this book, will be used as synonyms. Solidarity is a word with diffuse meanings that may be expressed by the use of different terms or functional equivalents, such as fraternity, brotherhood, unity, community, etc. This onomasiological aspect of the concept of *solidarity* is problematic, but not to the same degree in different ideologies and different periods. In the classic Marxist period, the equivalents to the concept of solidarity are relatively easy to identify. They are brotherhood, fraternity, (class) unity, internationalism and the like. In modern social democratic and Christian democratic language it is more complicated; feelings of community or of interdependence may certainly be seen as equivalents, but what about identification with the common good, cooperation, charity, compassion, citizenship? Generally, I have not regarded the last group of concepts as functional equivalents to solidarity.

The second element is the *term* itself, which at some point in time came to be the common way to epitomise the idea and replace equivalents. When this happens, the different meanings of the concept need to be made clear. This is the semasiological aspect of the term *solidarity*. The third element is *context*. Ideas and terms must be understood in light of the situation in which they appear. The context is essential for understanding the particular meaning of the term being expressed. Three aspects of the context are important and should be distinguished. They are the conceptual context, the political context and the historical or structural context.

The conceptual context is the relationship between the concept of solidarity and other key concepts to which the concept of solidarity is associated in the texts studied. As we shall see, the meaning of the concept will vary in accordance with its integration within differing conceptual contexts or languages of solidarity. It will be necessary to analyse the idea of solidarity as it is expressed by functionally equivalent terms, how the term solidarity was introduced and later established as hegemonic among other equivalent concepts,[2] and the relationship between the concept and other key concepts in solidarity discourses. In addition, I will examine the extent to which other languages rival or compete with the language of solidarity in the most recent programmes. I shall use the terms *language* and *discourse* when referring to relatively stable relationships between key concepts such as solidarity, freedom, equality, etc.

The political context is constituted by the relationship to other political parties and by the strategic alternatives that are perceived. Who were the important actors and what alternatives did they face when they formulated their ideas of solidarity? The historical *or* structural context refers to economic, national and international constraints. This particular contextual element has created a range of dilemmas since this book is not a general political history of social democratic and Christian democratic parties. Historical analysis must be limited to what is necessary for understanding the different political contexts of solidarity rhetoric. But what is necessary? Some readers may find the historical analysis too extensive, while others may find it wanting in events or persons they consider crucial.[3]

Sheri Berman concludes her study of Swedish and German social democratic parties in the interwar period by directing attention to two factors that are especially important for ideas to be influential in politics – *carriers* and *institutionalisation* (Berman 1998). Carriers are key people – most often, but not always – party leaders who are able to make others listen. Carriers are able to make some ideas prominent, but if these ideas are to be enduring, they must be anchored and integrated in an institution

---

[2] This refers simply to other terms that have approximately the same meaning and are used in the same contexts as solidarity. Merton's famous concept *functional equivalent* referred to social structure and the alternatives or substitutes of a particular social structure serving the same function – see Merton (1957).

[3] For general expositions of labour movement history, I refer to Hobsbawm (1994) and Eley (2002).

or organisation. The carriers to be included in this study are people in formal leadership positions such as party leaders and prime ministers, and those who have been seen as being the leading theorists within the social democratic and the Christian democratic political traditions.

The ideologies and values presented by carriers may be institutionalised in two ways. A weaker form of institutionalisation is found when a party adopts a resolution that expresses the carrier's ideology or values. A stronger form is found when the carrier's ideology or values are integrated into the party programme. I have chosen to analyse platforms and electoral programmes as representative documents and indications of accepted party language and rhetoric.[4] *Platform* refers here to a text approved by a party congress and stating the general principles, theories and basic values of the party. The functions of a platform are generally to depict the *Weltanschauung* – the world-view – of the party, the analysis of capitalist society, its laws and mechanisms and long-term goals, the strategy of the party and the relationship between classes. A platform *describes*, *explains* and *prescribes* action. *Programme* refers to a text that is usually more concrete, containing formulations about short-term goals, reforms and proposals. Programmes are usually election programmes. Sometimes, programmes were – and are – adopted at party congresses and may contain statements that are found in platforms.[5] Both serve as a means of political agitation and commit elected representatives to the policy of the party. Generally, platforms should be considered a more reliable source for the analysis of ideology. However, since many election programmes start and/or end with a paragraph expressing general ideology, the line between the two types of document is often somewhat blurred, making it necessary to include both types in the analysis. To

[4] Ian Budge and his colleagues have studied party programs from 1945 to 1998 with a quantitative approach, and they describe the role of programmes in different nations and parties in more detail. Budge and his colleagues are mainly preoccupied with the general left-right dimension in politics – see Budge, Robertson, and Hearl (1987) and Budge *et al.* (2001).

[5] In the British Labour Party and the Swedish Social Democratic Party, the party's national executive body has, more often than not, adopted election programmes. Parties sometimes use the term *manifesto* as a synonym for *programme*. The same practice has been adopted in this text. In the Marxist–Leninist tradition, the distinction between electoral programme and platform is somewhat problematic. Communist parties usually approved *theses* at their congresses. Those documents analysed the political situation, at home and abroad, and formulated strategy and tactics for the years to come. Theses were closely scrutinised by party leaders and representatives from other communist parties, and were often the subject of much discussion. Thus, for PCF and PCI, it has been necessary to study theses approved by party congresses. Finally, although less systematically, I have looked at congress resolutions to substantiate or revise conclusions reached in the analysis of platforms, programmes and theses.

simplify, the plural form *programmes* will refer to election programmes and party platforms.

In the Marxist – and later the Marxist–Leninist – tradition, platforms and programmes have been generally considered to be important documents that must be scrutinised meticulously before approval, to ensure that a correct analysis was being made. In the social democratic tradition, programmes have been regarded more as *a test* of the ability to transform theory and principles into practice. This is why social democrats have taken programme writing very seriously (Wright 1999). These are good reasons for picking platforms and programmes as representative key documents. However, there are obviously some problems connected with this method. First, since illiteracy was widespread in the last part of the nineteenth century, oral agitation and speeches may have been more important than written party documents. Second, platforms and electoral programmes were often simple and terse documents. Ideology and principles were seldom elaborated from the 1870s until the turn of the century. With the increasing influence of Marxism, however, that was soon to change.

Part II of this book is about *programmatic* beliefs. They are a complex of ideas lying between a comprehensive ideology and a particular political position. Like ideologies, programmatic beliefs are abstract and systematic and marked by the ambition to integrate assertions, theories and objectives. Programmatic beliefs provide general frames for political action, without specifying in concrete terms what should be done to realise the goal mentioned.[6]

Programmes and political texts are usually differentiated in terms of style. Their contexts and audiences are different. They express distinct political languages and constitute pieces of rhetoric. Rhetoric, here, denotes the art of prose and does not imply that what is said is not meant. It is used here about speech or writing that is intended to be effective and persuasive. In this text, language and rhetoric are used as synonyms.

Some linguists consider the special style of programmatic texts to be propagandist – a style that aims at reinforcing or changing existing basic values while at the same time provoking political action. The style is often emotive, filled with values and vague enough to address the largest possible audience (Bergsdorf 1983). Although there is some truth in this description, we should not exaggerate the instrumentality of political platforms and programmes. They are not created simply to communicate a

---

[6] Berman understands programmatic beliefs as providing guidelines for practical activity and the formulation of solutions to everyday problems (Berman 1998). I find that this establishes too strong a link between programmatic belief and action and prefer to view this as more open.

message from the party to the voter. Such documents are negotiated texts; they are scrutinised by leaders, committees and members, to ensure that they contain the correct language and symbols. There is a general concern that they must not arouse suspicion of ideological confusion, or worst of all, direct heresy. They may represent a compromise between different internal factions with different opinions about what political concepts and language are most suited to present the party. They are often a compromise between the wish to convince and influence the electorate, adjustments to anticipated reactions from voters, and the need to reassure party activists about adherence to party traditions. Ideological concepts are seldom, if ever, introduced into such texts by accident. Ideological concepts have their own constituencies and are introduced into platforms and programmes after careful consideration. Preoccupations with 'correct' theory have varied between parties and nations. In general, debates were more heated on the continent than in Scandinavia and in the United Kingdom.

Third, studying a large number of programmatic texts from different nations and in different periods does not reveal the motivations and strategies of those actors who formulated those texts. Parties appear as relatively homogeneous as internal conflicts and discussion in parties are disguised. Compromises that make texts inconsistent remain hidden. Besides, ideology and political ideas that are vivid, but not well articulated might be neglected. Although programmes are scrutinised and discussed thoroughly before they are adopted, *solidarity* may also appear or not appear accidentally in early programmes. Hence, we should be somewhat careful when interpreting the appearance or non-appearance of the term in that phase. However, reliability has been increased by comparing across time and countries, by studying congress resolutions and speeches and articles of leaders and theorists from the same period. Finally, one might argue that a comparative study of the idea of solidarity in the labour movement should have included a comparative study of this idea in the trade unions of different nations as well. However, a line had to be drawn. In any case, because of the central position of programmes, especially in the labour movement, these objections are not strong enough to making programmes a main source of the following study (see also Svallfors 1996).

The selection of political parties has been based upon several criteria. First, only parties that have declared solidarity as a basic value have been included. These are labour movement parties and Christian democratic parties. As mentioned above, liberal and conservative parties have not been preoccupied with the idea of solidarity and have consequently not been included. The special role of fascism has forced me to make an exception and I have included two fascist parties that rose to power in the interwar period – the Italian and the German. Right-wing populist or nationalist parties have sometimes had their own ideas of solidarity, but these have not been included because they have not been as influential in the development of the concept of solidarity and because they do not constitute any kind of continuity in its use. The rise of right-wing populism in recent years may be a good reason to include such parties. However, in most nations they have not risen to the size and influence of the other parties included here, and some restrictions had to be placed on the scope of this work.

Second, it has been important to include parties in nations where different ideological tendencies have been predominant. The German SPD has been considered a model for early social democracy and has influenced the social democratic parties of Sweden, Norway and Denmark. The British Labour Party represents another tradition, and the socialist parties of Southern Europe, a third distinct ideological tradition within the European labour movement.

Third, the parties included should be large or influential in their countries. Although these parties changed from being *socialist* to *social democratic* at different points in time, I shall use these terms as a description of them. I have included the communist parties in Italy and France, which have been the two largest communist parties in Western Europe. The selection of Christian democratic parties is discussed in Chapter 8.

Aspects of solidarity

We may analytically distinguish (and question) four aspects of the concept of solidarity:

* What is seen as the basis or foundation for solidarity?
* What is the objective or function of solidarity?
* How inclusive is it – who is included and who is excluded?
* How strong is the collective orientation – to what degree does it allow for individuality and individual freedom?

The self and its identifications constitute the foundation for feelings of solidarity. The continuum of self and its identifications can be seen as moving from 'I' to 'All'. The most narrow category is referred to as *self-interest*, but, even here, the self is seldom completely isolated and identifies with a restricted group sharing some common interest. The recognition of *sameness*, of belonging to a larger group or community, characterises the next category on the continuum. A feeling of interdependence can constitute the basis for solidarity with others. Political or religious affiliations are a further expansion in the identification of the self with others.

Finally, a more universal category is reached, and an altruism encompassing all human beings finds expression. Each category on this continuum, based on the self and its identifications, will have its own objectives and its own boundaries for including or excluding others.

The *goal* or *objective* of solidarity can be to realise certain personal interests that are not possible to attain without establishing a relationship to others. It can be to increase strength and influence in confrontation with an adversary. Also, community with other human beings can be a goal in itself – eventually associated with an idea about what constitutes a good society.

Should solidarity be limited to one's own family, or should it encompass the local community, one's profession, one's class, one's nation or the whole world? Does it encompass only men or are women fully included? Is it reserved for people of a particular ethnic origin or is it for people of all races? The self and its identifications raise the distinction between 'we' and 'the others', always a central theme in social theory. I am particularly interested in how political programmes have formulated the relationship between those who were included and those who were excluded. I want to *map* the progressive enlargement of solidarity, from including only workers, to including also members of other classes (peasants, fishermen etc.), other people living in the Third World, immigrants, etc. Finally, solidarity may be characterised by a weak or a strong collective orientation.[7] This refers to the degree in which an individual is expected to submit to collective interests and understandings. It is about the preparedness to relinquish personal autonomy and the freedom to choose other ways of acting than those that are expected and desired by the group. In particular, my interest here is to determine when, and to what extent, socialist parties recognised that solidarity and individual freedom might contradict or come into conflict with one another. When does the autonomy of the individual appear in party programmes?

Thus, solidarity entails two core themes in social theory – the relationship between an 'I' and its identifications with a 'we', and the relationship between a 'we' and a 'they'. Almost all examples of solidarity imply inclusion and exclusion and a consideration of the relationship between the freedom and autonomy of the individual and the individual's

---

[7] The term *very strong* has been used when it is argued that individual freedom should be suppressed or sacrificed for the sake of solidarity; *strong* when emphasis is placed on the collective, and individual freedom has not been made an issue; *medium* when the relationship between the collective and individual autonomy constitutes a dilemma, and a compromise that preserves individual freedom is seen as being necessary; *weak* when individual freedom is more important than solidarity. Finally, the term *none* has been used when collective solidarity is not attributed any value at all.

Table 0.1 *Examples of how different aspects of solidarity may be configured*

Aspect	Example 1	Example 2	Example 3	Example 4
Foundation	The self identifies and recognises common interests with a small number of others	Recognition of 'sameness', the self identifies with others in a larger community	The self extends its identifications to others sharing a political ideology or a religious affiliation	The self identifies universally with all others/ Altruism Empathy
Objective	Realise common interests	Create and sustain community and feelings of togetherness	Strengthen class feelings and identifications; realise the will of God	A good society or world
Inclusiveness	Restricted to a small and specified number	All those who are deemed the 'same' (the race, the nation, etc.)	The class or the class alliance All believers	All human beings
Collective orientation	Strong: individual autonomy readily submits to common interests			Weak: the individual preserves its autonomy

preparedness to subordinate that freedom and autonomy to the group.[8] This discussion of solidarity can be summarised in the following way (see Table 0.1).

As we shall see, aspects of solidarity may be found in differing configurations. The aspects may be clustered the way they appear in the examples above, or be mixed together in varying ways creating different constellations and categories.[9] As a result of this variability, there are many different concepts of solidarity. The concept of solidarity may be purely descriptive, normative or include a mixture of descriptive and normative elements. It may imply inclusion and exclusion, or only inclusion.

[8] A fifth aspect might have been added – expectations of obligations and duties. Different concepts of solidarity often contain explicit or implicit ideas about the duties of individual members of the collective, reciprocal obligations, etc. However, the sources applied in this study – see above – seldom make this a theme, and consequently I have left this aspect out of the analytical scheme.

[9] Not all contributors have treated all four aspects explicitly and, consequently, their ideas do not always fit neatly into our scheme. For instance, some theorists have been less preoccupied with the *objective* than with the *function* of solidarity. This will be indicated in the tables applied.

It may embody utilitarian characteristics or altruistic ones, or both. We find the concept of solidarity as a political concept in history, and in our own lives, as well as being an analytical concept in sociology, and a normative one in social philosophy – and as a mixture of political, normative and analytical elements in all three.

Previous research

Despite the significance of the concept of solidarity in political debate, few have bothered to make a theoretical or empirical investigation of the concept in recent years. It is also rather striking how seldom the concept of solidarity is included in the index of books and reports within the social sciences. In the few instances when this does occur, the references offer scant and general formulations without providing a definition or very much discussion. However, the interest is growing and contributions to the analysis of the idea of solidarity may be classified into four groups: studies contributing to the history of the idea, to sociological theory, to modern social theory, and to empirical sociological analysis.

First, a renewed interest in the historical roots of the concept of solidarity has surfaced in recent years, especially in Germany. The German social scientists, Andreas Wildt, Kurt Bayertz and Rainer Zoll, and the Swedish social scientist, Sven-Eric Liedman, have traced the historical and philosophical roots of the concept.[10] Their contributions have inspired and aided this work. Second, there are interesting contributions within social philosophy, particularly from Jürgen Habermas and a few others participating in this tradition.

Third, most contributions are found in sociology. This is not surprising, since a main current within sociology has tried to answer Georg Simmel's question: what makes society possible and what constitutes social order? Some would argue that social order, social cohesion and solidarity are strongly related phenomena. A large number of authors have discussed Durkheim's two concepts of solidarity. A contribution, in this tradition, has been made by Bryan Turner and Chris Rojek, in *Society and Culture: Principles of Scarcity and Solidarity.* They have contributed to the understanding of solidarity as a sociological concept, but their theme is more concerned with the social order in general than with the idea of solidarity in particular (Turner and Rojek 2001). Michael Hechter's *Principles of Group Solidarity* represents a pioneer work in trying to develop a rational

---

[10] See Wildt (1998), Bayertz (1998), and Bayertz (1999), Liedman (1999), and Zoll (2000). Note Wim van Oorschot and Aafke Komter's discussion of different concepts of solidarity in sociological theories, which inspired me to look into Weber's ideas – see Oorschot and Komter (1998).

choice theory of solidarity, and Patrick Doreian and Thomas Fararo have edited a book that furthers Hechter's work (Hechter 1987; Doreian and Fararo 1998).

Fourth, sociology and political science have seldom made empirical investigations of the idea of solidarity. But here, too, we find a growing interest in recent years in empirical investigation of the idea of solidarity. The Danish sociologist Søren Juul's *Modernity, Welfare and Solidarity*, was published during the final phase of my work. It discusses concepts of solidarity in sociology and social theory and gives an extensive empirical analysis of survey data from Denmark about individual attitudes of solidarity with family, friends, neighbours and foreigners (Juul 1997). On the basis of a Dutch survey, Wim van Oorschot has analysed attitudes of solidarity in terms of welfare arrangements, and John Gelissen has done the same on the basis of survey data from eleven countries in Western Europe (see Oorshot 2001; Arts 2001).

However, political science has not contributed very much to the study of solidarity. I have found no analysis of the idea of solidarity in political theory, even if Habermas' contributions might as well be classified as political theory, with the exception of, in Germany, Hauke Brunkhorst's *Solidarität. Von der Bürgerfreundschaft zur globalen Rechtsgenossenschaft* and a few contributions in an anthology edited by Kurt Bayertz (Bayertz 1998; Brunkhorst 2002). Brunkhorst is inspired by Luhmann's systems theory and the communicative theory of Habermas, and finds the roots of the modern idea of solidarity in Roman civil law, in Jewish and Christian ideas of fraternity, in the idea of friendship in Aristotle, and in the republican ideas of the French revolution. He asserts that solidarity is one of the few concepts of moral thought that can be reconciled with a model of political community based upon the state. The main strength of Brunkhorst's contribution is his exposition of the *precursors* of the concept of solidarity in ancient Greek philosophy, in Jewish and Christian belief and in the republican tradition. However, he does not follow the development of the concept in the nineteenth and twentieth centuries. The labour movement concept of solidarity is only briefly mentioned and the Catholic concept is absent.

Neither Brunkhorst nor any of the other authors mentioned above provide an empirical and comparative approach to the study of the development of *different concepts* of solidarity in European politics. By and large, the studies mentioned above take the concept for granted. They do not dismantle the concept or identify its different aspects. They do not analyse the different meanings of solidarity in the different political traditions of Western Europe, nor have they investigated how the concept has developed and changed within these different traditions. They have not systematically discussed the *validity* of the different ideas of solidarity.

In exploring the concept of solidarity in nineteenth century France, J. E. S. Hayward noted that the 'survival of a concept is generally only secured at the price of an intellectual odyssey in the course of which it is transformed out of all recognition' (Hayward 1959). This book documents a journey where the concept of solidarity was transformed, if not out of all recognition, then to have different connotations in terms of the four aspects mentioned above.

This study finds great variation in the ideas of solidarity, from the beginnings of its usage in Western Europe. We will follow the different strands within social theory and Western European politics and discover how different theoretical, political and religious traditions have created and developed their own understandings of the idea of solidarity. We will see how the *term* solidarity eclipsed other terms and how the concept has changed within Western European political discourse. Finally, we will see what the concept of solidarity means today. My ambition is to analyse and contrast the different ideas of solidarity and to determine *how* and *why* those ideas developed. In so doing, I will identify the significant *actors* in this process and differentiate between their varying *contexts*.

Guidance for the reader

Today *solidarity* is a key concept in three different types of discourse: the academic discourse of social scientists and social philosophers, the political discourse of social democratic and socialist ideology, and the Christian discourse of social ethics. At the same time, the extent of the phenomenon of solidarity, in our contemporary Western societies, is a frequently discussed issue. Readers might be interested in one or more of these topics. As a consequence, I have tried to compose this book in a manner that would allow for an intelligible reading for those who only choose to read selected chapters.

The first part of this book analyses the idea of solidarity in three different traditions. Chapter 1 analyses the conception of solidarity in social theory and I trace the concept of solidarity from its appearance for the first time, in early nineteenth-century France, in the works of Charles Fourier, Pierre Leroux and Auguste Comte. Chapter 2 follows the development of the political concept of solidarity as it was developed in Marxist and socialist theory in the last part of the nineteenth and the first decades of the twentieth centuries. Chapter 3 traces the development of a Catholic concept of solidarity, by analysing papal encyclicals, and proposes a modern Protestant concept of solidarity. The different ideas of solidarity are summarised in the conclusion to Chapter 3.

The second part of this book is composed of a series of empirical investigations. Chapter 4 analyses the process that made *solidarity* a key concept in social democratic ideology by studying the role of solidarity in platforms and election programmes of various socialist parties from their establishment in the late nineteenth century up until today. Chapter 5 concentrates on the four aspects of solidarity mentioned above and discusses the concept of solidarity within social democratic parties in a comparative perspective.

Chapter 6 analyses the idea of solidarity in three Christian democratic parties: the Catholic Italian DC; the German CDU, an interconfessional Catholic and Protestant party, and, finally, the Norwegian Christian People's Party, Lutheran. Those who are not interested in all three of these parties will be able to selectively concentrate their reading on the national party preferred. However, I would recommend the last part of this chapter to all readers of this book. Here, the social democratic and the Christian democratic concepts of solidarity are compared and contrasted. Chapter 7 draws the attention to the modern *languages* of social democratic and Christian democratic solidarity and discusses other key concepts to which solidarity is linked in the programmes of these parties.

The third part of this book is about the idea of solidarity in social theory and the prospects for solidarity in the first decades of the twenty-first century. Chapter 9 returns to social theory and discusses some of the main contributions to the discourse on solidarity in modern social theory, left-wing and critical theory and modern – and critical – Catholic and Protestant theology. The chapter concludes with a proposal for a modern concept of solidarity. Chapter 10 sketches briefly, and some might say too hastily, the challenges to solidarity in our modern world. Finally, I raise and address the following question: how does individualisation, class fragmentation, consumerism and globalisation affect the phenomenon of solidarity in contemporary Western society?

Part I

Three traditions of solidarity

1   Solidarity in classic social theory

The phenomenon of group loyalty and sharing resources existed long before the idea of solidarity developed. The core social units of precapitalist society were the family and the extended family. Ties of kinship were the basis for reciprocal loyalty, constituting specific duties and moral obligations. Moral norms required family members to help each other, remain together and defend each other against external threats and hazards. Outside the bounds of family in feudal society, peasants would help one another in the fields or when building houses. In some countries during the nineteenth century peasant solidarity developed a sophisticated cooperative movement that protected against the hazards of life and the growth of a market economy. Craftsmen established guilds that controlled the recruitment of apprentices, organised education and established security funds for their members (Christiansen 1997). Neighbours sometimes helped one another with food and money, when untimely death disrupted the household economy. Help with funeral expenses and looking after the neighbours' children, were not uncommon practices. The historian Knut Kjeldstadli has called the pre-working-class solidarity of the nineteenth century 'the community of ordinary people' (Kjeldstadli 1997). This involved an exchange of favours and services and reciprocal help between people. This behaviour was an everyday practice, the fulfilment of the widespread belief that 'if I help you then you will help me, if and when the need arises'.

The obligation to reciprocally assist one another existed in preindustrial societies and was based on common identity and a feeling of sameness with some, and of difference to others. These feelings were created by the cleavages of preindustrial society (Bartolini 2000). The cleavages followed cultural as well as functional lines of conflict, long before the class conflict was strong enough to predominate.

Historically speaking, the phenomenon of solidarity existed before the idea was formulated. The idea existed before the term became widespread, and the term was in general use before its modern meaning had developed. A Christian idea of *fraternity* was developed in the early days of the Christian era, and was coined to identify and parallel the close relationships within the family to the development of community between Christian friars. A political idea of *fraternity* or *brotherhood* developed during the French revolution, and France was the birthplace of the *term* solidarity as well. In the first part of the nineteenth century, French social philosophers reflected upon the period of social and political unrest in the wake of the revolution. At the same time, they witnessed the early development of capitalism and the increasing influence of liberalism. These experiences prompted French social philosophers to find a way to combine the idea of individual rights and liberties with the idea of social cohesion and community. Here, the concept of solidarity was seen as a solution. The concept was a broad and inclusive one and it aimed at restoring the social integration that had been lost. In Germany, where Marxism became an early and dominating influence in the labour movement, the concept of solidarity developed later and was adapted to express the need for cohesion and unity in the working class and in the labour movement. This idea was more restricted, since it referred solely to workers, and more inclusive, since workers across national borders were included. It did not aim at integration and it implied conflict and divisiveness (class conflict) as well as unity. In the latter half of the nineteenth century, Catholic social teaching inspired a third tradition of solidarity. Within Protestantism, the development of an idea of solidarity did not take place until after World War II.

In this and in Chapters 2 and 3, we will see how the idea of solidarity was developed in these three areas – classic sociology, socialist theory and Christian social ethics. The first objective is to trace the historical origins of the concept in social theory. The second is to map out how key contributors to classic sociology, the socialist tradition and to Christian ethics have configured the aspects of solidarity differently. In this way, different conceptions of solidarity will be explicated and used as a referential framework for the empirical study of the idea of solidarity in political parties in succeeding chapters.

Prelude: from fraternity to Charles Fourier and Pierre Leroux

If there is a precursor for the term solidarity, it is the concept of *fraternity* or *brotherhood*, which points to the close relations and the feelings of belonging that exist within the family and extends this understanding to other voluntary associations and groupings. The history of this concept begins when a relationship between people outside the family is referred to by analogy as a relationship between brothers. According to the *Geschichtliche Grundbegriffe*, the concept of fraternity was occasionally used in the ancient Greek and Roman worlds, but played a more significant role in the early Christian era. The Christian idea of brotherhood was a constitutive one for communities of friars. In the Middle Ages, the Christian idea of brotherhood was applied to the more mundane and profane relationships between men of the same profession, such as merchants, artisans and apprentices. In this way, the concept developed and changed, referring to the community and the cohesion of a social group. To a great extent, the concept lost its religious connotations (Brunner, Conze and Koselleck 1972). During the Enlightenment, the continuing process of secularisation further contributed to this development.

French lawyers already applied the term *solidarité* in the sixteenth century, referring to a common responsibility for debts incurred by one of the members of a group (Hayward 1959). The term was included in Napoleon's famous legal code, the *Code Civil*, in 1804. The transformation of the legal concept of solidarity into a political concept seems to have begun in the latter half of the eighteenth century. French historians of language have noted that revolutionary leaders, such as Mirabeau and Danton, occasionally used the term solidarity with a meaning that transcended the legal concept (Zoll 2000). During the revolution of 1789 the Jacobins made *fraternité* a key concept together with *freedom* and *equality*. Feelings of brotherhood were to be a means of realising equality, and the Jacobins established *societies of brotherhood* among revolutionaries to achieve the goals of the revolution. Fraternity or brotherhood came to denote a feeling of political community and the wish to emphasise what was held in common. Occupational differences and differences in the financial status of revolutionaries were downplayed, and the concept was part of the practical programme implemented to change society and its institutions. Brotherhood had now become a political concept that was close in its meaning to the concept of solidarity that would develop in the nineteenth century and become hegemonic in the twentieth century.

Andreas Wildt argues that the concept of solidarity was not politicised until the 1840s (Wildt 1998). He does not, however, concretise the criteria for what he would call a political concept. If *politics* means activities to influence the decisions of the state or activities of the state, we may discern a political concept of solidarity in Charles Fourier's *Theorie de l'Unité*. Charles Fourier (1772–1837) is often considered a forerunner of socialism. In 1821, he published this voluminous work in which he describes a utopia – *The Phalanx* – consisting of 1500 to 1600 people living and working together in harmony in common households (Fourier 1822a) and (Fourier 1822b). Here, *solidarity* is used in four different ways. First, there is the principle of insurance, the legacy of the *Code Napoleon* concerning the common responsibility of a group of people for insurance and the repayment of debt. Second, there is the preparedness to share resources with people in need. Third, there is the more general application to describe a feeling of community – *solidarités socials* and *solidarités collectives*. Fourth, there is Fourier's argument for the introduction of a guaranteed minimum income and for family support. He used *solidarity* to refer to public support for families and male providers in need – *la garantie familiale solidaire* (Fourier 1822b). The second and third ways of using the term *solidarity* are similar to the ways in which the concept is used today. These meanings were included in the meaning *solidarity* came to have in the Marxist and socialist tradition in the next hundred years. The fourth meaning has clear political implications and is close to the association between solidarity and the welfare state that is found today.

Fourier recognised the tension between collective organisation and individual freedom, but assured his readers that his harmonious utopia would allow for individual freedom because its members would own property and stock, and would use this ownership as a basis for the freedom of choice. In other words, class differences would still exist. Contrary to the commonly held assertion, one might argue that Fourier's ideas do not qualify him to be seen as a forerunner of socialism. What did inspire socialists later on were Fourier's fierce attacks upon competition, commerce, family life and capitalist civilisation.[1]

We might say, with Skinner, that the illocutionary force of Fourier's concept of solidarity was not strong. The concept was applied casually, it was not well defined or thoroughly discussed, and it disappeared from his later texts (Liedman 1999). Fourier's compatriot, the typographer, philosopher and economist, Pierre Leroux (1797–1871) was the first to elaborate on the concept of solidarity in a systematic way when he published *De l'Humanité*, in 1840 (Leroux 1985 (1840)).[2] Leroux was a pre-Marxian communist, and he later claimed – in *La Grève de Samarez* (1859) – that he was the first to introduce the concept of solidarity and the concept of socialism in philosophy (Leroux 1979 [1859]).

---

[1] For an early critique see Gide (1901). As a whole, the very extensive writing of Fourier is characterised by a strange combination of acute observations, peculiar speculations and detailed fantasies about society and his own prescriptions for utopia, i.e. detailed architecture and equipment in the rooms of the *Phalanx* (Fourier 1876).

[2] Leroux was elected to the Constituent Assembly in 1848 and later reelected to the Legislative Assembly. For a presentation of Leroux, see Peignot (1988).

This may be true, but only if we accept the idea that Fourier had not contributed to philosophy some years before, which is a matter of some controversy. There is no doubting that Leroux made an important contribution to the transforming of the legal concept of solidarity into a social concept.

Leroux's point of departure was his criticism of three other positions – Christian charity, the idea of a social contract as a foundation for society, and the conception of society as an organism. He criticised Christian charity for being unable to reconcile self-love with the love of others, and for considering the love of others an obligation, and not the result of a genuine interest in community with others (Leroux 1985 (1840)). Besides that, equality played no role in Christian charity, he complained. He wanted to supplant the concept of charity with the concept of solidarity, arguing that the idea of solidarity would be a more able one in the struggle for a justly organised society. He rejected Hobbes' and Rousseau's idea of a social contract, and saw the social contract as a misconceived notion because it presupposed an atomised view of the individual. Finally, he denounced the organic conception of society because he feared that this way of understanding social life would result in authoritarianism (Le Bras-Chopard 1992).[3]

Leroux conceived solidarity primarily as a relationship. Society was nothing but the relationships between the human beings that constitute a people. Socialism, Leroux wrote, is the organisation of greater and greater solidarity in society. Leroux's concept of solidarity was more social than political, and he did not believe that solidarity should constitute any rights for citizens, or that it should intend to influence the decisions or the activities of the state – (cf. also Wildt 1998). These two pre-Marxian concepts of solidarity are summarised in Table 1.1.

Compared to Fourier, Leroux brought the discussion of solidarity closer to the ideas developed in the classic works of sociology. Whereas Fourier's concept was very restricted and limited to his proposed utopia, the *Phalanx*, Leroux broadened the foundation and the inclusiveness of the idea of solidarity. At the same time, he tried to balance his position between an atomised view of the individual, in liberalism, and the authoritarian potential of the idea of society as an organism.

---

[3] Leroux understood society as based upon the triad of family, property and homeland. The problem for him was that the relationships between the three were not well organised. The family was based on the authority of the father, and property was based on man himself being a property. Thus, property served to oppress the proletariat. He argued for reforms and hoped that the bourgeoisie could be persuaded to implement peaceful changes. In this respect, Leroux's ideas, like those of Fourier, had a certain utopian flavour.

Table 1.1 *Fourier's and Leroux's conception of solidarity*

	Foundation	Objective	Inclusiveness	Collective orientation
Fourier	The household/ the *Phalanx*	Harmony	Very restricted (members of the Phalanx)	Medium: personal autonomy is preserved through private property
Leroux	Similarity Identification with others	Improved social relationships	Broad: the entire society	Medium: not made into a theme, but there is a general criticism of authoritarianism

A follower of Fourier, Hippolyte Renaud, brought the political idea of solidarity to broader public attention in 1842 with the pamphlet *Solidarité*. It was a very popular item and was reprinted several times (Wildt 1998; Liedman 1999). Although we might say that the immediate perlocution-ary effect was strong, this concept of solidarity was naïve and based upon the world-wide diffusion of Fourier's idea of a *Phalanx*, with people living in harmony and happiness.

During the 1840s, the term solidarity spread to Germany and England. It was adopted and developed by socialists in the upheaval in France in 1848. After this revolution the term was definitely accepted as a political concept, even if the end of the Second Republic in 1852 relegated the concept to obscurity again for some years. It did not reemerge again as an important concept until Leon Bourgeois and the middle-class *solidarists* revived it in the 1880s, often with reference to the ideas of Leroux (Le Bras-Chopard 1992).

Comte: time, continuity and interdependence

Concern about the idea of solidarity was part of a wider discourse con-cerning the constitution of social order and society. This preoccupation with social order must be understood in light of the development of cap-italism in Western Europe in the nineteenth century. Modern capitalism had disruptive effects upon local communities and family ties. Rapid urbanisation, the crisis within the Austro-Hungarian Empire, and the growth of anti-Semitism were inducements for sociologists to be partic-ularly concerned about social order and social integration (Turner and Rojek 2001). The fragility of the phenomenon of solidarity was part of the general concern about the conditions of society and the precarious-ness of social integration. Although Fourier and Leroux had introduced the concept of solidarity in the first decades of the nineteenth century, it was the father of positivism, Auguste Comte, who brought the concept of solidarity into sociology.

In his book *Système de politique positive* published in 1852, Auguste Comte opposed the increasing influence of individualist conceptions of economy and production and the accompanying *laissez-faire* ideology in the first part of the nineteenth century (Comte 1973 (1852)). His ambition was to formulate a 'religion of humanity'[4] that would create an altruistic system of discipline that would be able to tame egoistic instincts. The individual personality was not to be sacrificed, only subordinated to the social concerns that would promote social advancement.

Comte was preoccupied with the integrative mechanisms of society. The first is embodied in the different roles taken by women. According to Comte, there are three kinds of social functions in society – reflection or intellectual activities, moral affections and practical activities. Different groups fulfil these functions. The main provider of reflection is the priesthood, whereas women are the main providers of affection, and practical leaders of activity. The problem is that these groups focus in an unbalanced way on intellect, affection and practical achievements in life. The priesthood tends to underestimate feelings, while women tend to exaggerate their importance. This creates serious inconvenience and disturbs the general harmony of society. Women's integrative function is found in their three different roles as mother, wife and daughter. These are, at the same time, three different modes of solidarity: *obedience*, *union* and *protection* – corresponding to the three forms of altruistic instinct, *veneration*, *attachment* and *benevolence* (Comte 1973 (1852)).

The second integrative mechanism is *continuity*, according to Comte. The special mark of human society is the faculty of cooperation between generations. Human society is characterised by subjective bonds and the continuity between generations. Humanity accumulates and capitalises upon the resources of previous generations, and man is fundamentally a being that is conditioned by *time*. Time makes possible the transmission of collective experiences and resources, and this ability of humankind distinguishes it from all other forms of life. Man is not simply an economic being determined by the material aspect of the social structure. In the long run, culture imprints itself on the collective and contributes to improving the human condition, Comte argued.

The idea of solidarity is included together with his concept of continuity. Solidarity follows from continuity and is an important factor in social

---

[4] Comte defined *religion* as a state of complete harmony peculiar to human life – a state when all parts of human life were ordered in their natural relation to one another and where reason and emotion were balanced and integrated.

life. 'Continuity, not Solidarity, is the great moving force of man's destinies, especially in our modern times', wrote Comte (1973 (1852)). Our interdependence in the past develops bonds that make us more interdependent in our present social organisation. We are dependent upon the past for its accumulation of experiences and resources, and we are dependent upon others in our own day for the production of goods and services. Because wealth is created by the effort of many, the individual is not free to use his wealth as he pleases. Wealth is always entrusted to someone tacitly for a social purpose. Comte directed attention to two aspects of the division of labour. On the one hand, he saw the division of labour as an expression of human solidarity. On the other hand, in the new industrial society that was developing the division of labour was also a source of disorganisation. It could not be considered the foundation of the unity between human beings (Cingolani 1992). These were aspects of the division of labour that Durkheim would elaborate on fifty years later.

The third integrative mechanism for Comte was *the religion of humanity* – a common set of values and ideas. Only this could produce personal unity and integrate reason and feeling within each individual, and create social unity between individuals. Affection based upon reflection unites men universally in the same feelings and in the same beliefs, and in this way restores harmony in society.

Comte's criticism of the *homo economicus* in *laissez-faire* ideology did not lead him to collectivism or communism, which he thought ignored both natural and affective differences. Thus, Comte's positivism represented a third alternative between utopian liberalism and utopian communism. In hindsight, his theories about the location of the affections, reason and practical ability, about the belief in the homogenising effect of reason and intellect, and his ambition to create a harmonious society without contradictions or conflicts, are easily dismissed. But his emphasis upon interdependence and upon our debts to previous generations are ideas that were built upon in the decades to come.

Leon Bourgeois further developed Comte's theories about the *debt* owed to previous generations (see Chapter 4). Theories about interdependence were formulated in the social ethics of German Catholicism, and later made explicit in papal encyclicals from the latter part of the nineteenth century. In Germany in 1887, Ferdinand Tönnies developed his famous ideal types, *Gemeinschaft* and *Gesellschaft* or the distinction between community and society (Tönnies 1957). According to Tönnies, the development of capitalism made community weaker so that it gradually was replaced by *society*. Traditional social ties and personal relationships were weakened and economic rationality and a means–end orientation replaced cooperation and feelings of community.

Although *the term* solidarity is not always used, other classic sociologists such as Simmel, Durkheim, and Weber were concerned about the fragility of this phenomenon. Living at a time when liberalism was triumphant, they searched for mechanisms that would constitute social order and an integrated society. Simmel captured this search in the formulation of the title of his famous essay, *How Is Society Possible?* There were, of course, different proposals in answer to this challenge. Some noted the role of religion as the social cement of traditional society. Others found that solidarity should be considered the social fundament, and that solidarity was a prerequisite for the survival of society (Juul 1997).

Durkheim: social norms and shared values

The most famous and probably the most cited work in classic sociology on solidarity is Emile Durkheim's *The Division of Labour in Society*, published in 1893. Being part of the French tradition from Leroux and Comte, Durkheim's work represented a continuing dialogue with, and critique of liberalism, and the theory of a social contract in the writings of Hobbes, Locke, Spencer and others. Hobbes' view of *force* as an integrative mechanism in society did not pass unnoticed. The dissolution of traditions and social bonds that he observed in his own day persuaded him to formulate the basic question of sociology: *What holds society together?* His answer was that society was not a product of rational calculation, self-interest or social contract. Relationships based upon self-interest are the least stable of all. 'Today it is useful for me to unite with you, and tomorrow the same reason will make me your enemy', he said (Durkheim 1984 (1893)). Society is based upon social norms, shared values and rituals, and solidarity is one of the normative mechanisms that integrate members of society, he insisted.

Durkheim distinguished between two forms of solidarity, *mechanical* solidarity in a traditional society, and *organic* solidarity in a modern society. Mechanical solidarity develops in a simple and homogeneous society with a low degree of differentiation. People are linked together by their *sameness* in living conditions, life-styles, common culture and beliefs and by religion and rituals. According to Durkheim, all human beings have two kinds of consciousness, an individual consciousness that is characteristic of the person, and a common consciousness shared with all other members of society. In a traditional society, the latter form of consciousness is dominant within each individual. Durkheim's concept of mechanical solidarity integrates a material and a subjective element. Solidarity is strong in traditional society, because people *are* alike and because they *think* alike.

Contrary to traditional society, modern society is characterised by a high degree of occupational specialisation and social differentiation. According to Durkheim, citizens are not tied together by tradition and inherited social norms but by their interdependence created by the increased division of labour and specialisation. Modern society produces great differences in living conditions, culture and ideology. The increased division of labour reduces the space available for common consciousness, and individual consciousness becomes more dominant. *Organic* solidarity refers to the factual interdependence in modern society where occupational differences create a complex interdependence between the activities of different producers.

Durkheim is somewhat unclear about the relationship between mechanical solidarity in traditional society and organic solidarity in modern society. In some of his writings, he argues that the first simply disappears as a consequence of the increasing division of labour. At other times, when he argues in more detail, he maintains that the two forms of solidarity are, in fact, facets of the same social reality. Our common consciousness continues to exist in modern society, but it is a reduced entity. The advance of our individual consciousness has had this effect.

What worried Durkheim was that the process of weakening mechanical solidarity might leave a moral vacuum that would not automatically be filled. When mechanical solidarity is reduced, social life will suffer if a new form of solidarity does not take its place. Social progress does not consist of the dissolution of social life, but rather, on the increasing unity in society, and the only mechanism that can produce this is the division of labour, he argued. Because the increasing division of labour increases interdependence and the need for interaction and collaboration, law and morality will develop too. Human consciousness and morality are shaped by the influence of others in the group in which we take part. Law and morality represent the bonds that bind individuals to one another and to society. Morality is the source of solidarity, and morality is 'everything that forces man to take account of other people, to regulate his action by something other than the prompting of his own egoism . . .' (Durkheim 1984 (1893)).

Durkheim believed that the new organic solidarity of modern society would develop only if certain conditions were met. The division of labour would only produce solidarity if it were allowed to develop spontaneously. For Durkheim, this meant that all that prevented the free development of individual talents and abilities must be altered. The distribution of social functions should correspond to the distribution of natural abilities, and no obstacle should prevent an individual from obtaining a position commensurate with his talents. Thus, the established order had to be changed so that the lower classes gained access to new functions in society. This was a question of justice for Durkheim. 'Justice is the necessary accompaniment to every kind of solidarity', he said – a formulation that Habermas would repeat one hundred years later (see Chapter 9). Grave social inequities would compromise solidarity. Modern society strives to reduce inequality as much as possible by helping in various ways those who are in a difficult situation. The equality between citizens is becoming ever greater and this development should continue, he argued.

Durkheim's pioneering contributions reflecting upon the concept of solidarity brought to light a range of themes and issues that continue to be discussed in social theory: the relationship between similarity and difference, and the relationship between solidarity, justice and equality, the law as an integrating force, the phenomenon of increasing individualism, and the loosening ties within the family, in other groups, and in the traditions of the local community. All of these issues have been made subjects of discussion for social theorists including Habermas, Luhmann, Giddens and others. Some elements of his theories are close to the social democratic concept of solidarity that Bernstein formulated and that came to be reflected in social democratic party programmes in the twentieth century.

Table 1.2 summarises the two conceptions of Durkheimian solidarity. Social interaction, in a broad sense, is a necessary precondition for both of Durkheim's concepts of solidarity. Social interaction refers here to social relationships and ties that bind individuals to groups, organisations and ultimately to society itself. The number and the intensity of these ties are important and variable characteristics of social interaction. They will determine how inclusive or how exclusive solidarity in society will be. Durkheim observed an inverted relation between the degree of solidarity and the degree of openness towards foreigners. 'The weaker solidarity is, that is, the slacker the thread that links society together, the easier it must be for foreign elements to be incorporated into societies' (Durkheim 1984 (1893)).

Durkheim 1 and Durkheim 2 differ in terms of two of the aspects emphasised here – the foundation of solidarity and how these forms of solidarity encompass the relationship between the collective and the individual. In a society dominated by mechanical solidarity, common consciousness 'envelops our total consciousness, coinciding with it at every point. At that moment our individuality is zero. In such a society, the individual does not belong to himself – he is literally a thing belonging to society' (Durkheim 1984 (1893)). Durkheim 2 – organic solidarity – entails a more complicated relationship between the collective and individual freedom. In modern society individuals are at once more autonomous and

Table 1.2 *Durkheim's mechanical and organic conceptions of solidarity*

	Foundation	Objective/ function	Inclusiveness	Collective orientation
Durkheim 1/ Mechanical solidarity characterises traditional society	Social interaction, homogeneity, social norms, shared values, rituals, and common consciousness	Social integration	All who are alike (this can be understood broadly or narrowly)	Medium/strong: common consciousness dominates individuality
Durkheim 2/ Organic solidarity characterises modern society	Social interaction, social norms, interdependence is a consequence of the division of labour, and complementary diversity characterises society	Social integration	Varying: dependent on the number and intensity of ties that link the individual to groups, organisations, and ultimately to society	Medium/weak: the dilemma is acknowledged, accepted and discussed Defence of liberal democracy

more mutually interdependent. The ever-increasing division of labour transforms social solidarity and creates the conditions for the individual's greater freedom and greater dependence upon others.[5]

Durkheim did not return to the distinction between mechanical and organic solidarity (Crow 2002). He continued, however, to be preoccupied with two issues that are of interest here – how shared beliefs unify society and the relationship between solidarity and individualism. He continuously insisted that common interests were not sufficient to sustain cohesion in a social group, and that a common moral code was also necessary. Emotions reinforce the commitment to solidarity, and the more intense social relationships are, the stronger the sentiments of solidarity. What he called *moral individualism* was necessary to counteract the destructive effects of egoistic individualism. This presupposes the fact that people are sufficiently aware of their interdependence and their mutual obligations in complex modern societies. This understanding would reinforce solidarity in society. He continued to worry about the dangers of egoistic individualism. He sought different ways to bond the individual to society, but he was afraid that the bonds he observed were not strong enough to restrain egoism (Seigel 1987).

[5] Durkheim seems to postulate this relation, as he maintains that 'there exists a social solidarity arising from the division of labour. This is a self-evident truth, since in them [modern societies] the division of labour is highly developed and engenders solidarity' (Durkheim 1984 (1893)).

Max Weber: solidarity in social relations

Max Weber formulated a view of solidarity that differed from the group-oriented and integrative conception of Durkheim in two respects. First, whereas the tradition of Comte and Durkheim was mainly preoccupied with solidarity as a macro phenomenon binding society together, Weber was more inclined to conceive solidarity as a phenomenon at the micro level (Oorschot and Komter 1998). Solidarity was a special type of social relationship. In this respect, he picked up the thread from Leroux. Second, Weber saw solidarity as arising from the pursuit of economic advantage and honour. Thus, solidarity did not only integrate, but was divisive as well (Bendix 1960). Here, as in other respects, Weber's contributions are a result of the closer dialogue with his compatriot, Marx, than with the French tradition from Comte to Durkheim.

Weber's concept of solidarity follows from his key ideas; *social action, social relationship* and *social class*. For Weber, action is social when the individual gives it a subjective meaning that takes account of the behaviour of others and lets this orient his own course of action (Weber 1978 (1922)). Social relationships develop when many actors take into account the actions of others. A relationship is symmetrical when each actor gives it the same meaning. However, complete symmetry, Weber maintained, is rare. Generally, the parts of a social relationship orient their actions on a rational basis (*zweckrational – goal-oriented*), but in part they are also motivated by their values and sense of duty. Weber's exposition here is not explicitly about solidarity, but we may deduce that in a social relationship based on solidarity we will find varying degrees of identical reciprocal expectations and a mixture of instrumental and normative elements.

Although we find the term *solidarity* only sporadically in Weber's text, *Economy and Society*, the idea of solidarity is integrated in his discussion about the relationship between *Vergemeinschaftung* and *Vergesellschaftung*. *Vergesellschaftung* refers to actions based upon considerations of material advantage or utility, irrespective of personal or social considerations. He contrasts this with actions that are invoked by a sense of solidarity with others. Thus, *Vergemeinschaftung* represents communal actions based upon a sense of community, including those that are shared by family members, friends, professional colleagues or other social groups with an internal code of conduct (Oorschot and Komter 1998). As a general rule, Weber maintains, a communal relationship based upon *Vergemeinschaftung* is associated with another based upon *Vergesellschaftung*. Most often, elements of both types of action are interwoven, as all individuals are engaged in the pursuit of both ideal and material interests. Parents

Table 1.3 *Weber's conception of solidarity*

Foundation	Objective	Inclusiveness	Collective orientation
Interests and honour Norms and duties	Realise interests and increase power	Restricted: social groups or professions	Medium? Not explicitly formulated, acceptance of dilemma

look to the economic aspects of the marriage of their children, and even businessmen develop a sense of ethical conduct in their commercial relationships. The feeling of being part of a 'we' characterises the experience of solidarity. For Weber, every 'we' presupposes a 'they', those others who are excluded from the group or community.

In his analysis of social status and social stratification, Weber describes how social groups combine honour and the monopoly over ideal and material goods and opportunities, to distance themselves from others. The feeling of belonging together is always associated with the exclusion of others. All social actions that defend or preserve status differences are based upon the feeling of belonging together, he maintained. Weber did not apply the term solidarity to discuss how workers developed into a class, but his analysis of the development of class-consciousness almost implies class solidarity. Class-consciousness succeeds most easily when the following conditions are met: (1) when a group is able to identify immediate opponents (workers against entrepreneurs, but not against stockholders); (2) when large numbers of people are in the same situation; (3) when they are concentrated and easier to organise; (4) when a group has goals that are easy to identify, to identify with, and to understand, and when there are others, outside of their class (the intelligentsia) who are able to formulate and interpret these goals. This way of reasoning echoes that of Marx and Lenin.

Because solidarity is constituted by a mixture in the elements of community and society that bind people together (*Vergemeinschaftung* and *Vergesellschaftung*), and because this mixture has to be studied empirically, Weber's idea of solidarity may be broadly inclusive or narrowly limited. The mixture of the two may vary from group to group and from time to time, he wrote. Because his concept of solidarity applies to social relationships in general, it may be applied in more contexts than the concept of solidarity in the Marxist tradition, as will be made clear in Chapter 2.

Weber wanted to distinguish between two kinds of social relationships – the one that is governed by reciprocal expectations, and the other that is maintained by the exercise of authority. The latter implies the acceptance of a legitimate order and the rights of certain individuals within that

legitimate order to exercise power. In Weber's view, it is possible to understand the workings of a society by making an analysis of the conditions
that promote the solidarity that is based upon legitimate authority and
the solidarity that is based upon reciprocal expectation. Weber's concern
with authority, and with power and domination are further reasons for
placing his ideas closer to those formulated by Marx than to those that
were formulated by Durkheim.

The discourse in the development of social theory in the early days of sociology

The different ideas of solidarity in classic social theory are summarised
in Table 1.4. As we have seen, Fourier, Leroux, Comte and Durkheim
primarily understood the idea of solidarity as a means of restoring harmony and social integration in society. All of these thinkers were writing
in a society that was still trying to come to terms with its own most recent
history, with the violence and the terror of the revolution and with the
reversal of fortunes that transformed that revolution into the rise and
fall of Napoleon's empire. The need for a stable order, for harmony and
social integration, was felt everywhere, and this mood is tacitly reflected in
this early French discourse. Certainly, another answer must be added to
this first. The emergence of capitalism, and the problems associated
with the early phases of capitalism impelled these thinkers to find ame-
liorative solutions, without raising the spectre of yet another social revolt
or upheaval.

Of course, their understandings of the idea of solidarity do vary, and
their discourse is a complex and detailed elaboration of their differences
and similarities. Their discourse seems to underscore the need to have a
broadly inclusive understanding of solidarity, to include and encompass
all essential parts of society in the great social task that is embodied in
their common goal, the promotion of a harmonious society. The most
important distinctions, in a discussion of the idea of solidarity, are to be
found in the mechanical and organic forms of solidarity in the writings
of Durkheim.

All of these French writers are deeply concerned about the dilemma
found in the relationship between individual freedom and in the collective requirements of solidarity that are imposed by groups, organisations,
communities and societies. They all recognise that the strong social ties
integrating the individual to the group will conflict with a high degree
of individualism, but none of them argue that personal freedom should
be abandoned. The concern about this relationship exists throughout
the French discourse, but it is most clearly expressed in the texts of

Table 1.4 *Conceptions of solidarity in classic sociology*

	Foundation	Objective/function	Inclusiveness	Collective orientation
Fourier	The household/the *Phalanx*	Harmony	Very restricted	Medium: personal autonomy preserved through private property
Leroux	Similarity Identification with others	Improved social relationships	Broad: the whole society	Medium: not made a theme, but a general criticism of authoritarianism
Comte	Time and continuity Interdependence	Social harmony Integration	Broad: all	Medium: acceptance of the dilemma/subordinate but do not sacrifice individual freedom
Durkheim 1 Mechanical (traditional society)	Homogeneity Social norms, shared values, rituals Common consciousness	Social integration	Broad: all	Medium
Durkheim 2 Organic (modern society)	Interdependence is a consequence of the division of labour	Social integration	Broad: all	Medium: the dilemma is accepted and discussed
Weber	Interests and honour Norms and duties	Realise interests and increase power	Restricted: social groups or professions	Medium Not explicitly formulated Acceptance of the dilemma

Durkheim. It may be argued that the French discourse has an element of nostalgia, a tendency to look back at the past and to idealise conditions existing before the revolution of 1789, to a society that had all but disappeared. In particular, Comte and Durkheim have elements of this backward-looking view in their discussions of solidarity. But their conceptions were relevant in their own day and Durkheim's writings also look to the future. However, neither of these two had the strong future orientation that was to characterise the concept of solidarity in the labour movement.

Weber's idea of solidarity represents a different approach. Whereas Comte's and Durkheim's ideas of solidarity are located in a prepolitical tradition, Weber's concept is closer to a political idea of solidarity. He locates the basis for solidarity in the interests, norms and duties of *groups* that want to realise their interests. He was not a revolutionary and his own writings do not directly engage the Marxists of his day, but Marxist thinking did have its effects upon his own thinking. His writings about solidarity diverge from the French discourse and are closer to the Marxist tradition that will be discussed in Chapter 2.

2   Politics: solidarity from Marx to Bernstein

Marxist and socialist theory developed side by side with classic sociology, but only partly in confrontation with it, as Marxist theorists saw their theoretical contributions primarily as part of their political struggle. The concept of brotherhood or fraternity in the French revolution was made into a key concept in the bourgeois revolutions in Europe in 1848, but the defeat of bourgeois democrats meant a setback for the concept of brotherhood as well. However, in the first decades of the nineteenth century, the idea of brotherhood between *workers* started to spread. The concept of brotherhood in the first labour organisations referred to a proletarian mental attitude that should stimulate class-consciousness and the insight that workers had common interests (Brunner *et al.* 1972). In Germany, Ferdinand Lassalle (1825–64) made *solidarity* a theme in his writings in the 1850s. He distinguished between *corporatist* and *human* solidarity. Corporatist solidarity is developed in the sphere of labour, but is too restricted and should be universalised into a general human solidarity, Lassalle maintained (Zoll 2000).

Marx developed his theories and conceptual language as an integrated part of the labour movement struggle that was in the process of developing. The essential innovation of this language was its instrumentality in uniting the working class and constituting it as a subject in the struggle against a defined adversary – the bourgeoisie. The new way of understanding the idea of solidarity was a part of this project. Although Marx only rarely used the term solidarity, he developed a theory of working-class solidarity that was further developed in two very different directions by Karl Kautsky and Georg Lukács, respectively. Mikhail Bakunin made solidarity a key idea in anarchism, but the defeat of anarchism made this a cul-de-sac. Finally, Eduard Bernstein and the Swede, Ernst Wigforss, were the first to formulate a social democratic idea of solidarity and to reflect on the problematic relationship between collective solidarity and individual freedom.

Marxism: Karl Marx

Marx broke with the utopianism of Fourier and Leroux, but created, as we shall see, his own version of utopianism. He formulated what came to be known as the idea of class solidarity – in this book referred to as *classic class solidarity*. Marx described how the development of industrial capitalism destroyed social bonds and older forms of community where people were firmly integrated in local and social structures. In the *Communist Manifesto*, he and Engels described how the bourgeoisie had put an end to all 'patriarchal idyllic relations', torn asunder ties and 'left remaining no other nexus between man and man than naked self-interest, than callous cash payment' (Marx and Engels 1959 (1848)). Contrary to most of the classic sociologists, he did not witness this development with much regret.

At the same time as capitalism broke down social bonds and relationships, it created new social conditions that brought workers closer to one another, Marx maintained. The number of workers increased, workers were concentrated in large factories in the towns, and this physical proximity reduced mutual competition and enhanced solidarity. The working class was 'disciplined', united and organised by the very mechanisms of the process of capitalist production itself. In addition, the workers were confronted with the same prospects for the future and these prospects did not give hope of an individual escape (Dahl 1999). Modern means of communication made more contact between workers possible, and facilitated agitation and the establishment of worker organisations across national borders. All this created the preconditions for working-class solidarity.

According to Marx, the competition between capitalists and their desire to survive the economic battles and to maximise profits would make the conditions of life and the interests of the proletariat more and more equal. Differences between different types of labour would be obliterated and wages reduced to the same low level (Marx and Engels 1959 (1848)). Although this thesis was not corroborated by events, it represents a postulate about the relationship between the social structure and solidarity that became fundamental for later social scientists; solidarity develops out of a social structure with a high degree of homogeneity.

Gradually, in the later decades of the nineteenth century, the term solidarity was adopted in the language of the German labour movement. Nonetheless, in the writings of Marx the *term* solidarity is a hard one to find. It appears nowhere in the subject indexes of the forty-seven volumes of the *Collected Works* of Marx and Engels. It is briefly mentioned in

The German Ideology in a passage about the free development of individuals in communist society.

> Within communist society, the only society in which the original and free development of individuals ceases to be a mere phrase, this development is determined precisely by the connection of individuals, a connection which consists partly in the economic prerequisites and partly in the necessary solidarity of the free development of all, and finally in the universal character of the activity of individuals on the basis of the existing productive forces. (Marx 1998a (1846))

More or less equivalent terms such as *community* (*Gemeinschaft* and *Gemeinwesen*), *association* and *unity* occur more frequently. In his early texts, Marx referred to *brotherhood*, but came soon to the opinion that the concept of brotherhood was so generic that it could easily obscure class interests. In *The Class Struggles in France*, he mocked the concept of brotherhood as the snug abstraction from class contradictions and the sentimental smoothing out of conflicting class interests (Marx 1998b (1895)). The *Geschichtliche Grundbegriffe* asserts that Marx wanted to exclude the concept of brotherhood from the vocabulary of the labour movement, after the collaboration between the working class and the democratic bourgeoisie in the revolution in 1848 had ended (Brunner *et al.* 1972). The continuous appearance of terms such as *brothers, fraternal feelings* etc., raises some doubt about this. References to *brotherhood* and to *fraternal feelings* continued to appear in writings by Marx that were meant to promote agitation in the actual struggles of the labour movement. Here, he often mentions *worker unity, feelings of brotherhood between workers* and *the community of action*. In the *Communist Manifesto* of 1848, the words *brother* and *brotherhood* had disappeared and been supplanted by the famous rallying call: Workingmen of all countries, unite! Here, Marx and Engels declared that the struggle *itself* would create unity:

> Now and then the workers are victorious, but only for a time. The real fruits of their battles lie not in the immediate result, but in the ever-expanding union of the workers. This union is helped on by the improved means of communication that are created by modern industry, and place workers of different localities in contact with each another. It was just this contact that was needed to centralise the numerous local struggles, all of the same character, into one national struggle between classes. (Marx and Engels 1959 (1848))

What is interesting in this famous passage of the *Manifesto* is not the disparagement of the results that might be achieved in the day-to-day struggle, but the use of the concept of *practice* which had been laid out in the *Thesis on Feuerbach* a few years earlier.

The metaphor of fraternity and of being brothers continued to turn up in Marx's texts. When he addressed the founding conference of the International Workingmen's Association, in 1864, he told his audience that socialists should not underestimate the 'fraternal bonds that should unite workers in each country and inspire them to unite in the struggle for liberation. This underestimation would always punish their ambition and result in defeat', he said (Marx 1971 (1864)). Later, addressing the Council of the International Workingmen's Association, he declared: 'It is one of the great purposes of the Association to make the workmen of different countries not only *feel*, but act as brethren and comrades in the army of emancipation.' Thus, Marx expressed the idea of solidarity by the use of several other terms, and the term *solidarity* itself was not firmly established as an integrated part of his vocabulary.

In *The German Ideology* Marx elaborated on the feeling of community among people in capitalist society. He believed that community (*Vergemeinschaft*) could not be genuine in a capitalist society. Individual members of a class could engage in communal relations with others, but because their relations were determined by their common interests against a third party, and because people do not participate as individuals but as members of a class, this relationship is not a genuine one. When a class is oppressed and community is part of the relations of that class, people appear as average representatives of their class and their individuality remains undisclosed. In such a situation community is illusory. Community becomes independent of the individuals themselves and even a new fetter for them. Thus, only when people join freely together as individuals in a society where revolutionaries are in power and private ownership of the means of production is abolished, can a true community of individuals emerge, a genuine and free community prevail, and people enjoy their common freedom (Marx and Engels 1976 (1846)). In his contributions to social theory Marx argued that a genuine feeling of community can only exist in the future. The daily struggle of the working class does not, in itself, produce a true community.

The relationship between his theoretical conception of genuine community in a future socialist society and the feeling of being brothers in a present capitalist society is not at all clear. Marx asserted that under communism there would be no conflicts between the self-interest of different individuals, and no conflict between individuals and the community/the public/collective interests (Lukes 1985). Only under communism would the individual be free to develop his own personality, to realise himself and to cultivate creativity. Exactly how individual self-realisation and being in a community with others is mediated or reconciled is not clear. How can abolishing private ownership of the means of production not induce people to feel more solidarity with family, friends and others they know personally, than with strangers and people of different ethnic origin or from other nations? Why would individuals in a society without the private ownership of the means of production not experience any conflict between their own strivings for self-realisation and the need to acknowledge and give room to the strivings of others? The idea of *Gemeinschaft*, community or solidarity, under communism does exist, but Marx does very little to elaborate or clarify this idea in his writings.

Neither is the relationship clear between the instrumental interest in worker unity and the normative feelings that workers have of being brothers in a capitalist society. On the one hand, in his theoretical contributions Marx argued that workers establish a communal relationship based on common interests against a third party; on the other, he frequently used concepts like *fraternal feelings*, and *being brothers*, in his political texts – metaphors that certainly imply affection and a normative orientation. Generally, in his theoretical work, Marx was careful to emphasise the instrumental aspects of worker unity more than the normative and affective aspects. The Leninist tradition developed this instrumentality even further, whereas Bernstein and the social democratic tradition further elaborated upon the normative and affective aspects. This dualism in Marx's concept of solidarity is probably due to what Steven Lukes has labelled the paradox in the view of morality in Marxism (Lukes 1985). Morality is a form of ideology and represents an illusion without content, at the same time as the texts of Marx and of his successors abound in moral judgements, in condemnations and in explicit references to moral values.

We may conclude that Marx had two different ideas of solidarity. The first is what came to be known as the classic concept of working-class solidarity under capitalism which he described by using terms like *unity*, *brotherhood*, etc. The second is solidarity in postcapitalist society – under communism. This is what we may call *ideal solidarity*, which Marx described with the concept *Gemeinschaft* (*community*). These two different ideas have been summarised in Table 2.1.

Whereas the idea of a genuine community of individuals was referred to *in a future society*, where private ownership of the means of production had been abolished and where the proletariat was in power, conceptions of unity, union and association were relegated to the realm of political practice, to trade-union meetings, rhetoric and propaganda. The true theoretical contribution of Marx in this field of study is not what he wrote about solidarity, but rather the two theories that emerge from a study of his work. The first is the conception of the relationship between social structure and solidarity – that solidarity is contingent upon specific economic and social structures. The second is that solidarity is the result

Table 2.1 *Marx's two ideas of solidarity*

	Foundation	Objective	Inclusiveness	Collective orientation
Classic Marxist solidarity	The working class: physical proximity/ common situation/ similarity in social and political practice/common adversary/discipline	Realise interests: revolution, socialism-communism	Restricted to the working class, but the confines of the working class are not clear; includes workers across national borders	Strong: personal autonomy is not a theme; Bourgeois democracy is disparaged
Ideal Marxist solidarity	Abolition of the private ownership of the means of production	A genuine community?	Unclear: all those who had not been exploiters in capitalist society?	Unclear/medium: the relationship between individual interests and collective interests are discussed but not seen as being problematic

of specific forms of political practice. These two theories have inspired social inquiry that has proven to be very fruitful for later social research.

The road to revisionism and social democratic theory: Karl Kautsky

The most influential theorist and interpreter of Marxism in Germany, and throughout Europe in the latter part of the nineteenth century, was Karl Kautsky. He played a key role in the formulation of political programmes and by writing authoritative texts on Marxism and socialist theory. In Chapter 4, I will describe his role as a primary contributor to the SPD's Erfurt programme in 1891 when the party consolidated itself on a Marxist platform. Here, Kautsky's contribution to the development of the idea of working-class solidarity in socialist theory will be analysed. Kautsky published an official interpretation of the Erfurt programme – *The Class Struggle*[1] in 1892, which Kautsky himself characterised as *the catechism of social democracy*. This work was regarded as the official interpretation of Marxism at that time; it became a very influential document in the international labour movement and was translated into many languages. Citing the *Manifesto*, Kautsky developed the theories of

---

[1] I refer here to the Norwegian translation – see Kautsky (1915). For a version in English, see Kautsky (1971).

Table 2.2 *Kautsky's idea of solidarity*

Foundation	Objective	Inclusiveness	Collective orientation
A working-class feeling of community that emerges when common interests are recognised; a general feeling of togetherness	Socialism/ a society built upon solidarity	Broader: the working class and other ill-situated groups; even farmers in some situations	Strong? Individual freedom is not made into a theme

Marx and elaborated extensively upon the idea of solidarity. His work introduced the term to new audiences and contributed to its widespread use.

Kautsky maintained that the goal of social democracy was to transform society into one where the economy was based upon solidarity. He utilised *solidarity* both as a general concept, meaning the feeling of togetherness in general, as 'servants may have in the families in which they live', and more particularly as the feeling of community that develops among workers when they recognise their common interests (Kautsky 1915). Whereas the first usage has some similarity with Leroux's concept of solidarity, the other usage points to the specific Marxist idea. This double meaning made possible a gradual transformation from the last to the first among social democrats in the succeeding decades. Similarity, in working conditions brought about by industrialisation, Kautsky argued, arouses feelings of solidarity in the proletariat, and these feelings are bound to become increasingly stronger as long as capitalist production endures. This will result in the moral renaissance of the proletariat. The feeling of solidarity in the modern proletariat stretches out to embrace the entire working class and becomes an international force. As the working class increases in number and becomes more dominant in society, the ideas and feelings of the industrial proletariat will influence the way of thinking of *every* wage earner. Finally, this same feeling of solidarity will grow to encompass independent artisans and even, under certain conditions, some farmers (Kautsky 1915).

Kautsky's interpretation of Marxism was particularly innovative in two ways that affected the concept of solidarity. First, he adopted the term into Marxist theory. Second, he widened the concept to include groups outside the working class. Although *The Class Struggle* preserved the privileged role of the working class, it did not repeat the formulations from the *Manifesto* that characterise different segments of the middle class, farmers, artisans, merchants, etc., as reactionary, unless they voluntarily joined the revolutionary working class. Although Marx did open up the possibility of an alliance between the working class and these other social categories, it was quite clear that these groups would be subordinated to the working class in any alliance.[2]

Kautsky was obviously eager to find a way to formulate what the relationship between the working class and other classes should be in more positive terms. He insisted that the workers' party should develop into a *national people's party* that represented all those who worked and who were exploited. However, Kautsky considered Marxism to be a *science* and believed that morality was alien to science. This prevented him from developing his idea of solidarity further and from introducing ethical elements into the concept (Lukes 1985). After Kautsky, socialist theory developed in two distinct and diverging directions – social democracy and Leninism. The first continued Kautsky's hesitant step towards broadening the concept of solidarity: the second stressed a pure working-class conception of solidarity.

Revisionist theories of solidarity: Eduard Bernstein and Ernst Wigforss

The great revisionist of Marxism, Eduard Bernstein, took up Kautsky's discussion about solidarity and developed the modern idea of solidarity that became so influential, particularly in the northern part of Europe. In 1899, he presented a fundamental critique of Marxist theory and political analysis in *Voraussetzungen des Sozialismus (Preconditions of Socialism)*. Bernstein noted that by and large Marx's predictions had remained unfulfilled: the petty bourgeoisie and the middle class had not been proletarianised, and the working class had not become a majority in society. Capitalism had survived economic crises and recessions, and because there was no prospect of an imminent breakdown of capitalism, social democracy could wait no longer for the demise of capitalism and had to develop a concrete policy of reform and seek alliances with other classes and groups in order to establish a new majority in Parliament. Because socialism was a long-term and unclear goal, individual freedom could not be temporarily sacrificed as Leninists would later argue. Increasing differentiation in the class structure and a reduction of social differences between the industrial working class and other groups cleared the way

---

[2] See also Marx's polemics against Lassalle in *Critique of the Gotha programme* (Marx 1971 (1875)).

for a broader conceptualisation of solidarity, Bernstein argued (Bernstein 1973 (1899)).

In 1910, Bernstein published *Die Arbeiterbewegung – The Labour Movement*. Here an entire chapter was devoted to the concepts of rights and to the ethics of the labour movement (Bernstein 1910), themes that so far had been alien to Marxist theory. According to Bernstein, socialist ethics consisted of three core ideas: the idea of equality, the idea of community (*Gemeinschaft*) or solidarity, and the idea of freedom or autonomy. The problem was that these ideas had to be balanced against one another. Solidarity had to be balanced against individual freedom or autonomy, and equality had to be balanced against individual freedom. It is not possible to have unlimited solidarity if one wants to preserve individual freedom, and it is not possible to create equality and at the same time have maximum individual freedom, he argued.

Whereas, on occasion, Marx had spoken in a derogatory manner about those who understood equality as being an essential part of socialism, Bernstein argued that equality was a key socialist idea. Although the demands for equality were inherent in the modern working class, because of the capitalist transformation of working conditions, Bernstein believed that the working class had to recognise that equality was not possible in an absolute sense and that it had to be restricted.

Solidarity, he maintained, developed when workers understood that they could reduce their dependence on employers voluntarily, by uniting with fellow workers and by pooling their strength in trade unions. This voluntary act is the expression of an ethical commitment.[3] The more capitalism develops, the more workers recognise that the individual employee is dependent upon the superior power of the employers. The feeling of belonging together is reinforced and grows into a well-developed understanding of solidarity which becomes the strongest intellectual factor within the labour movement. The feeling of solidarity is stronger in the labour movement than in all other groups, and no principle or idea within the labour movement is more cohesive than the insight necessitating the exercise of solidarity. No other norm or principle of social law can compare to the binding power of this idea.

The third key idea for Bernstein was *freedom* or, as he sometimes preferred, *autonomy*. For Bernstein, equality was a historically contingent concept, but freedom was an ideal of humanity. There is no civilised

---

[3] It is interesting to note that Bernstein refers to solidarity as 'the technical-legal concept of solidarity that has been taken into general use' – indicating that solidarity was not yet firmly established as a political concept at the time (1910) or that this only recently had become the case.

Table 2.3 *Revisionism: Bernstein's view of solidarity*

Foundation	Objectives	Inclusiveness	Collective orientation
A feeling of belonging together among workers and others Ethics	Reform Socialism Freedom	Broad: the working class, the middle class and other populous groups	Medium: emphasis on individual freedom Acceptance of the difficulty in determining a proper balance between solidarity and individual autonomy

nation that does not appreciate the idea of freedom, because freedom is a yardstick of culture, he stated. Workers may acquire more freedom due to their greater collective efforts, but only if they resign themselves to the relinquishment of some personal freedom. By voluntarily relinquishing some personal freedom when they unite in a labour union, workers may be able to overpower the social forces that are allied against them. For the worker, sacrificing personal autonomy and engaging in collective action may result in material gains and in an increase in one's own relative freedom, he reasoned.

Bernstein observed that the contemporary working class had not sufficiently developed the idea of freedom. He believed that the worker would learn to aspire to and develop a free personality through engagement in the labour movement. The road to personal freedom can only be reached by travelling together freely on the path of collective association. The industrial worker will be able to acquire personal freedom through the achievements of his trade union, where on equal terms with the other members of the union the individual becomes a voluntary agent of the common will of the collective.

Bernstein brought earlier socialist reflections concerning the idea of *solidarity* a significant step further. He was the first to integrate the three concepts of equality, solidarity and freedom into socialist discourse. He did this half a century before the SPD adopted those three concepts in the Bad Godesberg programme in 1959. He emphasised the ethical aspect of solidarity and was the first socialist theorist to discuss the problematic relationship between these three key concepts of contemporary social democratic ideology. Yet, he is not very clear on how to rank the relative importance of solidarity to personal freedom. He praises both: the first as the most important concept in social law, and the second as the yardstick for civilised nations.

Bernstein's idea of solidarity is, in many ways, closer to Durkheim's than to that of Marx since he emphasised *values* and the relationship between solidarity and individuality. We should note, however, that another key figure of revisionism developed similar ideas about solidarity at about the same time that Bernstein did. The Nestor of Swedish social democracy, Ernst Wigforss, published ideas that were similar to Bernstein's in exactly the same year and criticised orthodox Marxism for being reluctant to introduce moral and ethical thought into socialist discourse (see Chapter 4). Thus, with Berntstein and Wigforss a process that transformed the classic Marxist concept of class solidarity had been initiated in the labour movement.

With Bernstein and Wigforss, elements beyond self-interest were introduced into socialist conceptions of the foundations of solidarity. As we shall see in Part II of this book, this change was part of a more general tendency within the labour movement in Western Europe in the first decades of the twentieth century.

Austro-Marxism: a third alternative?

In the years prior to World War I, a group of Marxist thinkers in Vienna sought to establish an alternative to what they saw as the revisionism of Bernstein and the dogmatism of Kautsky. After the split in the international labour movement, following the revolution in Russia and World War I, they also positioned themselves as being an alternative to Leninism. Most prominent among the Austrian Marxists were Max Adler, Otto Bauer, Rudolf Hilferding and Karl Renner. This group made an important contribution to the development of a modern Marxist social science – non-dogmatic, but critical of the developing revisionist tendencies within social democracy (Bottomore 1978). Particularly influential were Max Adler's philosophical and sociological contributions. Adler was inspired by neo-Kantian philosophy and he was prone to ask the basic question of sociology: *How is society possible?* My concern is to determine to what extent the Austrian Marxists formulated a third alternative, between Bernstein and the Leninists (see below), in their ideas about solidarity.

In *Die Solidarische Gesellschaft*, in 1934, Adler distinguished between two types of society. The first is characterised by the solidarity of primitive people in the distant past, and our knowledge about these societies is limited and uncertain (Adler 1964 (1932)). All written history is about class contradiction and class struggle, he declared, referring to Engels. This other type of society is characterised by the exploitation of one group by another, by class formation, by the contradictory interests that develop between classes and by a social life that is determined by the divisions and cleavages in a society based upon exploitation. This type of society lacks solidarity because societal solidarity is not possible in a society characterised by the exploitation of one group by another. According to Adler, the statement that societal solidarity is only possible in a classless society is a tautology. In a capitalist society solidarity is based on the recognition of common interests that develop when members of the same exploited class understand their social conditions, understand that they share a common economic destiny, and join together in common suffering and hope. Such a class will develop an ideology with an ethical idea about the general interest. The next step is when the revolutionary class interest is integrated with a more idealistic view about the general interest in society. Except for this emphasis upon societal ethics, Adler's conception of solidarity is very close to the one that Marx formulated. The scheme is as follows: *class situation→ class interest→ class consciousness→ class community/ solidarity (Gemeinschaft)*.

Adler's idea of solidarity does not really transcend the classic Marxist concept described above. He mentions ethics, but his interest in Kant's philosophy does not extend to Kant's ethics. Even if Austrian Marxism did promote an alternative socialist position that was different to that of both Bernstein and Lenin, it did not represent an original contribution or a renewal of Marxism in terms of the idea of solidarity. This seems to be confirmed by an analysis of the party programmes of the Austrian Social Democratic Party (see Chapter 5).

Leninism

Solidarity did not become an important concept in the Leninist school of thought which inspired the direction taken by the Marxist parties within the international labour movement. Lenin himself was not very preoccupied with solidarity, and the concept is not found in *What Is To Be Done?* (Lenin 1967 (1902)) or in *The State and Revolution* (Lenin 1964 (1917)), two of his most important theoretical contributions. Lenin was concerned with uniting the working class on a politically correct platform. Without a platform built upon *his* interpretation of Marxism, unity was neither desirable nor possible. He was more preoccupied with drawing lines of demarcation against groups with whom he disagreed, than on elaborating upon matters that united different groups. He stated briefly that a task for the party was to 'unify all forces in the name of the people', but this referred to an aim of the party, i.e. unifying forces under its own banner, and does not say anything about how attitudes and feelings of individuals within different classes can be unified. Opponents and heretics in the party or elsewhere in the revolutionary movement were to be fought ruthlessly and vanquished. Although class solidarity and political unity are different ideas and are not easily confused analytically, it may have been difficult for some to distinguish between the two in practice. The paradox in the Marxist view of morality is even more pronounced in Leninism, and normative aspects that are associated with the idea of solidarity were of no interest to Lenin.

In his books and articles, Lenin emphasised the need for *discipline* in the struggle against capitalism. Contributions that discuss and elaborate ideas like community or solidarity are hard to find. His strong dislike of any kind of sentimentality and his eagerness to avoid all concepts that encourage a mood of solemnity may explain his avoidance of these ideas. Linguists have drawn attention to Lenin's struggle against smooth and glib phrases with a low degree of precision. Words like *freedom* or *equality* are seldom found. His severe style of writing and his contempt for sentiment, pathos and declamatory concepts have had an enduring impact on the language of political programmes in Leninist parties (Tynjanow 1970; Kasanski 1970; Jakubinski 1970).

Nevertheless, another Leninist, Georg Lukács, did develop a Leninist idea of solidarity in his book *History and Class Consciousness*. Lukács discussed the relationship between individual freedom and solidarity and criticised the freedom found in capitalist society. It is the freedom that an isolated individualist has to reify private property and a freedom against other individuals, one that entitles egoism and the pursuit of private interests. In capitalist society, ideas of solidarity and interdependence are at best useless 'normative ideas' (Lukács 1971 (1923)). Individual freedom in existing bourgeois society cannot be built upon solidarity, but only upon the lack of freedom of others. It is a corrupted and corrupting privilege, according to Lukács. Normatively speaking, the individual should not only abstain from individual freedom but also subordinate himself to the collective will of the communist party. Bourgeois freedom will only transform the party into a loose collection of separated individuals and prevent them from developing an effective collective will. The subordination of the individual will help the party to realise its goal – a new society where freedom and solidarity is combined in a relationship between free individuals who feel solidarity with one another.

Lukács' Leninist idea of solidarity represents a further development of Marx's contention that genuine solidarity is not possible in a capitalist society. To achieve genuine solidarity and genuine freedom one must temporarily sacrifice individual freedom. The problem here, of course, is incorporated into the question: What is temporary? If the revolution is believed to be imminent, the Leninist position can be more easily defended. If the prospect of revolution is one that can only be imagined in

Table 2.4 *The Leninist conception of solidarity*

Foundation	Objectives	Inclusiveness	Collective orientation
The working class, its common situation and the similarity of its social and political practices/its common adversary, and its need for discipline	Revolution The dictatorship of the proletariat Communism	Restricted: the working class, but only the revolutionary part of it	Very strong: bourgeois democracy is disparaged, the sacrifice of individual freedom and autonomy is required

the long term, then a call to sacrifice individual freedom will appear to be overly romantic and dangerous. This was a contentious issue in the discussions between Leninists and social democratic revisionists. Moreover, the Leninist position not only implied a short-term sacrifice of individual freedom, since the revolution would necessarily be followed by a period of proletarian dictatorship, but also a sacrifice without a time limit. As we know, in practice this entailed the permanent abolition of individual freedom in the name of the working class and the institution of dictatorship *by* and *for* the communist party.

Whereas Lukács' idea of solidarity was a logical corollary of Leninist ideology, another Leninist developed a more fruitful approach to the concept. Antonio Gramsci, one of the fathers of the Italian communist party, had witnessed the defeat of the workers' councils in Turin in 1919. He found the cause of defeat in the inability of the Turin working class to develop solidarity with other exploited groups and with the peasants in surrounding areas (Macciotta 1970).

Among Gramsci's contributions to Marxism, and to sociology in general, was his concept of culture and cultural hegemony, and his concept of solidarity was integrated in his reasoning on these concepts. For Gramsci, the dominant patterns of moral philosophy are essential components of the culture of a society. In all societies, a class or a group has a cultural hegemony which is an essential part of the domination of this class or group over other classes. Consequently, the working class not only had to concentrate its activities on conquering the state and its apparatuses. It had also to create another cultural hegemony in civil society. Besides, it had to develop a culture that could overcome the fragmentation of the working class itself and its separation from the peasants. Capitalism could be defeated and the revolution could be successful only through the establishment of a social force or block that constituted itself as an alternative to capitalist domination. The worker must 'step out of the sphere of individualism' and competition with other workers. The principle of unity and solidarity is a critical one for the working class and it requires a change in the psychology of workers and peasants (Gramsci 1973b (1919)). The working class should create bonds with other social groups and develop an alternative culture based upon attitudes and values that differ from the hegemonic capitalist attitudes and values (Gramsci 1973a). The most elementary change would embody an economic and corporative sense of solidarity. The next step would be the development of consciousness about the solidarity of interests between all of the members in a broader social and political alliance, but still restricted to economic matters only. A third step would be to create a consciousness that transcended the corporative group and was in the interest of other social groups as well. This would indicate the aspiration of becoming a hegemonic force, according to Gramsci.

Gramsci enriched Marxist theory with his emphasis upon culture, moral understandings and psychology. He used the term solidarity more often than the other Leninists analysed here, although he alternated between solidarity and other equivalent terms such as unity. But he was part of the Leninist tradition, and he, too, emphasised the need for *discipline* in the communist party and in the working class and its allies (Gramsci 1973a). Although he was preoccupied with normative questions, he did not incorporate in his work ideas about solidarity that are found in the works of Bernstein, probably because he belonged to the tradition that understood Bernstein's revisionism as a betrayal of true Marxism.

Finally, Mao Zedong continued the approach of Leninist tradition in terms of solidarity. In the texts of Mao, *unity* is a central concept, particularly regarding the unity within the communist party itself, and the unity between the party and the masses.[4] The concept of solidarity is hard to find in his theoretical works, but he did employ the term frequently in speeches and in materials used for political agitation. The term *solidarity* is reserved mainly for denoting the relationship between the Chinese Communist Party and what Mao regards as the working-class parties in other countries. Besides, it is used about the relationship with countries that he considers progressive or friendly. Thus, generally Mao Zedong was as tepid as Lenin in his attitude towards the term solidarity. As we shall see in Chapter 8, this is also reflected in the programmes of Marxist–Leninist parties.

---

[4] See, for instance, *Reinforce the Unity of the Party and Carry Forward the Party Traditions* and *Opening Speech at the Eighth National Congress of the CPC*, in Zedong (1957).

Anarchism: Bakunin

In power, Leninists perverted the liberating aspects of socialism and Marxism and did not provide any room for solidarity or for individual freedom. The strong focus on the party in Leninist tradition directed attention away from the normative and ethical aspects of solidarity within the working class. The concept of solidarity became far more important in the tradition within the trade union movement that was least concerned with party matters. The anarchists failed to achieve political power and became almost irrelevant in politics, although their ideas did influence the ideas of segments within the trade union movement in France, Italy and Spain. The only country where anarchism did become important was Spain, especially in the period before and during the Spanish Civil War (1936–39).

One of the protagonists of anarchism, Mikhail Bakunin (1814–76), integrated the concept of solidarity into his theoretical and strategic contributions to a far greater degree than did Leninists. For Bakunin, solidarity was a necessary element in every society. Solidarity is a quality that is found in the individual which makes him join with others and create a community (Bakunin 1992a; 1992c). The proletariat is 'the carrier of the standards of humanity', and the guiding principle for the proletariat is solidarity. He defined it in this way:

All for one – one for all, and one by virtue of all. This is the motto, the fundamental principle of our great International [Working-Men's] Association which transcends the frontiers of States, thus destroying them, endeavouring to unite the workers of the entire world into a single human family on the basis of universally obligatory labour, in the name of freedom of each and every individual . . . And there are two ways to realise this wish. The first is by establishing, first in their own groups and then among all groups, a true fraternal solidarity, not just in words, but in action, not just for holidays, but in their daily life. Every member of the International must be able to feel that all other members are his brothers and be convinced of this in his practice. (Bakunin 1992d)

Bakunin's preoccupation with the idea and practice of solidarity was not an isolated phenomenon among anarchists. Some decades later, Kropotkin described solidarity as the basis for social integration and as a moral idea (Zoll 2000). The idea of anarchist solidarity was integrated in an organisational programme that emphasised the development of trade unions and other organisations, such as consumer and producer cooperatives, common funds for struggle, etc. In this way, anarchists developed a consistent and coherent theory and practice of working-class solidarity. Whereas Leninists overstated the importance of the party and endowed

Table 2.5 *Aspects of solidarity in socialist theory*

	Foundation	Objectives/ Function	Inclusiveness	Collective orientation
Classic Marxist solidarity	Class interests Recognition of 'sameness'	Realise interests: revolution socialism	Restricted: only the working class, but in all nations	Strong: Individual autonomy is not made a theme
Leninist solidarity	Class interests Recognition of 'sameness'	Realise interests: revolution the dictatorship of the proletariat Socialism	Very restricted: only the 'conscious' part of the working class, but in all nations	Very strong: Individual autonomy is explicitly suppressed
Classic social democratic solidarity	The common interests of the great majority of people Acceptance of difference Ethics and morality	Realise interests: reforms Socialism Create a sense of community	Broader: almost all groups; the nation?	Medium to weak: individual freedom is valued and the dilemma is recognised

it with dictatorial powers, anarchists did not see the necessity of a party in the struggle for power within the labour movement and within society as a whole.

Conclusion: Marxist, Leninist and social democratic solidarity

If we ignore the anarchist concept of solidarity, because anarchism failed to achieve political power, almost universally, in Europe, there are three diverging concepts of solidarity identified in socialist theory. I have labelled them *the classic Marxist*, *the Leninist*, and *the classic social democratic* concepts of solidarity. These concepts are summarised in Table 2.5.

The socialist ideas of solidarity did not refer to premodern societies, with integrated local communities that were strongly bonded together, as do some of the classic sociological concepts. Socialist concepts of solidarity reflect the experiences of workers and militants under capitalism. The importance of solidarity often reflects an urgency; the necessity of joining together in order to avoid defeat by adversaries. The concept was filled with connotations promising a different and much better future, and was seen as being an important instrument in the struggle to achieve a desirable future. These concepts differ in many other respects, first and foremost in the way they are founded and in the role of ethics and morality in constituting solidarity.

The classic Marxist concept is founded upon the recognition of class interests and the community between fellow workers. The goal is to realise the interests of the working class by revolutionary means and by the establishment of a socialist society. This is a restricted concept; it includes only the working class, although the exact confines of that class are not clear. National borders do not limit working-class solidarity. The emphasis upon the collective is strong, and there are no significant worries about how individual freedom and collective solidarity are to be reconciled.

The foundation for the Leninist conception of solidarity does not deviate from the classic Marxist concept. The goal is to realise the interests of the working class by revolution and by the establishment of a dictatorship of the proletariat. In principle, this kind of solidarity should be able to encompass the entire working class. However, Lenin emphasised the view that unity could only be founded upon a correct analysis – his own analysis – and consequently, only the revolutionary segments of the working class that are in line with his thinking are included. The emphasis on the collective is very strong, and individual freedom in bourgeois society is a gravely disparaged ideal.

Finally, classic social democratic solidarity is founded upon a much broader definition of interests. It entails the interests of the working class and the interests of other popular classes, or strata, and includes an acceptance of difference among these classes and groups. In addition, there is an ethical or moral component constituting the foundation for solidarity. The goal is to realise the interests of the majority by concrete reforms that will eventually lead to a fully democratic and socialist society. Solidarity should create a feeling of community between those who are included. The social democratic concept is clearly broader than the classic Marxist concept. Emphasis on the collective is classified as medium to weak, since individual freedom is highly valued. The potential contradictions between individual autonomy and the requirements of collective solidarity are clearly recognised.

Since so much differs in the socialist concepts of solidarity, i.e. the role of ethics, class and other populous groups, the place of individual freedom, etc., it may be more appropriate to consider these conceptualisations within the confines of the distinctive discourses in which they appear. This will be done in Chapters 4, 5, 7 and 8.

3   Religion: solidarity in Catholicism and Protestantism

Religions and churches had organised the belief system in society long before liberalism and socialism developed as coherent ideologies. Religion created a common language and a frame of reference for communication between believers. It created meaning, purpose and a sense of community, and established rules of behaviour for believers that regulated their relationship to one another and to those who did not believe or who believed in another religion. It developed norms and rules about the relationship between the individual, the family, civil society and the state. Durkheim saw religion as the social cement of society, and social scientists have argued that it was the sharing of religious rituals that created the solidarity found in societies of old (Turner and Rojek 2001). Thus, religion was a bond between people long before ideas of nationhood or class existed. When the idea of class solidarity was developed, the development was in conflict with established loyalties to religion.

The Roman Catholic Church developed hegemony and was for many centuries the only powerful religion in Western Europe. In the sixteenth century the Reformation brought about a split dividing western Europe into a predominantly Catholic south and a predominately Protestant north. There were zones of mixed religions, most notably from Ireland to the Alps. When the political parties of the labour movement were established in the latter half of the nineteenth century, their socialist ideology brought them into conflict not only with bourgeois and petty bourgeois political opponents, but also with Christians and their churches. In some countries, especially those which were Catholic, religion created a stronger identification for many people than did membership in a class, and Christians established their own parties. Popes and bishops allied with the political right, and the pope formulated encyclicals in order to give Catholic workers an alternative to socialism. In northern Europe, the Protestant Church was subordinated to the state, but it, too, found ways to ally itself with powerful groups in society.

We have seen that the early labour movement had an idea of solidarity that was well fitted to the theory of class struggle – a theory that was alien to Catholic and Protestant theology and social ethics. It should be no surprise that the term *solidarity* was not integrated into the mainstream of Christian social ethics until the term was dissociated from the theory of class struggle. In early Christian theology, however, we are able to discern four aspects of Christian teachings that almost 2,000 years later were used to found the Christian idea of solidarity. The first is embodied in the Christian development of the Greek word *agape*. The word signifies a key idea in Christianity and means the love that God has for all human beings as well *as* the love that all human beings should have for one another (Jackson 1999). God's love of humankind is a precondition of the admonishment to *love thy neighbour*. The universality of this demand makes the relationship between 'I' and the 'other' a central theme. Second, *loving thy neighbour* is closely associated with the concept of *charity*, which was seen as being the expression of the highest form of God's love. The reciprocal love between God and humankind is manifested in acts of charity, which are expressions of an unselfish *love of thy neighbour*. The third element, already mentioned in Chapter 1, is derived from the early Christian friars who developed an idea of *fraternity* denoting the preparedness to share with others as one does in a family. Finally, the great body of social ethics that is common to Judaism and to Christianity points to the *Brotherhood of Man*, the understanding that all people are brothers and sisters, and children of God, so to speak. This social ethic vibrates between its own affirmative and critical qualities. The Apostle Paul taught Christians to obey their worldly authorities, but the universal and the egalitarian character of the command to *love thy neighbour* necessarily imposes a potential critical tension upon Christians and their relationships to those who wield worldly power (Brunkhorst 2002). These four aspects of Christian teaching can be seen as being fundamentals of the Christian concepts of solidarity that developed in the twentieth century.

The Christian road from an idea of charity to an idea of solidarity implies, in principle, two important steps. First, Christians had to find a way to engage themselves in this world without forsaking the world to come. Second, the way to bridge these two worlds had to include formulations legitimating collective action. Christian engagement in the living conditions of a suffering humanity had to allow for organisation within a political movement in this world in order to do God's will on earth. As we shall see, this process was a complicated one, and particularly so for Lutherans.

This chapter traces the concept of solidarity in key documents that present Catholic and Lutheran understandings of social ethics. An attempt is made to address the following questions. When and to what extent was the concept of solidarity integrated into Catholic and Lutheran theology and social ethics? What are the similarities and differences that exist in the discourses about solidarity in Catholicism and in Lutheranism?

We will follow the development of the idea of solidarity by studying various papal encyclicals that were issued from the late nineteenth century up to our own day and age. Although Vatican staff and advisers participate in the process of drafting encyclicals, the texts are the sole responsibility of the pope in office. As a genre, papal encyclicals have something in common with the texts of Marxist leaders and theorists since all aim to guide the social and political practice and behaviour of their readers. Encyclicals are educational texts that are meant to guide members of the Catholic Church in their daily lives in society. The following analysis is restricted to the language in papal doctrines, and to an understanding of the ethical guidelines this language is meant to illuminate, and says nothing about the perlocutionary effects upon Catholics, or the extent of solidarity among Catholics.

Studying the development of the idea of solidarity within Lutheranism is a more complicated matter since there are no authorised texts that can be interpreted in the same way, with the exception of the texts written by Luther himself. Protestantism has taken many directions and is a pluralistic movement. There is more room for different interpretations of the relationship between religion and politics. In Lutheran Protestantism, my point of departure is Luther's conception of the two kingdoms and the conventional interpretation of his understanding of the relationship between religion and politics. We shall see how this conventional interpretation has changed and how the change has provided the space necessary for the introduction of the idea of solidarity into Lutheran theology.

Catholicism

For Catholicism, and particularly for the Catholic Church, the path from religion to politics was a short one. There are several reasons for this. First of all, the papal state was a worldly power, and in its capacity as such it is obliged to relate to the politics of this world. The second reason developed from the rediscovery of Aristotle's moral and political texts in the thirteenth century. These texts laid the foundation for the growth of the idea that political society was a human creation (Skinner 1980). Until then the Augustinian idea that the political order was ordained by God prevailed. Thomas Aquinas (1226–74) and other Catholic theologians systematised the Aristotelian idea of *natural law* and understood the laws of nature as reflecting the will of God. Natural law was valid for society, as God had already provided the rules and standards of conduct that are binding for human behaviour and social life. Legislators have the duty to find the true and objective solutions to social conflicts and are able to do so by logical deduction and by their interpretations of natural law. Natural law and its application to society can be apprehended by the use of man's reason. Human reason is sufficient, and all human beings are capable of determining morally correct action on their own by applying their God-given human reasoning powers. The Church is obligated to assist man in his efforts to find true and objective solutions to social conflict. The efforts of Aquinas and others to integrate Aristotelian thinking into the theology of the Church helped to legitimate the Church's interference in politics, and this conceptually new platform helped to further bridge the gap between religion and politics.

A third reason for the Catholic Church to engage in politics is based upon social ethics and its concerns about the social integration of society. Social integration was a subject in Catholic social teachings centuries before classic sociologists formulated their concerns about social developments in the modern era. The Catholic Church taught that man was able to earn his reward in heaven as a consequence of his own good deeds. Giving individually to charity was in the interests of all those who were able to give. In his main work, the *Summa Theologica*, Thomas Aquinas formulated principles that were further developed in later papal writings. Those who have an excess of property and money should not regard this wealth as something that belongs exclusively to them, but have a responsibility to assist the needy. Whatever one owns that is superfluous to the preservation of one's own vital interests should be given to the poor and needy. This is a duty, not of natural law and not of human law, but of Christian charity, according to Thomas Aquinas. But he also transcended the notion of individual charity and formulated a number of principles that are relevant for the governance of society, too. The individual should be integrated into the social group and into society. Society and government have a responsibility to impose taxes in order to finance those measures that would increase the social integration of society. This concern about social integration may be seen as being one of the origins of Catholic ideas of solidarity. Catholic solidarity particularly denotes attitudes that are necessary for bringing about and enhancing social integration within society.

Rerum Novarum *and* Quadragesimo Anno

The teachings of Thomas Aquinas were revived in the sixteenth century when the Dominicans and Jesuits developed their answers to the challenges of Protestantism and humanism. Two of his ideas are of special interest in this particular study. The first idea rejects the view that political order in society is invented by God. Thomists argue that political order is brought into being by citizens, in their concerted action (Skinner 1980). They claimed that the political order develops from man's original state in nature, where freedom, equality and independence were the rule. The second idea concerns the social nature of man. Man's freedom and independence is not complete, and his original state could not have been one of solitude or isolation (for a detailed analysis of Thomism, see Skinner (1980)). According to Thomas, man's inherent nature predisposes him to live a social and communal life. Man is at once free and independent, but no human being is self-sufficient and all are destined to live their lives in community with others. Thomists concluded that individual freedom and feelings of community are values that should balance one another.

The Catholic Church had taken a defensive posture for centuries. The Lutheran reformation had seriously reduced its influence in the north. The French revolution resulted in a serious setback for Catholicism in France, and the establishment of the new Italian state in 1861 had isolated the Catholic Church even there. Everywhere, the Church had struggled against modernity and been defeated. It was an isolated institution, politically and philosophically, when Pope Leo XIII issued the encyclical *Rerum Novarum* in 1891. As we shall see in Chapter 6, this encyclical reflected the reformism that had developed in Germany in the later part of the eighteenth century, and this more open cultural and philosophical spirit had won the pope's favour (Raguer 1990).

With *Rerum Novarum*, Pope Leo XIII opened the Church to modernity by addressing the burning social questions that had accompanied the rise of industry and the emergence of the working class. He declared the old alliance between the throne and the altar to be obsolete, and he reiterated and revived the Church's concerns for the practice of compassion and justice in society. The poor and the underprivileged were recognised and on the Church's agenda. Leo XIII developed themes from the works of Thomas Aquinas and underscored his view that the well-off had an obligation to give charity to the needy and that the Church should feel obliged to promote systematic assistance to the poor. He expressed his concerns about the situation of the working class and he called for a just wage, arguing that the Church should be more engaged in ameliorating social problems. He regretted that the old guilds and other institutions that had united people were collapsing and that class struggle was replacing feelings of interdependence and reciprocal understanding. Different classes should live together in harmony and balance (Leo 1983 (1891)).

A network of institutions should exist between the individual and the state. These intermediate institutions would express the human need that individuals feel to unite with one another, he professed. The state should not interfere in the activities of these intermediate institutions, but protect and support them. Here, Leo XIII formulated what Pius XI would further develop and what become a lasting contribution to Catholic social teaching – the principle of subsidiarity.

Leo XIII's concerns for promoting social integration represented an attempt to modernise the Church, and it brought the Church closer to participation in practical politics. Nonetheless, Leo affirmed the paternalist tradition, and he rejected the idea that the poor and the working class should take political action. He believed that necessary changes must be initiated by those who enjoyed privileges and by all those who benefited from the existing order. Change should not be forced by concerted action of the underprivileged. His key concepts were *friendship* and *fraternal love*. One hundred years later, John Paul regarded the idea of 'friendship' in the *Rerum Novarum* as a precursor to the Catholic concept of solidarity (Giovanni 1991). The ingrained paternalism in papal reasoning still promoted a form of *noblesse oblige* and may have prevented him from recognising the political right to act in concert for the working class and the poor of his day.

However, decades passed before the Church took further steps to modernise its social teachings in line with the spirit of Leo XIII's encyclical. The outbreak of World War I was a serious defeat for the idea of working-class solidarity and for the authority of the Catholic Church. Catholics joined the national armies and fought against one another, and criticised the pope for not supporting them (Raguer 1990).

In his encyclical entitled *Quadragesimo Anno*, in 1931, Pius XI elaborated upon the themes discussed by Leo XIII forty years earlier. As did Leo, Pius directed his encyclical against the reckless competition and untamed individualism of capitalist society. He wrote avidly in opposition to collectivist socialism and revolutionary Marxism. These popes emphasised the importance of the family and heralded the family as the *core unit* of society. They underlined their support for the role played by voluntary organisations in society as well. However, *Quadragesimo Anno* discusses the idea of a just wage and the principle of subsidiarity in more concrete terms. Since employers need labour and labour needs employers, Pius insisted that the one part could not demand something harmful or destructive of the other part. Whereas the definition of a 'just' wage had been unclear in *Rerum Novarum*, the idea of a just wage was now strengthened and clarified by the suggestion that a *socially just family wage* could be defined as a wage that was sufficient for a worker to provide for himself and his family. In return, workers should not make claims that would ruin their employers (Pio XI 1931).

Pius' elaboration of the idea of subsidiarity grew out of his concerns about the fragility of the social order. Leo XIII had seen that industrial capitalism brought about the dissolution of social ties and social institutions. Pius XI had seen the development of the modern state in its totalitarian version, and he worried that the state might destroy civil society by absorbing the functions of professional and social organisations. On the other hand, he recognised that many problems could only be solved by the state. The state had to acknowledge that it was a part of the hierarchic order of subsidiary organisations. He warned that 'as it is wrong to take from the individual and entrust to society what may be managed by private initiative, it is an injustice, a sin, and a disturbance of the right order if larger and higher organisations usurp functions that might be provided by smaller and lower instances' (Pio XI 1931).

This became a classic formulation of the principle of subsidiarity, and the idea was definitively integrated into Catholic social teachings with the publication of this encyclical. The state has a social responsibility, but its role should be *subsidiary*. It should take responsibility only when the individual, the family, voluntary organisations and local communities were unable to fulfil their roles. In addition, society and the state should support intermediating organisations when these did not have sufficient resources to fulfil their obligations.

Quadragesimo Anno was more explicitly political and more concrete than *Rerum Novarum* in many respects, and especially in its criticism of capitalism. It convinced many Catholics that the Church should be an agent of social change in society. It represented a continuation of the concerns voiced by Leo XIII regarding social integration and the social organisation of society. Pius' elaboration of the idea of subsidiarity implied a careful balance in the rights and responsibilities of the individual, the family and of other societal organisations, including the state.

French and Spanish Catholics did use the concept of solidarity in the decades before *Quadragesimo Anno*, and in Germany, Heinrich Pesch, the father of German *Christlicher Solidarismus* had integrated the concept into his social ethics and economic analysis (Pesch 1998 (1924)). Although German Catholics played a key role in preparing *Quadragesimo Anno*, Pius XI did not introduce the concept of solidarity into his encyclical. Since the main theme of *Quadragesimo* is social integration, this seems somewhat strange. One hypothesis that may explain its absence could be that the concept of solidarity was still too closely associated with the labour movement and with its alien ideas regarding class struggle.

Leo sought to transcend, and not to supplant, personal and private charity, and he introduced the notions of *justice* and *social charity*. Because the market economy was a 'blind force and a violent energy, it had to be restrained and guided wisely to be useful', he wrote (Pio XI 1931). Society needs the aid of more noble principles to guide it than a totally free market economy could ever offer. *Justice* should inspire the institutions and the social life of society and constitute the social and legal order to which the economy should conform. *Social charity* should be the spirit of this order, guarded and maintained by public authority. This combination of justice, social charity and public authority represented a new step in the direction of a Catholic concept of solidarity.

Pius broke new ground for the Catholic Church, retreating from Leo's severe paternalism when, in 1938, he published his encyclical entitled *Firmissimum*. In it he accepted the fact that resistance and rebellion were justified in extreme situations (Dorr 1983). Still, decades would pass before the concept of solidarity was to be found in a papal encyclical, even if the concept of solidarity had been integrated in German Catholicism several decades earlier (Nell-Breuning and Sacher 1954; Herder 1959). Yet the concept does not find papal authorisation until the papal encyclical published in 1961. When this happened, the idea of solidarity had to be balanced against the already fully developed concept of subsidiarity. The relationship between the two was to be a distinguishing mark of Catholic social ethics.

Mater et magistra

However, at this time the reputation of the Church was tarnished, and under the papacy of Pious XII the Church had to acknowledge that its authority had been weakened (Riccardi 1990). In this troubled climate, John XXIII was elected pope in 1958. He was to become a very popular pope and a great moderniser within the Church. He organised the Second Vatican Council and opened the Church up to participation in ecumenical activity. This greatly improved the Catholic Church's relationship to the other Christian churches. John reoriented the relationship between the Church and the world by emphasising that the Christian form of presence in the world should not be one of power, but one of service. He modified the Church's antagonistic position towards the communist countries and he introduced the term *solidarity* into papal writings and teachings.

The term *solidarity* is found for the first time in a papal encyclical in John's *Mater et Magistra* in 1961. Here, John called for government action to assist people in need and to reduce economic inequalities in society and the world: 'The solidarity of mankind and the awareness of brotherhood to which Christ's teaching leads, demand that the different nations should give each other concrete help of all kinds, not only to facilitate movements of goods, capital and men, but also to reduce inequalities between them' (John 1964).

A second reference to solidarity, more in line with earlier encyclicals, is also made. Here, the concern for enhanced social integration is reiterated: 'Workers and employers should respect the principles of human solidarity in organising their mutual relations and live together as befits Christians and brothers.'

In these few sentences, the essence of the Catholic concept of solidarity is made clear. Compassion and collective action are called for to help the poor and the underprivileged. Individual charity is transcended because the needs of the poor are simply too massive. Intermediating institutions, or the state, if necessary, need to act in order to reduce the inequalities that are found in the world community. But solidarity is also needed for cross-class integration. Solidarity is called for to integrate the different classes in society; their conflicting interests must be transcended in order to establish peace and harmony. *Mater et magistra* linked solidarity to justice, and pointed out that justice was a central concern for the issues of poverty and peace. It stressed the right of the poor to have a fair share of the goods of this world and insisted that the rich should do much more than simply give alms. Moreover, John prudently argued for the establishment of a new economic world order.[1]

Catholicism and the Third World: Populorum Progressio

During the 1960s, the Catholic Church became increasingly preoccupied with the situation in the Third World. The Second Vatican Council in Rome in 1962 had 40 per cent of the 2,500 participants hailing from the Third World. Even so, the Second Vatican Council was dominated by the traditional conflict between conservatives and liberals regarding liturgical matters. Third World issues and economic injustice within the First World were not really central issues, even if the conference did take up some of the themes from *Mater et Magistra* and called for justice and solidarity in the document *Gaudium et Spes*. Still, the concept of solidarity

---

[1] The right, represented by *Fortune* magazine, attacked *Mater et Magistra* for being 'wedded to socialist economics and increasingly a sucker for Third World anti-imperialist rhetoric'. It was criticised from the left by liberation theologians for showing insufficient concern for the freedom of the person (Goulet 1983). An established scholar of Catholic social ethics, John Dorr, characterises *Mater et Magistra* as being 'an opening to the left, but more as a decisive move away from the right' (Dorr 1983).

was only used in an elusive and abstract way. The document argued for more equality and for better regulation of international trade, but this was done in a non-committal way, speaking of 'an end to excessive economic and social differences' (Vatican 1968).[2]

Pope John XIII's successor, Paul VI, continued to work for improved relationships with other religions and to increases in the diplomatic activities of the Vatican. His encyclical *Populorum Progressio* in 1967 represented a new step in the development of a more precise concept and language of solidarity. Paul had travelled extensively in Africa and in Latin America before he was elected pope and called for solidarity and more concrete and concerted action in the struggle against hunger and misery in the world (Paolo VI 1967). An entire chapter of *Populorum Progressio* was devoted to the 'Solidaristic development of humanity'. Paul argued here that free trade was unfair if it was not subordinated to the goals of social justice. He condemned racism, called for agreements on trade and proposed the establishment of a world fund to assist poor nations. As previous popes had done, he denounced violence in the struggle for a more just world, but accepted the fact that revolution can be justified in some situations. This gives expression to an important change of attitude compared to previous papal encyclicals.

The general political unrest and the more radical mood in the First and in the Third Worlds in the latter part of the 1960s greatly influenced the development of Catholic social teaching. In Latin America, a theology of liberation developed that was inspired by Marxist analysis and language (Tombs 2002). In 1968, Catholic bishops gathered in Medellín, in Colombia. They pointed to the massive structural injustices in their part of the world and committed themselves and their churches to give 'effective preference to the poorest and most needy sectors of society' and accepted the obligation of solidarity with the poor and the marginalised (Dorr 1983). Elements from the Medellín declaration were later integrated into Paul VI's *Octogesima Adveniens* in 1971.

However, church authority was further reduced, and many believe that this was in part a result of the more open and democratic atmosphere at, and subsequent to, the Second Vatican Council. Certainly, the widespread social action and the tumultuous atmosphere in 1968 and in the years that followed also had an effect (Riccardi 1990). As pluralism gained strength, the authority of papal teachings gradually decreased.

---

[2] Allum (1990) and Dorr (1983) each give a different account of the Second Vatican Council's discussions about poverty and liberation. I do not agree with Allum's claim that poverty and liberation were major themes. The documents from the Second Vatican Council clearly show that the council was mostly concerned with liturgy and the vernacular (see *The Documents of Vatican II* (Vatican 1966)).

The continuing secularisation of society further weakened the hold of the Church.

John Paul: a complete language of solidarity

It was Pope John Paul II who finally made solidarity a dominant theme in Catholic social teaching. He expanded the concept and declared that solidarity was a key value for the Church, and he established a complete language of solidarity and defined the relationship between solidarity and other key concepts in Catholic social teaching.

John Paul II succeeded Paul VI in 1978. His papacy has been characterised by two particular developments. On the one hand, he made the message of the Church more relevant for the challenges of modern society. He gave great attention to poverty, war, international relations and ecumenical work. On the other hand, he tried to put a stop to the radicalisation of the Church in the Third World. He rejected liberation theology and installed conservatives in Church offices, forcing the radical elements within the Church in Latin America to be on the defensive (Tombs 2002).[3] Besides that, he reaffirmed positions on cultural and sexual matters that are very difficult to justify or support from a modern world perspective.

John Paul's Polish origin, and his association with the labour union struggle of Lech Walesa and *Solidarność* in Poland, may have helped to take the papacy one step further in its elaboration of the concept of solidarity in the encyclical *Laborem Exercens*, in 1981. Returning to the themes of *Rerum Novarum*, first addressed ninety years earlier, he wrote about wages and social issues, including health care and social insurance. For the first time in an encyclical, *worker* solidarity was made into a theme – and described in a positive way:

> solidarity and common action addressed to the workers . . . was important and eloquent from the point of social ethics. It was the reaction against the unheard of accompanying exploitation in the field of wages, working conditions and social security for the worker. This reaction united the working world in a community marked by great solidarity. (John 1989a)

John Paul frankly recognised that worker reaction to injustice was justified 'from the point of view of social morality' and he saw the need for new labour movements in different parts of the world. 'This solidarity

---

[3] In 1979, John Paul went to Puebla, in Mexico to take part in another conference of Latin American bishops. Although the Puebla meeting was preoccupied with the plight of the poor and the need for solidarity, it was considered a setback for liberation theology, and a warning for those who wanted to further politicise the Church.

must be present and is called for by the presence of the social degrading of the subject of work, by exploitation of the workers and by the growing areas of poverty and even hunger', he argued. This did not imply adopting socialist conceptions of class struggle. In an extensive paragraph on 'Conflict between labour and employers in the present phase of history' he gave priority to labour, but emphasised capital assets and did not view employers as being the personal adversaries of workers. Even if the struggle for justice might lead to confrontation, he urged workers and employers to acknowledge that both 'must in some way be united in community' (John 1989a).

The next step was taken in *Sollecitudo Rei Socialis* in 1989, which made *solidarity* a key concept in Catholic social teaching. Again, the point of departure was the relationship between rich and poor. Since nations and individual human beings are dependent upon one another economically, culturally and politically, solidarity is the adequate moral and social attitude, he wrote. Solidarity is not a diffuse feeling of compassion, but a firm and lasting commitment to the best for all. Those who have resources and influence should feel responsibility for the weak and share their resources with them. The weak should not be passive or behave in a destructive way, they too should do the best they can for everyone, while demanding their legitimate rights. Solidarity helps us to see *the other*, whether the other is a person, a people or a nation. In so doing we see the other not as a means with a capacity to work and to be exploited by low wages, but as a 'neighbour' with whom we share 'the banquet of life, where we all are invited by God on the same conditions' (John 1989b).

Finally, in *Centesimus Annus*, in 1991, John Paul developed a complete language of solidarity. On the basis of his own re-reading of *Rerum Novarum*, 100 years after it was published, he linked solidarity to a defined set of other key concepts. These are *personalism, love, the common good, subsidiarity, freedom* and *justice*. *Personalism* means that every human being is seen as a person. An individual becomes a person through his or her relationships to others, and the social character of a human being does not fulfil itself in relation to the state, but is realised in different intermediating groups, beginning with the family. An individual becomes a person through his/her ties to other persons by membership in the family, and by economic, social, political and cultural ties to other groups. Solidarity, John Paul declares, begins in the family, with the love between spouses and the reciprocal care between the generations. Other intermediary organisations activate networks of solidarity and mature into real communities, and in so doing strengthen the social fabric.

The concept of solidarity is closely associated to the concept of the *common good*. Cultural development demands the involvement of the whole person, the capacity for self-control, personal sacrifice, solidarity and the preparedness to support the common good. 'An elementary principle of every sound political organisation' is that the more defenceless a person is, the greater the need for the care and interest of others, including intervention by the state. This is 'the principle we today call solidarity' and it 'is valid, as well, in every nation as well as in the international order' (Giovanni 1991). John Paul argues that the Church has a 'preferential option for the poor'.

The ideas of solidarity and the common good are linked to the idea of *justice*. The love for humankind, and especially for the poor, is made concrete in the support of justice. Today, justice does not only mean giving from one's overabundance; it means aiding entire nations that are marginalised and allowing them to enter into the circle of economic and human development. To achieve this, it is necessary to change life-styles, ways of production and consumption, and the structures of power that rule the societies of today, John Paul argued.

He continued to claim that Catholic solidarity should be based upon an extensive welfare state and a well-developed system of labour laws. A person should express his own personality through work, be protected against unemployment, have the right to unemployment benefits and the right to requalify for other forms of employment, if necessary. A person should have the right to a decent salary that can provide for a family *and* for modest savings. On the other hand, the welfare state might make society less responsible. Therefore, *subsidiarity* must balance and delimit solidarity and public interference. Superior instances should not unnecessarily interfere in the life of inferior instances, but should support such instances. John Paul repeats the words of Leo XIII about subsidiarity.

With the publication of *Centesimus Annus*, John Paul authorised a complete language of solidarity in Catholic social teachings, and defined solidarity's relationships to other key concepts such as *the person, the common good, justice* and *subsidiarity*.

The continuing problem of the Vatican has been how it should relate the Catholic Church to modernity. The establishment of a language of solidarity has to some extent lessened this problem. However, John Paul II's conservatism on cultural issues has created new problems. He has consistently called for solidarity in society and internationally in the world community. Still, his policies towards national and social liberation movements in the Third World and the role of many of his bishops in the struggle for reforms in Central and in South America raise concerns about the distance between Church theory and Church practice. Besides that, one

Table 3.1 *The Catholic concept of solidarity*

Foundation	Objective	Inclusiveness	Collective orientation
Human equality in the eyes of God/the family/human interdependence	Social peace and harmony/social integration/ enhancing the conditions of human life	Very strong: all classes; the poor and the needy; the Third World	Weak: personalism Subsidiarity

could well argue that his position on HIV/AIDS, and on the use of contraceptives and family planning in Africa and elsewhere, are far from expressions of solidarity in their practical effects.

The Catholic concept of solidarity

As we have seen, the concept of solidarity has emerged and developed in Catholicism from two very different sources. The first is the preoccupation with social integration, with its origins in the works of Thomas Aquinas. In this tradition, the emphasis is upon a universal understanding of solidarity, stressing consensus and the community between all human beings. The second source is found in the concern for the suffering peoples of the Third World. The urgent problems of the poor nations and the Vatican's increased understanding of those problems and the influence of the Catholic churches of the Third World, especially in Latin America, paved the way for the introduction of the concept of solidarity into encyclicals and other ecclesiastical texts. With the confluence of these two strands a Catholic concept of solidarity was established. These strands of ideas were developed in the long and continuing confrontations with liberal capitalism and with socialist collectivism.

The foundation of solidarity is formulated somewhat differently in papal texts, depending on the context. Generally speaking, solidarity is founded upon the equal worth of each and every human being in the eyes of God. Sometimes the family is seen as being the basis for solidarity – a basis that might become a model for other social relationships. Occasionally, the general interdependence in society makes solidarity the adequate and necessary response to *others*. Here, self-interest does not have the significant role to play that it has in the classic Marxist and in the classic social democratic concepts. In Catholicism, the expression of solidarity aims at developing social peace and harmony and social integration. The Catholic idea of solidarity is the attitudinal correlate to social integration. Social integration is the aim and attitudes expressing solidarity are the means that assist in bringing about social integration. Sometimes, *increased equality* is mentioned, i.e. enhancing the relative positions of those who are without resources.

From the emphasis on social integration, it follows logically that Catholic solidarity is the broadest and the most inclusive sort. Transcending class boundaries, it is explicitly meant to encompass all classes of people across all social and economic barriers and divisions. The Catholic ambition is to unite employers and employees, workers and the middle class, women and men, into a community where cooperation and mutual understanding reign. In this way, Catholic solidarity clearly distinguishes itself from classic Marxist and social democratic concepts.

The collective orientation of Catholic solidarity is weaker than the collective orientation in the classic Marxist and/or the social democratic ideas of solidarity. Collective aspects are carefully balanced against the emphasis on the individual. *Personalism*, the idea that one becomes a person through one's relationships to others, makes the relationship between the individual and society *an issue*, and dampens the collective aspects of solidarity. The concept of subsidiarity reinforces the reservations that hinder a strong collective orientation. The conceptual context of Catholic solidarity is very different from the conceptual context of the classic Marxist concept. The same is true, only less so, when comparing the Catholic conceptual context to the social democratic conceptual context. The conceptual contexts of all three have ideas of justice and freedom, although these ideas are not exactly the same (see Chapter 7). The inclusion of *subsidiarity* in the Catholic conceptual scheme, and the stronger emphasis upon *equality* in the classic social democratic scheme, constitute the most important differences between these two.

A main problem in papal texts has been the role of struggle and conflict associated with the concept of solidarity. If people live in undignified conditions, if they are oppressed or exploited, if they are without influence over their own lives, should they not have the right to confront their oppressors with collective action and give expression to their conflict? The Catholic Church has struggled with this question for a very long time. Successive popes have gradually and hesitatingly begun to recognise that solidarity with the poor and with the oppressed should also imply *their* right to engage in confrontation and through their collective action make use of several forms of resistance.

The Catholic idea of solidarity is clearly closer to Durkheim's concept of organic solidarity than to the concept of the Marxist and early social democratic traditions. As we shall see later, the differences between the Catholic and the current social democratic concepts are less pronounced.

The solidarity of the labour movement has traditionally entailed a willingness to organise redistribution through the state. Catholic social teaching has stressed the role of voluntary associations and has assigned the state to a subsidiary, although necessary, role. The labour movement drew a sharp line between solidarity, on the one hand, and charity or altruism, on the other. There is no clear distinction between those concepts in Catholic social teaching (Kersbergen 1995). This was exemplified in John Paul's *Centesimus Annus*. Here the commitment to charity and solidarity is mentioned jointly without any distinction between the two. Both begin in the family, and both are necessary to overcome the contemporary and very widespread individualistic mentality, he argues.

Today, John Paul's criticism of the economy and of the social organisation in capitalist society is harsh and probably more severe than almost any other well-known participant in public debate in Europe. The widespread authority of the current pope and the hierarchical organisation of the Catholic Church would lead one to believe that the importance of the idea of solidarity in modern Catholic social teaching would influence the attitudes of Catholics in their relations to 'others': the poor, the unemployed and immigrants. However, the political and the perlocutionary effects of Vatican teaching about solidarity are not at all clear. The increased pluralism that has followed in the footsteps of the Second Vatican Council has reduced the authority of papal teaching (Allum 1990). Moreover, a well-known phenomenon concerning the Church's teachings, one that has been identified throughout the history of the Church, points to the filtering process that occurs when Church teachings are disseminated throughout the different layers of ecclesiastic hierarchy and given different interpretations. By the time the Catholic laity hears about changes in Church doctrine several intervening interpretations may have been made. In addition, individuals make their own reinterpretations. The increasing individualisation in our own day and age has changed the function of religion. The Pope is still listened to, by Catholics and others, but his words no longer have a strong authority among the Catholic laity in matters relating to society and politics.

Protestantism

Protestantism includes two main strands: the teachings of Luther and those of John Calvin. These two had very different understandings of the relationship between Christian belief and worldly political engagement. Luther proposed the *Zwei Reiche Lehre* (*The Doctrine of Two Kingdoms*) and the reformed Church proposed the *Königsherrschaft-Christi-Lehre* (*The Doctrine of the Kingdom of Christ*). Generally speaking, Protestant social teachings have been less explicit than Catholic teachings, and neither Lutheranism nor Reformed Protestantism has paid as much attention to the concept of solidarity as has Catholic social teaching. Reformed Protestantism has a much less complicated path to political engagement than Lutheranism. John Calvin saw the world as being *potentially* Christ's kingdom, and urged Christians to struggle to make the world conform to the laws of God. God was a King above all other Kings and worldly authorities. The worldly authorities should conform to the will of God, and their sovereignty should be limited. If they did not do so, citizens had the right to resist. After the massacre of the Huegenots, in France, in 1572, Reformed Protestants maintained that resistance was not only a right, but a duty (Hudson 1970). The Reformed Protestant Church did not prevent its members from engaging in politics, or from the pursuit of political power for the achievement of worldly political objectives that were in accordance with Calvin's understanding of the 'rule of God' (Johnston 1991). However, the only Protestant political party included in this study is the Lutheran Christian People's Party (KrF) in Norway. For that reason, I will concentrate on Lutheran Protestantism in the following.

The process that led many Lutherans to adopt the idea of solidarity had two distinct phases. In the first phase, Lutherans had to abandon the traditional interpretation of Luther's teaching about the two kingdoms (see below) and engage themselves more actively in politics. The next phase was to include the concept of solidarity in a political interpretation of the relationship between the rich First World and the poor peoples of the Third World.

Two realms: the kingdom of God and the kingdom of the world

Luther formulated several doctrines that distinguish Lutheran Protestantism from Catholicism. Foremost among these are the primacy of scripture (*sola scriptura*), the priesthood of all believers, the separation between the kingdom of God and the kingdom of the world and the freedom and obligation of service for all Christians. The first two emerged simultaneously and contributed to the fragmentation of Protestantism into a great variety of churches and denominations. The primacy of scripture calls upon all Christian believers to return to the Bible, and to consult the Bible independently for guidance. The priesthood of all believers proclaims that all Christians are capable of interpreting the Bible and that they have the right and the responsibility to do so, and that ecclesiastical hierarchies like those found in the Catholic Church should not interfere. This doctrine undermined all attempts to create a single, powerful and united Protestant church and laid the foundation for a profound individualism (Porter 1957). As a consequence, whereas it has been possible to identify a specific Catholic view concerning the idea of solidarity on the basis of papal encyclicals, no parallel undertaking can be made when it comes to Protestantism.

Luther's distinction between the two realms or kingdoms separates God's rule from worldly authority. Heaven is ruled by the word of the gospel and this world is ruled by human law and by the sword. Since the world is evil, governments have to rule with law and by the sword. In Luther's understanding, the world is a violent and brutal place, and is very similar to the one depicted by Thomas Hobbes more than 100 years later. Luther believed that governments should be allowed to exercise worldly power and that citizens were required to be obedient. The power of government should be restricted to 'life and property and external affairs on earth' (Luther 1957 (1520)), and the individual was not obliged to obey when governmental demands were contrary to scripture, personal conscience or the laws of the land.

Luther's third doctrine was formulated in the famous paragraph: 'a Christian is a perfectly free lord of all, subject to none. A Christian is a perfectly dutiful servant of all, subject to none.' The Christian concept of love and the Lutheran idea of service acknowledge a concern with the sufferings of humanity, but this concern was characterised more by individual charity than by any form of collective solidarity. As in Catholic countries, Protestant churches and congregations organised assistance to the poor and established institutions for orphans and asylums and hospitals.

The relationship between obedience to worldly rulers and the duty to protest and resist is disputed, and some would say contradictory, in the writings of Luther.[4] The doctrine of the two kingdoms brought about a harmonious relationship between the state and the church in many nations where Protestantism was influential (Ramet 2000). The doctrine was not conducive to the formulation of ideas of solidarity if these were interpreted as being critical of governmental practices. The political implications of Luther's teachings are that the church should not have any jurisdictional or coercive powers to regulate Christian life. This should be left to the secular authorities. The Church was nothing more than

---

[4] See Skinner (1980) and Frostin (1994) for detailed and thorough analyses of different positions on this issue in Lutheran and Calvinist thinking. Frostin maintains that 'it is impossible to summarise Luther's different statements and positions in his two kingdoms doctrine, into one that is not self-contradictory, because Luther changed his view. He was, at first, concerned about the opposition of the world as a power against God, but later saw the world not only as the place of sin, but also as God's creation.'

a community of believers and secular rulers that shared the faith, were given the authority to appoint priests and to make decisions concerning church property (Skinner 1980).

The idea of solidarity seems to have been introduced into Lutheranism and into Reformed Protestantism through two separate but interconnected channels.[5] First, many German Protestants passively accepted the German fascist regime after 1933, and this painful fact laid the ground for a new interpretation of Luther's doctrine of the two kingdoms. In the *Barmen Theological Declaration* of 1934 the prominent theologian and reformed Protestant, Karl Barth, repudiated '(the) false teaching that the church can and must recognise yet other happenings and powers, images and truths as divine revelations alongside this one World of God . . .' (quoted in Moltmann 1984a). According to Barth, there is no area of life in which man does not belong to Jesus Christ. No state and no government nor any other power or institution in the world can change that belonging. Lutheranism was also influenced by the life, deeds and the writings of the theologian Dietrich Bonhoeffer, who was jailed and killed by the Nazis for his participation in the conspiracy to kill Hitler during World War II. Bonhoeffer's prison writings, where his motives and actions are discussed and justified, were later published and have undoubtedly inspired Lutherans to revise their understanding of Luther's doctrine of the two kingdoms. After the war, the teachings of these two men gained great influence in their respective churches. Another important influence, in the last part of the twentieth century has been the ecumenical movement. An increasing awareness of the poverty and social problems of the Third World has paved the way for the introduction of the idea of solidarity into Protestant social ethics.

From Luther to the Lutheran World Federation

As there is no single authorised representative spokesman for Lutheranism in modern times, I have chosen to study resolutions and documents from the Lutheran World Federation (LWF). No other organisation can be considered a better representative for what might be called Lutheran social ethics.

---

[5] Luther sometimes referred to a concept of brotherhood. However, according to his teaching of the two kingdoms, he differentiated between the brotherhood of believers and that of the world, which he rejected as being particularistic. Brotherhood should be restricted to the spiritual sphere of the kingdom of God and not applied to the social sphere of the world. Luther's concept of brotherhood did not imply any solidarity in the modern meaning, one which implies the redistribution of material goods in order to achieve more equality between people.

The LWF is a free association of churches whose combined membership approaches 55,000,000. Although the LWF has not been authorised by member churches to decide upon theological issues,[6] documents and resolutions from LWF general assemblies are probably the most representative Lutheran texts to be found. Lutheran churches have channelled much of their own ecumenical commitments through the World Council of Churches (WCC). The WCC is a meeting place for Lutherans, Reformed Protestants, Eastern Orthodox, Anglican, Methodist, Baptist and a large number of non-Catholic churches. The Roman Catholic Church is not a member, but it does send representatives to important WCC events.

The Lutheran World Convention was constituted in Eisenach, Germany, in 1923. It grew out of the ambition to establish stronger unity between the Lutheran churches. Its goal was to heal the wounds that World War I had inflicted upon Lutheran unity, and to provide assistance to Lutherans whose lives had been devastated by the war. After World War II, it was reorganised into the Lutheran World Federation (LWF) which was established in Lund, Sweden, in 1947. Among its objectives were:

- to cultivate the unity of faith and confession among the Lutheran churches of the world
- to promote fellowship and cooperation in study among Lutherans
- to support Lutheran groups in need of spiritual or material aid
- to foster Lutheran participation in ecumenical movements. (LWF 1948)

In the period just after the war, the LWF had three primary tasks. The most important was providing aid to refugees and others who were suffering because of the war. In addition, the LWF was busy assisting sister churches and redefining Lutheran theology. At that time, the LWF was not concerned about general political issues, such as economic and social inequality and poverty in the Third World. The terms *fellowship* and *brother* were used, but these terms generally referred to the relationships between Lutherans. Assistance to those in need was expressed by using concepts like Christian love and charity rather than by the use of the concept of solidarity.

The inability of many German Lutherans to resist cooperating and complying with the Nazi regime made the critical rethinking of Lutheran

---

[6] After 1979, the LWF debated whether or not it should be a federation or a *communion* of Lutheran churches. The distinction points to the fact that the unity between churches has increased and to the fact that ecumenical work in the LWF has been given priority. Gunnar Staalsett, the LWF general secretary from 1985 to 1994, has been a protagonist in this development.

identity and the reinterpretation of Luther's teachings about the two kingdoms urgent. Karl Barth's critique, although outside Lutheranism, did
make an impact. Two influential members of the LWF were the Swede,
Sven Nygren, the first general secretary, and the Norwegian bishop,
Eivind Berggrav, who had been a prominent symbol of the struggle against
the German occupation of Norway. Both of these men insisted that it was
necessary to reinterpret Luther's conception of the two kingdoms. The
Church did not owe obedience to the state when the state violated justice. Injustice was an offence against the natural rights of all, according to
Berggrav. Other prominent Lutherans who had stood up against fascism
shared this view, and their interpretation found support in the new LWF.

The door was opened for a more active involvement in politics and
for greater engagement in discussion about social ethics. Eventually, the
idea of solidarity became a part of the LWF vocabulary, but many years
passed before the idea of solidarity was introduced into key documents
of the LWF world assemblies. From the very beginning, the LWF was
dominated by the German churches, which still enjoyed a great deal of
prestige with the Scandinavians churches, and by the Lutheran churches
in the United States. The Lutheran churches in the United States were
conservative and critical of what they regarded as the liberal theology of
the Scandinavians.

The second LWF world assembly took place in Hanover, Germany, in
1953. The assembly was preoccupied with inner church matters, but the
relationship between the church and the state was also on the agenda.
Berggrav elaborated upon his view that Christians have an obligation to
resist when a state or a government does not respect the law. Besides that,
he warned against the development of a welfare state which he believed
would create a new danger, because it would 'sterilise the social welfare
work of the church' and regulate individual lives. The church should claim
a place for parents and children, and for social welfare work, he declared.
The resolutions adopted at the assembly in 1957 introduced *justice* as
an important concept and declared that love and compassion should be
'translated into the structure of justice'. Civil liberties, racial integration,
concern for 'the uprooted and for people in areas of rapid social change,
and the care for the mentally and physically disabled' should be realised
in recognition of human rights (LWF 1957).

At the next conference in Helsinki, Finland, in 1963 key lecturers
focused attention upon the *north–south* and the *east–west* divides. Different
speakers called for a Christian 'genuine brotherhood' between different
races and with the developing countries. An appeal was made for Christian unity and not for a more general solidarity with others, even though

one lecturer from the Third World referred briefly to the 'solidarity of the Church with the world', alternating between the terms *solidarity* and *compassion*.[7]

The changing political climate following the student revolts in 1968 affected the LWF and the WCC, and both organisations developed a more pronounced political language. The WCC conference in 1968 was held in Uppsala, Sweden, and was a breakthrough for a more radical political commitment and for the development of a more specific political language in the WCC with greater concern for Third World issues and for justice and peace.[8] A parallel development took place in the LWF, and the LWF assembly in Evian, France, in 1970 also took a decisive step towards a more active involvement in social ethics and politics. The focus was now on human rights, the relationship between the rich nations of the North and the poor nations of the South, and the relationship between Eastern and Western Europe. The assembly warned that because of their traditions Lutherans might take a neutral stand towards social problems, and passed resolutions condemning racial discrimination and violations of human rights. The harsh effects of unjust social and economic systems result in hunger, misery and hopelessness and mean that human rights are being violated, the Assembly declared (LWF 1970). In short, the LWF Assembly in Evian represented 'a breakthrough in the Lutheran discovery of responsibility for the world' (Schjørring *et al.* 1997). A Lutheran language of social ethics and politics had now been established. The key term in this new language was *justice*, but *solidarity* was not yet an important concept.

In the early 1970s, the LWF became increasingly preoccupied with controversial social, political and economic issues. This development was confirmed at the 1977 LWF Assembly – the first to be held in a Third World country, in Dar es Salaam, Tanzania. The Assembly declared that the Church is called upon to be *in* the world and must develop a critical commitment in its own society as an expression of its solidarity with the world (LWF 1977).

The documents from the Assembly in 1984 and themes of the working groups clearly show that the gap between Lutheran social ethics and

---

[7] See the lecture *The New Song of Praise*, by Andar Lumbantobing, a university president from Indonesia.
[8] See the documents from the congress in WCC 1968. A study of key documents and resolutions from WCC conferences indicates that the WCC developed a social ethic and a political commitment somewhat earlier. The WCC took up Third World issues and called for 'more than charity' already at the conference in New Delhi in 1961 and increased its commitment to Third World issues in the succeeding years (WCC 1962; 1966).

politics had dwindled. The major themes of the working groups included racism, social and economic justice, a new partnership between men and women, the information age and peace and justice. This new political consciousness was reconfirmed at the Assembly in Curitiba, Brazil, in 1990. The Assembly reflected a strengthened involvement in the situation of the poor in the Third World, violations of human rights, the environment and pollution and discrimination against ethnic minorities (LWF 1990). Finally, the documents prepared for the assembly in 2003 witness a strong commitment to justice and call for the globalisation of solidarity as a response to the globalisation of the economy – 'a globalisation imposed by impersonal market forces that set us against each other' (LWF 2003a).

We have seen the gradual development of a Lutheran social ethic and the gradual appropriation of political language. Luther's distinction between the two kingdoms has been effectively abandoned. The resolutions of the LWF demonstrate that the Lutherans of today are willing to commit themselves very strongly to political solutions for the burning problems in society and in the world. Their gradual approach to political engagement has been accompanied by the search for a new language that can express this newfound commitment. *Justice* is the key concept in this language. This is not a very precisely defined term, although it does refer to a more equal distribution of resources. *Equality*, in itself, does not appear to be a central concept in the Lutheran language. Other concepts that are central are *human rights*, *oppression* and *discrimination*. The term *solidarity* is found in resolutions and texts from the LWF now and then, but it has not been a key concept – with the exception of Third World issues. *Solidarity* is used in a general and in a self-explanatory way, and has not been defined precisely, and there has not been a parallel to the elaboration of this concept that is found in Catholic social teaching.[9] To the extent that it is possible to discern a Lutheran concept of solidarity, the aspects of this concept are depicted in the table below.

Somewhat different to the Catholic and the social democratic concept, the Lutheran concept of solidarity seems primarily to be an instrumental one, as a means to bring about justice. It is never formulated as a value in itself, as is the case in Catholic social teaching.

---

[9] This is the case for the WCC as well. Resolutions and key texts from WCC conferences indicate that the political language developed from 1968 is closely related to that of the LWF. However, the concept of solidarity is found more frequently in the WCC than in LWF resolutions. The fact that the WCC seems to have developed a political language somewhat earlier than the LWF and the stronger emphasis on solidarity in WCC resolutions, may be due to the presence and participation of Reformed Protestant theologians, such as Jürgen Moltmann in the WCC (see Chapter 9).

Table 3.2 *A Lutheran concept of solidarity*

Foundation	Objective	Inclusiveness	Collective orientation
Man is created in the image of God The love of one's neighbour Christian servitude	To realise the kingdom of God on earth Welfare for all	Those who suffer The poor and the needy The Third World	Weak: modified by the Bible and by one's own conscience

Lutheran and Catholic solidarity

We have seen that neither Catholicism nor Lutheranism developed and integrated a concept of solidarity until the later part of the twentieth century. Whereas social theorists began to make the concept an object of reflection in the first part of the nineteenth century, as did socialist theory in the later part of the same century, the two dominant Christian religions in Western Europe did not do so until much later.

The Catholic concept of solidarity grew out of two quite different concerns: worries about social integration in industrial society and concerns about the Third World, dating from the 1950s, with an introduction of the concept in an encyclical in 1961. Lutherans, and Protestants in general, link the idea of solidarity with their concerns about the unfavourable situation of the Third World. This involvement begins in the 1950s and there is a breakthrough in 1968. The introduction of *solidarity* in Protestant social ethics has not been as prominent as it has been in Catholicism. The idea was introduced by Protestant radical dissidents and made its way into the ecumenical movement, which has generally proved to be more radical than most of the individual Protestant churches. From the LWF and the WCC the concept of solidarity has spread more broadly within Protestant circles. However, the concept of solidarity has not been integrated into mainstream Protestant social teachings to the same extent as has been done in Catholic social teaching. The Protestant discourse of solidarity is not as rich and as well developed as the Catholic one, and the concept is not as well integrated into a language with well-defined relationships to other key concepts.

Why has the idea of solidarity in Catholic and Protestant social ethics lagged behind developments elsewhere? One reason is that Catholicism and Lutheran Protestantism first had to bridge important gaps. In order to be able to engage in politics at all, Lutheran social ethics had to overcome an important doctrine, in Luther's thinking, the distinction between the two kingdoms. In Catholicism, the introduction of the idea of solidarity into social ethics had a political and a conceptual hindrance that first had to be overcome. Politically, the gradual and continuing deradicalisation of socialist and communist parties in western Europe reduced traditional Catholic hostility against the parties of the labour movement. During the elections in Italy, in 1948, Pope Pius XII had described the choice between the Christian Democratic Party and the Communist party as a choice between *good* and *evil*. His successor, Pope John XXIII, reformed the content and style of communication of the Church and reduced the direct intervention of the Church in politics, a policy continued by Paul VI (Wertman 1982). In France as well, the clergy and Catholics in general no longer intervened in politics in order to express hostility towards the socialist and communist left, and accepted a greater degree of political pluralism within their own ranks in this period (Donegani 1982). After 1968, many groups of Catholics approached socialism, Marxism and the parties of the left. This contributed to a more open dialogue between Catholicism and the political left.

A second reason for the lag in development of the idea of solidarity in Catholic and in Lutheran thinking is the close connection the idea of solidarity has had to other concepts of importance to socialist theory, concepts like *class conflict* and *political agitation*. The conceptual space shared by the dominant conception of solidarity in the labour movement was long associated with ideas about class struggle, the expropriation or nationalisation of industry, or the means of production, and to other limitations in the rights to private property. When Christians finally adopted the concept, it was at a time when this concept had been transformed into a broader and more altruistic one in most of the large and influential parties within the labour movement in Western Europe. This may have facilitated the introduction of the idea of solidarity in Catholicism and Protestantism.

Today, the differences between the Catholic and the Protestant ideas of solidarity are not very great, although there are still some distinctions. The foundations for their ideas of solidarity are the same. Man is created in the image of God, and all men are equal in the eyes of God. The call to love thy neighbour and the Christian obligation to serve others constitutes their common basis for giving expression to solidarity. Catholic social teaching will often add that human beings are interdependent and that the family is sacred. When the sharp distinction between *the two kingdoms* in the Lutheran tradition had been reinterpreted, it became easier to see the goal of solidarity as the realisation of the kingdom of God on earth. In later Protestant texts, the goal is sometimes simply referred to as *the welfare of all*. The clearest differences are to be found in the terms of inclusiveness and in the collective orientations of these somewhat different ideas of solidarity. Protestant solidarity focuses mainly upon the poor and the needy, referring more often than not to the Third World, but the poor in developed nations are also included. The Protestant concept is not *explicitly* a cross-class conceptualisation, as is the Catholic concept. Neither does it emphasise social integration as does the Catholic idea. This does not imply that Protestants view class conflict more favourably, but rather that the integration of classes in society is simply not made into an issue or theme in this particular connection. Finally, in Lutheranism the collective orientation is particularly weak. Whereas in Catholicism the concept of *the person* represents middle ground between individualism and collectivism, the collective aspects of Lutheran solidarity are strongly qualified. The collective must never force the individual to do anything that contradicts the dictates of conscience. In Lutheranism, the individual is obliged to adhere to the personal interpretation of Scripture that is most in keeping with the dictates of his or her own conscience.

Conclusion: concepts of solidarity in social theory, socialist theory and religion

The first part of this book distinguished between seven different conceptions of solidarity. These different conceptions are found in social theory, in socialist theory, and in Catholic and Protestant social ethics. Table 3.3 sums up how four key dimensions vary in the eight concepts that are being investigated.

A key distinction can be made between conceptions that understand solidarity as being *norms contributing to social integration* and conceptions that understand solidarity as being a *relationship* between members of a more or less specified group. The first conceptualisation is found in the writings of Comte and Durkheim. Here, solidarity is the result of the existence of norms and values that bind the different parts of society together.

The second conceptualisation is found in the writings of Leroux, in Marx and within Marxism, and in the writings of Weber. Here, solidarity is about interpersonal relationships that bind a group of people together. When a group is so defined, solidarity is seen as being a force that includes and excludes. In this understanding, solidarity integrates *and divides*. Several versions of this concept can be distinguished, depending upon what it is that constitutes the glue that binds people together in social relationships. This glue might be the rational pursuit of one's own interests, affective feelings, or a feeling of ethical obligation, or a mixture of some or all of these elements. In the development of Marxist thinking up to and including Kautsky, there is a discernible dislike for altruism and ethics,

Table 3.3 *Concepts of solidarity in social theory, socialist theory and Catholic social ethics*

	Foundation	Objective/Function	Inclusiveness	Collective orientation
1. Durkheimian solidarity (mechanic)	Homogeneity Interaction Social norms, values Common consciousness	Social integration	All who are alike (broad or restricted according to this)	Medium/strong: common consciousness makes individuality low
2. Durkheimian solidarity (organic)	Social norms, values and rituals Interdependence Complementarity Interaction	Social integration	Varying: dependent on the number and intensity of ties that link to society	Medium/weak: dilemma accepted and discussed defence of liberal democracy
3. Weberian solidarity	Interest and honour Norms and duties	Realise interests and increase power	Restricted: social groups or professions	Not explicitly formulated Acceptance of dilemma
4. Classic Marxist solidarity	Class interests Recognition of 'sameness'	Realise interests: revolution socialism	Restricted: only the working class, but in all nations	Strong: individual autonomy not made a theme
5. Leninist solidarity	Class interests Recognition of 'sameness'	Realise interests: revolution the dictatorship of the proletariat socialism	Very restricted: only the 'conscious' part of the working class, but in all nations	Very strong: individual autonomy explicitly suppressed
6. Classic social democratic solidarity	Popular interests Acceptance of difference Ethics and morality	Realise interests: reforms socialism create sense of community	Broader: all popular social forces/The nation?	'Medium': individual freedom is a value and the possible conflict between individual autonomy and collective requirements/expectations are acknowledged
7. Catholic solidarity	Man is created in the image of God/All human beings are equal in the eyes of God/The family/Love thy Neighbour/Human interdependence	Social peace and harmony Social integration More equality	Very strong: all classes The poor and needy The Third World	Weak/medium: modified by personalism and subsidiarity

and the role of affective feelings is ambiguous. Marx, Lenin and Lukács play down affective aspects in their theoretical contributions, but affective aspects were emphasised in political practice and agitation. The early social democrats, Bernstein and Wigforss, added ethical elements to the idea of rational self-interest, and these two elements form the foundation for socialist and classic social democratic solidarity. The Catholic concept cannot be classified in accordance with this distinction, since it aims at social integration and refers to social relationships.

When considering the basis for solidarity, both of the Durkheimian concepts emphasise interaction. The organic Durkheimian concept refers to a solidarity that is based upon the recognition of interdependence in modern society and on the sharing of norms, values and rituals. The objective or function of solidarity is to develop social integration in society. Its degree of inclusiveness remains somewhat ambiguous. On the one hand, diversity opts for a broad and inclusive concept; on the other, emphasis upon interaction and communication makes the concept more restrictive and non-inclusive. The collective aspect of this concept is not clearly defined, but it should probably be understood as being medium to weak. Durkheim valued individual freedom and autonomy highly, and discussed the relationship between the individual and the collective, maintaining firmly that solidarity and individual autonomy could be reconciled.

The Weberian concept is an open one in terms of the foundation of solidarity. Here, solidarity may be based upon interests, honour, norms and duties and is most often a mixture that might be revealed through empirical analysis. People join hands to realise their own economic interests or to increase their own power, and Weber points to the proliferation of professional groups when offering an example. This kind of solidarity is not inclusive. It is restricted and is often directed against competing groups. Not much is said about the relationship between the individual and the collective, but the problem is recognised and acknowledged.

As we have seen in Chapter 2, both the classic Marxist and the Leninist concepts are based upon the recognition of class interests and upon the community between fellow workers. The goal here is to realise the interests of the working class through revolution and by the establishment of a socialist society. This is a restricted concept which only includes the working class, although the confines of that class are unclear. However, national borders are not considered to be confines for working-class solidarity. The emphasis upon the collective is strong, and there are no significant concerns about how one can reconcile individual freedom and collective demands to toe the line. The Leninist concept is more restricted and collective. Lenin's insistence that unity could only be based upon correct analysis would mean in practice that only revolutionary segments of the working class were included. The emphasis upon the collective is very strong and no value is placed on the expression of individual freedom.

Classic social democratic solidarity is founded upon a broader definition of interests. Other classes and groups that are considered part of the working populations in addition to industrial workers are included. Ethics and morality are also seen as being essential fundamentals for the development of solidarity. Emphasis on the collective is classified as medium to weak, since the value of individual freedom is clearly stated and the potential conflict between this value and the need for collective discipline is openly recognised.

Finally, the Catholic and the Protestant ideas of solidarity are founded upon the belief that man is created in the image of God and that each and every human being is equal in the eyes of God. Catholic social teaching, which is more explicit, emphasises human interdependence and the family. Protestants, more often than not, mention the Christian duty to serve other human beings. The Catholic concept is in some ways closer to the Durkheimian concepts, since social integration and harmony are goals that are held in common. The Catholic concept is more inclusive than the Protestant concept, something which may simply be a consequence of the importance placed upon social integration. The Catholic concept time and again emphasises the importance of expressing solidarity across class boundaries and between rich and poor in modern society and between rich and poor nations. The Protestant concept most frequently directs attention to the poor and the needy in the Third World, and to those poor who suffer in the rich nations of the world. Both Catholic and Protestant solidarity imply a weak degree of collective orientation. In Catholicism, the individual is made a theme by the introduction of the concept of the person and by the stress on intermediating institutions in the concept of subsidiarity. These are collateral ideas that help to frame the Catholic concept of solidarity. In Protestantism, the individual has the right and the duty to make a personal interpretation of the scriptures and to insist that the dictates of conscience are respected.

It has been possible to differentiate between the eight concepts of solidarity in this study by closely examining four particular variables. But do these variables point to a necessary core in the idea of solidarity (cf. Freeden in the previous chapter)? Variations found within the four variables are not always easily discerned, but all the concepts studied point to two necessary values, that an individual should identify with others, to some degree, and that a feeling of community should exist between the individual and (at least some) others, and as a consequence it can be argued that all these ideas of solidarity imply some sort of inclusiveness. However, the strength of identification and the degree of inclusiveness may vary, and variations can also be found in the foundations of the idea, in the goal the idea supports, and in the degree that the idea has a collective orientation. If we do propose that a necessary core exists, based upon the four variables examined, we are forced to admit that there is a high degree of variation within each variable and that each combination changes the meaning of the concept being studied.

The political and religious concepts that are described here are located in different discourses or languages. As we shall see in more detail in the discussions of the social democratic and the Christian democratic concepts of solidarity in following chapters, these are associated in different ways with other key concepts. The meaning of the different concepts of solidarity can be established by studying the way in which each one is associated with other related concepts. Furthermore, as we shall see in Chapter 7, the location of the concept in a specific morphological system with other key concepts continues to increase the plurality and possible variations in the meaning of the concept.

The different versions of the concept of solidarity having been established, it is now time to turn to the world of politics in order to study the development of the concept of solidarity in various political parties of Western Europe. How, when and why are these ideas of solidarity *reflected* in the institutional ideologies of social democratic and Christian democratic parties in Western Europe?

Part II

The idea of solidarity in politics in
Western Europe

4   European variations of solidarity discourses in social democracy

The discourse about solidarity in European social democracy developed in societies that shared many common characteristics and that went through the processes of industrialisation and urbanisation. Not only was the working class more or less excluded from governmental institutions and political influence, it was confronted with dangerous working conditions and miserable housing conditions, and a bourgeoisie that defended its privileges and resisted change. It had to relate to farmers, smallholders and an urban petty bourgeoisie that identified neither with the working class nor with the bourgeoisie. The growing labour movement needed an ideology that united the class, and this is what Marxism offered. Within this common frame, national characteristics varied and influenced both the general ideology of the labour movement parties and the extent and the kind of solidarity discourses that were developed.

This chapter describes the process that made social democratic parties adopt an idea of solidarity; how different equivalent terms for this idea were replaced with *solidarity* and how this concept was transformed. It discusses national characteristics and throws light on why social democracy in some countries introduced the new and modern concept and developed a full discourse on solidarity earlier than others, and the contexts in which socialist and social democratic parties adopted a modern and broad concept of solidarity.

Class structure, trade unions and political parties

The growth of the idea of solidarity in the labour movement tradition has often been seen as a result of some kind of 'sameness', but this 'sameness' should not be taken for granted. On the one hand, the development of industrial capitalism brought workers together in factories and local communities in the cities. On the other hand, we should not paint a romantic view of a homogenous working class, with a high degree of internal loyalty, sharing resources and standing united against the common external enemy. Although varying between countries, the working class was marked by heterogeneity and divided by sectional interests, different social origins, regional cleavages or local differences and – in some countries – by religious and linguistic differences. In Britain, for example, Marshall, Newby, Rose, and Vogler claimed that internal heterogeneity and divisions built on sectional interests had always characterised the working class (Marshall *et al.* 1988). In Italy, Ferrera suggested that the extremely fragmented class structure and internal differences in the Italian working class explain why the Italian welfare state became weak and fragmented (Ferrera 1993). Although there are those who regard the working class in the Scandinavian countries as more homogeneous than elsewhere (Moody 1997; Bartolini 2000), the Norwegian historian Øyvind Bjørnson draws a different picture of an extremely heterogeneous class in his analysis of the working class in Norway from 1900 to 1920 (Bjørnson 1990).

Looking back on the history of class formation, Przeworski asserts that there is no automatic path from Marx's concept of 'class-in-itself' to 'class-for-itself' (Przeworski 1980). Classes are not only created by objective positions in production, but they are the result of struggle, and it is not only relationships of production that determine the outcome of these struggles. Class struggles are structured by the totality of economic, political and ideological relations; they have an autonomous effect upon the process of class formation. If this is so, solidarity is not an automatic result of capitalist development, but a result of the combined structures of economy, politics and ideology.

This approach naturally leads us to focus more on the strategy that political actors applied to develop coherence and solidarity in the class. Building on the approach of Przeworski, Esping-Andersen emphasises that class formation implies both a constructive and a destructive strategy (Esping-Andersen 1985). The labour movement must establish class as a legitimate and meaningful political agent and define the boundaries for inclusion in the class. Not only must it have a strategy to overcome market fragmentation and individualism, but it must also supplant alternative sources of worker identification, such as religion, ethnicity or localism, and early 'corporative' worker organisations, such as guilds and fraternal organisations.

What then was decisive in making working-class solidarity supersede older forms of solidarity? Stefano Bartolini asserts that a key factor in explaining the degree of cohesiveness of the working class in different European nations is the degree of cultural homogeneity/heterogeneity, especially religious and linguistic homogeneity (Bartolini 2000).

Historians such as Hobsbawm and Kjeldstadli emphasise three types of crucial factors for the development of working-class solidarity. First, workers gradually recognised the many points of resemblance they shared. They lived under the same economic scarcity. They were socially segregated. Urbanisation had brought people close to each other in blocks of flats that stimulated communication. They shared the same differences in relation to other classes with better living conditions. They acknowledged a common adversary – employers. The possibility of individual social mobility was small, and they gradually came to recognise that they could not improve their lot by individual action, but only by collective action, strikes, mutual aid and voting (Hobsbawm 1994; Kjeldstadli 1994). Second, solidarity was developed through struggle and organisation. Labour movement practice was decisive in creating solidarity within the class (Bjørnson 1990). Beyond a certain threshold, the labour movement developed through its own activities an internal alliance within the working class. Through strikes, demonstrations, meetings and a web of organisations the labour movement created a sense of belonging and an understanding of common interests (see Marx's view on practice in Chapter 2). In some countries, trade unions and political parties, youth organisations, choirs, athletic organisations and the like created strong subcultures with internal cohesion and solidarity. Finally, a third component was needed – a self-imposed morality (Kjeldstadli 1994). The movement grew out of enlightened self-interest, through recognition that solidarity meant a common struggle for a common goal against a common enemy. It was *enlightened* because one could not count on having something in return in the short run. Out of this enlightened self-interest developed a morality with its own weight, an inner commitment to solidarity. Without this ethical aspect, the labour movement could not achieve unity. A hypothesis would be that the interplay of working-class homogeneity/ heterogeneity and the strategies and practices chosen by political parties were decisive in determining the extent to which labour movements succeeded in uniting the working class in different countries.

While trade unions were important in bringing about worker unity in the workplace and among workers from different branches, political parties needed to have a broader view. Parties were required to reflect on all aspects of society, including the relationship between the industrial working class and other classes and social categories. In addition, parties had to develop a view on how national interests, the interests of the working class and those of oppressed workers in other countries might be reconciled. Political parties needed to integrate as well as have a language with concepts that might assist in accomplishing these aims.

The establishment of both trade unions and political parties may be considered an expression of the idea of solidarity. Both types of organisations aimed at overcoming the isolation of individual workers and the fragmentation of the working class. In trade unions the idea of solidarity implied that the individual worker would sacrifice his freedom in order to enter into a personal work contract with employers. In return, his fellow workers would do the same, so that they could negotiate collectively with employers. In labour movement parties, the idea implied that the worker should renounce narrow or sectional interests when necessary in order to work out a platform that expressed the interests of other segments of the working class as well.

The political parties of the European labour movements were formed by the specific national traditions out of which they grew, but also by being exposed in different ways to the diverse strands of European radicalism in the late nineteenth and the beginning of the twentieth centuries. Prominent among these strands were revolutionary Marxism, pragmatic trade unionism and anarcho-syndicalism. The birthplace of Marxism was Germany, and the most important political expression of a theoretically sophisticated Marxism was the German SPD. In France, Marxism was combined with anarcho-syndicalism, whereas pragmatic and reformist trade unionism were to be characteristics of the British Labour Party (Bartolini 2000). We shall see to what extent solidarity became an important concept in the parties belonging to those traditions.

First, however, we shall look into documents of the First International – an organisation regarded as the organisational expression of unity between the working class in different countries.

The First International

Recognising the increasing international character of capitalism, Marx was strongly engaged in opposing capitalism with an international organisation that could forge links among the workers of different countries. Hence, when the First International was established with Marx as a central founding leader in 1864, this was in itself an expression of the idea of solidarity. The statutes – written by Marx – referred explicitly to the significance of solidarity: 'all efforts aiming at that great end [the economic emancipation of the working class] have hitherto failed from the want of solidarity between the manifold divisions of labour in each country and in the absence of a fraternal bond of union between the working class of different countries' (First International 1934).

Solidarity is used here with a meaning close to how it was used in *The German Ideology* (see Chapter 2) and the concepts of *unity* and *association* in *Manifesto*. The concept of solidarity of the First International was certainly close to the classic Marxist concept. It would be an exaggeration, however, to say that *solidarity* was a central term in the First International. This term still had to compete with others to express the idea.

The First International did not turn out to be an effective expression of worker unity or solidarity. During its eight years of existence, the movement was marked by internal struggle culminating in The Hague Congress in1872 when Marx defeated and expelled his opponents, among them Bakunin and other anarchists. In the documents from The Hague Congress, *solidarity* was never mentioned. This is not surprising since the whole congress was preoccupied with internal strife (Gerth 1872). The congress demonstrated that it was not possible to develop sufficient unity to establish an international workers' party. In the following years the term *solidarity* was, however, more frequently used in socialist and trade union agitation. After the defeat of the Paris Commune in 1871 it became associated with the working-class struggle and the labour movement (Liedman 1999).

Germany: a model, but a late-comer

Throughout much of its history the German Social Democratic Party (*die Sozialdemokratische Partei Deutschlands* – SPD) has had a special status in the family of socialist and social democratic parties in Europe. Not only Marx, but also many other leading Marxist and socialist theorists were German, for example Kautsky, Bebel and Bernstein – the latter also generally regarded as the father of modern social democratic theory. A strong organisation and early electoral successes contributed to the prestige and influence of the SPD. The social democratic parties in the Netherlands, Austria, Denmark, Sweden and Norway in particular were much influenced by the ideology and politics of the SPD. But whereas the social democratic parties in Scandinavia became 'natural government parties' from the 1920s and 1930s, the SPD had to endure the next 100 years in isolation, being a party of opposition most of the time, with the exception of a few years during the Weimar Republic. This contrast between electoral and organisational strength on the one hand, and lack of influence on the other, was due in the early phase to the authoritarian character of the German Reich. It was not a parliamentary monarchy as in the north, and members of the *Reichstag* had little influence. After the Weimar period, the SPD did not succeed in entering into government again until 1966, in coalition with its chief adversary, the Christian democrats.

The early SPD: from Gotha to Heidelberg

The SPD[1] was founded as the result of a merger between the supporters of Ferdinand Lasalle and Marx in Gotha in 1875, and the platform of the new party necessarily had to be a compromise. Although there can be no doubt about the strong international orientation of the labour movement and the SPD at this time, the platform did not refer to worker solidarity or any equivalent concept (SPD 1875).

The new party faced an authoritarian regime and a conservative bourgeoisie not much influenced by the liberal ideas of this period. Bismarck was determined to fight the labour movement by almost any means and he banned the party in 1878. The SPD went underground and the leadership directed its activities in Germany from abroad. This endured for twelve years, with the result that the party became radicalised, more tightly organised and more disciplined than before. The SPD was a party and a movement at the same time. Political, social and cultural suborganisations and activities fortified the bonds between members and created a strong shield against other parties and social groups. Some have characterised this as 'ghettoisation', others have labelled the party/movement a *Solidargemeinschaft* – a community of solidarity (Lösche and Walter 1992; Lösche 1998).

The SPD was the dominant and most influential party in the Second International which was founded in 1889. At the Second International's foundation congress, the banners *Proletarier in aller Länder, vereinigen wir uns! (Proletarians of All Nations Unite!)* expressed the idea of international working-class unity (Second International 1889). The statutes referred specifically to 'the international union and action of the workers in the struggle against jingoism and imperialism . . .' (Second International 1986). The idea of international worker solidarity was strong, but the founders apparently did not consider it important to include those formulations concerning *solidarity* that had been part of the statutes of the First International. The term *solidarity* is not to be found at all, and in the years to follow, *solidarity* did not occur frequently in resolutions passed by the Second International. However, the programmes of the new working-class parties reflected the fact that the idea of international worker unity was strong and most parties stressed the need for such a unity in their programmes but chose phrases other than *solidarity* to express it.

When Bismarck lifted the ban, the SPD assembled in 1891 in Erfurt in Germany to approve a new platform. Karl Kautsky, August Bebel and

---

[1] With the name *Sozialistische Arbeiterpartei Deutschlands*. I have preferred to use the present day name, SPD, throughout the text, also in the period when the party was split between Majoritarian Socialists and Independent Socialists (USPD) from 1917 until 1922.

Eduard Bernstein formulated the draft, which reflected the radicalisation of the party and consolidated it on a Marxist platform. Inspired by the *Communist Manifesto*, the congress met under the banner, 'Workers of the world unite!' (Steenson 1991). In the years to come, the Erfurt programme was regarded as an expression of scientific socialism.[2] The programme came to initiate a long period of dissonance between theory and practice in the SPD. On the one hand, the Marxist analysis and terminology of the programme conveyed a revolutionary message to opponents and potential allies. On the other, day-to-day issues in the party's minimum programme dominated political practice, and socialism was deferred to a distant future (Carr 1991).

In terms of solidarity, the Erfurt programme stated that the 'interests of the working class of all countries are the same . . . [and] in recognition of this, the German Social Democratic Party feels and declares itself one with class conscious workers of all countries' (SPD 1891). This and such equivalent formulations as 'brotherly feelings' and 'internationalism' came to be used in the years to come, both in the German and in other Marxist and socialist parties in Europe. However, the term *solidarity* was not used in the Erfurt programme, which remained unaltered until after World War I. Until this time the term did not seem to be important and was only occasionally applied in key SPD documents.[3] The absence of *solidarity* in the Erfurt programme is conspicuous because the main author of the programme, Karl Kautsky, made solidarity a theme in his 'catechism' that explained and elaborated on the programme – *The Class Struggle* (as mentioned in Chapter 2). This book was considered the correct interpretation of Marxism in that period and demonstrates that the term *solidarity* was not alien to socialist theory and rhetoric. However, the increasing threats of war in the first decade of the new century made the party appeal for international working-class unity, and in this context the term *solidarity* was used more frequently.

The SPD congress in 1921 approved a new programme, which was completely silent about solidarity; without reference to common interests, brotherly feelings or solidarity with the working class of other countries (SPD 1921).[4] The congress met again in Heidelberg in 1925 and

---

[2] In the introduction to Kautsky's *The Class Struggle*, the Norwegian socialist Olav Scheflo described the programme as 'the red guiding principles for social democratic party engagement, not only in Germany, but in all civilised countries' (Kautsky 1915).

[3] At most of the congresses it is not mentioned at all and appeared only sporadically in resolutions, motions and greetings from foreign guests to the congresses during this period.

[4] Neither is it found in the statutes of the reestablished Second International in 1920. This organisation never became very influential, riven with continuous conflicts about its relationship with the Communist Party.

approved a new programme prepared by Kautsky and Rudolf Hilferding. This programme clearly reflects the schizoid relationship between reformist practice and Marxist rhetoric. First, the *idea* of solidarity was now, for the first time, expressed with the same *term* and not with any other functional equivalent such as brotherhood or proletarian internationalism. *Solidarity* was now in the process of becoming the most important term to express the idea of solidarity. Second, *solidarity* was still applied in the classic Marxist sense – as the international solidarity of the proletariat: 'The German Social Democratic Party is conscious of the international solidarity of the proletariat, and resolute to fill all duties that grow out of this' (SPD 1925).

This is the traditional concept of international class solidarity as it had been applied sporadically in the period from 1880 to 1914. However, it is interesting to note that the programme applied *solidarity* in another way as well. It declared that when capitalist relations of production were transformed to socialist, society would develop from general divisiveness to 'free self-government in harmonious solidarity'. What is most interesting in these formulations is the combination of the concept of *transformation* (rather than revolution) with the concept of a harmonious society. This came to be the typical social democratic conception of change in years to come. Thus, the programme preserved the Marxist concept, but simultaneously signalled the new social democratic concept that was to come.

Inability to form alliances

Similar to other social democratic parties, the SPD was confronted at an early stage with the need to relate to the farmers and the middle class. To what extent did the SPD formulate the relationship between the working class and such other classes as a question of solidarity?

The Erfurt programme of 1891 signalled no ambition to include farmers in a solidarist alliance and did not argue for any reforms in the interests of other groups than the workers. The relationship with the farmers came to be an object of internal conflict and debate for three decades, with Kautsky and the left wing rejecting any programmatic openings towards the farmers. After 1920, however, it became increasingly obvious to party leaders that other classes and groups were not proletarianised to the extent that Marxist theory had predicted: wages increased, the number of white-collar employees grew, and rather than becoming more polarised, the class structure became more heterogeneous (Lösche and Walter 1992).

Establishing links with other social categories was not made a theme until the Görlitz programme in 1921 with Bernstein as a member of the programme committee. Now, the SPD declared that SPD should be: 'the party of the working people in cities and rural areas . . . striving for the unity of all people active in physical and intellectual activities – those having to live by their own labour' (SPD 1921).

Thus, the working *class* was replaced with the working *people*, and the programme listed a long range of groups that were threatened by the development of capitalism – white-collar employees, civil servants, teachers, authors and small property-owners. Four years later the Heidelberg programme introduced *die Mittelschichten*, the middle class, and succeeding programmes reflected the increasing importance of this class. Although the term *solidarity* was used for the first time, it was not applied to the relationship with other classes. At last, in 1927, the SPD was able to formulate an *Agrarprogramm*, and finally accepted that the law of capital concentration did not apply to agriculture (Przeworski 1985). Although this development witnessed an increasing understanding of the need to relate to other classes than the working class, the SPD was not able to make the necessary programmatic concessions and formulate an effective policy to achieve this. Neither were party leaders or theorists able to formulate an overarching ideology of solidarity that could contribute to new social alliances. The German labour movement had to experience a political catastrophe, and decades were to pass before the SPD could try this road with greater conviction.

This is not the place to discuss the collapse of the Weimar Republic. Suffice to say that one contributing factor, although not the most important, was that the SPD had not been able to break out of its isolation and forge a lasting social and political alliance with the parties of the centre and those social groups represented by them. Neither was it possible to unite the working class because of rivalry with the sectarian Communist Party. After Hitler came to power in 1933, both the SPD and the Communist Party were banned. In the years to come, Social Democrats as well as communists had to flee the country or were put in concentration camps.

A broader concept of solidarity alone might not have prevented what happened, but the SPD's inability to formulate a class compromise and an ideological concept to justify this certainly did not help. In Scandinavia, social democratic parties succeeded in building a social and political alliance, and this laid the foundation for an alternative development. In her study of German and Swedish social democracy in the interwar period, Sheri Berman attributes the outcome in Germany to the stronger adherence to Marxism in the SPD, and to the separation of the roles of party leader and of party theorist. Kautsky was never a party leader, but was the predominant theorist over a long period

(Berman 1998). Here it might be added that the SPD stuck to a traditional Marxist concept of solidarity restricted to the working class longer
than the social democratic parties in Scandinavia.

The introduction of modern social democratic ideology

After World War II, the challenge facing the reestablished SPD was to
develop a policy and a political language that was adapted to the new
situation. The presence of the Soviet Union in Eastern Germany and the
need to expand electoral support beyond the working class into the *Mittelstand* made it necessary to tone down the radical language of the 1920s
and 1930s. However, continuity was needed as well, both in programmatic content and language, as the Marxist ideology and language were
still alive among party members. The SPD tried to solve this dilemma
by preserving demands for a *planned economy and socialisation*, but on
the other hand it rejected concepts such as class struggle, it emphasised
democracy and it appealed to the middle class.[5] In 1945, the leader Kurt
Schumacher declared that the struggle for the old and new middle classes
was a key problem and that a democratically oriented middle class was a
precondition for building a new order (Schumacher 1973 (1945)). Yet,
neither he nor the party was able to formulate a political basis for a class
alliance between the working class on the one hand, and the farmers and
the middle class on the other, as one of solidarity in those years.

The platform of 1947 signalled a farewell to classic dogmatism. It
declared that 'Social democracy unites humanitarian attitudes, religious
and ethical obligations to form a power to change the world' – reflecting
a move from class interest to ethics as a foundation for politics. A new,
extensive and detailed SPD programme (50 pages) was adopted in 1952
and extended in 1954. Still, central concepts of the Marxist analysis of
society were preserved. These first postwar programmes did not contain
any references to solidarity.[6]

However, both the political and the conceptual context were in a
process of change. The political context was the enduring dissonance
between party rhetoric and the political mood of the country, which
became increasingly problematic during the 1950s. Tired of political
isolation and of being in opposition, the SPD became more and more
eager to win government power, and a discussion about Marxist and

---

[5] For a linguistic analysis of SPD language in general for those years, see Svensson (1984).
[6] The programme cited the declaration of the First International of 1951, but the emphasis
of the new First International on the need for solidarity was not reflected in the SPD
programmes of 1952 and 1954, although these programmes were full of proposals aiming
at developing a German welfare state (SPD 1990 (1952/54)).

socialist concepts such as *planned economy* and *expropriation* was initiated (Bergsdorf 1983).

The fundamental change of both content and language in SPD programmes came in 1959 with the Bad Godesberg programme. The programmatic revision of 1959 left behind socialist principles of the nationalisation of industry and accepted a market economy. The programme declared the basis of democratic socialism to be 'Christian ethics, humanism and classical philosophy' (SPD 1959). *Social democracy* and *social democratic* would now be used more than terms such as *socialism* and *socialist*.[7] Thus, the conceptual context of the solidarity rhetoric had definitely changed.

This programme was also the definitive breakthrough for both the idea of and the term *solidarity* in SPD programmes and rhetoric. The term was frequently applied with old and new meanings side by side. The *foundation* of solidarity was now both ethics, and workers' interests in the struggle against employers. The objective was no longer socialism, but reforms and improvements. Solidarity was used in a much more inclusive way, referring to German participation in international cooperation, and the relationship with the 'underdeveloped' nations. The collective orientation was toned down, and the concept of the individual was introduced. Socialists were to struggle for a society where 'each human being should develop his personality in freedom'. On the other hand, each human being should also be a serving member responsible to society and cooperate in the political, economic, and cultural life of humanity. The individual had been introduced, but the relationship between collective solidarity and individual freedom was emphasised in a way that distinguished social democracy from liberalism.

Finally, *solidarity* was included in the paragraphs about *die Grundwerte des Sozialismus* (the basic values of socialism), and in association with concepts such as *justice, freedom* and *responsibility*. This was done in a way similar to Bernstein's contribution almost fifty years earlier, but one which had not yet been seen in social democratic party programmes.[8] However, the concept of solidarity in the Bad Godesberg programme is not identical

---

[7] From the establishment of the SPD these terms had been used interchangeably without any significant difference of meaning.

[8] According to Wildt, Tenfelde claims that solidarity became an important concept in the German social democratic party (SPD) first after 1945, while Wildt asserts that solidarity became a normative concept early in Liebknecht and Bernstein, and refers to texts from 1871 and 1910 respectively (Wildt 1999). However, this boils down to what is meant by 'important'. As has been documented here, both Kautsky and Bernstein emphasised the importance of the concept. As seen above, it was the Bad Godesberg programme that first elevated the concept of solidarity to programme language and integrated it into a modern social democratic discourse.

with the classic social democratic concept as formulated by Bernstein. It differs in one important aspect – the objective. In Bernstein's concept the objective of solidarity was reform and socialism, but in *modern social democratic solidarity* socialism is omitted as an objective. In this respect, the concept of solidarity in the Bad Godesberg programme is the *modern* social democratic concept. What makes the Bad Godesberg programme so remarkable is that this modern concept is included in a full *language* of solidarity. The Scandinavian social democratic parties had been early in formulating a modern *concept* of solidarity, but the SPD was the first to formulate a full *language* of solidarity within a programme.

The programmatic renewal of Bad Godesberg represented an attempt to broaden electoral appeal. It signalled an opening to the middle class and to groups that so far had been remote from the party. Solidarity and the other basic values in the programme such as justice and freedom came to be recurrent themes in SPD programmes.[9] It did not, however, bring the SPD into government power at the next election in 1961, although electoral support increased notably.

The student revolt and a new ideological renewal

The CDU/FDP coalition broke down in 1966, and a great coalition government of the CDU and the SPD was established. Although the SPD now entered government in 1966 for the first time in more than thirty years, the coalition was disputed in the party. Many feared that welfare arrangements would be dismantled (Brandt 1976). In 1969, the coalition collapsed, and the SPD entered into a new coalition with the liberal FDP with Willy Brandt as chancellor. Brandt saw the alliance with the FDP in a strategic perspective. He was convinced that the FDP was a key to an alliance with groups that the SPD never had been able to attract alone – *der Mittelstand* (Baring 1998).[10] Brandt wanted to use a prudent language that would not jar on anybody's ears (Bergsdorf 1983). Concepts such as *continuity* and *innovation, reform* and *freedom* were often used. Brandt's successor, Helmut Schmidt, took further steps in this direction.

---

[9] In their analysis of the development of the SPD from a class party to a people's party Lösche and Walter assert that the basic values of democratic socialism soon were scarcely mentioned and were supplanted by pragmatic issues (Lösche and Walter 1992). As can be understood, I find this only partially true – the SPD was pragmatic, but its programmes reflected a concern with social democratic values.

[10] This was a main theme in his speech to the congress in Hanover in 1973. The phrase *Die neue Mitte (The new centre)* was coined in 1972. This referred to the alliance between democratic socialism and social liberalism and the two political parties, the SPD and the FDP, that represented these ideological traditions (Brandt 1974).

The student revolt became more explosive in Germany than in most other nations in Western Europe. As elsewhere, the student movement was antagonistic to social democracy and branded it as part of the establishment. Brandt wanted to integrate the new radical currents in the party, but at the same time to keep a distance from 'extremists'.[11] Small groups of the student movement ended up as bewildered terrorists and criminals, but a large number of young people came flocking to the SPD from 1968 on when the extra-parliamentary movement started to ebb away. A new generation of activists with higher education and employed in the public sector entered the party where they met elderly skilled workers and trade unionists who viewed the party as their home. With experience from the student revolt and extra-parliamentary activities the new members criticised the party for not having an ideological purpose (Padgett and Paterson 1991).

The new generation was soon to influence programme rhetoric. A programme document of 1975 stated that *freedom, equality and solidarity* should be the basic values of the party, and included a whole paragraph on the concept of solidarity. For the first time in any political programme of the labour movement parties analysed here, the concept was not applied in a self-evident way, but explained and elaborated upon extensively:

Solidarity expresses the experience and insight that we may live together as free and equal human beings only when we feel responsible for each other and help each other. For us, solidarity has a universal human significance; hence, it may not end at national boundaries. From the basic value of solidarity grows an obligation for everybody toward fellow human beings and toward society. (SPD1975)

Thus, the basis of solidarity was further separated from class interest and founded in equal worth, feelings and cognition of the individual. Solidarity should include the whole of society, every human being, and should extend beyond national boundaries.

In the second half of the 1970s, two political currents existed side by side in the SPD. One represented the working-class tradition, and promoted economic growth and defended the welfare state. The other was rooted in the new middle class, and was more preoccupied with ecology, feminism and pacifism. A basic value commission under the leadership of Erhard Eppler was appointed to build a bridge between the two (Eppler 1998). In the following years, the importance of solidarity was repeatedly emphasised in SPD documents. After the collapse of the SPD/FDP government, the SPD found itself in opposition again in 1982, and this was to last for a long time. In spite of continuous high unemployment rates

---

[11] In his biography, Brandt mentions that he had personal experience with radical youth, as his two sons were participating in radical activities (Brandt 1976).

and stronger appeals for solidarity, the SPD did not succeed in returning to government until Gerhard Schröder defeated Helmut Kohl in 1998.

After the electoral defeat of 1982, the strategic choice for the SPD was between hunting voters in the centre or establishing a better relationship with the new social movements – the feminists, ecologists, pacifists and anti-nuclear activists. The answer to this dilemma was a compromise between old and new politics (Sassoon 1996), and in 1983 the SPD changed position on the issue of the deployment of new nuclear missiles in Germany. Ecology, gender emancipation and shorter working hours were put on the SPD agenda.

In 1984 the party congress in Essen decided that it was time to replace the Bad Godesberg programme. A 'Basic Values Commission' with Willy Brandt as leader was set up resulting in the Irsee draft in 1986. The ideology of economic growth had been the foundation of social democratic politics for many decades. Now, on the left the Green Party appealed to the young and educated middle class. Within the SPD awareness grew that social democratic politics had to come to terms with the limits of environment and ecology. Thus, growth had to be 'qualitative', building on science and technology, humanism and ecology (Padgett and Paterson 1991). A new electoral defeat in 1987 contributed to a more radical policy. These changes prepared the ground for a later rapprochement between the SPD and the Green Party.

A new commission chaired by Jochen Vogel and Oscar Lafontaine, who was elected leader of the party in 1995, prepared the draft for a new programme – the Berlin programme in 1989. As the Bad Godesberg programme had represented the break with a Marxist past, the Berlin programme forty-one years later meant a renewal of social democratic ideology with its emphasis on growth, the male breadwinner model and welfare expansion. With the aim of bridging the gap to the new social movements, ecology and feminism were integrated into SPD programme language (Meyer 2001). The programme assured the traditionalists that trade unions would be the core of the new reform alliance between old and new social forces. There was no mention of any anti-capitalist positions. At the same time, a new peak of solidaristic rhetoric was reached. The programme referred to *solidarity* or *solidaristic* not less than twenty-two times, almost excessively, and it expanded on previous formulations:

> Solidarity, cannot be enforced. It means to be prepared to stand up for each other beyond legal obligations to do so. Solidarity has characterised the labour movement in the struggle for freedom and equality. Without solidarity, there can be no human society.
>
> At the same time, solidarity is a weapon of the weak in the struggle for their rights and the consequence of the insight that man needs his fellow human

beings . . . Those who experience hardship should be able to count on the solidarity of society.

Solidarity also requires that people in the Third World should have a life worthy of human beings. We who live today decide on conditions of life for the next generations, and they have a claim on our solidarity.

Solidarity is also necessary to enhance individual possibilities for development. Preconditions for individual egoistic individualism and autonomy cannot be created and secured only through common action.

Freedom, justice and solidarity depend upon each other and support each other reciprocally. (SPD 1989)

The most remarkable aspect of the concept of solidarity here compared to the previous programme is the very broad inclusiveness. *Solidarity* is used again in the context of social policy – *Sozialpolitik als verwirklichte Solidarität* (social policy as solidarity put into practice). Solidarity should entail relationships between the young and the elderly, men and women, majority and minority ethnic groups. For the first time, a social democratic programme formulated the relationship between the present and future generations as a question of solidarity. Finally, this is also the first time in a SPD platform that *solidarity* is applied within a *productivist* logic. Solidarity should also imply *solidaristic effort* to achieve prosperity, meaning *working* and not struggling together against a common adversary. This shift echoes one made by the Danish Social Democrats in 1934 and the Norwegian Labour Party in 1939. The close association between solidarity, justice and freedom was repeated.

However, the fall of the Wall eclipsed the Berlin programme, and the programme did not play an important role, either in the party or with the public. Lafontaine's sceptical attitude to a rapid reunification between the two German states was in clear conflict with the mood of the voters at the national election in 1990. A new electoral defeat was the result. The SPD programmes of the 1990s did not bring much that was new in terms of solidarity, although the excessive use of the concept in the 1989 programme was played down somewhat. The 1990s continued to be a frustrating period for the SPD. Rapid changes of SPD leadership, unclear identity and low credibility in terms of economic policy did not attract new voters, and Helmut Kohl and the Christian democrats seemed invincible. Finally, Gerhard Schröder brought the SPD back to government with his media appeal in 1998, although in a coalition with the Green Party. Schröder made *Neue Mitte* – the new centre – his slogan, emphasising the interests of the middle class. The title of the SPD election programme, *Employment, Innovation and Justice*, illustrated the introduction of elements from the modernising political language of Tony Blair in German social democratic traditionalism. The programme emphasised the *renewal of a social market economy, modernisation, innovation in economy, state and society* and *ecological innovation*. It appealed explicitly to the middle class, promised to reduce taxes and to facilitate more private enterprise (SPD 1998b).

In terms of solidarity, the programme repeated what had been said in previous programmes, but added a call for solidarity between East and West Germany. The collective aspect was modified, as the individual was given a more pronounced place. The goal of the welfare state, the programme said, was to 'stimulate personal responsibility and individual initiative, not guardianship'. The programme further emphasised that 'we must continuously determine the relationship between solidarity and individuality'. Thus, the programme echoed Bernstein's discussion almost ninety years previously about the problem of reconciling solidarity and individual freedom. In addition to Schröder's media appeal and the weakened position of Kohl, this mixture of modernity and tradition was conducive to bringing the SPD back to government in 1998.

Present basic values

Today, the SPD conception of solidarity is based on the worth of the individual as described in the UN Declaration on Human Rights – man is born free and equal in terms of worth and rights (SPD 1998b). Thus, all individuals should feel a responsibility to ensure that others are living under conditions worthy of human beings. At the same time, the SPD has preserved a link with the classic social democratic tradition where the objective of solidarity was to realise interests. This is illustrated in the 1998 platform, which states that solidarity is also a weapon for the weak in their struggle for their rights. The universal idea of equal human worth implies a very broad and inclusive idea of solidarity that in principle leaves nobody out and establishes a special responsibility for the weak. A wide range of groups and issues that should be included in solidarity are listed – the relationship between men and women, future generations, the Third World and cultural minorities. The platform also represented a long step from the uncomplicated idea of the relationship between the individual and the collective in the classic Marxist concept, as the relationship between solidarity and individuality was discussed as an important issue (see Chapter 5).

The platform emphasises that freedom, justice, and solidarity are the basic values of the SPD. *Justice* stems from the equal worth of all human beings. Justice claims equal freedom, equal chances in social and political life, and more equality in the distribution of income, property and power, as well as more equality in access to education and culture.

There are three interesting characteristics of the German social democratic discourse on solidarity. First, compared to other European social democratic parties, a modern social democratic *concept* was developed later than in Scandinavia, but earlier than in France, Italy and Spain. The interesting question of the timing of the transformation of *solidarity* into a modern social democratic concept in different parties is further discussed in Chapter 5. It suffices to direct attention to some factors that might explain why this took place at a later stage in the SPD than in the Scandinavian sister parties. Most important is probably the fact that the SPD revised its *general* programme language later than the Danish and the Norwegian sister parties in particular. This was again probably due to the less egalitarian class structure that made it more complicated to adopt a strategy for alliances with first the rural and then the urban middle classes (see Chapter 5).

Second, when finally developed in the Bad Godesberg programme in 1959, it was part of a more fully integrated conceptual context with other ideological key elements of what came to be the modern social democratic *language* of solidarity as well. This language was formulated earlier than in Scandinavia. Third, as in most other social democratic parties, we have noted the strong correlation between the introduction of solidaristic rhetoric and general deradicalisation of programme content and rhetoric, as was the case in the Bad Godesberg programme. In recent years, the challenge for SPD ideology appears to be how to combine its concept of solidarity with defence of the traditional working class and the impressive German welfare state with emphasis on innovation and tax reduction for the middle class.

Discourses on solidarity in Scandinavian social democracy

As they do today, the Scandinavian countries shared many characteristics in the early phase of the labour movement. They were small, relatively egalitarian countries with a weak bourgeoisie – although it was somewhat stronger in Sweden than in the neighbouring countries, whereas the agricultural sector was more important in Denmark. They were homogeneous in terms of ethnicity, religion and linguistics, and they shared a common history with internal migration and trade. Industrialisation took place at a late stage compared to the UK and Germany, and the SPD and the debates among German Marxists and socialists influenced the labour movement. The Danish Social Democratic Party was established through successive attempts in the 1870s, the Norwegian Labour Party

(DNA) in 1887 and the Social Democratic Workers Party of Sweden (SAP) in 1889.

Early programmatic beliefs

In Denmark, the first platform of the Social Democratic Party in 1876 – the Gimle programme – was very similar to the Gotha programme that the German sister party had approved the year before. As for the Gotha programme, the Gimle programme was pre-Marxist, and it was short and combined some theoretical statements with a concrete reform programme. Like most other socialist parties of the period, it declared its commitment to the idea of solidarity. The party said that it was 'convinced about the international character of the labour movement and was prepared to sacrifice all and to fulfil all obligations to bring about freedom, equality and brotherly love between all nations' (Socialdemokratiet 1876).

In Norway, the founding congress of the DNA in 1887 declared in its short programme the need for a party that could develop solidarity between the workers in the cities and the countryside and take care of their common interests (DNA 1887). This way of using solidarity represented a deviation from what generally was seen as correct Marxism, because other socialist parties preferred to state the need for worker unity. This was the case in Sweden when the SAP approved its first programme in 1897. It was inspired and influenced by the 1891 Erfurt platform of the SPD. It included the standard formulation about solidarity and declared, as the SPD platform had done, that the interests of the working class are the same in all capitalist countries and that Swedish social democracy should be at one with the social democracy of other nations (SAP 1897). This idea of solidarity – without the term actually being used – was repeated in succeeding platforms in 1905 and 1911. The election manifesto in 1914 was approved under the threat of the imminent war and declared that the party would struggle for 'peace and brotherhood between the working people in all nations, liberated from capitalist exploitation' (SAP 1915). As in most other European socialist parties, the SAP had not replaced terms that were functionally equivalent with the term *solidarity* prior to World War I.

Thus, the early programmes of the Scandinavian labour parties all expressed the idea of solidarity – although with different concepts and terms. Only the DNA applied the term *solidarity* from the beginning. The new DNA programme of 1891 was a fully developed programme. Here, and in documents in the ensuing years, solidarity was used in the classic Marxist sense, referring to *workers' association* and *solidarity* in the struggle for equal rights and duties for all oppressed persons and peoples and calling for unity with 'class-conscious workers in all countries' (DNA 1891). However, a pure Marxist concept of solidarity was to survive less than two decades in DNA programmes – from 1891 to 1909. After the turn of the century, DNA membership and electoral support increased sharply. New industries increased the number of workers, and unionisation was boosted. DNA became a well-organised party with a concrete political programme adapted to the national situation (Friis and Hegna 1974). In terms of solidarity, this was reflected in a shift in the programme in 1909, which represented a step away from the classic Marxist concept. The words *workers' association* and *solidarity* were again used, but this time emphasising the common interests of wage earners, merchants, industrialists of small means, and farmers. This early broadening of the concept is a parallel to the ideas of Swedish social democratic leaders of the same period, but in Sweden this was not reflected in the party platform until after World War II.

The early broadening of the idea of solidarity reflected the special characteristics of the class structure in Norway. Norway was less urbanised than other countries in this study. There was no strong urban industrial proletariat: the differences between workers, artisans, fishermen and smallholders were small,[12] and the class structure was probably more egalitarian than in the other nations studied here, and more conducive to ideas about equality.[13] Many DNA leaders had their roots in the rural periphery, and rhetoric about solidarity and holding together seemed natural to them (Furre 1991). Besides, electoral considerations might have contributed to this as well, as the party gradually shifted its emphasis from class struggle to political influence in popularly elected bodies.

In Denmark the process of industrialisation started earlier than in Norway and Sweden, but developed slowly, occurring mainly in the 1890s. Consequently, class struggle and worker organisation developed later, but collaboration between trade unions and employers and the first negotiated regulations of conflicts were soon to follow (in 1899 and 1910) (Olsen 2001). Danish socialism was early influenced by an evolutionary optimism combined with ideas about a gradual transformation of capitalism. Although the new programme in 1888 represented a step towards Marxism in certain aspects, it cannot be said to be Marxist

---

[12] Already in the 1850s an alliance of workers, artisans, cotters, smallholders, and rural workers constituted a popular movement – the Thrane movement – with the slogan of uniting against the rich and powerful. See Pryser (1977).

[13] A pietist and religious movement in the early nineteenth century had contributed to such egalitarianism as well – see Chapter 6 which discusses the Norwegian Christian People's Party.

and said nothing about working-class solidarity.[14] From 1904 Danish social democrats frequently criticised the SPD for its theoretical and verbal radicalism (Bryld 1992). Increased collaboration between the Social Democratic Party and liberal and agrarian parties was soon to follow.

However, electoral progress and increased political strength in the 1890s and the first decade of the new century made socialists more self-conscious. This may explain the radicalisation of the new platform in 1913 – the first and only Marxist platform of Danish social democracy. Now both the concept of, and the term, *solidarity*, were introduced in a conceptual Marxist context and applied with the classic Marxist meaning. The programme stated that the party identified with and declared 'solidarity with the class conscious international working class, whose task in world history is complete liberation with no respect to gender, race or nationality' (Socialdemokratiet 1913). The Marxist theory of classes, polarisation and crisis was included, but nothing was said about revolution and the strategy for socialism, and the reform-oriented practice from the previous years continued (Bryld 1992). A party historian regards the theoretical considerations in the programme as a ritual initial prayer before the congress could get down to what it saw as more important – the actual and concrete challenges in politics (Olsen 2001).

Alliances and ideology

The language of the early SAP programmes was radical and socialist, but certainly not revolutionary and Marxist, as the programmes concentrated on concrete reforms and the need for universal suffrage. The 1920 platform introduced Marxist analysis and terminology and demanded that private ownership of the means of production should be abolished in industry, transport and finance. Natural resources should be socialised, and a planned economy should be introduced (SAP 1920). However, the platform did not represent any change in terms of the idea of solidarity or the term itself. Hence, the party did not formulate a Marxist idea of solidarity or adopt the term solidarity in its platforms in this period. When the concept of solidarity appeared in a platform twenty-four years later, it was as a social democratic idea.

What is peculiar to the Swedish social democratic party compared to those of Norway and Denmark on the one hand, and elsewhere on the continent on the other, is that this absence of institutionalisation of both the idea and the term solidarity was combined with two other

---

[14] Here it was said that 'socialism is not only a national or local issue, but presupposes theoretical and practical support of the workers in all countries' (Socialdemokratiet 1888).

characteristics. First, like the sister parties in Scandinavia, but contrary to most other socialist parties, the Swedish SDP developed a strategy of alliances with peasants and later white-collar groups at an early stage, and this was reflected in party programmes. Second, SAP leaders and ideologues were early in developing an idea of solidarity that was parallel to that of Bernstein, but contrary to the Scandinavian sister parties this idea was not clearly formulated in party programmes until after World War II.

Since the turn of the century SAP leaders had been conscious of the need for increasing electoral support from smallholders and people of humble means in the countryside (Svensson 1994). The platforms of 1905, 1911 and 1920 gradually developed the idea that an alliance between the working class and smallholders, merchants and artisans was necessary (see Chapter 5); the road to an alliance between the working class and these other groups was opened. The foundation of a broad concept of solidarity had been laid, although many years were to pass before the platform of the party formulated the relationship between different classes in a language of solidarity.

This programmatic development – or lack of it in terms of solidarity – was paralleled by theoretical and ideological contributions from party leaders and ideologists. Ernst Wigforss, the foremost ideologist of Swedish social democracy, combined a talent for theoretical reasoning with pragmatic politics and was a key carrier in the introduction of a social democratic concept of solidarity in the Swedish labour movement.[15] In many ways, he was a Swedish Bernstein preoccupied with the ethical aspects of socialism. Already in 1910 he had published an article about 'Socialism and morality' where he argued for Marxism, but criticised Kautsky and orthodox Marxism for its reluctance to introduce morality and ethics in socialism (Wigforss 1941 (1910)). Like Bernstein, Wigforss thought that the idea of socialism could not be based solely on the scientific understanding that socialism would follow capitalism, but should be based on ethics and social indignation as well.

'The point of departure for a new moral in the labour movement should be solidarity developed in class struggle', he said. Solidarity should be

---

[15] I agree with Tilton who criticises other students of Swedish social democracy for exaggerating the pragmatic and weak ideological character of the party (Tilton 1990). There is not necessarily a contradiction between pragmatism and ideology as long as pragmatism is confined and given a direction by an ideology. Compared to Norwegian and Danish social democracy, SAP platforms are characterised by a more ideological language. At the same time Swedish social democratic leaders from Wigforss to Palme have continued to be more interested in ideology than social democratic leaders in Denmark and Norway.

based not only on the recognition of the individual worker that his egoistic interest is best secured through class struggle, but also on unselfish
feelings and solidarity with the class. Because the labour movement is
founded on instinctive feelings, not calculating and egoistic motives,
it constitutes a real morality – in this case a class morality, he said.
Wigforss, however, transcended the idea of class solidarity based on
morality and argued that a solidarity that includes the whole of society
represents a superior morality (Wigforss 1941 (1910)). Thus, before the
SAP had approved its Marxist platform and before Bernstein had published his revisionist idea of solidarity, Wigforss formulated an idea of
solidarity that was different in key aspects from the classic Marxist idea.
It added feelings and moral content to interest as the basis of solidarity
and this made it possible to broaden the idea of solidarity so that it could
encompass the whole of society. Later social democratic leaders such as
Hjalmar Branting and Per Albin Hansson further developed this concept.
Like Bernstein, Wigforss located his reasoning about solidarity in a discourse with other values that decades later came to be integrated in social
democratic programmatic language – *freedom*, *democracy* and *equality*.
Tilton has noted that he integrated these values with economic efficiency
and industrial democracy (Tilton 1990). The combination of these ideas
came to be a distinguishing characteristic of Swedish social democracy.

Branting and Hansson: solidarity with the whole of society and the idea of a 'people's home'

Two years after the Russian revolution, the SAP leader Hjalmar Branting
viewed with disgust the results and the establishment of the dictatorship
of the communist party. Branting argued that socialism could not be
introduced if other classes were subordinated to the working class. In
the moral field a strong sense of solidarity should grow and develop.
This feeling of solidarity could not be restricted to the working class,
but should embrace the society that the workers would inherit and lead.
The workers should learn to regard their opponents not as enemies who
must be wiped out with fire and sword, but should seek to win them by
persuasion. 'Only in this way could a true socialism be created', he said
(Branting 1948). In 1920, Branting formed the first Social Democratic
government.

Branting's point of view that worker solidarity should be transformed
into a broader societal solidarity was picked up by his successor Per Albin
Hansson. In 1926 Hansson formulated ideas that he developed into his
concept of *the people's home* (*folkhemmet*). Worker solidarity and societal
solidarity should fuse together, and the solidarity that had elevated the

working class to its present position in society should not be seen as opposed to the general interests of society (Hansson 1948). In his key speech about *the people's home* in Parliament in 1928, Hansson applied 'the home' as a metaphor for a society based on solidarity.[16] He did not apply the concept of solidarity in this speech, but argued again for mutual understanding and agreement across class boundaries (Hansson 1948).

When the economic world crisis reached Sweden, social democratic leaders did not believe that this would result in the collapse of capitalism. Wigforss argued that it was not the time to struggle for the socialisation of the means of production, but for increased economic planning. The separation of the two meant in practice abandoning classic Marxist teaching (Lewin 1992). An ideological reorientation was initiated after the party came into government, and the party congress of 1932 buried demands for socialisation of the means of production expressed in the 1920 platform, making that platform even more irrelevant as guidelines for the party (Bergström 1989). Per Albin Hansson directed attention to the situation of smallholders, farmers and the middle class and succeeded in reaching a compromise with the farmers' party and farmers' associations. In 1935 Hansson described society as an *organism*, signalling a further step away from the concept of capitalist society as riven with antagonistic conflicts and approaching a Durkheimian view on solidarity and society (Hansson 1982b (1928)).

In the ensuing decades, from 1936 to 1976, the party dominated Swedish politics and was permanently in government alone or with others. Although both Branting and Hansson had broadened the concept of solidarity to include not only the working class but also society in general, the term *solidarity* was not introduced in the programme of the party until after the war.

The class and the nation

In Norway, the late 1920s and the 1930s was a period when the DNA was brought closer to social reality. Unemployment and the harsh living conditions of the voters made the need for immediate reform urgent. Social democratic pragmatic ideology gradually supplanted Marxism, but this process accelerated in the 1930s, and this was to have implications for the idea of solidarity.

---

[16] The good home is characterised by community and fellow-feeling – it is a place where nobody is privileged and nobody is a stepchild. In a good home, equality, thoughtfulness, cooperation and helpfulness prevail. Hansson said in society, social and economic barriers that separate the privileged and underprivileged, rulers and subjects, rich and poor should be broken down.

A protagonist in this process was the historian Halvdan Koht who had come to the DNA from the liberal party. In *Communism and the national idea* from 1923, Koht laid out his idea about how the rise of the working class and the nation-building process should be integrated. Increasing integration was a general law in history, he argued. Increasing numbers of human beings, nations and other forces were being drawn together in cooperation. At the same time, he noted, echoing Durkheim, another law leads to separation. Eventually people become increasingly different in their roles in working life, in their abilities and ways of thinking; every human being becomes an individual. Koht reinterpreted Marx's famous statement in the Manifesto that 'workers had no home country' to mean a regret and complaint that capitalism had deprived workers of their own country as it had done with their homes and private lives (Koht 1977 (1923)). Communism and national feelings were not opposites, and the development and building of the nation was not only about national independence but about the growth of national unity as well. All class revolt entails a broader notion of unifying all classes on a national basis. Thus, a 'communist' society would be a society devoid of class struggle and with strong collaboration between all classes. A living 'feeling of community' and 'solidarity'[17] would develop out of the struggle and broaden into a national feeling, he wrote.

Koht's idea of solidarity was different from the classic Marxist concept in several respects. First, he extended the basis to ethics and even to religion. Similar to Bernstein and Wigforss, Koht directed attention to the ethical aspects of socialism but did not abstain from citing the national and Christian hymn: 'Let people live together as brethren – as is appropriate for Christians' (Koht 1977 (1923)). Thus, contrary to Wigforss, he signalled a positive attitude to religion. This theme was to be picked up by other Norwegian social democrats three decades later. Second, Koht's concept of solidarity had a strategic aspect. He wanted to prevent fascists and the political right from monopolising national feelings. He argued that the labour movement should not let the political right have a monopoly on national values, but make those values its own, and in this way attract new groups of voters to the DNA (Slagstad 1998).[18] The goal was to raise true national feeling as opposed to having class objectives disguised in a national rhetoric. Third, Koht's concept was, in consequence, more inclusive than the Marxist concept of solidarity. Altogether, this

[17] In Norwegian, 'levande samfundskjensle' and 'samkjensle' directly translated mean 'feelings of togetherness' (Hansson).

[18] In 1930, Koht presented a party programme for language and culture. Here, he argued that 'the sense of solidarity among working people should be strengthened by creating a true popular culture instead of class culture'.

conception of solidarity cannot easily be classified according to the different categories listed in Chapter 3. It represents a mixture of aspects of Durkheim's organic concept and aspects of the classic and the modern social democratic concept of solidarity.

National integration and solidarity in production

During the late 1920s and the 1930s, the labour movement in the Scandinavian countries entered into social and political alliances with the farmers and/or their political organisations. At the same time, the relationship between trade unions and employer organisations was institutionalised with rules and procedures for wage bargaining and strikes. The idea of class solidarity was clearly inadequate in this situation, as it would have alienated groups that were necessary to establish such alliances and made impossible a political platform that could achieve a majority in Parliament. As seen above, political leaders developed new ideas of solidarity that expressed a preoccupation with national integration and collaboration.

A special version of the idea of solidarity is found in some of the social democratic programmes in those years. In Denmark, the world crisis struck Danish agriculture and industry in the early 1930s and made broader economic and social solutions more urgent. The 1934 platform was influenced by this and reflected the social democratic party's search for a broader alliance to support a reform programme. Now, solidarity was found in a new version: 'The working class accomplished much through solidarity and cohesion, but the whole people should take part, when those who understand the significance of production, unite around the battle of our time . . . Everybody might contribute through honest effort in work' (Socialdemokratiet 1934).

This was a farewell both to Marxism in general, to Marxism as a programme language, and to the concept of solidarity applied in the platform of 1913. The concept of solidarity now introduced was a premonition of a *productivist* concept of solidarity, five years before such a concept was introduced in the programme of the Norwegian sister party. Cooperation in production should increase economic growth, and make it possible for everyone to have a fair share of the wealth that was produced. The concept of solidarity was now in the process of being transformed from a class-specific concept to a more inclusive concept that embraced all the people. The following year, the social democratic leader Thorvald Stauning expressed this clearly in a speech to the party congress: 'Now, the people are permeated by the spirit of democracy, of feelings of solidarity, and of comradeship, now the country is owned not by the upper class, but by the whole people' (Sonne 1974).

In Norway, whereas the DNA 1933 programme still contained many elements from Marxist theory and phraseology, the programme of 1939 must be definitely described as social democratic or even as social-liberal. References to the Marxist foundation of the party were removed. When solidarity reemerged in the 1939 programme for the first time since 1921, the conceptual context had definitely changed. Solidarity no longer referred to struggle against a defined enemy. Instead, a productivist logic marked the new way of thinking. The necessity for efficiency, for the organisation and utilisation of all labour and the productive potential of the nation was emphasised. This was dependent upon the 'solidarity, societal responsibility, discipline, and the active participation of the working people in all constructive effort'. Production capacity should be more efficiently utilised to improve the standard of living, and the state should still have a key role in a system-planned economy (DNA 1939).

The aim to create a concept of national solidarity, the broadening of the concept to other classes and the productivist version of the concept must be understood in the light of the growth of German fascism. DNA leaders urgently needed a strategy that would prevent a 'solution' to the social crisis similar to that created in Germany.

After the war: production and programme revisions

Whereas Sweden was neutral during World War II, Denmark and Norway were occupied by Germany. After the war, social democratic governments in all three nations were faced with the task of reconstruction and economic growth. The experiences of the war had contributed to a new feeling of solidarity. In Norway, in particular, hardship, and collaboration between the labour movement and members of the bourgeois parties had created a stronger feeling of community. A new generation of social democratic leaders became members of the government – Tage Erlander in Sweden, Einar Gerhardsen in Norway and Hans Hedtoft in Denmark.

In Denmark, the first postwar platform in 1945 further developed the productivist logic of the 1934 programme, and called for a solidaristic effort to increase production and living standards (Socialdemokratiet 1945). The emphasis was on full employment, social security and democratisation of industry and socialisation of the means of production had definitely been abandoned. In Norway, the immediate task was to rebuild the economy and society, as a joint effort involving all classes and social groups. The need for reconstruction of the economy was reflected in the idea of solidarity. The DNA programme of 1945 reinforced the productivist flavour of the previous prewar programme and reflected a further step in developing a new concept of solidarity. Now, solidarity referred to 'economical solidarity between all branches of work and economic life' (DNA 1945). Conflict between labour and capital had disappeared, and solidarity meant community across previous demarcation lines between the two. The platform *Basic View and Guidelines* of 1949 has been characterised as making the DNA into 'one of Europe's least dogmatic social democratic parties' (Lange 1994). The goal should still be a socialist society, but the choice of means should be a pragmatic issue, the platform stated. Solidarity should mean that 'each individual' had a duty to work and to feel responsible for others. 'On the other hand, society shall have responsibility for everyone and secure rights in every field of society, irrespective of race, religion, gender and income.' Solidarity should be expressed through a reciprocal contract: Everyone should do his or her duty, and the government would take responsibility for public social security arrangements (DNA 1949). This discourse with its emphasis on industrialisation and increased productivity reflected the modernisation strategy of the DNA, and became an intermediate station on the road to the modern concept of solidarity. Social democracy came to be the main voice of a productivist ideology in Norway (Slagstad 1998). The SAP platform of 1944 also reflected, even if less pronounced, a productivist approach. For the first time, the platform also stated that the right to participation in economic life should be matched by 'a duty to take on work and tasks that are required for an efficient organisation of production' (SAP 1944).

The productivist version of the concept of solidarity in this period in Scandinavia represents a special case of the discourse on solidarity in Western Europe. Although many social democratic parties in this period had changed strategy and emphasised economic growth and social reform instead of class struggle, they did not legitimise this through the development of a solidarity discourse. In stylised form it might be contrasted with the classic social democratic concept of solidarity as seen in Table 4.1. As in the classic Marxist idea, solidarity is founded on interests, but on a different conception of interest. Now solidarity is not based on class interest against employers, but on the common interest of workers and employers to increase production. This productivist concept lacks the emphasis on ethics as a foundation for solidarity.

The objectives of this solidarity are not structural reforms or substantial changes in the capitalist economy, but an increase in the standard of living for the broad masses of the population. This solidarity is broad and inclusive and encompasses not only working people and their allies

Table 4.1 *A productivist concept of solidarity*

	Foundation	Objective	Inclusiveness	Collective orientation
Classic social democratic solidarity	Popular interests: acceptance of difference ethics and morality	Realise interests: reforms Socialism. create sense of community	Broader: all popular groups, The nation?	'Medium': individual freedom accepted and dilemma recognised
Productivist solidarity	Common interests between employees and employers	Increased standard of living through collaboration concerning increased production and efficiency. Social security	Broad Inter-class	Unclear? Strong?

as the classic social democratic concept, but also – although of necessity – their previous adversaries, the employers. The collective aspect of the productivist concept was strong, as the state should provide security through social policy measures in return for the productive effort of the individual, without this relationship being regarded as problematic.

Although Sweden was neutral during World War II, the experience transformed further the idea of solidarity, making it broader and more inclusive.[19] In the SAP platform of 1944, the rhetoric was definitely softened and adjusted to the actual policies of the party. Although still somewhat marked by Marxist ideology, concepts such as exploitation, class struggle and impoverishment were removed. Planning and control supplanted socialisation of the means of production. Economic life and industry were to be rationalised and made more efficient. In this way the conceptual context was changed.

A new concept of solidarity was now introduced into this context. Solidarity was introduced in a discourse about 'the old ideas about human dignity, humanity, freedom, emancipation, solidarity and cooperation . . .' These values had been inherited from previous traditions and 'transformed by the influence of new experiences'. The new idea of solidarity was based on a 'mutual feeling of belonging together' (SAP 1944). It was inclusive and denoted a general feeling of community; it was not restricted to the working class or to other social democratic parties. This was a somewhat belated confirmation of the alliance between the working class and farmers that had been established decades ago, but was now

---

[19] See Hansson speech 'A national manifestation' in 1943. Here he repeatedly called for national solidarity and community (Hansson 1982b (1928)).

formulated in a way that might appeal to the growing middle class as well. From then on, a broad conception of solidarity has been a recurrent theme in social democratic ideology and language in Sweden. A more detailed action programme launched the idea of a solidaristic wage policy that came to be a key concept in the following decades (Bergström 1989). This referred to a system with equal wages for equal work irrespective of the individual enterprise or business. Workers in profitable enterprises should refrain from demanding maximum wage increases, at the same time as less profitable enterprises were squeezed out of business. This brought about a continuous rationalisation of Swedish industry and together with the broad conception of solidarity certainly contributed to the long social democratic hegemony in Swedish politics.

The reintegration of ethics

The clear productivist concept of solidarity was soon left behind and replaced by another discourse. In Sweden, Per Albin Hansson's successor – Tage Erlander – appointed Olof Palme as his personal secretary in 1953. Both were to strongly influence the development of social democracy in Sweden in the ensuing decades (Tilton 1990). For Erlander, ideology should serve to give purpose and direction to concrete social reforms. His idea was to make social democracy realise equality and solidarity on the one hand, and democracy and freedom on the other. State action should expand educational opportunities, increase job choices and improve health care, and in this way individual freedom would be expanded as well. Similar to Durkheim and Koht, he argued that the increased differentiation of modern societies made cooperation and solidarity necessary in order to integrate society; this was also necessary for individuals to realise their potential. These ideas should be concretised through social reforms. At the same time, the SAP reoriented its search for a class alliance and attention was shifted from smallholders to the increasing number of white-collar employees in the public sector. At the same time, social democratic leaders were eager to replace the term *workers* with *wage earners* (Svensson 1994).

The platform of 1960 reflected Erlander's ideas and the ambition to appeal to other wage earners than workers. Solidarity was used several times, and with a plural meaning. Now, it was applied to a feeling of interdependence not only among workers, but also among 'different groups', about a 'general social policy', the relationship between rich and poor nations, and included 'all the peoples of the world' (SAP 1960). This concept of solidarity had a streak of Durkheim's concept of organic solidarity, as it stressed the interdependence, inclusiveness and integrative aspects. Except for the Bad Godesberg programme, the discourse about solidarity here was more extensive than in other social democratic parties at this time.

In Norway, the new social democratic leader, Gerhardsen, established a system with corporatist arrangements where consensus could be built (Slagstad 1998). Now the foundation was laid for a long period of truce between the social democratic government and private enterprise. The 1953 programme left the explicit productivist concept behind and inaugurated a return to the development of a modern concept of solidarity. It took up a theme from prewar programmes and declared the need for solidarity between people living in the cities and farmers and fishermen. Besides, for the first time in a social democratic programme in the nations studied here, solidarity was applied to the relationship with the nations of the poor and underdeveloped world, which has since been a permanent theme in DNA programmes (DNA 1953).

The same year, 1953, the party appointed a committee to draw up a cultural programme. This reflected the party's ambition to influence not only the economy and politics, but the values and culture of society as well (Bergh 1987). The chairman of the committee, Helge Sivertsen, presented the programme at the congress in 1955 and signalled a reorientation of party attitudes to religion. The party should differentiate between the Christian religion and the institutionalised Church. The former was close to the values of the labour movement, whereas the latter had positioned itself closer to the political adversaries of the movement, Sivertsen argued (Midttun 1994). The congress of 1959 approved the programme, picked up the thread from Koht, and made solidarity the governing idea in the programme. Solidarity should be based on 'love of one's next, not on class hate' (Bergh 1987). Sivertsen argued that the labour movement should transfer the Christian idea of brotherhood to practical politics. This was not only similar to, but also reinforced what had been said about Christian belief in the Bad Godesberg programme and represented a new confirmation of the farewell to the Marxist conception of solidarity. The DNA now based its concept of solidarity on ethics.

The productivist version of the idea of solidarity was to be transitory also in Denmark. The 1945 social democratic platform contained statements that pointed towards the integration of Danish social democracy in mainstream social democratic ideology, both in general and in terms of solidarity. First, the conceptual context was in a process of change and a broader ideological context gradually developed. In the 1953 platform, the concepts of *democratic socialism* and *capitalism* were reintroduced. However, what is most interesting about the programmatic language from

1961 and during the 1960s is the scarcity of ideological and value-laden concepts in the programmatic language. This probably reflects the strong pragmatic character of Danish social democracy. The permanent minority position of the party among voters and in Parliament may have induced this cautious use of ideological concepts. In many ways, this programme language had more in common with the language of the British Labour Party than with the German, Swedish and Norwegian social democratic sister parties at that time.

Second, solidarity was gradually made broader in terms of the groups and issues that were specifically included. The 1945 programme declared that social solidarity had to be equally as important as international solidarity. In the first decades after the war, the concept of, and the term, *solidarity* did not appear frequently and until 1969 it was found only a few times, referring to international relations and the poor nations, intermingled with the concept of social justice. Thus, the social democratic concept of solidarity existed in the programme language of Danish social democrats, but it had not yet been made a core ideological concept and no full language of solidarity had been developed. Third, the relationship between the collective and the individual was increasingly given more attention (see Chapter 5).

The basic values of Scandinavian social democracy

The student revolt in 1968 was strongly anti-social democratic, but was to have important consequences for the development of the programme language, if not so much for practical politics in Scandinavian social democracy. In Sweden, Olof Palme, who succeeded Tage Erlander as chairman and prime minister in 1969, was receptive to the international issues that the student revolt brought onto the agenda.[20] In Norway, the student revolt made the DNA leadership conscious of the need for an ideological response to meet the large young cohorts now in the process of entering the electorate.[21] In Denmark, the language of the student revolt was soon reflected in the programme language of social democracy.

Olof Palme recognised that idealism and demands for justice were important aspects of the student revolt (Palme 1968). The first SAP platform after 1968, that of 1975, was more influenced by Marxist rhetoric

---

[20] Palme was personally engaged in international issues, strongly committed against apartheid in Southern Africa and probably the only Prime Minister in Western Europe who took part in early demonstrations against the US war in Vietnam.

[21] The chairman and later Prime Minister Trygve Bratteli and a group of party members travelled to other European countries to study and discuss ideology and politics. Among others they met Enrico Berlinguer, general secretary of the PCI (personal interview with the previous DNA leader Reiulf Steen 12.05.2001).

than the previous one from 1944, criticising capitalism and arguing for economic democracy. It declared solidarity to be a basic value, together with freedom, equality and democracy, and an entire paragraph was devoted to each of these basic values. The foundation of solidarity was not seen as (class) interest, but 'empathy with the conditions of others and a willingness to show compassion for each other' (SAP 1975). Olof Palme was head of the programme committee, and empathy[22] pervaded his speeches during the US war in Indo-China during the 1960s (Palme 1969).

In Norway, social democracy picked what it deemed suitable from the new radical rhetoric and integrated it into its own programme language. Since 1968, all DNA platforms and electoral programmes have referred to solidarity, continuing traditions from earlier periods in stating the need for international solidarity, broadening the concept to include new groups and aspects, and making the concept more important. From 1968 to 1981 a modern social democratic concept of solidarity was gradually institutionalised. First, the conceptual context was developed. From 1969, solidarity was mentioned together with justice, equality and freedom.[23] Now, the term solidarity appeared with increasing frequency and importance in programmes. In 1977 solidarity was made part of the title of the election programme, together with employment and the environment, and for the first time a separate paragraph was devoted to defining the concept.

Second, the basis of solidarity was now definitely anchored in ethics, values and even religion. Koht and Sivertsen had prepared the ground, and contributions from the theologian Tor Aukrust came to be the ideological foundation for a redefinition of the relationship between socialism and religion in the DNA in the 1970s. In 1973, the party appointed a new committee to review the relationship between democratic socialism and religion. Again, Sivertsen headed the committee, and Aukrust and Bishop Alex Johnson were among the members. The report concluded that democratic socialism was in accordance with Christian teaching about right and wrong and juxtaposed love of one's neighbour and solidarity (DNA 1974). The gulf between the rich and the poor world

---

[22] In an article in 1973 Palme warned that 'the feeling of community and solidarity could fail' if the capacity for empathy with other peoples and nations was absent. He argued strongly for solidarity as a force directed against that 'kind of financial power that is exercised in the name of the free market' (Palme 1973).

[23] It is interesting to note that the last three are exactly the same as the ethical criteria listed by the theologian Tor Aukrust four years earlier in his key contribution to Christian social ethics, *Man in Society* (Aukrust 1965). Aukrust, who has been characterised as the 'theologian of consensus of the Norwegian social democratic state' (Slagstad 1998) was familiar with the Bad Godesberg programme of the SPD and referred to this several times in *Man in Society*.

should be bridged, and living conditions should be made more equal because this was what both democratic socialism and Christian belief would imply. In a speech to the 1975 congress, Sivertsen emphasised that in 'all fields of life, love of one's neighbour should be the guidelines for action. In society, love of one's neighbour means solidarity and justice and solidaristic distribution of goods on earth' (Sivertsen 1975). The 1975 congress represented a further step in shifting the basis of solidarity from personal and economical interests to ethics. A congress resolution stated that the DNA saw 'a clear connection between the Christian message [about love of one's neighbour] and politics based on solidarity'. At the same time, the party recognised Christendom as a 'substantial part of the cultural legacy of our nation' (Midttun 1994).[24]

In Denmark, the changed ideological climate after the student revolt brought social democracy back to European mainstream rhetoric. The platform, The New Society, in 1969 declared solidarity with the Vietnamese people, and the peoples of the Third World and stated that 'societal solidarity should be a characteristic of welfare policy' (Socialdemokratiet 1969). The preoccupation with freedom, self-respect and participation of the individual in the programme was conspicuous, and may have reflected the atmosphere of personal liberation that characterised the Danish student revolt.[25] The first new platform after the oil crisis of 1973 – the platform of 1977, *Equality, Well-being, Solidarity* – now made solidarity a key concept in Danish social democracy (Socialdemokratiet 1977). In general, this programme represented a turn to the left in terms of programme language. *Equality, justice* and *solidarity* were the key concepts, and gender emancipation was emphasised: solidarity was mentioned no less than twenty-one times. The concept was made more inclusive in terms of groups and issues that were specifically mentioned. It referred to aid to the Third World, the relationship between men and women, and a general identification with society as a whole. It was applied to a wage policy that should encourage wage restraint to prevent unemployment, to a policy of sharing work through leave-of-absence and to reduced economic growth in order to counteract ecological problems. It was claimed that solidarity should encompass all citizens, and there was no trace of the old concept of working-class solidarity against employers.

---

[24] The 1981 platform emphasised empathy and compassion for the weak, poor and needy as constitutive of solidarity. At the same time, it mentioned self-interest, but emphasised that self-imposed restraint was needed in pursuing own self-interest (DNA 1981).

[25] Generally, the Danish student revolt was marked more by liberal attitudes to drugs and alcohol, sexual liberation and personal self-realisation than the revolts in Sweden and Norway where orthodox Marxism came to be more dominant.

The problem was that the programme was eclipsed by the wave of liberal and individualist ideology that also struck Denmark around 1980.

The effects of individualism in the 1980s

In Scandinavia as elsewhere, the influence of individualism and liberalism increased during the 1980s. The social democratic parties met this challenge with somewhat different approaches.

In Sweden, the strong liberalist and individualist ideology of the period influenced the language in SAP programmes to only a small degree. In 1986 a social democratic programme for citizenship and freedom of choice stated that

Democratic socialism entails both the inviolable freedom of the individual and at the same time society's positive measures to broaden and guarantee this freedom. It regards both the formal limits of freedom and the material possibilities to realise freedom. It gives all equal worth in freedom and prevents the strong from oppressing the weak. (SAP 1986)

The new platform in 1990 did not add much in terms of solidarity. The concept was now explicitly broadened to include the relationship between men and women, and the platform stressed more clearly than before the value of individual freedom and autonomy (SAP 1990). This was probably a muted reflection of the liberalist and right-wing offensive during the 1980s. The modest way this was done reflected the hegemonic position of social democracy in Swedish society.

In 1991 a centre-right coalition won the election and established a government. The next year the government and the SAP agreed on austerity packages with cuts in social welfare, to protect the value of the Swedish currency. Unemployment rose to a peak of more than 8 per cent in 1993, a level unheard of in Sweden for many decades. A new social democratic government came to power in 1994 and continued the policy of austerity (Marklund and Nordlund 1999). Many believed that the era of the Swedish welfare state built on solidarity had come to an end. However, the rhetoric of solidarity in social democratic programmes did not change significantly during this period. Although the programme of 1998 indicated a further softening of socialist rhetoric, the concept of solidarity was mentioned several times, this time also to include responsibility for generations to come, and love of other human beings (SAP 1998). Thus, the emphasis on solidarity was somewhat reduced, but broadened to include even more aspects and groups.

In Norway, the DNA government recognised in 1977–78 that the international economic setback was no longer temporary and it abandoned its

Keynesian policy. Support for employment in key industries was reduced, a policy of wage restraint was introduced, and unemployment increased. In 1981, the DNA suffered an electoral defeat, whereas the Conservative Party triumphed and came to power. The 1980s also became the era of individualism in Norway. The DNA developed a double-sided response to the new situation – a combination of modernisation of programmatic content and insistence on solidarity values. The 1981 platform represented an adjustment to the market ideology of the period.[26] The public sector should be modernised and made more efficient; public monopolies should be abolished; socialism should no more be the goal of the party.

This turn to the right was accompanied by the most extensive and elaborate exposition of the social democratic concept of solidarity in any document in the labour movement tradition. The 1981 platform elaborated on the idea of solidarity in a way that constitutes the most explicit exposition of how solidarity is used in political discourse in Scandinavia. Several implications or aspects of solidarity were described: empathy and compassion for the weak, poor and needy; equality, self-imposed restraint in pursuing own interests; community and collective arrangements (DNA 1981).

After the electoral defeat in 1981 the DNA toned down the language of solidarity and become increasingly preoccupied with individual freedom. During the election in 1985, the DNA leadership launched 'Action Freedom' to be debated among the members. At the congress in 1987, the state and public bureaucracy were presented as problems for social democracy (Benum 1998), and all later programmes have been preoccupied about the relationship between individual and community. This development must be seen as a defensive response to the new liberalist ideological climate of this period.

The present language of solidarity

Today, all the Scandinavian social democratic parties have integrated a full language of solidarity into their programmes. However, the most recent SAP platform – that of 2001 – also reflected the growing concern about the individual, and made the relationship between solidarity and individualism a theme. The platform declared that 'each human being shall be free to develop as an individual and be master of his own life'. Contrary to the liberal idea of individual freedom, however, it emphasised

---

[26] Einar Førde – an intellectual and political scientist who led the revision of the platform, declared to the congress that 'we must dispose of all allegations that we are hostile to the market' (cited in Slagstad 1998).

that this presupposes equality – that all human beings are given the same opportunities to shape their own lives. Solidarity should not exclude a striving for individual development and progress, but only egoism that permits the exploitation of others to own advantage (SAP 2001). It is an interesting change of nuance between this formulation and that of the 1998 programme of the SPD, which declared that solidarity was necessary to enhance individual self-realisation. Although mentioning that free, strong and autonomous individuals today demand more freedom to chose, Swedish social democrats seem to be somewhat less prepared to give way to the individualist mood at the beginning of the new century. Thus, the new climate of individualism has not made Swedish social democracy reconceptualise its ideas about individual freedom and collective solidarity. To the degree that the party has made concessions to this new climate of opinion, it has been by formulating more clearly the theme of individualism and individual freedom, but at the same time adhering to earlier positions that this can only be guaranteed by collective effort and equality.

In Norway, the DNA 1993 programme signalled a renewed interest in solidarity, and the programmes of 1997 and 2001 made solidarity an important theme, a core value along with freedom and equality.[27] These programmes defined solidarity in increasingly broader terms, of the number of issues and groups that should be included, and this was combined with a preoccupation with individual freedom of choice and personal self-realisation. The individual and the community were said to be interdependent, and the relationship between the two should continuously be reflected upon (DNA 1989, 1996).[28]

Conclusion: unity and variations in Scandinavian social democratic languages of solidarity

The Scandinavian social democratic parties differ from their European sister parties in that the Marxist idea of solidarity, in party programmes,

---

[27] See DNA (1992; 1996; 2000). In the programmes approved in 1996 and 2001 the concept is mentioned sixteen and seventeen times, compared to four and five times in the programmes approved in 1985 and 1989.

[28] In the following years, the DNA made what was coined *The Solidarity Alternative* a key slogan. This was a strategy for growth, competitiveness and employment. The strategy entailed cooperation on prices and wages structure among trade unions, employers and the government to curb inflation, secure low nominal wage increases and make industry more competitive. Besides, active labour market and educational policies should allow for structural adjustments in the labour market, while a flexible fiscal policy should stimulate or decrease demand according to the situation. This strategy proved to be successful in reducing unemployment, but at the same time it led to increased profits for business and industry and to a more unequal distribution of income.

was transformed at an early stage into a broader and more inclusive concept. Concepts in Marxist language such as unity and proletarian internationalism disappeared, and equivalent terms and concepts such as fraternity were replaced with solidarity (except in Sweden). Besides, these parties were the only ones that adopted a productivist idea of solidarity in their programmes, although this idea was found only in the years immediately prior to and following World War II. Moreover, these parties also demonstrated an early concern with the individual in their programmes.

In addition to this common preoccupation with solidarity, each of the three Scandinavian social democratic parties exhibits some peculiarities. Despite the strong preoccupation with solidarity among Swedish social democratic leaders from Wigforss to Hansson, the concept of solidarity was only much later included in party programmes, and the classic Marxist idea of solidarity was never found in SAP platforms. It was only partially reflected in the Marxist programme of 1920. Nor did later party programmes reflect the broader conception of solidarity that Wigforss, Branting and Hansson had formulated. Such a concept was introduced later than in Norway and Denmark. This discrepancy between leaders' language and programme rhetoric is probably explained by the long interval between the platform of 1920 and that of 1944. From 1944, however, solidarity has been both an important idea and term in programme language – and generally has been applied in the same way as in the German and the Scandinavian sister parties.

What distinguishes the language in SAP programmes from that of the Scandinavian sister parties is that the idea of solidarity was integrated in a stronger and more continuous socialist rhetoric. Swedish social democracy preserved elements of Marxist analysis and rhetoric and argued for reforms of the capitalist economy also when this had been abandoned in Norway and Denmark. Even if the 2001 platform does not contain any concrete proposals for change in the structure of power or private property, it represents continuity in terms of rhetoric. It is still written in a style inspired by Marxism, applying concepts such as class, contradiction, exploitation and struggle, whereas such concepts are virtually absent from the recent programmes of Norwegian and Danish social democracy, and contrary to the sister parties the SAP still declares itself to be anti-capitalist. Thus, the conceptual context of the idea of solidarity has differed from that of the Scandinavian sister parties.

How should we explain the continuity and strength of socialist rhetoric in Swedish social democracy? One possible hypothesis may be found in the class aspect of social democracy in Sweden. Class differences were historically deeper in Sweden than in Norway and Denmark. Large industries were more developed, and in the countryside small farmers were opposed to the owners of large estates. Thus, politics has been more strongly influenced by class and class antagonism than in Norway and Denmark. Whereas social democracy in most other European countries to a much larger extent had to break down existing religious, linguistic or regional loyalties in the working class, the Swedish social democrats had almost no other loyalties to break down in order to establish hegemony in the working class (Therborn 1989). Therefore socialist ideology may have been easier to establish and preserve. A second reason, and one related to this, is that these differences are due to the comparatively stronger position of the workers' trade unions in Sweden – especially compared to Denmark. A third factor might be that contrary to both Norway and Denmark, Sweden was not a member of NATO and was less influenced by anti-communism and cold war ideology. This made the political atmosphere different, both generally and in the trade union movement. Its formally neutral position was associated with stronger contacts with Third World countries and leaders, largely due to the personal commitment of Palme.

A fourth hypothesis may be sought in the special characteristics of social democratic leadership. In her comparative study of the programmatic beliefs of the SAP and the SPD in the interwar period, Berman maintains that integration of the functions of theorist and political leadership in the SAP brought about a stronger coherence between theoretical ideas and political practice (Berman 1998). In the SPD these roles were separate, with Kautsky – who was never a leader of the party – as the predominant theorist. According to Berman, this led to an inability to implement a policy of class alliance, and to a prolonged period of political isolation for the SPD. A similar approach is probably fruitful in terms of explaining why the SAP preserved a socialist rhetoric longer than the social democratic parties of Norway and Denmark. Swedish social democratic leaders were generally well educated. Branting, Erlander, as well as Palme had university degrees; they were very familiar with the contributions of socialist theorists, and may have been more inclined than their colleagues in Norway and Denmark to formulate their politics in terms of theories and visions.[29] In Norway especially, the social democratic part of the labour movement was characterised by anti-intellectual attitudes for decades, and this made the party less inclined to preserve a radical rhetoric.

---

[29] The Danish leader Stauning was a tobacco worker, and the Norwegian Gerhardsen had been a road worker before advancing up the levels of party organisation. Neither was concerned with theory. In Norway, most Marxist intellectuals remained outside the party after the split-up with the communists. The influential secretary of the party for almost a quarter of a century was notorious for his hostile attitude towards intellectuals.

The DNA was the first to include the term *solidarity* in its programmes and to make it into a broader concept that included social groups other than workers. The DNA was the party that earliest, maybe most frequently and in the most possible plural way, has applied the concept of solidarity in platforms and electoral programmes. The Marxist class-restricted notion of solidarity was abandoned earlier in platforms and political programmes than in all the other parties studied here. As in Danish and Swedish social democracy, it has widened the concept to explicitly include wage restraint and to urge industrial workers to abstain from collective action for own economic interests. Moreover, the DNA distinguishes itself because more than the Swedish and Danish sister parties it has redefined its attitude to religion and repeatedly declared that religion could be the basis for solidarity.

Compared to Swedish social democracy, the DNA programmes of the last half-century are marked by a weaker socialist rhetoric. The programme language is more pragmatic, and deradicalisation of content has been stronger, for instance concerning industrial democracy. Social democratic leaders such as Einar Gerhardsen and his successor Trygve Bratteli did not enjoy ideological debates: Gerhardsen because he preferred to build consensus and Bratteli because of a strong technocratic orientation. The modern ideology of solidarity was, however, formulated by academics. Halvdan Koht formulated the idea that the rising working class should have a responsibility for national integration. Although the modern social democratic concept of ideology was formulated before they grew up, it was intellectuals such as Einar Førde and Gudmund Hernes who came to elaborate on the concept in DNA programmes. Their contribution was not to insist on socialist traditions that had been buried decades before, but to take part in modernisation, and in adjustment to what they saw as challenges in a new situation.

In Denmark, early social democratic programmatic language differed from that of the Scandinavian sister parties by being less influenced by Marxism. This is probably best explained by the weaker position of the working class and the stronger influence of an agricultural sector more oriented to the right. Danish social democracy acknowledged early that it could not win a majority alone and that it was necessary to make concessions to groups on the right. The weak influence of Marxism and a strong reformist pragmatism were reflected in the programme language, and until the late 1960s the programme language of Danish social democrats was positioned between the German and the Norwegian tradition on the one hand, and the British on the other. Most interesting in the development of a Danish social democratic language of solidarity is the change from a pragmatic rhetoric, similar to that of the British Labour Party to the adoption of the general Western European social democratic solidarity language. The student revolt, the economic setback and the development of a common social democratic language resulted in the adoption of a modern social democratic concept and language of solidarity in the 1970s. When the 1977 platform declared *Equality, Well-being and Solidarity* (the title) as basic values, the Social Democratic Party again joined the mainstream of European social democratic rhetoric.

United Kingdom: an anomaly of European social democracy?

The British Labour Party grew out of the tradition of British trade unionism. This tradition was not much influenced by continental Marxism, more by the hegemonic liberal political culture of England. When the labour movement was in the process of being organised, Liberalism had already become a dominant ideology – contrary to the situation in Germany, Scandinavia and Southern Europe. Whereas the state had to play an active role in protecting the development of capitalist production elsewhere, the British state had been more active in securing colonies and raw materials for production. However, the specific characteristics of British socialism were also to influence the development of political language – Fabianism, pragmatic reformist socialism and the strong influence of the trade unions. Besides, a tradition of Christian socialism had developed in the later part of the nineteenth century (Jones 1968). Thus, the ideological and political climate was quite different to elsewhere in Western Europe, and the British Labour Party came to develop a more pragmatic ideology than was the case in social democracy on the continent and in Scandinavia – perhaps with the exception of Danish social democracy.

Early Labour Party programmes

The Labour Party (it took this name in 1906) was established in 1900 when political activists of the working class felt that the Liberal Party could no longer represent their ambition for social reform. The Trade Union Congress took an active part in its foundation and came to influence the new party in successive decades. The idea of solidarity was strong in the British labour movement – particularly in the trade union movement. This movement was characterised by a strong collective orientation and saw its collective capacity as a way to enhance the freedom of the individual worker. Thus, the individual should have restricted freedom in relation to the collective. Unity became a core value, and strikes were an opportunity to exercise solidarity with others who were in conflict with their employers. From the 1920s, the Trade Union Congress (TUC) unified the industrial working class – contrary to the fragmented character of trade unions on the continent (Minkin 1991). Naturally, this ideology influenced the Labour Party, but as we shall see, the concept of solidarity and a language of solidarity were not institutionalised in the Labour Party in the same way as in most other social democratic parties.

The documents of the first annual Labour Party conferences were marked by British pragmatism and written in a political language distinctively different from the Marxist language of other European socialist parties of the time. No references to the idea of solidarity are found in early electoral manifestos and key documents – neither a Marxist nor a social democratic concept. The language in these documents is very concrete and down to earth, arguing for specific reforms with almost no references to ideology, values or emotional concepts. The election manifesto of 1910 declared that it was 'time to unite', and that 'those who suffer [should] join to remove their suffering' (Labour 1910). Although this was an equivalent for solidarity, this is the closest and sole reference to anything associated with the idea of solidarity. From 1910, programme appeals were directed to *the people*, *the nation* or to *all citizens*, and this indicates the weak Marxist influence on Labour Party ideology.

The absence of a Marxist concept of solidarity in early Labour Party programmes must be understood as a natural consequence of the general absence of Marxist ideology and phraseology in Labour programmes. Thus, what is to be explained is why there was no strong Marxist influence in Britain. McKibbin has tried to answer this question by directing attention to a range of characteristics (McKibbin 1990); the class structure was fragmented; enterprises were small; workers' wages were sufficiently high to permit a certain level of consumption and social life, and associational life could in some ways compete with politics for workers' attention. At the ideological level, the working class rallied around national symbols and ceremonies such as the monarchy and the British Empire. The relationship between parts of the working class and the middle class was relatively egalitarian, often strengthened by a common adherence to religion and participation in local church activities. Individual rights had a strong position. Finally, a political elite of Marxist intellectuals did not exist among the middle class as on the continent and in Scandinavia. However, as Marxist parties developed in other countries with a fragmented and heterogeneous working class and an egalitarian relationship to other classes (cf. Scandinavia) ideological factors such as the hegemony of liberalism and the legitimacy of the parliamentary system have probably been more influential impediments to the development of Marxism.

A step to the left and a cautious introduction of values: 1918

Labour Party election programmes did not possess a language to express values before World War I, but the party apparently found such a language in the years after the war. Reflecting as elsewhere the radicalisation of the working class after the Russian revolution and the war, the party approved a new constitution in 1918 with the famous Clause Four that was to be the subject of much later struggle. It demanded 'common ownership of the means of production and the best obtainable system of popular administration and control of each industry and service' (Mowat 1968). The new programme in 1918, *Labour and the New Social Order*, argued for democratic control and public ownership over industry, and social reforms. At the same time, it introduced ideological concepts such as *social justice* and *freedom*. These were elaborated upon in the 1923 programme, Labour's Appeal to the Nation. Now, we find also an appeal to 'all citizens' to 'take a generous and courageous stand for right and justice . . . and to hold out their hands in friendship and good-will to the struggling people everywhere who want only freedom, security and a happier life' (Labour 1923). The concept of *friendship and good-will* represents a functional equivalent of the social democratic idea of solidarity. It is broad and includes not only the working class, but also *all citizens* and it is directed towards the general goal of a better society.

The election manifestos in 1924 and 1931 represented a continuation in this respect. Here, we find prudent referrals to a classic social democratic concept of solidarity – expressed by terms such as *brotherhood* and the need to *stand together* or *stand by each other* (Labour 1924, 1931). Such terms were not – as in Scandinavia – transformed into or replaced by *solidarity* in the years to come. They simply disappeared without being replaced with *solidarity* or any other equivalent term.

In 1924, Labour came into government under the leadership of Ramsay MacDonald, but the government became a disappointment for Labour supporters and was quickly brought down because of what was regarded as MacDonald's sympathetic attitude to the new Soviet state (Mowat 1968). He became Prime Minister again after the 1929 election, but the world crisis triggered off a crisis in the party as well. Unemployment and foreign debts increased. Foreign banks demanded cuts in public expenditure as a condition for new loans. When the majority of the party would not accept this, MacDonald formed a coalition government with the Liberals and the Conservatives. The crisis strengthened the Conservatives, and at the next election Labour lost support and did not form a government again until after World War II. During those years, nothing was added in terms of the idea of solidarity in party programmes.

After the war: pragmatic ideology, but demands for radical reforms

Although the programme language was pragmatic, British social democracy continued to argue for radical reforms, and nationalisation of key industries and economic planning continued to be important issues. The Christian socialist R. H. Tawney, who made *equality* a central theme, and the liberal William Beveridge, inspired the Labour Party's ambition to develop a welfare state (Padgett and Paterson 1991). Labour pragmatism was stated boldly in the election manifesto of 1945: 'The members of the Labour Party, like the British people, are practical minded men and women' (Labour 1945). This pragmatism and a widespread desire for social reform brought a great victory at the election in 1945.

As in Denmark and Norway, but unlike the German SPD at that time, the Labour programmes in the early post-war years – the 1945, and particularly the 1950 programme – were infused with a productivist logic. Increased production and increased welfare were knitted together. If a welfare state was to be developed, it was necessary to produce and to export more, especially to the United States; enterprise should be encouraged (Labour 1950). The introduction of a National Health Service and National Insurance in 1948 expressed the same idea of solidarity that made social democrats in other countries the advocates of the welfare state. As in Denmark and Norway, this was wrapped in an ideology and a language of solidarity, but together with other terms: 'All must work together in true comradeship to achieve continuous social and economic progress' (Labour 1945). Contrary to the Scandinavian sister parties, however, Labour evaded the concept of solidarity.

The Labour government did not succeed in giving a boost to the economy, and was defeated at the election of 1951, the Conservatives returning to power. Repeated electoral defeats for Labour in the 1950s created doubt in the party about nationalisation and public ownership, but the trade unions and the left wing were able to defend these positions. In the years to come, however, Labour rhetoric was developed further. Hugh Gaitskell tried to reduce the emphasis on state control and broaden the party's appeal. Whereas 'revisionist' intellectuals had contributed to the introduction of solidarity in social democratic language in other countries, this did not happen in the UK. Anthony Crosland, the most important intellectual in British mainstream social democracy, was not preoccupied with solidarity in his great work *The Future of Socialism*, which was published in 1956, even though he, as other social democrats, was preoccupied with the ethical aspects of socialism and argued for equality. He denounced aggressive individualism and discussed how *cooperation* could be enhanced, but not in a way that could be seen as equivalent to the discourse about solidarity that Wigforss, Koht or Blum had presented (Crosland 1994 (1956)).

However, *Social justice, fair distribution* and *peace* and *equality of opportunity* now became frequently applied concepts in programme rhetoric. The manifesto of 1959 even included a chapter on 'Our socialist ethics', which emphasised the equal value of every human being, justice and human rights, but nothing about solidarity (Labour 1959). A few programmes faintly reflected the broader idea of solidarity that was found in the Scandinavian and German social democratic parties after the war, as they occasionally referred to *brotherhood of man, an expanding community* and *acting cohesively*. These broad and general concepts were applied at the same time as Harold Wilson tried to limit the number of strikes, but the unions complained that he was too concerned with pleasing the middle class (Fielding 2003). The 1970 programme declared that the goal of Labour was to 'create a strong, just and compassionate society' (Labour 1970). However, the (illocutionary) force of these statements was not strong. The idea of solidarity was not discussed or elaborated upon, and the programmes were consistently immune to the *term* 'solidarity'.

Labour returned to government with Harold Wilson in 1964, was ousted by the Conservatives in 1970, and returned again to government from 1974 to 1979 after an industrial recovery. When in power again, Labour soon abandoned the radical election manifesto and the promises about nationalisation and redistribution of wealth. On the one hand, the party had to struggle with the structural problems of the British economy; on the other, it had to manage internal conflicts between a right wing of so-called modernists and a left wing of trade unionists and socialists. This conflict increased sharply after the electoral defeat that brought Margaret Thatcher to power in 1979.

The Labour Party had run for election in 1979 with an election manifesto containing the customary slogans about *justice* and *fairness* – this time supplemented by *individual freedom* – combined with proposals for greater worker influence in the workplace, equal rights for women and greater social and economic equality (Labour 1979). However, Margaret Thatcher was triumphant and initiated a conservative hegemony that lasted until the victory of Tony Blair in 1997.

Labour responded to the right turn of Thatcher by taking a clear step to the left before the 1983 election, making mass unemployment a main issue. The election manifesto argued for mass expansion in public investment and consumption, unilateral nuclear disarmament, renationalisation of key industries and repeal of conservative labour legislation. Demands for greater equality and equality of opportunity were repeated throughout the programme – more than thirty times (Labour 1983).

However, such demands were out of touch with the general mood of the electorate – only 16 per cent supported the idea of nationalisation (Heath *et al.* 2001). Gerald Kaufman – a Labour member of Parliament – characterised the election manifesto as 'the longest suicide note in history' (Bull 2000). For the first and only time in Labour's 100 year history, *solidarity* was found in an election programme. It was applied almost casually, referring to 'solidarity with the poor and oppressed all over the world'. It was interesting to note that it was found in this context of radicalised policy. As has been seen above, in other social democratic parties the general tendency was the opposite, as the use of solidarity paralleled a process of deradicalisation. The appearance of the concept of solidarity in the 1983 programme was to be an isolated incident, as it disappeared in the following programmes.[30]

The new Labour leadership under Neil Kinnock faced a problematic situation. The number of industrial workers was decreasing, and new voters who could bring the Labour Party into government were found in the middle class (Heath *et al.* 2001). Defeat meant that the content and rhetoric in election manifestos were more careful in the years to come. The new leader, Neil Kinnock, initiated a process to broaden the party's appeal and attract middle-class voters. This meant creating a greater distance from the trade unions and traditional Labourism (Fielding 2003). The election manifestos of 1987 and 1992 did not include radical proposals about worker influence, planning and disarmament, and the concept of solidarity did not appear again. The role of the trade unions was gradually reduced, and public ownership was abandoned, creating a greater distance from the trade unions and the political left. *Justice, fairness* and *individual freedom* were preserved as ideological key concepts, and calls for equality of opportunity were repeated, although less frequently than before (Labour 1987, 1992), but Labour was not yet able to broaden its electoral appeal to include a sufficient number of middle-class voters, and the Conservatives kept winning elections.

New Labour and new rhetoric

The election of Tony Blair as leader in 1994 brought about a change in both political profile and rhetoric. Two types of social theories influenced Blair's political ideology: Anthony Giddens' concept of a third way for social democracy and Amitai Etzioni's communitarian ideas (see

---

[30] A study of the large number of resolutions passed by the annual conferences 1981 to 1983 seems to confirm this. *Solidarity* is found only once, in a short reference to solidarity with the liberation struggle in El Salvador (see Labour 1981–83).

Chapters 9 and 10). Other communitarians have also influenced New Labour's ideas, such as Alistair MacIntyre and Michael Waltzer (Driver and Martell 1997). In terms of solidarity, communitarian ideas were most influential. In speeches and written texts Blair has been preoccupied with the communitarian idea that individuals are socially interdependent upon each other. Common values and institutions weave people together and create a feeling of community. This community is not based on class, but on the nation. Blair's idea of community is not only a description, but represents also an ethical value. Community is good because it creates a good society. At the same time, community means to balance individual rights with corresponding obligations and responsibilities (Blair 1997). Blair has now and then referred to the term solidarity, but this concept is not important in his vocabulary. Instead, he is concerned with inclusion and exclusion. His communitarianism is based on the duty to contribute in return, more than on fellowship and solidarity (Fairclough 2000). Being a declared Christian, his ideological position continues a tradition in British social democracy. His religious belief has made him oppose a selfish and individualist idea of self-interest on the one hand, and made him concerned about the relationship between the individual and the community on the other – see *Why I Am a Christian* (Blair 1997).

After a heated debate with the left, Clause Four of the Labour Party Constitution was changed (Fielding 2003). Demands for public ownership were dropped and replaced with a paragraph that brought Labour Party language closer to mainstream European social democracy while at the same time it distinguished itself from other social democratic parties with a stronger accent on communitarian values:

The Labour Party is a democratic socialist party. It believes that by the strength of our common endeavour, we will achieve more than we achieve alone; so as to create for each of us the means to realise our true potential and for all of us a community in which power, wealth, and opportunity are in the hands of the many not of the few, where the rights we enjoy reflect the duties we owe, and where we live together, freely, in a spirit of solidarity, tolerance and respect.

Besides, we find references to *justice, equality of opportunity, the enterprise of the market, a dynamic economy* combined with *the family* and delegation of decisions to the communities affected. Thus, the political language of the new constitution represents a mixture of conventional social democratic and communitarian values on the one hand, and the language of the market on the other hand.

What is peculiar is that only some aspects of this mixture were reflected in the programme that brought Tony Blair to power after the election in 1997. *New Labour because Britain deserves better* is primarily characterised by a language of modernisation. Traditional Labour concepts such as *jus-tice* and *equal rights* or *equal opportunity* are not found in this manifesto, but *fairness* is preserved – sometimes in the context of *fair taxes* (Labour 1997). Blair's preoccupation with community was not reflected in the manifesto, and the concept of solidarity found in the new constitution was left out. However, we find frequent references to concepts in communitarian language such as *responsibility* – sometimes qualified as *moral responsibility, personal responsibility or individual responsibility*. This was mixed with concepts from a language of *modernisation* – such as *British qualities of inventiveness, creativity and adaptability, quality, skill, innovation* and *reliability*.[31] The new language was accompanied by a move to the right in terms of content. New Labour now promised to retain nuclear weapons and Conservative trade union legislation, and not to increase taxes for the next five years.[32] How shall we explain this difference between the constitution and the election programme in terms of solidarity and collective orientation? A possible explanation could be the different audiences for the constitution and the programme. Both documents address party activists as well as the public. However, party leaders must take activists more into consideration when drafting a party constitution, whereas they probably are relatively more preoccupied with the public when it comes to an election programme. Thus, the absence of *solidarity* and collective orientation in the programme may be interpreted as an expression of Blair's ambition to present a complete 'new' Labour for the voters.[33]

The winner-takes-all character of the electoral system made the victory of Blair's New Labour appear as a landslide, but the party did not achieve more than 43 per cent of the vote (Holtham and Hughes 1998). It was not a victory of social democratic ideology. Politically, Blair had abandoned Labour's old demands for public ownership and control of key industries, but this was only to bring Labour up-to-date with what had long ago been the case in European social democracy. Nor was the renunciation of Keynesianism particularly sensational compared to other social democratic parties. More exceptional, perhaps, was his strong promise

---

[31] For an analysis of the communicative skills of Tony Blair, see Bull (2000). Bull attributes Blair's victory in 1997 to his ability to tackle the turnaround from the 1983 to the 1997 programme with a technique of *equivocation* – which is to use equivocal or ambiguous expressions. See also Fairclough (2000) for an analysis of the modernising language of New Labour.

[32] I do not intend to enter the debate between those who consider Blair's policy as more or less Thatcherite and those who stress continuity in Labour policy, but refer to Fielding's informed analysis (Fielding 2003). For an analysis of Labour programme positions on a left–right scale, see the analysis of Budge and Klingemann (2001) which demonstrates the clear movement to the right in the 1997 programme.

[33] See also Fielding's discussion of the concept 'New' Labour (Fielding 2003).

not to increase taxes, the emphasis on education and ambition to renew the public sector. However, what made Blair successful was his ability to combine adaptation to the new reality that had developed under Thatcher with modernisation of both politics and rhetoric.

Tony Blair and New Labour renewed the mandate in 2001 with a new electoral landslide. We note again the same discrepancy between Blair's own personal rhetoric and the language in the election manifesto. In spite of Blair's successful rhetoric about community, this is only vaguely reflected in the manifesto. The concept of community was only mentioned incidentally a couple of times. The concept of solidarity was still absent, although inclusion and exclusion were briefly made a theme. The values mentioned were *justice* and *equality of opportunities*. *Justice* was applied in a general and not a well-defined way as is customary among other social democratic parties. The programme signalled that education and other public services should be more open to the private sector and that corporation tax should be reduced, representing a new step away from traditional social democratic positions.

We must conclude that the communitarian concept of community has not been institutionalised as Labour ideology, although both Blair and other leaders make efficient use of communitarian rhetoric publicly. This possibly illustrates the fact that programmatic rhetoric is not what is most important in the politics of today.

Conclusion: no solidarity and no individuality?

The Labour Party is a member of the social democratic family in Western Europe. Just as other parties, it has struggled for the workers and the poor and argued for collective and public responsibility for welfare. As with the other social democratic parties, it has in some periods agitated for public ownership, and taxation of the rich, to redistribute resources – and as they have, it has abandoned former positions in order to adjust to the mood of the voters and the need for electoral support. However, in terms of political language and institutionalised ideology it distinguishes itself from most other social democratic parties in Western Europe.

For a long period the strong trade-union influence and the programme emphasis on public ownership represented an anomaly compared to German and Scandinavian social democracy. What is interesting is that the discourse on solidarity also is clearly different. The Labour Party never did institutionalise a Marxist concept of solidarity – either expressed in this term, or in other equivalent terms. Neither did it institutionalise in party programmes a classic social democratic idea of solidarity and transform this into a modern social democratic concept. We find only weak traces of a classic and later a modern social democratic idea of solidarity. The idea of solidarity was never declared to be a basic value, and the term itself was only mentioned once in a Labour programme that came to be regarded as a failure. In 2003, the party declared that it had five values: *Social justice, strong community and strong values, reward for hard work, decency* and *rights matched by responsibilities* (Labour 2003). Thus, the absence of the concept of solidarity is not only a question of linguistics, since we only occasionally find concepts that might be considered functional equivalents of solidarity. Whereas in other social democratic parties we find a programme discourse of solidarity, we find in Labour another discourse that represents a mixture of elements from communitarianism, liberalism and social democracy.

The almost continuous absence of the idea of, and the term, *solidarity* is combined with another peculiarity of Labour programmatic rhetoric. Given the strong hegemonic tradition of liberalism, it is strange to note that there are not many references to the individual in Labour programmes – except for the emphasis on individual freedom in the 1980s. As we have seen above, the individual emerged in the programmes of Scandinavian social democratic parties after World War II. In the decades to come, those parties came to be more preoccupied with the relationship between the collective and solidarity on the one hand, and the individual, individual freedom and self-realisation on the other hand. The Labour Party, however, has been surprisingly more reserved in this respect. The programme of 1945 referred prudently to the 'freedom of the ordinary man', the 1987 programme to 'the liberty of all individuals', and the last programme of 2001 declared that in terms of level of living the government should ensure 'that no individual and no community is left behind'. But that is all. Such formulations represent only a weak parallel to how the Scandinavian social democratic parties have emphasised the relationship between the individual and society, individual freedom and individual possibility to choose. Since 1994, the influence of communitarianism under Blair could perhaps explain this, but naturally not the absence in previous periods. Blair has repeatedly denounced the selfish and amoral individualism of the 1980s (Holtham and Hughes 1998). His repeated insistence that individual rights should be accompanied by duties and responsibilities may be seen as another indication of this sceptical attitude to liberalist individualism. Anyway, this combined weak presence of both solidarity and the individual distinguishes Labour from the sister parties in Northern Europe.

Why was solidarity never implanted in British socialism and social democratic ideology in the same way as it was in all other social democratic parties studied here? One simple answer might be that the word was not originally English, but French, and that it is still not seen as integrated in English. This would be to beg the question. The problem, to be precisely, is why this was the case. Alternative concepts such as brotherhood, fraternity or fellowship might have served the same functions, and the concept of solidarity was easily adopted into German, other Latin and Scandinavian languages. A study of the political theory of R. H. Tawney points to the fact that the concept of fraternity was common during the surge of working-class organisation and agitation of the 1820s and 1830s (Terrill 1973). When the working-class movement turned to the pursuit of political power, the emphasis on fraternity disappeared. Thus, neither was a functional equivalent to *solidarity* integrated into the political language of the Labour Party.

The second and probably most important factor contributing to the absence of the idea of solidarity in British social democratic ideology suggested here, is the pervading influence of Liberalism. Middle-class Liberalism had triumphed in the struggle against aristocracy and asserted itself as a dominant economic and political theory. The Labour Party was born into a nation where Liberalism already had established itself as a hegemonic ideology. The collective aspects of solidarity were bound to collide with Liberalism, as any kind of solidarity to some extent has to restrict individual freedom of choice. Other key concepts that were gradually integrated in Labour programmes were not that clearly in conflict with Liberalism and more easy to combine with the dominant national ideology. The concept of justice is not alien to Liberalism, and *equality* can easily be given an interpretation more in harmony with Liberalism. At the same time, those concepts might – as *solidarity* – be given flexible interpretations according to changes in the political situation.

A third and related explanation is that the Labour Party was never strongly influenced by Marxism. Thus, a social democratic concept of solidarity could not be developed by a gradual change of the Marxist concept. Change of programme rhetoric was not felt to be as impelling as in other social democratic parties as the circumstances changed. On the other hand, the left wing of the party had for a long time a stronger influence on programmes than in Germany and Scandinavia. This prevented deradicalisation of issues such as nationalisation and allowed for radical formulations about nuclear disarmament and so forth. Whereas the introduction of *solidarity* in other social democratic parties generally was associated with deradicalisation, the short visit of *solidarity* in a Labour programme was associated with radicalisation.

Fourth, an explanation of the weak presence of *solidarity* might be sought in the influence of Christians in the British labour movement. In the last part of the nineteenth century middle-class Christians discussed socialism actively and had integrated their socialist and religious beliefs. The misery and poverty of the masses led many Christians to look to socialism, and Christian socialist organisations were established (Jones 1968). Non-conformist churches had been more closely in touch with the working class than with the establishment, and this determined the attitudes of other socialists to religion and prevented the emergence of a strong anti-clerical tradition as in France (Pelling 1966). The socialist reformism developed by the influential Sidney and Beatrice Webb was inspired by religion (Beilharz 1992), and the Christian economist and social scientist R. H. Tawney was highly influential in the Labour Party in the first part of the twentieth century. Christian socialists were seldom Marxists, and naturally did not embrace the Marxist notion of class struggle. Tawney thought that fellowship should be based on both personal feelings towards others and on institutions that expressed those attitudes of solidarity (Terrill 1973). His concept of equality rested upon the humanist and Christian assumption that all men share a common humanity, which eclipsed all aspects of dissimilarity and gave men equal worth. Tawney thought fellowship implied not only feelings, but also good relationships that are institutionally based. Contrary to the restricted Marxist working-class concept of solidarity of that time, Tawney's concept of fellowship should in principle embrace all citizens. However, he did not succeed in making *fellowship* a key concept in British socialist ideology. Finally, Tony Blair's New Labour represents a new ideological mix. As a declared Christian, Blair stands firmly in the tradition of British Christian reformism.

Finally, when Kinnock, and particularly Blair, renewed the programme content and language in the late 1980s and early 1990s, they did not use the opportunity to introduce mainstream European social democratic ideology and the language of solidarity. At that time, this had been done in most other social democratic parties. Why was this the case? One reason might simply be that programme authors took further the value-poor genre of earlier authors. Another reason might be found in the fact that Kinnock, and particularly Blair, felt the need to renew social democratic language more profoundly than the introduction of mainstream solidarity rhetoric would allow. If earlier authors had existed in a Liberal hegemony, this was certainly even more true of Blair after the Thatcher era.

The continuous problem of the Labour Party has been to develop a platform that could encompass both the working class and the middle class. Whereas social democracy in Scandinavia managed to acquire electoral support from many in the primary sector and later among the new educated middle class, the liberal hegemony in Britain made this more complicated for the Labour Party. In Scandinavia an ideology of solidarity that included a preoccupation with the value of the individual, individual freedom, possibility of choice and self-realisation may have made such an alliance easier. In the UK, however, the trade union influence in Labour seemed to block a stronger foothold in the middle class. This influence increased from the late 1960s, and strikes and trade union militancy had created trouble for Labour governments (Marsh 1992). Thus, Blair was in need of a language that signalled a solid distance from trade union ideology and language. With Tony Blair the Labour Party chose a strategy different from other social democratic parties – to adjust to the prevailing liberal political hegemony, but at the same time to counter liberalist individualism with communitarian ideology.

Solidarity in Southern European socialism

In the three countries of Southern Europe that are included in this study – France, Italy and Spain – the early labour movement was influenced by a mixture of Marxism and anarcho-syndicalism. In France, socialists and anarchists – the last inspired by the heritage of Luis Blanc and Jules Guesde – had established themselves before the writings of Marx were known and were dispersed among different theoretical positions and groups (Steenson 1991). In Italy, Bakunin's theories were more widely known in the 1870s than the texts of Marx, partly because he lived there at some time. The *Communist Manifesto* was not translated into Italian until 1891. In Spain, the syndicalist tradition was possibly even stronger, and endured until its defeat in the civil war (Bartolini 2000).

The French Workers' Party – *Parti ouvrier francais* (POF) –and the Spanish Socialist Party (PSOE) were established in 1879, and the Italian socialist party – *Partito Italiano Socialista* (PSI) – in 1892. These parties were created in a Catholic society where religion was part of the identity of many workers, artisans and members of the urban and rural middle class, and a strategy was needed to unite these groups with the industrial and radical working class.

Early programmatic beliefs

The first programmes of these parties did not demonstrate any interest in the idea of solidarity. The POF programme was short and almost free of Marxist analysis and rhetoric, with no reference to worker unity or solidarity. Brevity and vagueness came to be general characteristics of socialist programmes in France until after World War I.

In Italy, a working-class party was created in a state that had been united only three decades earlier. The first PSI programme described society as divided into two classes – workers and capitalists – and did not mention farmers. It declared that the PSI wanted to be the class party of the workers, and argued for immediate reforms of wages, working conditions and working hours. The problem of combining a revolutionary rhetoric with a pragmatic practice was even more conspicuous in the PSI than in other socialist parties. The programme contained some theoretical considerations about the role of the party, although very brief.[34]

The first PSOE programme was also short. It called for the abolition of classes, nationalisation of key economic activities such as mining and transport, universal suffrage and other democratic rights. The programme contained no comments on unity or solidarity or any other similar idea. The aim of Pablo Iglesias – the founder of the party – was to create a working-class organisation and he consequently rejected the idea of an alliance with other classes. For a long time the party enjoyed little support from intellectuals and retained a weak intellectual and ideological tradition. However, the congress in 1888 followed the path of other working-class parties of Europe. The Marxist influence was clearer, and a more detailed and concrete programme of social and economic reform was approved. Now, we find the usual introduction of the Marxist idea of solidarity with proud statements about international worker unity and the need for stronger cohesion and unity for the struggle of the party to be successful (PSOE 1888).

All the three parties faced strong challenges. They were confronted with sharp differences and conflicts – between different regions and between the cities and the countryside. Compared to the UK and Germany, industrialisation was late and the working class fragmented because production units were small, and the agricultural sector was dominant. Besides, religion divided potential class allies. The Catholic Church was allied with the right – in Italy in conflict with the state as well – and all these parties became anti-clerical. Besides, the internal labour movement conflicts between Marxists, anarchists and socialist modernisers complicated the development of a coherent strategy to build bridges between the working class, smallholders and underprivileged and/or progressive forces in the cities.

Digression: Leon Bourgeois and middle-class solidarism

Before returning to the idea of solidarity in socialist parties, it is necessary to discuss another discourse of solidarity that developed in France.

---

[34] See the electoral programmes and platforms of 1895, 1900 and 1917, printed in Molaiolo (1982). As for other parties, the concept was occasionally used in other documents of minor importance.

As we have seen, it was in France that the concept of solidarity developed out of the legal tradition of the *Code Napoleon* and was introduced in social philosophy by Fourier, Leroux, Comte and Durkheim. When Durkheim elevated it to a key concept in his work *The division of labour in society*, in 1893, it had already been made a key term in politics as well.

Although the concept of solidarity was used in the early labour movement after 1848, it was not socialist ideology and rhetoric but middle-class politicians in the republican tradition of *Liberté, Égalité, Fraternité* that brought *solidarity* into the heart of politics in France. Continuous concern about social unrest in the decades after the French revolution made not only social theorists but also middle-class politicians concern themselves with social integration. After the defeat of the Paris Commune in 1871 neither the bourgeoisie nor the defeated working class were able to govern, and the urban petty bourgeoisie rose to power. During the 1880s and 1890s, members of the middle-class radical-socialist party sought to develop a pathway between bourgeoisie liberalism, working-class collectivism, and Catholic social teaching. They borrowed eclectically from all quarters, and the result was a complex social doctrine they labelled *solidarism*.

In 1895 Leon Bourgeois became prime minister and formed a government of the radical-socialist party. A year later he published the pamphlet *Solidarité* (Bourgeois 1912).[35] Bourgeois' social philosophy was an eclectic mixture of elements from Darwinism, Liberalism, Pasteur, Durkheim and collectivism, which at the same time drew sharp lines against *laissez-faire* capitalism and socialist collectivism. He was firmly entrenched in the secular Republican tradition and saw solidarism as an alternative to Catholic social teaching as well.

From Darwinism, Bourgeois adopted the idea of the brutal struggles among all creatures of nature. From Liberalism he took the idea of individual liberty, competition among men and the need for individual self-realisation: 'The history of societies, as well as of the species, demonstrates that the struggle of existence is the basic condition for all progress; it is the free exercise of abilities and creativity that bring about change . . .' (Bourgeois 1910; Bourgeois and Croiset 1902).

---

[35] Bourgeois was a strong supporter of the League of Nations and was awarded the Nobel Peace Prize in 1920. I base my remarks here mainly on the Danish translation of *Solidarité* with a highly complimentary introduction of Georg Brandes, the most prominent literary and cultural critic of late nineteenth and early twentieth-century Danish and Norwegian cultural life. I have also applied Hayward (1961), which is the most cited analysis in English, and Schmid's (1997) comprehensive exposition in Danish.

From Pasteur he learned to be concerned about bacteria and viruses, and developed the idea that men were dependent on one another and on their environment through invisible ties of bacteria and viruses. The health of each individual was dependent on the health of others and the general state of health in society. Metaphorically, he conceived society as a complicated organism where individuals and primary communities were the cells of the organism with the state as the regulating centre. This interdependence made liberal individualism inadequate as a social theory. Because natural interdependence was a scientific fact, a practical doctrine about moral and social interdependence should be developed as well, Bourgeois argued.

Echoing Comte and making deductions from the natural sciences and the metaphor of the organism, Bourgeois elaborated his theories on man's debt to society. Man was indebted to society because he had access to cultural and material capital accumulated by earlier generations. Hence, man had a debt to repay to society and was not free to pursue solely his self-interest. He noted that 'national economics' teaching about non-interference becomes in reality a justification for using force to violate others; in the free struggle of existence, the strong will knock down the weak, as we see happening in 'the non-compassionate free nature' (Bourgeois 1910).

The individual debt to society should correspond to individual duties. Individual energy and creativity should be harnessed not only for its own good, but for the common good of society as well. In this way, Bourgeois created a system of thought that accepted some basic tenets of Liberalism and rejected others. The challenge was to find a balance: 'The highest form of organisation is the balance between the individual and the total-ity, understood as the totality exists as much for the individual as the individual exists for the totality.' What is needed is a moral recognition and a practical teaching of reciprocal interdependency. This teaching was *solidarism*, and the associated movement is *le mouvement solidariste* (Bourgeois 1910).

Many aspects of Bourgeois' social philosophy were naive or obsolete, as were his analogies between biology and the social sciences. His insistence on the historical, social and contextual aspects of individual success or failure made him reject the liberalist idea of man as creator of his own success and fortune, and he argued for an active public social policy. Because society was responsible for the conditions the individual was born into, society had a responsibility for securing equal access to the common social and cultural heritage from earlier generations – through education, employment, social security and social services (Hayward 1961). As one might expect from their roots in the middle class, the

Table 4.2 *The solidarists' conception of solidarity*

	Foundation	Objective/ function	Inclusiveness	Collective orientation
Durkheim's organic solidarity	Social norms, values and rituals/ Interdependence because of division of work	Social integration (hold society together)	Very broad: all	Medium: acceptance of individual autonomy and recognition of dilemma
The solidarist idea of solidarity	Historical debt Interdependence because of viruses and bacteria	The common good of society Social reforms	Very broad	Medium: acceptance of individual autonomy and recognition of dilemma

solidarists were not *étatistes*, although they gave the state a central function as regulator. Solidarity, they believed, should be rooted in society, and the state should only be at the people's disposal as an instrument for society.

The theories of Bourgeois and the other solidarists about the relationship between the individual and society resulted in a programme with a specific mixture of public initiatives and voluntary and mutual organisations. They developed an extensive programme of social reform. Bourgeois proposed a progressive tax system and new taxes on inheritance and property to finance a new pension system, social insurance against accidents at work, unemployment and old age. There were already some pensions, but they were insufficient and had to be supplemented with public arrangements. At the same time, he wanted to develop or strengthen voluntary organisations such as trade unions, cooperatives of producers and consumers and other associations. Improvements in the educational system should strengthen moral education and increase moral consciousness. However, Bourgeois failed to get the support of a majority in Parliament, and after a year as Prime Minister he and his government had to resign in 1896.

As we have seen, the solidarist concept of solidarity is closely related to the Durkheimian concept that was described in Chapter 1. Table 4.2 gives a stylised description of the similarities and differences between the two.

The most important difference is simply that the solidarist concept represents a political idea and includes social reform as an objective, whereas the Durkheimian concept is more concerned about function than objective. Besides, in the solidarist concept of Bourgeois the basis of solidarity is seen as interdependence because of viruses and bacteria. This emphasis may have reduced the legitimacy of the concept in the decades that followed.

What is especially noteworthy in this context is that Bourgeois and the solidarists were among the first to make *solidarity* a key term and to integrate it into an ideology of welfare policy. As mentioned above, Fourier had used the concept in this context sixty years earlier in his utopian way. For both theorists and political parties in the socialist tradition, it was to take decades after Bourgeois before they started to associate solidarity with practical welfare reform in their programmes.

French *solidarism* was an expression of the need of the new ruling secular middle class to formulate an alternative ideology to liberalism and socialism as well as to develop social ethics that were neither liberal-individualist nor collectivist. The solidarists also wanted to formulate a social ethical alternative to the social ethics dominated by Catholic influences. They succeeded in accomplishing this, so that solidarism became a sort of official French social philosophy by the turn of the century. However, both the collective ideology of the working class and Catholic social teaching – which are discussed in Chapters 6 and 7 – became more lasting ideologies.

The SFIO and Jean Jaurès

After several splits and reorganisations on the French left, Jean Jaurès succeeded in 1905 in establishing the French Section of the Workers' International (SFIO) (the Second International). The party was always informally called the Socialist Party. The SFIO differed from the socialist parties in the North because it was not brought to birth by a trade union movement that sought political expression as in Scandinavia and the UK, but was to have a problematic relationship with a radical trade union movement. To a large degree the party became a socialist party without a clear basis in the working class (Todd 1991). It was also to be troubled for decades about how capitalist society could be transformed. Could a socialist society be built on the gradual transformation of capitalism without some sort of radical rupture, or would such a rupture be necessary at some point (Kergoat 1997)? Thus, the rhetoric of the SFIO and later its successor the PS continued to be more radical than the rhetoric of the social democratic parties of the North when those embarked on their process of revision of Marxist theories.

Jaurès criticised Bernstein for absorbing the working class into the other classes. He argued against Kautsky that Kautsky's Marxism caused an inability to act and to form political alliances (Jaurès 1900). He was pre-occupied with solidarity, but he did not, as did Bernstein, integrate the need for alliances with the idea of solidarity between the working class and other classes. On the one hand, he saw solidarity only as worker solidarity – and expressed this idea sometimes with the term *cohesion*, sometimes *unity*, and sometimes *solidarity*. On the other hand, he argued that 'proletarian egoism' was the 'sacred egoism of humanity'. Socialism did not need to seek a morality outside itself, because socialism by itself constituted a moral and developed historical solidarity into solidarity of conscience (Jaurès 1976b). Thus, his support for the classic Marxist idea that the proletariat represented the whole of society made it unneces-sary to develop a broader concept of solidarity. Like Bernstein and the Swede, Wigforss, Jaurès emphasised the moral aspect of socialism, but he was not able to broaden his idea of solidarity in the way that Wigforss and Bernstein had done.

In general, the SFIO discourse on solidarity seems to follow the same pattern as for the SPD until after World War I. Party programmes reflec-ted the classic Marxist idea of solidarity, and this was expressed by differ-ent functional equivalents such as *unité des travaillers* – worker unity – and *fraternal aid*. The few and sporadic times *solidarity* was applied, it was about international worker solidarity and most often associated with the perils of war. However, the SFIO seems to have been somewhat more familiar with *solidarity* than the SPD in the period 1905 to 1913, as it appears more frequently in programmes, statutes and greetings at con-gresses in this period.[36]

The SFIO was split when a majority decided to join the Third Inter-national at the congress of Tours in 1920, leading to the establishment of the French Communist Party – PCF. This was the beginning of a long period in which French politics represented an anomaly in Western Europe. The communists did not gain a majority at a party split in any of the other countries analysed here, and did not achieve such broad early electoral support as the PCF. Although the SFIO gained more votes than the PCF in the 1924 elections – 20.2 per cent versus 9.5 per cent – the PCF became a serious challenger to the SFIO on the left in the following years – a competitor with stronger influence in the trade unions and the industrial working class.

[36] The 1906 congress declared that in relation to war, the international solidarity of workers and socialists of all nations should be considered the first duty (PS 1906). In 1913, with the war only months away, the tenth congress received a great number of *adresses de solidarité* from socialist parties of other countries (PS 1913).

This may have made the SFIO stick to a more radical and revolutionary rhetoric than other socialist parties in the process of becoming reformist social democratic parties. The programme of 1928 still argued for the dictatorship of the proletariat – although somewhat more hesitantly than before. The idea of solidarity was made more inclusive, as it declared the SFIO to be the party of *human fraternity*. The term *solidarity* still had no place in the programme, either in referring to the situation in the colonies, or to social welfare reforms (PS 1928). Thus, the SFIO behaved in accordance with the general tendency in European social democracy and demonstrated little interest in the idea of solidarity during the 1920s.

In the 1930s, the idea of solidarity again emerged in SFIO documents, expressed both by the term and by other functional equivalents. The new tactics of the Third International resulted in communist support for the socialist government of Leon Blum in 1935. Now *solidarity* appeared in the declaration of the Blum government, when it briefly stated its 'solidarity with the present misery of the working class' (Blum 1977 (1936)). This way of applying the concept transcended *solidarity* as synonymous with international proletarianism or international unity. It referred to the broader concept that was under way and was to develop further after World War II. However, the Blum government was short lived and had to resign in 1937.

Socialist ideology in Italy and Spain until World War II

Both the PSI and the PSOE continued to be ridden by internal conflicts about political strategy, the need for political alliances, reform and the value of parliamentary democracy. In Italy, the industrial revolution from 1898 to 1907 increased the number of workers, and PSI's struggle against repression and corruption brought electoral progress in 1895 and 1900. In the PSI, one group wanted the party to be the instrument of modernisation in Italy and to compromise with liberals and democrats: on the other side were the syndicalists, maximalists and Marxists who wanted class struggle. The latter group won at the congress in 1912 (Grand 1989).

After World War I, an economic crisis erupted, an extensive and militant strike wave rolled over industry and workers councils popped up. The PSI approved a new programme in 1919 and declared again that it was a revolutionary party with ambitions to establish the dictatorship of the proletariat after the Leninist recipe. The election of 1919 further increased PSI support and they gained almost one third of parliamentary seats. However, the situation was not revolutionary, and the party was unable to lead the working class even if it had been so. Finally, after conflicts with the Third International, the PSI was split and a new Leninist party – the *Partito Comunista Italiano (PCI)* – was established in 1921.

Under the military dictatorship of Primo de Rivera from 1923 the PSOE oscillated between condemnation, collaboration and participation with the regime until 1929 – and were in government for a period (Share 1989). During the succeeding Second Republic, the PSOE became the strongest party in Spain and took part in the coalition government of 1931–36.

In this period, neither PSI nor PSOE programmes were concerned with the idea of solidarity, and neither party developed a new and broader concept of solidarity before Mussolini took power in Italy in 1922 and Franco was victorious in the Spanish Civil War in 1938.

The stalemate in French and Italian socialism after the war

After World War II, Leon Blum published his book, *Pour être socialiste, To be socialist*, where he reflected on the values of socialism. Here, he tried to introduce the classic social democratic concept of solidarity that had been launched by Bernstein and Wigforss about twenty-five years earlier. He emphasised equality, justice and solidarity as socialist values – all three key concepts that were later integrated in the programme language of social democracy. Man was 'born with a sense of equality, a sense of justice, and a sense of human solidarity'. This sense had been developed through the history of human struggle and represented a universal morality. It was this instinct of justice, solidarity and human morality that found its expression through socialism. 'Thus, socialism is a system of morality, almost a religion as much as a doctrine', he said (Blum 1945).

The SFIO programme after the war preserved a radical content and a Marxist language, still arguing for the abolition of private property and classes, nationalisation of key industries and financial institutions. As in other countries after the war, it emphasised increasing production as a condition for improving the standard of living. The SFIO had no strategy that could combine these two aspects, and the programme did not, as in Scandinavia, introduce a productivist idea of solidarity. However, the thread from the government declaration of 1936 and Blum's ideas were introduced in the programme. Here, *solidarity* was applied several times with the meaning of keeping or staying together, transcending the restricted concept of class solidarity and giving the concept a broader and generic sense (PS 1946). A broader idea of *solidarity* had been introduced, but not as broad as in Scandinavian social democracy.

The communists enjoyed considerable prestige both because of their active role in the Resistance and because of the contribution of the Soviet

Union in defeating Hitler. At the election in 1945, the PCF superseded the SFIO as the largest party of the labour movement. For almost thirty years – until 1978 – the SFIO was smaller than the PCF, confirming the extraordinary situation of French socialism. Also in Italy, the PSI was reduced to a junior partner of the PCI.

In spite of Blum's elaboration of the values of socialism and the emphasis on solidarity in the 1946 programme, the SFIO of the 1950s and 1960s did not make solidarity a key concept. The concept of solidarity emerged now and then in congress documents, but not in a way that indicated a strong interest in the concept. The Fundamental Programme of 1962 toned down the radical language of the programme of 1946, but repeated, although largely rhetorically, the commitment to revolution (Padgett and Paterson 1991).

Like the French SFIO/PS, the Italian PSI distinguished itself from the social democratic parties in Germany and in Northern Europe by a more radical political phraseology. It displayed a more uncritical attitude to the Soviet Union, was more strongly anti-clerical, and chose to ally with – and be subordinate to – the Communist Party. The relationship with the PCI and the need to respond to PCI strategy came to be a continuous concern of the PSI in the years to come, and the party was not able to develop an independent programme, either concerning economics or in terms of solidarity. At the end of the war the programme applied a concept of solidarity similar to the classic Marxism of communist parties, referring only briefly to 'international solidarity of the proletarian parties' (PSI 1945).

Following pressure from the US, which threatened to withhold Marshall Aid, the socialists and communists were thrown out of the postwar coalition government with the Christian democrats in 1947. These parties were defeated after a massive anti-communist campaign at the national election the following year, and a long period of political isolation for both the PSI and the PCI commenced. The PSI leader, Pietro Nenni, inaugurated a change of political strategy in 1955 and launched the idea of collaboration with the Christian Democrats. The PSI condemned the Soviet invasion of Hungary in 1956, signalling a different and more independent political position from the PCI. Whereas the congress of 1955 had repeated the Marxist–Leninist idea of proletarian internationalism and declared solidarity with 'the peoples that had defeated the class domination of capitalism' (PSI 1955), the congress in 1957 signalled a prudent minor change. The party again confirmed its solidarity with struggling workers and 'peoples that have broken capitalist domination and go forward on the road to socialism', but stated at the same time that 'PSI shall preserve its right to judge and criticise in a socialist fraternal spirit' (PSI 1957). In 1961, the PSI abandoned its anti-NATO position, removing one important obstacle on the road to collaboration with the dominant Christian Democratic Party.

Finally, in 1963, the PSI entered into a coalition government with the Christian Democrats, leading to a split in the party. Variants of this coalition were to endure until the moral and political breakdown of the PSI in 1992. It is interesting to note that this turn to the right in the 1960s does not seem to have been accompanied by any widening of the concept of solidarity, as was the case in other socialist or social democratic parties.[37] Still, the PSI programmes were entrenched in Marxist language and unable to develop a broader concept of solidarity.

The French master of rhetoric and the bankruptcy of Italian social democracy

For the French PS, the end of the 1960s brought both organisational and programmatic renewal. As in Germany and Italy, the student revolt revived political debate, socialist theories and political rhetoric. However, after a short period of strikes, political unrest and an election that confirmed the trust of the majority in President de Gaulle, politics returned more or less to normal. In 1968, the socialists reorganised and the party was reestablished as the *Parti Socialiste*, PS, and François Mitterand was elected leader three years later (Kergoat 1997). Similar to Brandt, Mitterand acknowledged the positive aspects of student radicalism at the same time as he rejected what he labelled the 'mishmash of quasi-Marxism', 'hotchpotch' and 'confusion' of the movement (Sassoon 1996). Mitterand was a pragmatic politician, but at the same time a master in applying radical socialist rhetoric. The new programme of 1972 – *Changer la vie* (Change life) – reflected the organisational reestablishment and the influence of CERES on party ideology and rhetoric. The programme represented a breach with orthodox Marxist rhetoric in the SFIO tradition, but preserved the idea of a radical breach with capitalism, and socialisation of the means of production (Kiersch 1979). Thus, the PS continued to have a more radical language than the social democratic parties of Scandinavia, Germany and the UK. In 1972, the PS and the Communist Party succeeded in establishing a common programme, reflecting a step to the left for the PS. This did not mean any change in terms of the insignificant role of *solidarity* in party rhetoric and programmes.

---

[37] I have not been able to find the 1963 programmes, but there is no mention of solidarity in the 1960 programme, nor in the theses adopted at the 1961 congress (see PSI 1960; 1961).

It was the master of socialist rhetoric, Mitterand, who made solidarity a more important concept in socialist programme rhetoric. His programme at the presidential election in 1981, *110 propositions pour la France*, described values and principles more eloquently than previous programmes. Socialist politics should be based on four main themes: *peace, employment, freedom* and *France*. Social justice was emphasised as essential as well. The programme declared the need to fight egoism and declared an ambition to make society more just and man more solidaristic. Improvements in social security and welfare were discussed under the heading of 'a solidaristic society' (Mitterand 1981). Solidarity had now clearly become a more central concept, but had not yet been elevated to a fundamental value, as was the case in the German and Scandinavian social democratic parties at this time.

Mitterand could hardly be said to have had a coherent political philosophy, and neither is a coherent idea of solidarity easy to discern. Nonetheless, he succeeded in combining traditional socialist rhetoric that appealed to party activists with pragmatic politics that communicated with a broader audience. However, the prominent role of solidarity in Mitterrand's presidential programme was no isolated incident. In the following years, he made solidarity a key concept in his rhetoric and applied it repeatedly and insistently in speeches on different occasions. What distinguished his political discourse from social democratic discourse in other countries, was the combination of his specific form of nationalism with the social democratic values of freedom, justice and solidarity (see, for instance, Mitterand 1995a; 1995b; 1995c).

Although the 1981 programme represented an important step towards modern mainstream social democratic ideology of the German and Scandinavian type, some more steps had to be taken for the PS to adopt a modern social democratic language of solidarity. The victory of Mitterand at the presidential election in 1988 again made solidarity an important concept in the political discourse on the future of social security and the welfare state (Chevallier *et al.* 1992). In *Letter to all the French*, he emphasised that solidarity should imply vertical redistribution 'from those who have much to those who have nothing' (Mitterand 1992).

In Italy, the PSI continued to be a coalition partner with the christian democrats in governments of the 1970s and 1980s, but the political results of this collaboration were not easy to see. The distance between radical Marxist rhetoric in programmes and pragmatic government politics was great, although the new PSI programme of 1978 represented a step from radicalism to social democracy. Now, a renewed PSI that built on mainstream European social democratic ideas and language intended to compete with the PCI and the DC for voters who sought alternatives to having two large blocks in Italian politics (Padgett and Paterson 1991).

The social democratisation of the party included a first cautious step towards the idea of solidarity that was part of social democratic ideology in Scandinavia and Germany.[38] The congress in 1978 adopted an extensive reform programme (106 pages), arguing for the restoration of public finances, decentralisation, public planning and intervention to create employment. Unlike most other social democratic parties, the PSI still preserved a radical rhetoric about *socialist internationalism*, but now included a general reference to the 'need for a strong solidarity between peoples of different nations' as well (PSI 1978). However, the PSI still did not use the concept outside the sphere of international relations. Even when the relationship between lay and Catholic workers was described, it was with the old concept of class unity and without any rhetoric about solidarity.

Three years later, the PSI leader Bettino Craxi launched the slogan 'Socialist Renewal for the Renewal of Italy' (PSI 1981). The path embarked upon in 1978 was continued and radical rhetoric further toned down. The theses declared that the PSI now was an 'undoctrinaire' party. It stood forth as the party of modernisation, but even now this was not accompanied by a stronger emphasis on solidarity, as was the rule for most other social democratic parties at crucial moments of deradicalisation. Craxi mentioned solidarity only once in his long speech at the congress in 1981 – about the need for collective solidarity against the processes of marginalisation in modern society – and in a way similar to that of other social democratic parties. Contrary to its rival on the left, the PCI, it was not much concerned with softening its anti-clerical policy to attract Catholics (see Chapter 8), and it did not develop a broad concept of solidarity as a key concept, as the PCI did in the following years.

The PSI did not demonstrate an ability to transform this rhetoric into practical politics in the following years. It continued to be a minor partner of the Christian Democratic Party, even when Craxi became Prime Minister in 1983. Craxi and the PSI gradually became more involved in traditional Italian clientelism and political corruption, and developed this system even further. As a result of the *Tangentopolis* ('Bribetown') scandal the PSI was dissolved in the early 1990s.

---

[38] As I have not been able to find the 1976 and 1979 electoral programmes, this impression is built on the analysis of theses, resolutions and other congress documents from this period.

Spain: Felipe Gonzalez and a step to the right

The PSOE kept alive the Marxist tradition during the years under Franco, who died in 1975. The PSOE that now emerged on the political scene was ambiguous in terms of ideology. On the one hand, contrary to social democratic parties of Northern Europe, the PSOE declared itself a Marxist class party, although democratic, as late as in 1976 (Padgett and Paterson 1991). On the other hand, the leadership was young and educated with a social democratic ideology inspired by German social democracy. Altogether, it had not much in common with the old socialist party from the pre-fascist period. The next years were to witness a turn to mainstream social democratic ideology both in general and in terms of solidarity.

However, the PSOE was not able to win the first election in 1977, but the centre-right party UCD won government power. Under the leadership of Felipe Gonzalez, who had been elected secretary general in 1974, a reorientation now took place in the PSOE. A great many members of the new middle class now joined the party – lawyers, teachers, intellectuals, artists, etc. – contributing to a change of both programme and party culture.

After the first oil crisis in 1973, unemployment increased steadily and affected 16 per cent of the workforce in 1982, making Spain the country with the highest level of unemployment in the OECD (Catalan 1999). The second oil shock in 1979 was followed by increased public debt and the need for reforms opened new opportunities for the PSOE. After a sharp conflict at the congress in 1979 about whether the PSOE should declare itself as a Marxist party, Gonzalez had his way and the status of Marxism was reduced.[39] The new PSOE election programme in 1979 reflected the change in the party and was a decisive step to the right. The programme was naturally concerned with the need for a consolidation of democracy. Nothing was said about socialism, and nationalisation of industry and other economic activities was abandoned. Spanish society needed a profound modernisation of the economic structure, and Spain should be integrated in Europe, the programme declared. Some elements of traditional socialist theory were preserved: economic planning should still have a central role, and the financial system should be built on nationalised and socialised institutions, whereas private financial

---

[39] The 1979 congress declared once more that the PSOE was a Marxist party. Gonzalez resigned in protest, but was reinstated at another congress the same year after a compromise had been reached – saying that Marxism was a critical and undogmatic instrument and that socialism should be an alternative that respects people's individual belief (PSOE 1979).

institutions should play only a limited role. The programme declared the fundamental principles of PSOE to be a *just, egalitarian*, and *free* society where citizens should be the real protagonists of their destiny. It argued for struggle against unemployment, and for social reforms, increased regional autonomy, and improved relations with Latin America (PSOE 1979).

After a new electoral defeat Gonzalez and his party analysts drew the conclusion that the PSOE had to reorient its policy towards new social strata in order to win a majority. The party should address 'all oppressed people, whether manual or intellectual workers' (quoted from Share 1989), and the party was rapidly transformed from a worker's party into a 'people's party' (Maier 1979).

The programme approved by the congress in 1981 has been labelled a 'Spanish Bad Godesberg programme' after the profound revision of the SPD programme thirty-two years earlier (Share 1989). The idea of a financial sector dominated by nationalised and socialised institutions had disappeared, and the market was described in more positive terms. This was the decisive step to leave behind socialist and classic social democratic positions and accept the ideology of modern social democracy. The change was accompanied by a programme language that emphasised solidarity more strongly than previous programmes. The new concept of solidarity was broad, inclusive and close to how solidarity was applied in other European social democratic parties in this period. The opening stated that the election represented an opportunity for relaunching progress and solidarity. Solidarity was applied both to the need to increase employment, to introduce fiscal reforms and to improve social services. The programme declared solidarity with peoples struggling for freedom and national sovereignty, defended human rights and adequate legal protection for refugees. Solidarity between the peoples of different regions was emphasised (PSOE 1982).

Although the PSOE now had adopted a modern social democratic discourse about solidarity, solidarity had not yet been elevated to the role of a basic value or principle – a status that was still reserved for *freedom* and *justice*. The combination of the popularity of Gonzalez, internal conflicts in the conservative UDC, deradicalisation of economic policy, a more positive attitude to the market and a stronger rhetoric of solidarity, resulted in a victory at the election in 1982. The election result has been described as a political earthquake, doubling the PSOE electoral support and the parliamentary group (Montero 1999).

This was the beginning of a period of fourteen years in government. Whereas the party had demanded socialisation of key productive sectors and the end of foreign domination by the great powers and multinationals before 1982, a process of privatisation of public enterprises now started. The overriding goals were to modernise and to prepare Spain to become a member of the European Union, and later to meet the Maastricht criteria for the single currency. The negative experiences of the French PS with deficit spending made the PSOE government choose a strategy of austerity and reduced public expenditure to curb inflation. Rationalisation and massive layoffs in industry resulted in increased unemployment. Cuts in social security and reduced benefits for the sick and the elderly were implemented. In general, this policy was more reminiscent of Thatcher's policy in the UK than the social democratic policy of the North. On the other hand, the party implemented an active reform policy in other areas, including education, public administration, regionalism, etc. Access to the EU in 1986 opened a period of strong economic growth. The PSOE liberalised the economy and adopted a market-oriented policy. Altogether, this policy did not conflict with the general mood of public opinion (Share 1989).

The PSOE programmes of the 1980s and the 1990s bear the hallmark of this policy. The aim of the party was to modernise and liberalise, and this was accompanied by a strong accent on solidarity in the programmes. Whereas previous programmes had also been concerned with modernisation of the economy and society, the 1986 programme emphasised the need for flexibility and for adaptation to rapid changes in the world economy. Besides, it declared the goal of the PSOE to be a more modern and solidaristic society. The social conception of the PSOE, it said, was based on a plurality of forms of life in solidaristic cohesion. 'Spain should defend for other countries the same principles on which are based the internal life of Spain – peace, freedom, redistribution of wealth, justice, participation and social cohesion' (PSOE 1986). We note here the introduction of the concept of 'cohesion', which may have been inspired by France, but solidarity was not yet mentioned among the basic principles.

The final step towards a fully developed language of solidarity was made in the election programme of 1989. Here, solidarity, full employment, social justice, peace and democracy were emphasised. The extension of solidarity to all citizens should be a final goal of PSOE policies, and reforms of the social security system, increasing minimum pensions and public pensions should strengthen solidarity, the programme declared (PSOE 1989). The concept of solidarity was extended to cover protection of nature, but not yet applied to the situation of women, although gender issues were extensively addressed in both this and previous programmes, and discussed as a question of *equality* between the genders.

Conclusion: present status of solidarity

The 1990s did not bring much new in terms of the idea of solidarity in Southern European socialism. Recent key documents of the PS demonstrate that the party of today has adopted mainstream social democratic rhetoric on solidarity. In 2001, the statutes declared the goals of the party to be *freedom, equality* and the *dignity of men and women, welfare, responsibility and solidarity* (PS 2001). However, the PS has generally preserved a more radical political language than most other social democratic parties in Western Europe. When, in 1999, Tony Blair and Gerhard Schroeder published a common manifesto with a strong social liberal accent, the French socialist leader Lionel Jospin characterised the document as more liberal than social, and refused to sign it. The same year the PS argued strongly at a meeting of the Socialist International that the International ought to maintain a critical attitude to capitalism (PS 1999). In spite of this, the PS of today is a full member of the family of European social democratic parties. In the first decade of the new century, the PS is confronted with the same challenges as most other social democratic parties: how might radical policies, collectivism and solidarity be reconciled with increasing individualism? how should broad solidarity meet the xenophobic demands for national solidarity against 'the others'? The presidential election and the election for the national assembly in 2002 made clear that the PS had no effective answers to these questions and that Jospin's more radical version of social democratic politics was not an adequate answer for many voters. However, the setback of the PCF in the election to the National Assembly definitely made the PS the dominant party of the centre-left.

Also, the Spanish PSOE has adopted the mainstream European social democratic language of solidarity, but unlike the French PS has not preserved a radical anti-capitalist language. It has combined a language of solidarity with a language of modernisation, reflecting the profound modernisation that Spain has experienced. Recent PSOE programmes indicate the aim of combining the language of social democratic solidarity with concern regarding intermediate institutions and individual freedom. The 1996 programme introduced the concept of personal responsibility and stated that support to voluntary organisations should preserve social cohesion, and the 2000 programme devoted more attention to the concept of the individual than earlier programmes (PSOE 2000). Thus, in this respect also the PSOE discourse on values has approached the discourse in mainstream European social democracy. However, the PSOE lost the elections in both 1996 and 2000. It faces the same dilemma as the French PS and the social democratic parties in the North. How should modernism, emphasis on individual freedom and personal responsibility, flexibility and intermediate institutions be combined with collective solidarity and public responsibility?

The Italian PSI did not succeed in transforming its Marxist concept of solidarity, and did not survive. Today, the inheritor of Italian communism has taken over the role of a social democratic party and established a social democratic discourse on solidarity (see Chapter 8).

The development of the idea of solidarity by the socialist parties in France, Italy and Spain initially followed the same path, but the trajectories soon parted and followed lines influenced by national contexts. They all took up the classic Marxist idea in the early phase and expressed this as did other labour movement parties in several different concepts and terms – worker unity, internationalism, fraternity, solidarity. None of the parties managed to formulate an idea of solidarity that transcended working-class solidarity and included potential allies in a community based on more than instrumental utility. None of them made *solidarity* a key term until the second part of the twentieth century; none managed to transcend the historical cleavage between socialism and the Catholic Church. Whereas the transformation of the concept of solidarity in Germany and Norway was associated with formulating an open attitude towards religion and its potential as a basis for solidarity, neither the PS, the PSI or the PSOE succeeded in doing the same in its programme.

Although France was the birthplace of the political term and concept of solidarity, French rhetoric on solidarity has had a cyclical character. Earlier than in other countries, social theorists such as Leroux, Comte, Durkheim and Bourgeois developed both a sociological and a political concept of solidarity. Thus, it is surprising that the parties of the labour movement did not make solidarity their own key concept after the political defeat of Bourgeois. Although the SFIO, as other parties of the labour movement, was preoccupied at an early stage with the idea of solidarity in the classic Marxist sense, it applied the term only sporadically. First, François Mitterand, almost one hundred years after middle-class *solidarism*, again made solidarity a central theme and term in French social democratic rhetoric – now as a modern social democratic concept. He was also was the person to formulate the specific trait of French social democratic rhetoric on solidarity – the specific combination of solidarity and nationalism in political discourse – a combination not found in any of the other parties studied here. This belated introduction of a modern social democratic discourse on solidarity can probably best be explained by the special characteristics of French socialism and socialist rhetoric.

First, the prolonged tradition of radical and revolutionary rhetoric in the SFIO/PS may have delayed changes in political rhetoric. Second, the existence of a large communist rival with a more solid basis in the working class may have worked in the same direction.

The Italian PSI was always a deviant in the family of European social democracy, being the object of continuing discussion and doubt about whether it in fact could be counted as a member of the social democratic family (Padgett and Paterson 1991). Throughout most of its history the PSI had a programmatic ideology closer to Marxism and stood to the left of social democratic parties in Germany, the UK and Northern Europe in terms of rhetoric. Its political practice was, on the other hand, more to the right of social democracy in most other countries studied here. Also in terms of the concept of solidarity, the PSI must be regarded as a special case. It did not complete the transformation of the Marxist idea of solidarity to a modern social democratic concept, and it never developed the extensive discourse about solidarity, justice and equality that other social democratic parties had adopted before the end of the 1980s. Neither did it redefine its relationship with religion, as did the German and the Norwegian social democratic parties.

The reasons for this might to some extent be sought both in the prolonged adherence to Marxist rhetoric in general and the dominant position of its rival, the PCI. However, when party ideology and rhetoric was finally in a process of transformation, the radical ideological climate of the first part of the 1970s had disappeared. The new, more liberalist ideological climate of the late 1970s and the 1980s may have made it less tempting to emphasise the collective aspects of the modern concept of social democratic solidarity that social democratic parties in Northern Europe had been developing. The continuing technocratic orientation of the party may have reduced the ability to formulate a new concept of solidarity as well.

In Spain, the PSOE did not have to compete with a strong, and at times dominant communist party, as was the case in France and Italy. The last two decades of the twentieth century witnessed a profound transformation both of Spanish society and of the PSOE. Spanish capitalism was modernised and integrated in the European Union. The PSOE was transformed from a party with a traditional socialist profile with nationalisation and public control of key positions of the economy in the programme to a party that was more concerned with privatisation and flexibility in the labour market. The rhetoric of redistribution and equality was toned down. Such a change of position has probably gone further in the PSOE than in most of the other social democratic parties studied here, with the possible exception of the British Labour Party. This development was accompanied by the introduction of a language of solidarity that we also find in other social democratic parties included in this study.

Spanish social democratic discourse on solidarity was marked first by the insignificant emphasis on the idea until the outbreak of the civil war. Here it has been suggested that this might have been due to the weak intellectual tradition of the party during that period. Second, it was characterised by the late introduction of the modern social democratic concept of solidarity in party programmes after the reestablishment of democracy. Other key social democratic concepts such as *justice, equality* and *freedom* were elevated to programme rhetoric before *solidarity* was introduced. The introduction of a full language of modern social democratic solidarity did not take place until 1989. At that time the Socialist International had been reinvigorated and had adopted the language of modern social democratic solidarity, and this probably encouraged the PSOE. As in most other social democratic parties, the modern concept of solidarity was introduced in a programme that at the same time meant a political turn to the right. The programme rhetoric of PSOE today in terms of solidarity parallels the general discourse of West European social democracy, using the concept frequently and with a broad and inclusive meaning. As with many other social democratic parties, the collective aspect of this concept has became more problematic, and was a theme in recent PSOE programmes.

A preliminary conclusion: three clusters of solidarity discourses

Summing up so far, we may discern three patterns in the development of solidarity rhetoric. First, we have noted the early appearance of *solidarity* in Scandinavian social democratic rhetoric. In Norway and Denmark the idea and the concept were early and continuously emphasised in programmes, and it is a strong and continuous line from Wigforss' discussion about the ethical aspects of solidarity to Per Albin Hansson's concept of *the people's home*. Second, in spite of the central role of German social democracy in the European labour movement and its generally assumed ideological influence on Scandinavian sister parties, the influence of solidaristic rhetoric probably has gone in the opposite direction. The SPD was slow to broaden and modernise its concept of solidarity compared to sister parties in Scandinavia. On the other hand, the extensive discourse on solidarity, justice and freedom as basic values in the Bad Godesberg programme came to be a crucial event in the development of social democratic programmatic rhetoric and ideology in Western Europe.

The second 'pattern' is hardly a pattern at all, as it consists only of British social democracy. The British case of solidarity rhetoric is simply that both a Marxist and a social democratic idea of solidarity were only faintly reflected in a few party programmes, and that the *term* solidarity has been missing in party programmes during the hundred years and more that the Labour Party has existed. This might most fruitfully be explained by the hegemony of liberal ideology in the UK, the absence of Marxist influence in the Labour Party, and perhaps the early Christian influence in British socialism as well.

The third pattern is the late transformation from a Marxist to a social democratic concept of solidarity in Southern European socialism and the late introduction of the term solidarity in party programmes. The variations within this group are clear. The 'up and down' character has characterised French solidarity rhetoric. The concept of solidarity was initially French. In the nineteenth century it was rooted in legal, social, philosophical and political discourses and became a hegemonic concept at the turn of the century in middle-class political discourse. Against this background it is strange that it was not integrated earlier into socialist rhetoric, although it was sporadically mentioned. Although Leon Blum discussed solidarity, justice and equality in the 1930s in a way that echoed Bernstein, solidarity was only mentioned occasionally in the SFIO pro-grammes after the war. It was François Mitterand who brought about a renaissance of the concept in French social democratic programme lan-guage in the presidential election of 1981 and in the years to come. The Spanish PSOE did not introduce a social democratic idea of solidarity until after 1981, which can be explained by the late social democratisa-tion of the party, due to the long period of dictatorship. The Italian PSI never adopted a modern language of solidarity and ended its history as a sad example of the ambition to combine modernisation with political corruption.

5   A comparative perspective on social democratic solidarity

In Chapter 2 we saw that early Marxist theorists formulated an idea about working-class unity and solidarity, but that they rarely applied the concept of solidarity in their texts. Chapter 4 concluded that this was the case in the party programmes in the first decades of the labour movement parties as well. Other terms such as *worker unity, (proletarian) internationalism* and *fraternity* or *brotherhood* were more frequently applied. Such terms were sometimes functional equivalents to solidarity, e.g. fraternity and brotherhood. At other times they referred to different specific aspects of solidarity such as unity in the struggle for tariffs and better working conditions, or to sympathy and material support for workers in other nations. Both *solidarity* and other more or less functionally equivalent terms were based on a notion of class interest, were restricted to the working class and implied a strong degree of collective orientation where individual autonomy had to be subordinated to the interest of the collective. Later, *solidarity* replaced the other equivalent terms and was gradually redefined and transformed into a new concept with a different foundation, goal, inclusiveness and degree of collective orientation. The transformation of the Marxist to the modern social democratic idea of solidarity entailed a change of all these four aspects of solidarity and the relationship between them.

This chapter systematically compares the variation between different social democratic parties in the development of a modern social democratic concept of solidarity. A periodisation is sketched and the changes of the four different aspects in the programmes of the eight social democratic parties included in this study are outlined.

Periodisation of solidarity discourses

The discourses on solidarity described here have demonstrated that the development of the discourse on solidarity was strongly integrated into the general political and ideological change in socialist parties. Both the transformation from a Marxist to a social democratic idea of solidarity and the introduction and increasing importance of the term *solidarity* were part of the general social democratisation of the parties discussed here. These changes took place in a process that varied from country to country. The periodisation of the development from the introduction of the term *solidarity* in party programmes up to a full language of social democratic solidarity that integrated *solidarity* and other key concepts such as justice and freedom is schematised in Table 5.1.

The transitional phase from a Marxist to a social democratic concept endured from twenty to more than fifty years, with the parties of Southern Europe being the latest to adopt the new concept. Although the idea of worker solidarity was widespread, only the Norwegian DNA used the term *solidarity* in its first platform when the first congress in 1887 declared that workers in the cities and the countryside should feel solidarity with one another. DNA programmes introduced the term fifteen years before the French SFIO, twenty-one years before the Danish social democrats, and twenty-four years before the ideological big brother, the German SPD.

The idea of worker solidarity was, however, strongly emphasised when the protagonists of German socialism – August Bebel, Karl Kautsky and Eduard Bernstein – compiled the Erfurt programme in 1891. Formulations like *brotherly feelings* and *internationalism* came to be used in the years to come, both in the SPD and in other Marxist and socialist parties in Europe, but the term solidarity was not used. The oscillation between different terms and the fact that the term was not found worthy of being applied in the programme itself reflects the fact that the *concept* had not yet been elevated to the status of a key idea.

After the Norwegian DNA, the next party to elevate solidarity to programmatic rhetoric was the French SFIO in its programme of 1906. In spite of the popularity of the concept in France in the later nineteenth century, it was not very frequently applied in early PS programmes. When used, it was also applied there in terms of international worker unity. The pre-World War I programmes of the Spanish and the Italian socialist parties made no mention of the concept of solidarity. The special role of anarchism and syndicalism in Southern Europe did not make the socialist parties of these countries inclined to take up the tradition of Bakunin and make solidarity an important term in programmes.

In the years prior to 1914, the shadows of war made international working-class unity precarious. The possibility that workers of one nation might fight against workers of another nation was contrary to Marxist principles and was abhorred by socialist leaders. In this situation a new rhetoric and new concepts that might make a more effective emotional appeal than the established rhetoric were needed. This may have made

Table 5.1 *The institutionalisation of a social democratic language of solidarity in party programmes*

	Introduction of the Marxist concept	Worker *solidarity* first mentioned	Transitional period	The introduction of a social democratic concept	Declared as a basic value	The introduction of a social democratic language of solidarity
SPD (Germany)	1891–1925	1925	1925–56	1956	1959	1956
SAP (Sweden)	1897–1920	1944	1920–44	1944	1975	1975
DNA (Norway)	1891/1909	1887	1909–39	1939–45	1981	1969–75
Socialdemokratiet (Denmark)	1913	1913	1913–34	1934–45	1977	1977
SFIO/PS France	1906	1906	1928–81	1981	1981	1981
PSI (Italy)	–	1943	–	–	–	–
PSOE (Spain)	1888		1888–1981	1981	1989	1989

solidarity a more central concept in socialist rhetoric in the first decade of the new century. As the threat of war came closer, the frequency of solidarity appeals increased. The resolutions passed by the Second International also demonstrate how the threat of war made *international worker solidarity* become a more frequently used concept. As 1914 approached, the condemnations of militarism and appeals for worker solidarity became more desperate. The congress in Copenhagen in 1910 called for a struggle against armament and war, urged for the 'realisation of international solidarity' and for the 'duty to worker solidarity with workers of other countries' (Second International 1976). In 1912 the French socialist leader Jean Jaurès presented the resolution on war, calling again for international solidarity and warned governments that a war might provoke revolution. The final collapse of international worker solidarity came at the meeting of socialist leaders in July 1914 in Paris. Against the background of Austria's declaration of war against Serbia and bellicose statements from Berlin and Paris, the Austrian socialist leader, Victor Adler, had to state that his party had no possibility of mobilising workers against the war. At that time, people were rallying for war in the streets of Vienna.

Still, the *term* solidarity was not considered important enough to be applied in platforms and election programmes by most of the socialist parties studied here during those years. Only the Norwegian DNA, the French SFIO and the Danish Social Democratic party mentioned *solidarity* in party programmes before World War I. *Solidarity* was infrequently applied, not integrated into programmatic language, and apparently not yet considered a highly effective symbolic expression – except in appeals against the war. When used in party platforms, election manifestos and resolutions from the Second International, *solidarity* nearly always referred to class solidarity with workers of other industrialised nations. It was rarely used about national, social and political issues. Nor was it generally used about the relationships between the working class and other classes or social groups, such as smallholders or the poor – although there are many programme formulations about social policy and the poor. Finally, it was not usually applied to the relationship between the working class and the peoples of the colonies in what is now called the Third World or in regard to the relationship between workers and immigrants from other countries. Thus, until World War I, the labour movement's concept of solidarity still adhered to the classic Marxist ideology – solidarity based on common interests among workers and expressed identification with other workers. This does not mean that socialists did not care about those issues. The protocols of the Second International and congress documents from the SPD, for instance, express a strong commitment to social policy, and much concern about the situation in the colonies and even about immigrant workers.

The outbreak of World War I revealed the paralysis of the international labour movement. Most working-class parties sided with their own governments and abandoned the idea of international working-class unity and solidarity against the war. A common interest in fighting national bourgeoisies, capitalism and imperialism, and also brotherly feelings engendered in the labour movements were insufficient to prevent the working class from siding with their own national governments. Conflict over the implications of international working-class solidarity, the strategy towards national governments, the national bourgeoisie and social alliances, initiated a process that eventually caused the labour movement to split irrevocably into a socialist/social democratic camp and a Marxist–Leninist camp. This split resulted in the two camps being poised against each other in bitterness, contempt and merciless struggle. Finally, after the Russian revolution and the First World War, radicalisation of the working class and many intellectuals resulted in the establishment of communist parties in most European countries. For a short period, the Austro-Marxists (see Chapter 2) tried to represent a third alternative, but did not succeed.[1] The split between social democrats and the Marxist–Leninists became permanent and lasted until the eventual breakdown of the Soviet Union.

In the 1920s, the idea of solidarity was generally absent from social democratic party programmes, probably due to the atmosphere of rivalry and conflict within the labour movement.

The transitional phase of socialist solidarity

In the social democratic parties, the transition from a Marxist to a social democratic concept of solidarity varied considerably. It first commenced in Scandinavia: with the Norwegian DNA programme in 1909, in Danish social democracy in 1913, in the Swedish SAP in 1920, and concluded in the period between 1934 (Denmark) and 1944 (Sweden). In Sweden

---

[1] As mentioned in Chapter 2, the Austrian Socialist Party, the SPÖ, tried before World War I to develop a Marxist critique of revisionism without accepting Marxist–Leninist dogmatism. We saw in Chapter 2 that Max Adler's discussion about the idea of solidarity did not result in a renewal of the classic Marxist idea. A study of SPÖ programmes demonstrates a conceptual development not significantly different from that of SPD programmes in terms of solidarity. Solidarity is not found in the programme until 1958, when the SPÖ declared neutrality in confessional issues and stated that it wanted to improve the relationship with the Catholic Church. In the new programme of 1978, solidarity was stated as a basic value together with freedom, equality and justice in a way that was similar to many other social democratic parties.

and Norway this process was further assisted by the ability of leaders and theorists to work out a new idea of solidarity which embraced both the people and the nation. In Germany, the SPD lacked leaders and theorists with such abilities in the inter-war years. In France, Leon Blum did not succeed in his attempts to formulate a new and broader idea. In Italy and Spain, the socialist parties were exiled or underground and were not allowed to function normally by fascist dictatorships. The Italian PSI never completed the transformation, and the Spanish PSOE completed the transition in a brief period when Felipe Gonzalez succeeded in defeating the left wing of his party in the early 1980s.

The introduction of a social democratic concept

Variations of a social democratic concept of solidarity were introduced into party programmes in Denmark and Norway in the 1930s, followed by the Swedish SAP in 1944 and the Bad Godesberg Programme in 1959. The socialist parties in France, Italy and Spain did not follow suit until the early 1980s.

World War II had a profound impact on socialist ideology and mentality and to some extent eclipsed earlier political and social conflicts. Socialists, communists, Christian democrats, liberals and conservatives joined together in resistance movements. The need for reconstruction and economic growth made class struggle not very attractive for most socialist leaders. All this reinforced the process of deradicalisation that had been at work before the war. The need for a rapid reconstruction and improvement in standards of living made collaboration between the labour movement and the industrial bourgeoisie and business interests imperative. Concepts such as class struggle and class solidarity felt awkward and less appropriate than before. This was reflected in party programmes and in the meaning that solidarity was now set to acquire.

From 1945 until the student revolt in 1968 the concept of solidarity in social democratic programmes was made more inclusive. At the same time, the social democratic parties broadened their electoral appeal. After the war, socialist and democratic parties were in government in the Scandinavian countries and the United Kingdom, but still in opposition in West Germany, France and Italy (after a brief interlude as part of a coalition government), and underground during the Franco dictatorship in Spain. For social democratic parties in government, the challenge was now to make the national economy grow and rebuild the country. For those in opposition the challenge was to break out of political isolation and increase electoral support.

When social democratic parties in Europe met at the congress of the new International in Germany in 1951, the final resolution reflected the dissolution of socialist doctrines that was in process. It appealed to the solidarity of all wage earners and declared solidarity with all peoples living under fascist or communist dictatorship (Socialist International 1990). Solidarity was applied in a general, non-specific way, meaning something positive. The resolution stated that not only material incentives were important to stimulate economic growth, but also personal satisfaction with work efforts, solidarity and the feeling of community that may arise when people are working together for the common good. However, it contained no reference to solidarity with the oppressed peoples of the Third World or to the fact that the UK and France were great colonial powers.

The programme of the new International reflected the ideological mood of the social democratic parties. In Sweden, the Social Democratic Party softened the radical rhetoric in the new platform of 1944. In Norway and Denmark a productivist concept of solidarity was developed. The antagonism between labour and capital disappeared and was no longer mentioned; solidarity had also come to imply community across previous demarcation lines between the two. Solidarity was now formulated in terms of a reciprocal contract: on the one hand, everyone should do his or her duty, on the other hand, the government should develop a welfare state. In France, Leon Blum's book in 1945, *Pour être socialiste*, presented the new concept of solidarity that was to be found so frequently in social democratic programmes and key documents some decades later (Blum 1945). The fundamental change of SPD programmes came in 1959 with the Bad Godesberg programme. The market economy was accepted, and the programme contained the full language of modern social democratic solidarity in a way that was not found in the earlier phases of social democracy.

This development must be understood in the social and political context of the period. The 1950s and 1960s were the 'golden years' of capitalism (Hobsbawm 1994). Economic growth was explosive, unemployment almost non-existent, and the prospects for continuously increasing the standard of living for the great majority of the population were good. Keynesian economic theory provided the social democratic governments with tools to manage economic fluctuations. In many countries, it was a tacit or explicit consensus between employers and labour organisations that wage demands should be within limits that did not eat into profits and investment. Increasing tax revenues made social reforms possible. Social democratic parties interested in government power could not jeopardise the excellent economic prospects. In addition, they had to forge new electoral alliances to muster a parliamentary majority. Social democracy abandoned structural reforms and in return received an increased standard of living and social reforms that created more predictability and security against the hazards of life.

For government parties, this atmosphere of progress and consensus left no room for an idea of solidarity that was associated with class struggle and concentrated solely on the working class. Parties that nourished ambitions about government power had to embrace larger segments of the population than the industrial working class. Whereas previously farmers had been important potential allies, political interest now had to be diverted to new white-collar groups in the private and public sectors. The new and broader social democratic idea of solidarity that was developing was more adapted to this situation.

The process described above entailed a change and a reconfiguration of all four aspects of solidarity that are focused on in this study. Not only was the concept made more inclusive, but also a new idea of the foundation and the goal of solidarity developed. Finally, the conception of the relationship between the individual and the collective was also changed. We shall look at these four aspects in more detail below.

Towards an inclusive concept: allied classes, women, the Third World, immigrants and the next generations

Generally, a broader social democratic idea of solidarity was developed through several phases. First, the classic Marxist concept was broadened from class to people or nation. This change was associated with a general deradicalisation of content and language in party programmes that took place at different periods in the various nations. Second, the concept was broadened to include the relationship with peoples of the Third World. This occurred in the first decades after World War II. Third, the concept was broadened to include aspects that gained increased attention after the student revolt in 1968 and in the second part of the twentieth century – feminism, environmental problems and immigration.

Solidarity between the working class and other classes

The classic Marxist concept of solidarity included only workers, although also workers in other nations. As Przeworski has noted, orthodox Marxist theory had no clear definition of who was to be defined as belonging to the working class (Przeworski 1985). Was the working class to be confined to industrial workers, or should it be defined to include all those who did not own means of production and were thus forced to sell their labour in order to survive? Kautsky, the most central interpreter of Marxism in the latter part of the nineteenth century and the beginning of the next, fluctuated between a narrow and a broad definition of the working class. The party programmes studied here have not been preoccupied with this issue. Generally, they apply the concept of working class without any discussion concerning who should be included. This is not surprising, as such a discussion might have alienated potential voters.

This was not a problem as long as the concept of working class was synonymous with poverty and squalid working conditions. The belief that capitalism would relegate increasing numbers of farmers, merchants and small industrialists to a constantly growing working class made this issue less important. In the long run, the working class would encompass all such groups. The introduction of universal suffrage and the need to participate in parliamentary politics changed the rules of the game. Pressure from below to achieve results and improve the situation of the working class made a strategy for electoral success necessary. Socialist parties gradually acknowledged that the petty bourgeoisie would not disappear. The working class would not necessarily become the majority, and socialist parties would not automatically achieve a majority in parliaments. Thus, it was necessary to win voters outside the working class, to form alliances and establish governments that represented not only the interests of workers. This insight grew out of the defeats of mass strikes in different European countries in the two first decades of the twentieth century (Przeworski 1980).

Irrespective of how the working class was defined, it became increasingly urgent for socialist leaders to broaden the appeal of their party to social categories that definitely were not regarded as members of the working class. Marx had defined categories that were not regarded as working class – farmers, artisans and merchants as essentially conservative or reactionary, meaning that they defended outdated modes of production. However, under some conditions they could join the revolutionary working class. Kautsky introduced the idea of a national *people's* party, and Bernstein called for an alliance between the working class and the middle class. In *Politics Against Markets*, Esping-Andersen, developing Przeworski's findings, emphasised the fact that the narrow idea of class solidarity would prevent socialist parties forming broader alliances. Since the goal of social democracy was to win an electoral majority, the definition of solidarity had to address the 'people', not the 'class', he says (Esping-Andersen 1985). It is certainly the case that socialist parties had to address not only the class, but it does not follow from this that a broader appeal had to be formulated in terms of *solidarity*. It is this issue that will be discussed here. To what extent was the transformation from class to people really formulated in terms of solidarity in party programmes? How and when did party programmes argue that the relationship between the working class and other classes or groups should be one of solidarity?

The Norwegian DNA, which had been the first to use *solidarity* in a party programme, was also the pioneer in another aspect: it was the first to apply solidarity in a wider sense than worker solidarity. The first programme approved at the inaugural congress in 1887 had reserved membership exclusively for those in manual labour, and declared the need for solidarity between workers in the cities and the countryside. The 1894 programme encouraged farmers to become members of the party, and the 1909 programme applied solidarity to the common interests of wage earners, merchants, farmers and industrialists of small means. From then on, similar formulations continued to appear in DNA programmes.

In Denmark, the first programme of the social democratic party in 1876 stated that compared to the working class, all other classes were reactionary. In a country where agriculture and independent farmers were dominant and the industrial sector very small, this position was difficult to combine with a successful electoral strategy. Already in the 1880s socialist leaders defined the working class broadly to include smallholders, small merchants and artisans (Bryld 1992). An agricultural programme in 1890 argued that land should be given to tenants and run by them, although owned by the government.

In spite of its Marxist character, the programme of 1913 expressed the will to give land to cotters, but did not mention tenancy. This signalled that the party had accepted that it could not win political power without an alliance with agricultural workers and many peasants as well (Socialdemokratiet 1913). The manifesto of 1934 addressed all social strata that 'suffered under the crisis of capitalism' and 'the workers of industry and agriculture, to farmers, cotters, fishermen, employees and businessmen in trade and industry . . .' (Socialdemokratiet 1934). Contrary to the Norwegian DNA this gradual programmatic reformulation of the relationship between the working class and other classes and groups was not formulated as a relationship of solidarity. For the first time after World War II in 1945, we find a general appeal to 'all forces to stand together in solidarity' (Socialdemokratiet 1945).

Already, at the dawn of the twentieth century, in Sweden, the aim of the social democratic party was to bring in smallholders and cotters. Even so, it took even longer than in Denmark before the party extended the concept of solidarity, restricted in the programmes to the working class, to other social groups (Svensson 1994). The 1905 platform called for the protection of small farmers, and the platform of 1911 declared that capitalism undermined the autonomy of small farmers, artisans

Table 5.2 *Solidarity between the working class and other classes as a theme in party programmes*

Party		Solidarity first mentioned	Solidarity with other classes
Germany	SPD	1925	1959?
France	PS	1906	1981
Spain	PSOE	1982	1982
UK	Labour	1983	
Italy	PSI	1943	
Denmark	Socialdemocratene	1913	1945
Norway	DNA	1887	1909
Sweden	SAP	1944	1960

and merchants, and that the small farmers were included among the exploited classes. The social democratic leader, Hjalmar Branting, argued in 1919 that worker solidarity should be broadened to a societal solidarity (Branting 1948). The following year, the 1920 platform stated the need for 'a union of all exploited classes' (SAP 1920).

In a newspaper article *People and class* in 1929, Branting's successor, Per Albin Hansson, argued in accordance with his concept of *the people's home* (see Chapter 4) which meant that the social democratic party should abandon a narrow conception of the working class and continue on the road to becoming a 'people's party' (Hansson 1982b (1929)). However, even the 1944 platform did not formulate the relationship between the working class and other groups as a question of solidarity. That did not happen until the 1960 platform. Surprisingly, even this platform did not mention farmers explicitly, but called for solidarity between 'different groups' of society – a rather diffuse concept. Thus, even in Scandinavia (with the exception of Norway) the concept of solidarity in party pro-grammes did not include classes and social groups other than the working class until after World War II.

As we saw in Chapter 4, the German SPD demonstrated an inability to form alliances with other classes and groups, and this was reflected in its reluctance to introduce a concept of solidarity that included more than the workers. Similar to other social democratic parties, the SPD was con-fronted with the need to relate to at least two other classes – the farmers and the middle class. Not until 1921 was the programme opened up to establishing bonds with other social categories, when the term *working people* was introduced. During the 1920s, programmes directed attention to the *Mittelschichten* and the farmers. Yet, the party did not mention a class alliance between the working class on the one hand and the farmers and the middle class on the other as a relationship of solidarity.

This occurred first when the Bad Godesberg programme of 1959 introduced the modern social democratic concept of solidarity and declared that solidarity was a fundamental value. Nonetheless, not even this programme *explicitly* argued that the relationship between these groups should be one of solidarity. This was done only implicitly, as the concept was no longer restricted to the working class but concerned the whole of society. Socialist parties in Southern Europe followed suit decades later.

It may certainly be argued that electoral logic made it necessary for social democratic parties to broaden their appeal if they were to win a majority. Social democratic leaders, particularly in Scandinavia, accepted this earlier than their counterparts in Germany and Southern Europe. Neither should it be disputed that the need for support from groups outside the working class led to deradicalisation of both political ideology and the programmes of the social democratic parties.[2] Yet, broadening the appeal, first to farmers and later to the middle class, could be achieved without necessarily seeing this as a question of solidarity. The analysis of programmes here has indicated that this was what happened and that the need for political alliances was not stated in terms of solidarity in programme rhetoric. Generally, social democratic parties did not view the relationship between the working class and other classes as one of solidarity in their programmes – neither in the classic Marxist nor in the classic social democratic sense. Leaders did this more often, but parties skipped this problem and later introduced a general and broader concept of solidarity that encompassed the whole of society.

Women – the forgotten solidarity

'Nothing underscores the Left's lost opportunities like socialism's difficulties with feminism', says Geoff Eley (2002). This was true in terms of solidarity as well.

Nevertheless, socialist parties were concerned at an early stage with the situation of women and demanded emancipation and equal political rights for women.[3] When the German SPD leader, August Bebel,

---

[2] At this point, the analysis here gives more support to Przeworski than to Esping-Andersen, who argues that broadening the appeal to segments outside the working class did not imply a deradicalisation of programmes (Esping-Andersen 1985).

[3] In the Erfurt programme, the SPD demanded full suffrage for women and the abolition of all discriminating laws. The Swedish SAP demanded universal suffrage in the programme of 1897, abolition of discriminating laws and introduction of maternity benefit in 1920. However, socialist parties were often reluctant to struggle actively for universal suffrage when male workers had achieved the right to vote (Esping-Anderson 1985).

published *Die Frau und der Sozialismus – Women and Socialism –* in 1879, this was a milestone in the labour movement struggle for the emancipation of women. More than a decade before the SPD programme was consolidated on a Marxist basis in 1891, Bebel argued that the oppression of women was not only a consequence of capitalism, but was also an aspect of the relationship between men and women. Whereas later Marxists such as Clara Zetkin focused on working-class women and subordinated feminism to the class struggle, Bebel stated that both women *in general* and workers had been oppressed throughout the whole history of mankind (Bebel 1879). Women had always taken on the burden of hard domestic work, while men had been the masters and devoted themselves to hunting, war and politics, and this was the case today as well. Bebel argued that in a future socialist society women would be free and on equal terms with men, with equal access to education, employment and political participation. Rationalisation of domestic work, introduction of large-scale kitchens and laundries and collective care for children and the elderly would liberate and emancipate women. Still, between 1875 and 1925, feminist socialists had to fight on two fronts: against governments and against their socialist comrades who did not want women in party positions of any authority (Anderson and Zinsser 1989). Unions did not pay much attention to the situation of female workers, and for a long time women had to struggle against the idea that if necessary, they should step down to secure employment for men. Socialist parties were to take a long time before they were able to regard the relationship between men and women as a question of solidarity.

Female Marxists such as Clara Zetkin and Rosa Luxemburg argued for *equality* and *emancipation* in the class struggle and society and wanted their male comrades to accept them as equals. Although they used the concept of solidarity in other contexts, they did not claim – as far as I have been able to establish – that men should exercise solidarity with their sisters in the struggle for emancipation (see e.g. Zetkin 1971 (1928); 1974a (1889)). Whenever a conflict emerged between socialism and feminism they, insisted that feminism should be subordinated to socialism. Zetkin criticised women for putting the narrow interests of their families above the general interest of society. 'As strongly developed as was her love of her family, as wretched and poor her social solidarity', she said and complained about the lack of solidarity *among women*: 'Most women have not as much as the faintest idea of the meaning of solidarity' (Zetkin 1974a (1889)). She maintained that women were often restricted, brutal and cruel towards everything outside their personal sphere, and this tendency was most prevalent among women of the petty bourgeoisie, and least strong among working-class women because they were more likely to understand and exercise the idea of solidarity. She asserted that the liberation struggle of working-class women should not be a struggle against men of their own class, as was the case for bourgeois women, because barriers between her and the male worker had been raised not by the male worker but by free economic competition in capitalist society. Thus, there was no need for feminist agitation, only for socialist agitation among women (Zetkin 1974b (1896)) – a position that clearly proved to be wrong.

In Germany, feminist socialists created the largest working-class women's movement in Europe (Anderson and Zinsser 1989). The SPD argued for the first time for the general right of women to employment, and for other issues related to the situation of women in industry, in the programme in 1921 (SPD 1921). After World War II SPD programmes devoted whole paragraphs to *Frau und Familie*, arguing for emancipation, equal pay and kindergartens (SPD 1952/54). A parallel development took place in Swedish and Norwegian social democracy in the same period.[4] However, this turn towards family policy may be seen as an expression of solidarity with women only to a limited extent, as it was most frequently based on the model of the male bread-winner and the existing division of work within the family.

Another two decades or so were to pass until gender was explicitly stated as an aspect of solidarity. The new women's liberation movements from the late 1960s and the 1970s brought political and cultural aspects of male domination onto the agenda again. The student revolt had revitalised the idea of solidarity in general, and soon *solidarity* became an issue in the feminist movement as well.

Social democratic parties were late in adopting this aspect of post-1968 solidarity language. The Danish social democrats were the first party to formulate the gender relationship as a question of solidarity in their programme in 1977; this was probably the result of ten years of struggle by the new feminist movement and the increasing influence of women in the social democratic parties. The SPD did not follow suit until 1989, and during the 1990s most other social democratic parties did the same. This belated integration of women, such a large, oppressed and discriminated-against part of the population, into the concept of solidarity is probably explained by the party culture, which was a male culture with historical roots in the industrial sector of society.

---

[4] In Sweden, social democratic platforms did not devote many words to the situation of women until 1944. The 1944 platform argued for paid maternal leave, initiatives to ease work at home etc. In Norway, the DNA programme of 1945 argued for equal pay for equal work and declared that 'In the future in Norway, every woman and man will have work and secure conditions.'

Table 5.3 *Gender emancipation formulated as a question of solidarity in party programmes*

Germany	SPD	1989
France	PS	
Spain	PSOE	1996
Italy	PSI	
Denmark	Socialdemocratene	1977
Norway	DNA	1997
Sweden	SAP	1990
UK	Labour	

The welfare state

What was the role of solidarity as a motive for the construction of the welfare state? In *The Politics of Social Solidarity* Peter Baldwin analyses the social and political forces underlying the welfare states of Scandinavia, France, the United Kingdom and Germany. His study is about the phenomenon of solidarity and not about the concept, as is the theme in this study. It is possible that Baldwin is right when he says that the welfare state grew out of a combination of collective identity and feelings of being 'the same' and of instrumental self-interests, but he does not document the first part of this statement. As seen above, a broad concept of solidarity including both the working class and other classes was institutionalised in party programmes but not until after important building blocks of the welfare state had been laid. Nor does he demonstrate that a concept of solidarity was at work in this process.

When the welfare state was born with the social insurance reforms in Germany in the 1880s, Bismarck and his followers did not formulate the rationale behind these reforms in terms of solidarity. It may be a little more surprising that neither did social democratic parties use the concept of solidarity when they argued for social reforms in programmes in the years before World War II.

Danish social democrats were the first to use solidarity in the context of social reforms when the programme of 1945 emphasised social solidarity and called for reforms in social security to reduce the need for poverty relief (Socialdemokratiet 1945). Norway followed suit in 1949; Germany and Sweden in 1959 and 1960 respectively. The social democratic parties of Southern Europe were latecomers also in this respect and did not follow suit until after 1980.

The concept of *the welfare state* does not seem to have been used in early programmes that argued for solidarity in terms of welfare arrangements.

The political language that was used in the struggle for the welfare state included neither solidarity nor the welfare state. The modern social democratic language with the association of solidarity and the welfare state was not developed until the last decades of the twentieth century. Thus, an institutionalised language of solidarity and welfare is a rather recent phenomenon.

At this point, the electoral benefits of constructing an ideology of solidarity were probably more obvious to social democratic leaders. Social reforms could be addressed to a large audience. As Baldwin has demonstrated, universal social security arrangements in Scandinavia appealed first to farmers and fishermen, and later to the increasing numbers of white-collar employees in both the private and public sector (Baldwin 1990). When labour market participation for women increased in these countries in the 1970s, a self-reinforcing process was set in motion. Women became supporters of the welfare state and the basis of a new and broader conception of solidarity. In Germany, the *Mittelstand* was the key to majority and government power, as it was in France, Spain and Italy.

Although social democratic parties had not been able to formulate the relationship between the working class and the new middle class in terms of solidarity, the introduction of social reforms could now constitute a new platform for parties in search of a new ideological formula. Leaving the old socialist concept of class alliances behind, it was possible to introduce a new and broader concept of solidarity by associating the concept with social reforms that addressed broader social strata than the working class.

The Third World

The classic Marxist concept of solidarity was international and referred to worker solidarity across national borders. From an early stage socialist parties had been preoccupied and engaged with international issues, and were early in adopting a belief in international cooperation, international class-consciousness, and anti-militarism in foreign affairs as guiding principles (Padgett and Paterson 1991). For instance, the SPD refused to support Germany's war against the revolt in Southwest Africa in 1905. Nevertheless, the exploitation of the colonies did not worry the Second International until 1907 and European socialists – with some exceptions – generally did not condemn colonial policy, and even supported it until 1914 (Eley 2002).

Lenin's view that the colonies should also enjoy national self-determination opened for a socialist critique of colonialism. Communist parties and the Third International became engaged early in the struggle against colonialism and supported national autonomy for Third World nations. It is a point for discussion whether this was an expression of loyalty to the Soviet Union or of solidarity. Socialist parties that were part of what became the social democratic camp for decades supported the colonial system and resisted national independence for the peoples of the Third World, although they often expressed sympathy for the living conditions of people in the colonies. Notwithstanding this, party programmes did not mention such issues associated with the idea of solidarity. The idea of solidarity with the Third World was not institutionalised in the programmes of social democratic parties until the second part of the twentieth century when the concept had been transformed to a social democratic concept. By then the concept had been broadened to include classes and groups other than the working class and the basis of solidarity had been reformulated from interests to a general compassion. In this situation the step to include people living in misery in the Third World was natural.

When social democratic parties came to power, solidaristic ideology and political practice grew apart in this respect. The social democratic parties in the UK and France accepted only reluctantly that colonies should be granted national autonomy. The British Labour Party had a close relationship with anti-colonial movements before World War II, but was less radical when it came into power after the war. The Labour government granted independence to India and Pakistan, but hesitated to do the same in Africa. The French SFIO had some responsibility for the war in Indo-China, fought against independence for Algeria and supported intervention in Egypt in 1956 (Eley 2002). Other social democratic parties supported France in the Algerian war and also the United States in the first years of the war in Vietnam. On the other hand, peoples of the Third World were frequently viewed with sympathy, and the need for improved living conditions was emphasised in party programmes.

Once again, the Norwegian DNA was a forerunner in using the language of solidarity about the relationship with poor nations.[5] The programme in 1953 declared a need to bridge the economic gap between nations and wanted the United Nations to be a 'centre of real international solidarity' (DNA 1953). In Germany, the Bad Godesberg programme

---

[5] The DNA government led Norway into NATO in 1949 against protests from its left wing. When, in 1951, the party leadership initiated a development project in the south of India, this was an expression of genuine concern with need and poverty in the world. At the same time, the leadership saw this as an opportunity to divert attention from increased spending on rearmament and to 'give people something positive' (Pharo 1987).

Table 5.4 *Solidarity with the Third World introduced in programmes*

Germany	SPD	1959
France	PS	?
Spain	PSOE	1982
UK	Labour	1983
Italy	PSI	1978
Denmark	Socialdemocrats	1961
Norway	DNA	1953
Sweden	SAP	1960

referred to the need for solidarity in the relationship between Germany and 'underdeveloped' nations. In the following years, the Swedish and Danish social democratic parties introduced similar formulations in their programmes but the socialist and communist parties of Southern Europe did not do the same until the late 1970s and the 1980s. From around 1960 until the beginning of the 1980s the concept of solidarity with the Third World became part of the modern social democratic ideology of solidarity in party programmes. Electoral considerations were hardly conducive to this development. The inclusion of this aspect of solidarity was not based on ideas about self-interest, but on an altruistic compassion for the plight of people living in the poor world. We could, however, discuss the distance between this ideology and political practice. Assistance from rich countries to Third World countries did not amount to as much as 1 per cent of GDP, and the terms of trade were not changed to the benefit of the Third World to any significant degree.

The next generation, nature and ethnic minorities

In the last part of the twentieth century issues that cut across previous political cleavages emerged. In the early 1970s, the MIT report *The Limits to Growth* gave rise to a debate about the effect of industrial and economic growth on ecology and the global environment (Meadows *et al.* 1972). In the 1980s, Green parties were established in some countries, or green ideas gained influence in established parties. In 1986, the UN Commission on Environmental Development – the Brundtland Commission – launched *sustainable development* as a key slogan to identify the need for development that combined economic growth with consideration for the effects on the environment and on nature. Environmental

Table 5.5 *Ecology, future generations and ethnic groups included in the concept of solidarity in party programmes*

		Nature, ecology	Relationship between generations	Ethnical groups
Germany	SPD		1989	1998
France	PS			
Spain	PSOE	1989		1993
Italy	PSI			
Denmark	Socialdemocratene	1977		1992?
Norway	DNA	1993	1997	1997
Sweden	SAP			
UK	Labour			

issues were gradually given more attention in the programmes of social democratic parties. The idea that global warming and the use of non-renewable resources require solidarity with succeeding generations was gradually reflected in party programmes.

In the same period, unemployment again became an important issue. After the oil crisis in 1973, unemployment rose strongly. In the 1970s, the Scandinavian social democratic parties coined the phrase: 'solidaristic wage policy'. This implied that workers in secure employment should demonstrate solidarity with the unemployed by exercising restraint in wage demands. Unemployment, the increasing number of refugees, and sometime later the war in the Balkans, made the relationship between ethnic majorities and minorities a burning issue. These changes were gradually reflected in the programmes of social democratic parties and to some extent in their concept of solidarity as well.

A fully-fledged inclusive concept of solidarity was developed when social democratic parties started to include such groups and aspects in this concept. These could be *future generations, nature, immigrants, refugees* and so forth. Generally, it was not until the last decades of the twentieth century that the concept of solidarity in party programmes was broadened to include these groups or aspects.

The Danish Social Democrat party was the first to state that environmental issues should incorporate the question of solidarity when this was emphasised in the 1977 programme. Other parties followed from the late 1980s and in the 1990s. Yet, social democratic parties have generally been reluctant or cautious in this respect. While generally including something about ecology and the need to protect the environment for future generations in their programmes, they balance this carefully against the need for economic growth and increased employment and only now and then do they emphasise this issue as a question of solidarity.

The last groups to be included in solidarity in party programmes seems to be ethnic minorities, refugees and immigrants. Social democratic parties made the situation of immigrants and refugees an issue in their programmes, but this was not formulated as a matter of solidarity until the 1990s. Danish and Spanish social democrats were the first to do this in their programmes of the early 1990s, and most other social democratic parties followed suit within a few years.

We have seen that social democratic parties have made their concept of solidarity continuously more inclusive. Electoral considerations probably explain the broadening from class to people or nation. The connection between solidarity and the concept of the welfare state might be seen in the same perspective, but it is more difficult to see the electoral advantage of arguing for solidarity with the Third World and with immigrants. These issues are highly controversial among the party electorates and it is not easy to evaluate potential gains and losses among electorates. Nevertheless, including such groups and issues might be understood in two other alternative ways. One is to regard it as an expression of a general humanist and altruist ideology of solidarity that emphasises the need for solidarity with all oppressed, discriminated against or needy groups. The other perspective is to see it as an expression of compromise. On the one hand, the parties may declare solidarity in their programmes, making left-wing critics more content. On the other hand, they may implement policies that make such solidarity real to only a limited extent, by keeping aid to the Third World at a low level and restricting immigration, and in this way not provoking critics on the right wing.

The foundation and the objective

The broadening of the concept of solidarity was accompanied by a change of what was considered as the foundation and objective of solidarity. However, either the early programmes were generally brief concerning the goals or objectives of solidarity, or they did not distinguish clearly between these two aspects. As in the Erfurt programme and most other Marxist programmes, *common interests* and the feeling of community that grew out of this were seen as the foundations of solidarity. The objective was the liberation of the working class and the replacement of private ownership of the means of production by collective ownership (SPD 1891). During this process of change in the Marxist concept the objective of solidarity was not often clearly spelled out in programmes. In the 'productivist' versions that developed in Scandinavia before and after World War II, the objective was to increase economic growth and create resources for improving the standard of living and for increased social security. When this concept was abandoned, solidarity was most frequently formulated as instrumental in relationship to other key values such as *social justice* and *equality*, or more vaguely to other values such as *social security* and *equal opportunity for everybody* (Socialdemokratiet 1977).

The foundation of solidarity was reformulated in two phases. First, the explicit reference to class interests disappeared. In most parties this happened before World War II. Second, in programmes after the war, the basis of solidarity was seen as *ethics, feelings of reciprocal responsibility, recognition of interdependence*, or *the feeling of belonging together*. The SPD programme in 1947 referred generally to human attitudes, and religious and ethical obligations. In the 1944 programme the Swedish SAP said that solidarity was founded on a mutual feeling of togetherness. When the new International met in 1951, it was stated that it did not matter whether Marxist, religious or humanitarian principles inspired socialist conviction. The Bad Godesberg programme declared 'Christian ethics, humanism and classical philosophy' to be the foundation of democratic socialism. From the 1970s on the SPD declared that solidarity was based on feelings of responsibility, obligations toward society and towards others. The Swedish SAP declared that this 'implies empathy with the conditions of others and a willingness to care, and compassion for each other' (SAP 1975). The DNA had started a process of gradually redefining this aspect with Koht's positive view on religion already in the 1920s, and Sivertsen's and Aukrust's contribution after World War II. In the 1970s, DNA programmes showed empathy and compassion for the weak – Danish social democrats referred to the equal worth of human beings – as the foundation of solidarity. A parallel process did not take place in the socialist parties in Southern Europe – probably because of their more pronounced lay character and the stronger historical conflict with a conservative Catholic clergy.

Class interest and self-interest as the foundation of solidarity have virtually disappeared and only remnants of this were occasionally mentioned in programmes in the last decades of the twentieth century. The SPD's Berlin programme of 1989 mentioned that solidarity still could be a weapon in a struggle, and the DNA 1981 programme mentioned self-interest as a basis for solidarity. Generally, the foundation for solidarity is sought in a mixture of elements – in interdependence, ethics, empathy and the recognition of the equal worth of all human beings.

The collective and the individual

Solidarity raises not only the issue of who is going to be included in the collective, but also the relationships *within* the collective – the relationship between the collective and the individual. In his study on the concept of *individualism* Steven Lukes demonstrates that the concept of the individual has different connotations in French and in German traditions. Whereas after the revolution of 1789 the French tradition saw individualism as a threat to social cohesion and community, the German tradition emphasised the positive aspects of individual uniqueness, originality and self-realisation (Lukes 1985). In the tradition of Marx a distinction was drawn between the situation of the individual under capitalism and under socialism and communism. In the *Communist Manifesto*, Marx argued that in bourgeois society, capital is personal and autonomous, whereas the individual worker is impersonal and dependent. In a society without classes, individuals will be united in an association where the free development of each individual is a precondition for the free development of all, he maintained (Marx and Engels 1848). In this way he sought to solve the problem of the relationship between the individual and the collective in the society that would succeed capitalism. Under capitalism working-class solidarity entailed the idea that the individual should subordinate his/her personal interests to the common interest of the collective, which might imply making sacrifices of some kind of personal freedom. As we have seen in Chapter 2, this expectation was most clearly and extremely formulated in Leninism, as in Lukàcs' *History and Class Consciousness*. How have social democratic parties conceived this issue in their platforms and programmes?

The old socialist idea was that the road to emancipation for the individual was through the emancipation of the collective – the entire working class. Collective struggle should result in better living conditions, social security and more influence, and this would create a basis for the development of individual abilities and talents. In consequence, socialist parties generally saw no need to make the relationship between collective solutions and individual freedom an issue in their programmes in the early phase, and the concept of the individual was not generally made a theme until after World War II.

Yet, in the first years after the war the concept of *each one* or the *individual*[6] emerged in social democratic programmes. This happened first

---

[6] In Danish and Norwegian '*den enkelte*' – is translated directly as *each one*. The 'individual' ('*individet*' or '*det enkelte individ*') is almost never applied in Scandinavian social democratic programmes, perhaps because it has been a key concept in conservative rhetoric. I shall here apply the concept 'the individual'.

Table 5.6 *The relationship between individual and collective in social democratic platforms and programmes*

	Party	Appearance of the individual	The relationship between individual and the collective a theme	Recognising a potential conflict between the two
Germany	SPD	1952–59	1998	1998
France	PS			
Spain	PSOE	2000		
Italy	PSI			
Denmark	Socialdemocratene	1945	1961	
Norway	DNA	1949	1969	1996–2000
Sweden	SAP	1960	1960	2001
UK	Labour			

in Denmark in 1945 and in Norway and Germany a few years later. At this time, one could hardly argue that all collective challenges had been met, although it may have been possible to imagine that material and social security could be achieved in the not too distant future. Other factors were probably more conducive to including the concept of the individual in programmes. First, experiences with fascist totalitarianism had resulted in a greater focus on the value and dignity of each human being. Second, the abandonment of Marxism, the general deradicalisation, and the increasing importance of the middle class may have made these social democratic parties more prepared to include the notion of the individual.

In Denmark, the *individual* was first mentioned in the 1945 programme where it was stated that the individual had rights and claims on society and that the social security system should be adapted to individual need. This preoccupation with the individual, or *each one* (*den enkelte*), was expressed also in the programmes of the 1950s. The 1953 platform declared that 'Democratic socialism builds on cohesion and solidarity, simultaneously requiring that each individual executes his duties according to his own ability.' Even if the individual had been made a theme, the emphasis remained on the collective, and the party was not too concerned about the subordination of the individual.

In the post-war programme of the DNA, the core principle in the modernising project of social democracy was to reconcile public regulation with democratic freedom. Nevertheless, when the concept of the individual was introduced in the platform of 1949 it was not to emphasise that the individual had rights and entitlements versus the government or society as was the case in the Danish social democratic programmes four years before. On the contrary, the DNA programme stated the need for society to 'instigate creativity and inventiveness in each individual', and said that society was 'obliged to require strong feelings of solidarity and responsibility from the individual' (DNA 1949). The individual was not considered as an autonomous person who should enjoy personal freedom of choice, but as somebody the government should take care of through social reforms and public policy. Twenty years were to pass until DNA platforms and programmes made the individual an issue again.

As mentioned in Chapter 4, the SPD's Bad Godesberg programme in 1959 introduced the concept of the individual. Even though the collective orientation was toned down, the programme argued that the common interest should be placed above the interests of the individual. Whereas Swedish social democracy had been convinced that the freedom of the individual could be realised only through collective public efforts, Olof Palme was concerned as early as 1960 that collectivism could become a danger for the individual. Collectivism could oppress the freedom of the individual and quell his/her distinctive character and autonomy, he maintained (Palme 1960). The same year, the new platform expressed the same concern, but emphasised at the same time that the freedom of each human being depended upon the common interest and the common effort of all citizens. Thus, although the notion of the individual was introduced, the old socialist idea that the liberation of the individual was dependent on collective effort was still present.

In Norway, the DNA's programmatic renewal in 1969 and the introduction of the three concepts of *justice*, *equality* and *freedom* together with *solidarity* were accompanied by a new concern about the individual. The DNA's vision of a socialist society was said to be a society with 'great freedom for each human being as long as it does not harm others'. Within the 'confines of community, each human being shall be free to choose a way of life and develop his/her own personality' (DNA 1969a). This was the first time personal freedom was made an issue in a DNA platform and described in relation to community and solidarity. Although this may be interpreted as a vague indication that this relationship could be a problem, this is not stated clearly. In the DNA platform of 1981, the relationship and 'interplay' between individual and society was emphasised anew, although still emphasising collective orientation more than individual freedom (DNA 1989). In Germany, Gerhard Schröder's and SPD's programme in 1998 moderated the collective orientation and emphasised individual initiative and personal responsibility. The programme declared that the equal worth of human beings should mean that individuals have the autonomy and freedom to decide about their own life in community with others, and that the individual could develop his/her individuality only in community with other persons. The freedom of others constitutes the boundary of the freedom of the individual, and solidarity is necessary to widen the life-chances of the individual. However, we note here that although the relationship between solidarity and individual autonomy is discussed, the emphasis is still primarily on a defence of the collective aspects.

Socialist parties in Southern Europe have not been particularly concerned with the role of the individual in their programmes. The Italian PSI did not make it a theme before the party was dissolved in 1992, and the French PS does not mention it at all in the most recent platform. The Spanish PSOE has introduced the concept of the individual, but does not mention the potential conflict between collective and individual interests or considerations.

The relationship between individual freedom and the individual's right to choose on the one hand, and collective solutions and solidarity on the other, currently constitutes the most burning problem and challenge for social democratic and other parties of the left. In their political practice they have been bound to try to find solutions to this challenge. They have modified and changed positions in social, housing and educational policy and in consumer politics – some of them in a way that might be criticised for abandoning solidarity to the advantage of individual choice or flexibility. Yet, they have not been able, or willing, to formulate their dilemma to any significant extent, or to state the preferred balance between the two in a language of solidarity. In modern social democratic programmes, the weakening collective orientation is expressed not only in the explicit references to the individual, but also in the emphasis on *freedom*. In the history of social democracy, the struggle for freedom has always been essential. Whereas freedom in the past referred to collective freedom through political rights and the development of a material basis for freedom through social security and equality, the connotations of freedom today are increasing individual freedom to choose in the market, to realise individual interests and personal development. However, when social democratic parties move into this field in their programmes, they also move into a territory that so far has belonged to their historic adversaries – the Liberal and Conservative parties.

The establishment of a language of solidarity

Although the changes described above took place at somewhat different times in the nations included here, the student revolt seems to have been an influential factor in the development of the concepts and political language that social democracy developed. The student revolt in 1967–68 was anti-systemic in its character, but did not come to influence the politics of the established parties to any great extent. The effects were much more significant at the cultural level (Sassoon 1996). Thus, the rhetoric of left-wing politics came to absorb some of the concepts that the student movement revived or brought to the fore. The term solidarity was one of these.

The student revolt was equivocal in terms of solidarity. On the one hand, it revived the idea and gave it broader meaning. Solidarity was no longer only worker solidarity – albeit across national boundaries; it came now to mean identification with all those who could be considered as oppressed, underprivileged or discriminated against. Students were to exercise solidarity with workers – and hoped for solidarity *from* workers in return. A movement for solidarity with the Third World and support for national liberation movements in Asia, Africa and Latin America developed. The peoples of the Third World were included in the concept of solidarity, not only the workers of those countries. Women, the disabled, ethnic and sexual minorities should be embraced and included in solidarity with those who were fighting for another or a better society. Feminism and ecology were also put on the agenda. In short, solidarity was made a vivid concept with a much richer content and connotations than had been the case so far.

On the other hand, the student revolt also represented a struggle against conformity and for the right to develop one's own personality independent of the parent generation. With Giddens, we may say that 1968 represents a key phase in the breakthrough of modern self-reflectivity. The French-German student leader Daniel Cohn-Bendit expressed this in his autobiography *The Great Bazaar*: 'Capitalist society had denied me the possibility of finding an identity that corresponded to my personal needs. My biography is the history of the destruction of my original identity and the attempt to find a new one in the process, in my behaviour and thinking, whereby the second still is dependent of the first' (Cohn-Bendit 1975, quoted in Baring (1998)). Thus, the values of the student movements were contradictory and combined an emphasis on collective solidarity on the one hand and an emphasis on personal freedom, self-realisation and the development of individual identity on the other. The 1968 project represented an attempt to reconcile these values in a new way, but, as noted by Donald Sassoon, the emphasis on individual self-realisation led to the hegemony of the individualist ideology of the 1980s (Sassoon 1996).

For many social democratic leaders the student revolt of 1968 signalled that times were changing. Social democrats – and communists – suddenly found themselves outside a social and radical movement of protest, and realised that the new radicals regarded them as the establishment, traitors and belonging to the political right of society. This was disquieting, because it raised the possibility that social democracy could be isolated not only from radical students, but also from the new mass of educated social strata of which students were a part, and the need for a revitalisation of social democratic policy was made a theme.

One early effect of the student revolt was that the ideological language of the left was radicalised. *Capitalism, class, imperialism* etc. were reintroduced in political language, also outside traditional Marxist spheres. In this vocabulary *solidarity* came to be one of the most popular concepts and was taken up also outside the social democratic and left-wing camps. Even so, it was only partially a revitalisation of the old concept. *Solidarity* was now more often used in the broad sense that had been applied in the Bad Godesberg programme. A broad and inclusive concept of solidarity was now integrated in the discourse of the New Left, together with old Marxist concepts such as class, imperialism and exploitation, and with newer concepts from Freudianism and modern social philosophy like *frustration, structural violence* and *liberation*.

To the cultural change of 1968, a fundamental economic change was added. After the first oil crisis in 1973, a new agenda developed. Profits were falling, and the long boom after World War II had ended (Brenner 2002), and Keynesian strategies to counter cyclical movements lost support and legitimacy. Unemployment increased all over Western Europe, and welfare retrenchment was discussed and implemented in many countries. Social democratic parties were now frequently in the awkward position of seeing both a need to restructure the welfare state to prevent further increases in expenses, and of defending the welfare arrangements they wanted to preserve. After 1968, the political atmosphere had created a need for a new and more radical language, and now – from 1973 – there was need for a language that could serve both to restructure and defend welfare arrangements.

In the project of revitalisation social democratic parties picked from the 1968 vocabulary what was suitable for them as *solidarity*. This was a symbolic concept with roots in their own history, and at the same time it had now become a fashionable concept with considerable popularity among the young. After the economic setback in 1973 it could be utilised both as an argument in the discussion on restructuring the welfare state and as an argument for preserving welfare arrangements. It is, in fact, impossible to disentangle the effect of the student revolt in 1968 from the economic setback in 1973 in this respect. A third factor that may have stimulated a revival of solidarity ideology was the transformation of the working class commencing in the latter half of the 1970s. Now, old industries with a core of class-conscious workers declined significantly. Employment in mining, coal, steel, shipyards, textiles, etc. was drastically reduced as industries closed down or moved abroad to countries with lower wages and poorer worker protection (Hobsbawm 1994). On the one hand, the political basis for classic working-class solidarity was reduced; on the other, the challenges for social democratic political leadership became more complicated. How could a more heterogeneous population be united behind a social democratic programme? Stronger emphasis on a broader concept of solidarity might contribute to that.

A few years after the 1973 oil crisis, all the Scandinavian social democratic parties approved programme documents that made *solidarity* a key concept. In Germany the concept became even more central in SPD programmes. In 1975 both the German and the Swedish social democratic programmes stated that *freedom, equality* and *solidarity* were their basic values – the Swedish programme also added *democracy* to the list. Two years later, the Danish social democratic party approved a programme titled Equality, Well-being, Solidarity, and the Norwegian DNA adopted a programme with the heading Solidarity, Employment, Environment. These were the years when Willy Brandt, Olof Palme and the Norwegian Thorvald Stoltenberg campaigned for a New International Economic Order (NIO) – a new internationalism based on reformism and Keynesianism across national borders.

The challenges of the 1980s

The 1980s brought further change in the class structure. The traditional industrial working class had declined during the 1970s, and in the 1980s the working class as a whole contracted. The economic crisis had created mass unemployment. New technology displaced employees, especially the unskilled and semi-skilled workers. It has been estimated that the number employed in manufacturing was reduced by 7 million in the six old industrialised countries of Europe (Hobsbawm 1994). Politically, the victory of Margaret Thatcher in the UK in 1979, and of Ronald Reagan in the USA a year later, inaugurated a liberalist offensive. In the years to come, social democratic parties which had been in government were driven out of office. Market ideology and individualism became hegemonic.

Social democracy could have responded to this development by adjusting to the new ideological climate and reducing emphasis on collective solutions and solidarity. Most social democratic parties chose a double-sided strategy. On the one hand, they partially adjusted policies to the new climate. When in power, they changed or softened their position on privatisation and implemented cuts in social security and welfare. On the other hand, they continued to emphasise solidarity in programmes and key documents. Although we may trace some concessions to the new liberal climate in programmes after 1981, social democratic parties in general did *not* chose to abandon their ideology of solidarity, but consolidated this concept as an integrated part of their programmatic ideology and rhetoric. In France and Spain, it was in this period that the social democratic parties adopted a language of social democratic solidarity.

A period of ideological and political uncertainty

The breakdown of the Soviet Union in 1989 represented a further blow to both socialist and social democratic ideology. Although social democratic parties had for long made it clear that Soviet-type planning was not their model, and nationalisation or socialisation of the means of production had been abandoned, the collapse of the Soviet Union discredited state planning and economic steering in general. Social democratic leaders now frequently accepted political positions that had been unthinkable a couple of decades earlier. By the end of the 1980s most parties had made a reappraisal of politics and programmes (Sassoon 1996). Most social democratic leaders now accepted some sort of privatisation of public enterprises.

Donald Sassoon has labelled the social democratic ideology from the 1990s as *neo-revisionism* (Sassoon 1996). This is not a well-defined and coherent ideology. It means that public ownership is definitely abandoned, and there is a sceptical attitude towards the possibility of regulating capitalism on a national basis. Financial institutions, energy and telecommunications should be deregulated or 'liberalised'. Despite such changes in practical policy most social democratic parties demonstrated continuity in terms of programmatic values and ideology in this period. The SPD programmes continued to insist that freedom, justice and solidarity were the basic values of the party (SPD 1998); the Norwegian DNA mentioned solidarity together with freedom and equality as core values; the French Socialist Party stated in its declaration of principles that the goals of the party are freedom, equality, and the dignity of men and women, welfare, responsibility and solidarity; and the PSOE included solidarity as a basic value together with responsibility, peace and freedom in the programme of 1996 (PSOE 1996). Although practical politics may vary, social democratic parties of today must be said to have a common ideology in which this combination of key values is more or less identical. This language is discussed in more detail in Chapter 7.

Discussion: structural and political context variables

How can we explain the differences between social democratic parties in terms of solidarity? Why were Scandinavian social democrats the first to elevate the concept into programme language? Why did the Germans do the same, later than the Scandinavians, but before Latin socialist parties?

We can conceive of four different types of explanation for this in terms of structural and political context variables: the different degrees of homogeneity in the class structure and the population in general, party electoral support, closeness to government power and the ideological tradition.

The first hypothesis could be that the more heterogeneous the class structure and the population in terms of religion and ethnic background, the more difficult it has been for a general concept of solidarity to develop. Solidarity may have required some sort of 'sameness' in terms of economic situation, privileges and cultural orientation. Where there is greater economic and social differentiation within the working class and between the working class, the farmers and the middle class, it is more complicated to develop a common identity and to build a bridge between those groups than in more egalitarian societies. Adherence to different religious beliefs, different linguistic or ethnic origins would probably also make it less likely that a broad concept of solidarity would develop within social democracy.

The Scandinavian countries have generally been regarded as more homogenous than the nations on the Continent and in the South of Europe. In his seminal work, Stefano Bartolini characterises the South as 'fragmented and socially heterogeneous' and the North as 'cohesive and relatively socially homogeneous', arguing that the interplay between structural, ideological and organisational cleavages, and class and other cleavages must be understood in order to grasp this difference (Bartolini 2000). Lane and Ersson summarise research on fragmentation in terms of class, religion and ethnicity in different European nations by ranking Norway as the least fragmented, followed by Sweden, Denmark, Germany, Italy, United Kingdom, Spain and France in that order (Lane and Ersson 1999). Although this picture changes somewhat according to indices and points of time, the Scandinavian countries appear to be more homogeneous than the other nations included in this study. Here, farmers were small and independent and generally did not employ many agricultural workers. Protestantism dominated completely, and linguistic and ethnic minorities were small. In Germany, France, Italy and Spain the relationship between the industrial working class and those working in agriculture was more complex. Germany had a large Catholic minority, France a Protestant minority. Italy did not develop a national language until after World War II and has remained permanently socially and politically divided along regional lines.

Second, electoral support might have induced social democratic parties to increase their appeal by broadening their concept of solidarity. This may have worked both ways: on the one hand, parties that had electoral support outside the working class may have found it expedient to broaden their working-class concept of solidarity so as not to alienate voters from other classes who already supported the party. On the other hand, parties could broaden their concept of solidarity so as to attract new voters outside the working class. The logic might be this: when a socialist party has started to broaden its electoral support and in addition attract voters from outside the working class, it may be induced to develop an ideology of a broader and inter-class solidarity so as to forge links between the working class and smallholders, peasants and the growing urban middle class. Such an ideology might have increased electoral support and broadened the political basis even further. As we have seen above, Scandinavian social democracy was more prone to formulating the relationship between the working class and other social classes as one of solidarity. At the same time these parties gained broad electoral support and extended their social basis to include groups outside the working class. On the other hand, the French PS and the Italian PSI also had a large share of their voters outside the working class without developing an inter-class ideology. These parties remained, however, comparatively small, possibly because they were not able to formulate a policy of cross-class alliance.

The third factor is that social democratic parties with large electoral support had more chances of achieving government participation than the smaller socialist parties of the South. In Scandinavia the social democratic parties were already in government when they broadened their concept of solidarity. The German SPD was eager to get into government when it introduced the broad social democratic concept of solidarity in 1959, as was the case for the Spanish PSOE in 1982. Being in, or close to government, might have influenced parties to seek a broad concept to transcend worker sectionalism and establish themselves as *people's parties*. Parties in, or close to being in government, know that being in government will make it necessary to take into consideration the situation of various classes and groups and not only the interests of the working class. A party in power needs an ideology that integrates and makes compromises between the interests of different classes and groups.

Finally, the specific ideological traditions of socialist parties might have influenced the decision to accept the new concept of solidarity. Orthodox Marxism continued to influence the programmes of socialist parties in France, Spain and Italy for a longer period. Thus, these parties were closer to the rhetoric of Marxist–Leninist parties than those of the North. As we shall see in Chapter 8, the Marxist–Leninist tradition was more ambivalent towards accepting the term and the modern concept of solidarity as part of its language. In France and Italy, especially, the socialist parties had to compete with communist parties that were larger, and more influential among the working class. This may have delayed a change of party rhetoric in the socialist/social democratic parties in those nations.

The social democratic parties of Scandinavia fulfil all the criteria. They existed in a homogenous environment. They acquired wide electoral support at an early stage and saw the possibility of entering into government. They observed the great debates in Germany and other nations about revisionism and the possibility of a gradual change to socialism from a distance. Marxism and Marxist rhetoric played a smaller role after World War II than in the parties of the South, although some elements continued to be a part of party programme language, especially in Sweden. All this made the introduction and the integration of a broad and modern social democratic concept of solidarity easier in the parties of the North than in those of Southern Europe.

A history of differences and of convergence

The variables discussed so far are all associated with the internal history of each nation. As the European labour movement has always been internationally oriented, we should not neglect the inspiration each national party has received from sister parties through reciprocal representation at congresses and membership in the Internationals. But the history of social democratic solidarity is not only a history about differences, it is also one of increasing similarity and convergence. The result of this process is that today all the parties included in this study with the exception of the British Labour Party declare solidarity, freedom and justice to be basic values.

The increasing similarity in terms of basic values in European social democracy is part of a more general convergence of social democratic ideology and politics as Donald Sassoon, among others, has shown (Sassoon 1999). Today, most social democratic parties agree that labour markets should be made more flexible. Taxes should not increase, but rather, be reduced. Low inflation should be a key issue and given higher priority than reducing unemployment. Public ownership should not be increased, and market mechanisms should be introduced in new sectors, and so forth. Most parties are worried about the future financing of the welfare state as well, and seek to develop a welfare policy that stimulates labour market participation, although they may find somewhat different solutions to the problems they face (Vandenbroucke 1999). We have noted that the convergence towards a common concept of solidarity has been accompanied by a general deradicalisation of ideology and rhetoric. In his study *In the Name of Social Democracy*, Gerassimos Moschonas demonstrates that this has happened at the same time as anchoring in the working class has been reduced, organisational structures have become weaker and relationships with trade unions less committed, while the role of leadership has strengthened. He suggests that these changes have been so profound that they represent not only a deradicalisation, but that they entail even a *de-social-democratisation* of these parties – meaning that they have lost their specific historical identity (Moschonas 2002). However, I am not sure if a discussion about the concept of a historical identity is fruitful, especially when Moschonas himself emphasises that change and flexibility have been enduring characteristics of these parties.

The tendency towards convergence is, of course, due to the external constraints that affect social democratic parties. To some extent globalisation limits their freedom of action. The European Union, the parameters of Maastricht and the central role of the European Central Bank restrict the ways in which national policy may be conducted. Demographic changes, if not identical, point in the same direction in most countries. Neither should we disregard political collaboration, contact and common discussions between social democratic leaders. It is not possible to understand the process towards similarity in programmatic language without discussing the contact between different social democratic parties through international organisations, conferences and exchange of programmes.

In this context, we must address the ideological renewal that took place in the Socialist International (SI) in the 1970s. The reestablished Socialist International in 1951 approved a resolution that signalled ideological pluralism and expressed solidarity with those living under dictatorship. These formulations of pluralism were echoed in the Bad Godesberg programme of the SPD in 1959. During the next couple of decades, the concept of solidarity emerged infrequently in political resolutions and texts from the SI especially in those related to the situation in Third World nations.

At the congress in Geneva in 1976 the SI adopted a language of solidarity. This congress initiated a renewal of the SI. Willy Brandt was elected chairman and started the process of renewal. The congress declared that the goal was to extend 'democratic socialism' to the Third World. Brandt directed the engagement of the SI more towards the Third World and recruited member parties from outside Europe. The congress initiated a process that during the next sixteen years saw the development of a new theoretical model for democratic socialism intended to be relevant to the industrialised nations as well as Third World nations. Besides, Brandt declared that the SI now would concentrate on three issues – peace and disarmament, North–South issues, and respect for human rights (Christensen 1992).

Thus, preoccupation with Third World issues was part of a general ideological renewal of social democratic ideology. The resolution from the Geneva congress made frequent use of the concept of solidarity and applied it to the relationship with the Third World, future generations and the environment, sometimes associated with *justice* (Socialist International 1977). Two years later, the SI congress in Vancouver stated that 'democratic socialism' should be dedicated to 'the achievement – on the basis of democracy, solidarity and justice – of peace and development for all mankind' (Socialist International 1979).

It is hardly a coincidence that until the renewed interest in ideology in the SI commencing in 1976, only the German and Swedish social democratic parties had developed a complete rhetoric of freedom, justice, and solidarity. Now, leaders and general secretaries of an increasing number of parties took part in discussions about the relationship between the rich and the poor worlds in the SI, and it was expected that the preoccupation with solidarity in SI debates and programmes would be reflected in the programmes of the national social democratic parties.[7] As we have seen, in the following years, the Danish, Norwegian, French and Spanish parties all made solidarity a more important theme in their programmes.

It would, of course, be too simple to assert that this timing in itself suffices to establish a one-way relationship of influence between the SI and the various national social democratic parties. The point to be made here is not that the SI influenced those parties to put emphasis on solidarity in their platforms and programmes. What happened was that the SI developed into a more central forum for discussion and reflection about ideology. Those who took part in these discussions were largely the same people who had influenced ideological development in the different social democratic parties of Western Europe. Consequently, they brought ideas from their national debates to the SI and vice versa. A parallel process of social democratic collaboration developed from the 1970s in the EU with the establishment of the Party of European Socialists (PES) in 1992 as the result. This ever-increasing closer

---

[7] Personal interview 12.05.01 with Reiulf Steen, chairman of the DNA 1975–81.

collaboration between the social democratic parties has contributed to the convergence of social democratic ideology and rhetoric in Europe (Hix 2000).

Finally, the influx of a new generation of social democratic activists and party officials has probably contributed to greater homogeneity in social democratic programmes. This generation was well educated and familiar with both classical socialist texts and modern social theory and foreign languages. They had received ideas from the common ground of the social sciences and had the ability to transform their predilection for ideological coherence into programme texts as members of programme committees and secretariats.

Conclusion: the modern concept of solidarity

The transition from a Marxist to a social democratic concept of solidarity and the establishment of a full social democratic language of solidarity has entailed a change in all the four aspects of solidarity and the relationship between these aspects as depicted in previous chapters. The concept has broadened to include not only workers, but a range of other groups and issues as well. The foundation is not seen as interests, but as ethics, humanism, empathy and compassion. The goal of solidarity is not socialism, but the creation of a feeling of community, social integration and sharing of risks. The relationship between loyalty and subordination to a collective on the one hand, and individual freedom and right to choose on the other hand, has been strongly reformulated.

The Marxist concept of solidarity, the classic social democratic concept that Bernstein formulated in the first part of the twentieth century, and the modern social democratic idea of solidarity as depicted in party programmes today is summarised in Table 5.7. The differences between the classic Marxist and the modern social democratic concepts are clear and need no further comment here. The differences between the classic social democratic and the modern social democratic concept are more interesting. First, the modern concept is institutionalised in party programmes and stated as a basic value, whereas the classic concept was mentioned only briefly in some programmes and was not declared to be a basic value.

Second, in both concepts, solidarity is founded not on 'sameness', but on the acceptance of difference. Solidarity should encompass persons from different classes, men and women, different age-groups and different generations and races. The extent to which social democratic solidarity should encompass not only the working class and the middle class but also the upper classes, is not always clear. But what is clear is that

Table 5.7 *The Marxist, classic and modern concept of social democratic solidarity*

	Foundation	Objective/ function	Inclusiveness	Collective orientation
Classic Marxist solidarity	Class-interests Recognition of 'sameness'	Realise interests: Revolution Socialism	Restricted: only the working class, but in all nations	Strong: individual autonomy not made a theme
Classic social democratic solidarity	Popular interests Acceptance of difference Ethics and morality	Realise interests: Reforms Socialism Create sense of community	Broader: all popular groups The nation?	'Medium': individual freedom accepted and dilemma recognised
Modern social democratic solidarity	Interdependence Acceptance of difference Empathy Compassion Ethics and morality	Create sense of community/social integration Share risks Self-interest?	Very broad: the whole nation The Third World Women Minorities	'Medium/weak?': individual freedom accepted and dilemma recognised Increasing emphasis on individual freedom to choose and on flexibility

the upper classes are expected to exercise solidarity with those who are less privileged. The modern social democratic concept is based on ethics and morality more than on class interest. How ethics are formulated varies – particularly in terms of how the view on religion is formulated. As we have seen in Chapter 4, the German SPD and the Norwegian DNA have formulated the most open and positive attitude to Christian belief. The Bad Godesberg programme declared bluntly that democratic socialism is rooted in Christian ethics, humanism and classical philosophy. In the DNA, there is a clear and continuous line from positive attitudes to religion of early ideologists such as Koht and Sivertsen, to more recent authors of programmes. This is contrary to the Swedish SAP, which does not formulate an explicit positive view about the Christian religion. In Southern Europe where socialist parties were part of a lay tradition, a history of strong conflicts with the Catholic Church have prevented these parties from reformulating their views on religion to the same extent as has been the case in the North. The anti-clerical tradition of French radicalism is echoed in the programme of the PS, which emphasises the secular character of the party.

Third, the modern concept of solidarity emphasises *interdependence*. The argument is that the need for collaboration in production and the economy creates interdependence between employees and employers. If both parties do not accept this, the result is reduced economic growth, smaller increases in salaries and fewer resources to develop or maintain the welfare state. Here, the heritage from Durkheim is clear and, as we have seen, some social democratic theorists were undoubtedly familiar with Durkheim.

Fourth, the concept of interest is reformulated. Solidarity is based upon *self-interest* and the *insight* that common arrangements providing for all when sick, unemployed, disabled or elderly is best for everybody. Thus, interest should be *enlightened self-interest*. The concept of self-interest is further modified in several ways, by emphasising *empathy*, *identification by society as a whole*, *self-restraint* and so forth. Empathy with and compassion for the weak and people in need will create the will to share resources and restrict individual pursuits. Besides, identification with society as a whole and self-restraint should prevent individuals from pursuing their self-interest in a way that harms social integration. For instance, workers' wage demands should be reasonable and balanced against the danger of increased unemployment. Finally, *community* and *collective arrangements* are key elements of social democratic solidarity. Solidarity implies togetherness and cooperation that give the strength and power to carry through common projects. Collective projects are necessary because individual action often is not sufficient, the programme declared.

Fifth, the goal of solidarity has been reformulated. The objective of the classic concept was to strengthen the struggle and to realise reforms. The traditional idea of solidarity as *a weapon in struggle* has generally disappeared from social democratic programmes in the later part of the twentieth century, but is still echoed in some party programmes. Today, this is toned down as an aspect of the modern concept. The need to develop a general feeling of community and the need for social integration are emphasised instead – also across class borders.

Sixth, as we have seen, the modern social democratic concept of solidarity is broader than the classic concept, although variations might be found until the end of the twentieth century. Generally the confines of solidarity are not formulated. Today, the concept includes the majority of the population, the weak, marginalised or poor in one's own country and the poor nations of the Third World. Gender issues are now frequently formulated in terms of solidarity, although the authors of the programmes seem to avoid demanding that men should exercise solidarity with women. Solidarity should include the relationship between generations and environmental issues as well. In recent years, solidarity is applied in some programmes to include also the relationship between the ethnic majority and ethnic minorities.

Finally, the collective orientation of both the classic and the modern concepts of solidarity have been weakened. In the later part of the twentieth century concern about the relationship between the collective and the individual began to emerge in party programmes. The individual and his/her preferences outside the realm of politics were given more attention. For a long time social democratic parties emphasised individual political freedom as a fundamental value, and today they accept the dilemma between individual freedom and collective solidarity in a society where both the market and the value of self-realisation are accepted.

Thus, the concept of solidarity is no longer associated with struggle against private ownership of the means of production, with radical redistribution of wealth or a threat to the privileges of the upper segments of society. Does it have an ineliminable core? We can discern three components of this: to seek collective solutions to social problems; to give the state responsibility for social welfare; and to have a sympathetic attitude to those most in need and to those who are discriminated against or oppressed. However, what this should mean in practical politics is not very clear. Neither is this ineliminable core easy to distinguish from the ineliminable core in another, competing concept of solidarity – the Christian democratic concept, which is the object of analysis in Chapter 6.

Nevertheless, the modern social democratic concept of solidarity gives social democratic parties a programmatic identity and provides continuity between the history of the labour movement tradition and the present. It does not, as did its precursors, direct attention to a more or less distant future, but to interdependence in present-day society. Thus, it is closer to Durkheim's organic solidarity than to the early labour movement idea of solidarity. In Chapter 7 I shall elaborate further on the flexibility of the social democratic language of solidarity.

6   The great challenger: the Christian democratic idea of solidarity

The social democratic parties did not monopolise the idea of solidarity in politics in Western Europe. The social democratic concept, both in its classic and in its modern version, was challenged from many quarters. Within the labour movement the communists insisted on regarding class as the foundation of solidarity and from outside the fascists agitated that the nation and the race should be the frame of reference for solidarity (see Chapter 8). The most permanent challenger in terms of solidarity, however, was to be social Catholicism and the political parties that saw Christian ethics as the foundation of solidarity.

As there is no plain road from socialist theory to socialist and social democratic politics, religious doctrines are not automatically reflected in Christian politics. Ideology – developed by Marxist and socialist intellectuals or popes, bishops and priests – is transformed into party ideology and politics through complicated processes. National history, cleavages in class structure and culture, political configurations, electoral considerations and other factors condition how and to what extent religion becomes an important factor in politics. In Western Europe religion has come to play a crucial role in politics in some nations, but not in others. Influential Christian democratic parties developed in Italy, the Netherlands, Belgium, Germany and Norway, but not in the United Kingdom, Denmark, Sweden and Spain.

In France, the Catholic Church had allied with the monarchy, and the revolution in 1789 initiated a long history of conflicts between the new secular state and the Church. French Catholicism wished to restore the monarchy and remained hostile to liberal democracy, even when Leo XIII attempted to make the Church adapt to a new epoch. In 1924, a group of more liberal Catholics established the *Parti democrate populare*, PDP, but the PDP did not have the same electoral success as the German and Italian sister parties of the time (Ormières 2002) (see below). After World War II, a Christian democratic party – *Mouvement Républicain Populaire* (MRP) – was established and achieved considerable support in the 1945 election. MRP emphasised social integration and cross-class politics and had an ambition to formulate a path between liberalism and socialism and a programme paralleling that of the German and Italian Christian democratic parties, but it never succeeded in uniting Catholic voters. There were many reasons for this: the liberal profile of the leadership was not in harmony with the conservatism of its voters; De Gaulle's establishment of his own party *Rassemblement du Peuple Français* (RPF) attracted many potential MRP voters; the majoritarian electoral system and the strong bipolarism of French politics made it difficult to be a party of the centre; the strong anti-clericalism of the republican tradition. Finally, the RPF became increasingly identified with unpopular government politics and points of view that were problematic for a Christian democratic party, as, for instance, the colonial wars in Indo-China and Africa (McMillan 1996; Durand 2002; Ormières 2002). The MRP has not been included in this study because it did not become an influential party, as did the Christian democratic parties in Germany and Italy.

In Spain, a Christian democratic party, PSP, was established in 1922 (Vincent 1996). However, the strong conservatism of Spanish Catholicism prevented the growth of a democratic alternative in the centre. During the dictatorship the Catholic hierarchy collaborated with the Franco government (Durand 2002). The continuous alliance between the Church and political authoritarianism contributed to the deep anti-clericalism of the republican and socialist left, which again contributed further to the alliance between Catholicism and Franco's authoritarian right. After the reintroduction of democracy in 1977–79, the new party of the right, *Partido Popular,* was a conservative and not a Christian democratic party. Thus, a Christian democratic party never became influential in Spain. Christian democratic parties have developed mainly in predominantly Catholic countries or countries where Catholics constituted a substantial minority, as in Germany. Protestant Norway is an exception, as a Christian party was established in the 1930s. Hence, the main variable deciding the establishment and growth of Christian democracy was not Catholicism, but the extent to which religious groups felt that liberal or radical parties were threatening their values (Mény 1990).

In his contribution to comparative research on Christian democracy, Kees van Kersbergen points to the fact that those parties are neither a substitute for conservatism nor a duplicate of social democracy (Kersbergen 1995). In Christian democratic ideology, an articulate social theory of capitalism emphasises the vital role of social organisation and the subsidiary role of the state. The market should be accepted, but politics should aim at social integration and the reconciliation of potential social conflicts. Thus, *mediation* is an essential function of Christian democracy.

The question to be answered here is what has been the place of *solidarity* in Christian democratic parties? To what extent has the development of a Catholic concept of solidarity been reflected in the programmes of such parties in nations where Catholicism has been influential? Has the introduction of *solidarity* in Lutheran World Federation documents been reflected in Christian democracy in those countries where Protestantism has been dominant? What is the relationship between a Christian democratic concept of solidarity and the modern social democratic concept? A study of party programmes of three Christian democratic parties will serve to throw light on these issues: *Democrazia Cristiana* (DC) in Catholic Italy, the interconfessional *Christlich-Demokratische Union* (CDU) in Germany where Protestants and Catholics joined together, and *Kristelig Folkeparti* (KrF) – *Christian People's Party* (CPP) – in Protestant Norway.[1]

Germany: Zentrum and CDU

Among the nations studied here, Germany was the first to see the establishment of a political party based on religion. As the German SPD came to be a model and inspiration for other social democratic parties, German Catholicism articulated early a political programme and came to inspire Catholics in other countries to follow suit.

The early political organisation of Catholics in Germany was due to their minority position and the need they felt to defend their interests against the Protestant majority and the Protestant state. Before Bismarck united Germany into a single nation in 1870, Germany was not only politically, but also religiously, divided. Most major states were religiously mixed, although Protestants were dominant in the north and east, and Catholics had their stronghold in the south and in the Rhineland (Carr 1991). After the Napoleonic wars, Catholics began to feel threatened by state authorities and started organising the defence of their Church. The revolution of 1848 stimulated the establishment of new Catholic organisations and newspapers. At the same time, a growing concern about the social consequences of industrialisation made Catholic intellectuals develop an interest in social problems (Schmidt 1987).

---

[1] One could argue that it was not the Christian People's Party (KrF), but the Conservative Party that should have been included from Norway as this party is associated with the European People's party as well. However, the Conservative party has never declared itself as a Christian democratic party and religion has not played the same important role as for the KrF.

Zentrum and Christlicher Solidarismus

After the war in 1866, Catholics became a minority of 37 per cent in a Protestant state with a Protestant emperor. The minority's need to defend its religion and interests resulted in the creation of a national Catholic party in 1870, *das Zentrum*. The Zentrum was unique among German parties because it had supporters in all classes – the aristocracy, the middle class and the working class. In 1871, it became the second largest party in the Reichstag.

Zentrum's political Catholicism was a mixture of conservative and liberal currents. It preferred corporatist institutions, and its attitude towards liberal democracy was ambivalent or unclear. The first programme, the so-called *Soester programme* of 1870, argued for the independence of the Church, the decentralisation of government and administration, the curtailment and just distribution of taxes. The Zentrum wanted equal status for capital and landed property on the one hand, and for labour and capital on the other, and wanted to protect and develop the *Mittelstand* (the middle class). It argued for laws that would remove the 'evils that threaten the moral or physical destruction of workers' (Zentrum 1952 (1870)).

The protagonist in developing Catholic social ethics was the Catholic Bishop von Ketteler. In 1864 he published *Die Arbeiterfrage und Christentum* (*The Worker Question and Christendom*). Here he argued for Christian trade unions, worker-producer cooperatives and assistance for those not able to work (Ketteler 1952 (1864)). Ketteler came to influence both German social policy and papal teaching in *Rerum Novarum*. The Zentrum soon made such proposals its own and made them key issues. In von Ketteler's texts and speeches and in the programme of the Zentrum, there are four aspects that came to be core elements of Catholic social ethics when Leo XIII published *Rerum Novarum* 20 years later (see Chapter 3). First, a boundary was drawn against liberalism. Second, the worker question was made a key issue. Wages ought to be raised to the real value of the labour; working hours should be reduced; children should not work; and mothers should not be allowed to work in factories (Ketteler 1979 (1869)). Third, *justice* was early to become a key concept. The fourth aspect came to be a continuous concern of German Christian democracy – the preoccupation with the *Mittelstand*.

Bismarck's *Kulturkampf* against the Catholics strengthened Catholics' feelings of being in opposition to the German state. After this conflict the Zentrum and the new regime came to be on more friendly terms in the latter part of the 1880s. In the *Declaration of Berlin* in 1909, the Zentrum emphasised that it was a political and not a confessional party, representing the whole German people. It wanted to defend the religious freedom of all citizens, although it had been necessary to pay special attention to the situation of Catholics because of the prolonged conflict with Bismarck. The Zentrum supported improvements for workers, but rejected class struggle. The aim should be a just peace between employers and workers, von Ketteler stated (Ketteler 1979 (1869)). Society should be based not on class domination, but on corporatism and the community of *professional* groups. The analogy to society as an organism was sometimes drawn explicitly (Galen 1979 (1877)).

After the turn of the century, the spiritual father of what was labelled *christlicher Solidarismus*, Heinrich Pesch, developed an extensive theory about how a market economy could be reconciled with solidarity. Pesch was familiar with the contributions of Leroux, Comte, Durkheim, Bourgeois and other French solidarists. However, he criticised the 'exaggerations of nineteenth-century sociology where an analogy between society and physical organisms had been proposed', and thought the idea of society as an organism was a reason why the concept of solidarity fell into disrepute (Pesch 1998 (1924)). Inspired by the line of reasoning in Leo XIII's *Rerum Novarum*, he sought to develop a doctrine of a middle way, avoiding the weaknesses of both individualism and collectivism and taking into account the interests of both individuals and society. He wanted to 'christianise' the economy and society according to the principles of the common good and argued for a corporate social order based on solidarity between workers, white-collar employees and employers (Pesch 1919, quoted in Uertz 1981). He integrated also other elements of papal teaching, such as the idea of subsidiarity and a just wage.

In 1900, Pesch published his voluminous *Liberalismus, Sozialismus, und christliche Gesellschaftsordnung*. Here he criticised what he called the *science of free economy* – Liberalism – for building only on natural instincts. The natural instincts of human beings to strive for their own personal interest must be subordinated to a higher order – that of reason and conscience. The *law of solidarity* is based on the interdependence of human beings, on their interest in cooperating to achieve the common good and on Christian duty. It is not only of reciprocal advantage to stay together, but a duty, because 'solidarity is based on human nature and is claimed by the natural law of God', he said (Pesch 1901). Pesch developed this line of argument further in 1905 in *Lehrbuch der Sozialökonomie* where he elaborated on *solidarity* and made it a key concept in his economic theory (Pesch 1998 (1924)). The principle of solidarity should be applied at three different levels: the whole human race, citizens of the same state and members of the same occupation. He associated solidarity with the idea of social justice and argued that this meant the private economy should be subordinated to the collective interest and common objectives of the national economy.

Ten years later, Max Scheler brought the concept even more strongly into focus in European social philosophy in *Der Formalismus in der Ethic und die materiale Wertethik*. His 'ethical personalism' was strongly inspired by Christian ideas. He defined solidarity as the coresponsibility of each individual for the moral well-being of all others. A high moral standard implied conceiving oneself not as an 'isolated person', but as a person bound to God, directing love in the world and seeing oneself as united in solidarity with the whole of humankind. Because a person is autonomous, morality becomes relevant, he argued (Scheler 1966 (1913–16)).[2] Scheler distinguished his concept of autonomy from that of Kant and argued that whereas Kant's concept is individualistic, his own concept does not exclude solidarity. Responsibility for oneself and coresponsibility for others does not arise *ex post facto*, but is closely associated and given from the start, constituted by the nature of moral community among persons, he maintained. This ambition to insist on personal autonomy and at the same time transcend Kant's individualism represents in some ways a religious precursor of Habermas' contribution in the last decades of the century (see Chapter 9).

Whereas concern about social integration had become an issue early in German political Catholicism, the preoccupation with solidarity among German Catholics was first reflected in a political programme in 1909, in Zentrum's *Declaration of Berlin*. The organic growth of the community of the German people depended 'upon the solidarity between all social strata and professional groups', it was stated in the programme (Zentrum 1952 (1909)). In the spirit of the Christian-social view of life, the Zentrum wanted to develop the existing feeling of fellowship in the German people to become a strong consciousness of community. Such formulations about cross-class solidarity, combined with the emphasis on a 'true Christian feeling of community' and on the family, were repeated in later programmes. All these elements later came to be core elements of Christian democratic ideology.

Thus, we note the early introduction of *solidarity* in Zentrum programmes, both compared to the German social democratic party, which included the term solidarity for the first time in the 1925 programme, and compared to papal encyclicals which did not do the same until 1961. Although not much applied at this time, a Catholic concept of solidarity had now definitely been brought into Christian politics in Germany.

---

[2] See also Bayertz (1998) about Scheler's contribution which does not mention Pesch, whose texts on solidarity were published earlier and in a much more accessible language.

This concept referred to feelings of community across class boundaries and feelings that should bring about integration in society. More than fifty years before the concept emerged in a papal encyclical and sixty-two years before it was taken up by the Christian democratic CDU, the Zentrum applied the concept of solidarity in a way that later came to be standard in Catholic social ethics.

After 1918, the Zentrum played an important role in German politics, often in coalition government, but sometimes negotiating from opposition. The social heterogeneity of the party became a problem under the increasing strength of fascism in the 1920s. The party moved to the right and was no longer able to fulfil its integrative function by providing a bridge between the right and the left of German politics (Lönne 1986; 1996). The Zentrum, as the Italian PPI, was not able to maintain its opposition to fascism and concluded by supporting the bill that gave Hitler general power in 1933. Some months later, the party decided to dissolve itself (Carr 1991).

German Catholicism, however, came to develop an enduring and special preoccupation with solidarity in the first decades of the twentieth century. The *christlicher Solidarismus* of Pesch later influenced Oswald von Nell-Breuning and other contributors to more recent Catholic social ethics. Pius XI appointed Nell-Breuning as one of the editors in the preparation of *Quadragesimo Anno*. Nell-Breuning formed an advisory group with other German Catholics and social scientists influenced by the *christlicher Solidarismus* of Pech (Uertz 1981). Although the concept of solidarity now seemed to be well entrenched in German Catholicism, the term was not used in the encyclical. In any case, both the idea of solidarity and the term were integrated in German Catholic ethics many years before a new Christian democratic party was established after World War II.

The reestablishment of Christian politics – the CDU

The *Christlich-Democratische Union Deutschlands* (CDU)[3] that was established after the war in 1945 was only partly a successor to the Zentrum. The traumas of the experiences in the Weimar Republic and the need for a

---

[3] Its sister party in Bavaria – *Christlich-Soziale Union* (CSU) – was established in 1946 with the support of the Catholic clergy in Bavaria and was inspired by all the classic themes of pre-war social Catholicism, from corporatism to federalism (Durand 2002). It constituted a working community with the CDU and became the representative of Christian democracy in Bavaria. As it was a junior partner of the CDU, I have chosen to concentrate on the CDU as the German Christian democratic party. On the establishment of the CDU/CSU see also Becker (2003).

clear rejection of totalitarianism made necessary a more profound political renewal and a new party that could claim to represent not only Catholicism but also Christian values in general (Broughton 1994). Moreover, their experiences during the war had made religion more important in the lives of many citizens (Conway 2003).

For German Catholics the road from religion to politics was not problematic. A Catholic party had existed before the war, and a Catholic party could still be seen as a logical consequence of natural law. Catholic bishops and associations were concerned with the increasing secularisation and felt a need for a stronger defence than a purely Catholic party might provide. Thus, they had a positive attitude towards the establishment of a broader interconfessional party (Narr 1966). For Protestants it was somewhat more complicated. As has been seen in Chapter 3, there was no easy bridge from Lutheran theology to Protestant politics. The Barmen declaration (see Chapter 3) and the terrible experiences with Nazism in the following years constituted such a bridge. Like many Catholics, many Protestants thought that secularisation and modernity made it necessary to engage in society in an organised political way and saw the establishment of an interconfessional party as the best choice (Buchaas 1981).

In this way, the new CDU could present itself as a non-denominational Christian party open to both Protestants and Catholics. This made it possible to attract liberals as well, and prevented the establishment of a liberal-conservative party of the kind that was found in the UK and Scandinavia. In a situation when the social democratic SPD still adhered to socialism and presented itself as a workers' party, the CDU was able to attract voters from all classes. Whereas the Zentrum had never been able to fully accept modern liberal democracy, the new Christian democrats supported liberal democracy firmly and deliberately developed a policy for integration, class reconciliation and solidarity between different groups.

However, the influence of Catholics in the new party was strong. After the separation into two German states, the balance between Catholics and Protestants had changed, the two now being more equal in numbers: 45 per cent of Catholics as opposed to 30 per cent before the war (Carr 1991). The Catholic Church supported the CDU, and the Catholic tradition was immediately reflected in the sceptical attitude to *laissez-faire* capitalism and the emphasis on public social policy.

The CDU programme of 1947, *CDU überwindet Kapitalismus und Marxismus* (CDU Defeats Capitalism and Marxism), was an expression of a desire to distance itself from both capitalism and socialism. The Ahlen programme, as it was called, represented the Catholic desire to

find a third way. It was a mixture of liberal market economy and socialist elements, with a certain anti-capitalist flavour, arguing for planning,
national control of key industries and worker influence in the management of industrial enterprises (CDU 1947). The last issue expressed the
Catholic idea that both employers and employees were necessary for the
production of wealth, and this came to be an enduring characteristic of
German political Catholicism. The CDU later came to deem this programme ambivalent – on the one hand, a programme oriented towards
the future, on the other, a regrettable mistake (Buchaas 1981).

The Ahlen programme and succeeding programmes during the next
two decades did not include any definition or discussion about what
it should imply to be a Christian party. The *C-element*, however, came
to be an issue after some years. What should it mean to be a Christian party? What should be the relationship between Catholicism and
Protestantism – and between Catholics and Protestants in the party? The
Berliner programme of 1971 was the first to make the Christian imprint
of the party explicit.

What succeeding party officials came to see as the anti-capitalist 'mistake' of the Ahlen programme was soon to be corrected when it became
clear that conservatives constituted an important part of CDU electoral
support.[4] The programme of 1949 *Die Düsseldorfer Leitssätze* – (The
Principles of Düsseldorf) – already signalled the acceptance of a 'social
market economy', defended by Ludwig Erhard, among others. The economy should be based on capitalism, the market and competition, combined with a conscious social policy that offered social protection and
security against negative side-effects on integration (CDU 1949). Public
intervention should conform to the market, and the social security system should be closely linked to labour market participation, with a strong
correlation between personal contribution and benefits. In this way an
optimal balance of economic utility and social justice could be achieved
(Buchaas 1981).

The concept of the social market economy expressed the fundamental ambition of economic thought from Thomas Aquinas to present-day
Catholicism to reconcile private property, in modern times capitalist competition as well, and social integration. The socio-economic order should
be based on the notion of human responsibility, which implies respect for

---

[4] For an extensive analysis of the ideological positions in German Catholicism before the
consolidation of the CDU, see Uertz (1981). Uertz refers to a strand of Christian socialism
within German Catholicism, strongly influenced by Dominicans, that put its imprint on
the Ahlen programme. In the following years, however, Christian solidarism, influenced
by Jesuits, came to be more influential in the programmes and actions of the CDU, see
also Lönne (1996).

the creation and the environment, the relationship between employers and employees and solidarity between all human beings (Durand 2002). Thus, the idea of a social market ideology came to be an important part of the complete discourse about solidarity that was institutionalised in CDU programmes during the ensuing decades.

The combination of a market economy and an active social policy became an enduring characteristic of German Christian democratic politics. The *Hamburger programme* in 1953 was the first extensive programme and came to be the only general programme of the party for the next fifteen years. It was approved without debate and with minimal discussion in the party before the congress (Buchaas 1981). Even now, the core values of Christian *solidarismus*, social justice and solidarity, were not found. The programme was perhaps most innovative in emphasising the need for a more active social policy (CDU 1953); and reform of the pension system resulted in a new electoral success in 1957.

In the tradition of Pesch, German Catholic theologians continued to be preoccupied with solidarity during the 1950s. Oscar von Nell-Breuning argued in his *Zur Christlichen Gesellschaftslehre* (*On Christian Teaching about Society*), that 'The basic law of Christian solidarity is opposed to individual and group egoism' which makes people place self-interest above the common good, and blocks social commitment (Nell-Breuning and Sacher 1954). The extensive *Herder's Social Catechism* declared *solidarity* to be a basic law. As a totality cannot exist without its separate parts, the separate parts of society cannot exist without community, the Catechism proclaimed (Herder 1959). Solidarity was necessary to integrate individuals and separate parts of society into an organic totality. Franz Klüber, a professor of Christian sociology, listed three basic principles of Catholic social teaching: the principle of the *person* (distinct from that of the *individual*), the principle of solidarity and the principle of subsidiarity (Klüber 1963). As we have seen in Chapter 3, this came to constitute the core elements of papal teaching on social ethics in the following decades.

The Berliner programme and the adoption of the concept of solidarity

It has been argued that the ideology of the CDU from the beginning was only a general background, a certain atmosphere, all-embracing and vague enough to recruit supporters among Catholics and Protestants. Pragmatism and Union were synonyms (Buchaas 1981). The Chancellor, Konrad Adenauer, and the policy of the CDU government were regarded as the best programme. Although there may be some truth in this, it seems somewhat overstated. It is a continuous identity in CDU programmes. At least from the late 1960s a programmatic renewal was under way, but this renewal represented more an elaboration than a fundamental change of ideology and identity.

At the end of the 1950s, the CDU initiated a programmatic discussion between Catholics and Protestants about the Christian identity of the party (Projektgruppe Parteiensystem 1978). The loss of government power after the liberal FDP switched sides and entered into a government together with the SPD in 1969 made a programmatic renewal more urgent (Hintze 1995). A committee with Helmut Kohl as chairman delivered a proposal that resulted in the approval of the Berliner programme in 1971. Here, most key concepts of the modern Christian democratic ideology were finally introduced. The programme stated that CDU politics were based on the principles of Christian responsibility. The aim, it was declared, was *the freedom of the individual*, recognition of a commitment to society, and *justice, equal opportunity* for everybody, the *solidarity between all citizens* and the *responsibility of the person*. The social market economy should be based on the contribution of the individual and social justice, competition and solidarity, personal responsibility and social security, the programme stated (CDU 1971). This was the definite integration of Catholic social teaching and the doctrines that had been developed by von Ketteler, Pesch and Nell-Breuning.

In 1975, Heiner Geissler, who had learned Catholic social teaching at a school run by Jesuits, launched the concept *die neue soziale Frage* (the new social question) in an attempt to renew CDU ideology and attract new voters among groups that did not benefit from the distribution of resources in society: women, retired persons and other groups. Geissler's ambition was to let Catholic social teaching and the Christian idea of man profile the party, thus reducing the image of market liberalism (Nullmeyer and Rüb 1993). In 1975, Geissler was elected general secretary and came to represent Catholic social teaching in the party leadership over the next couple of decades. The new CDU programme in the same year, the *Declaration of Mannheim*, was influenced by Geissler's ideas and presented the *new social question*. However, a more active social policy was blocked by the effects of the oil crisis and resistance from the conservative part of the party. Nonetheless, in terms of solidaristic ideology a new step was taken. The programme declared *freedom, justice* and *solidarity* to be the basic values of the party. Solidarity was now applied to the relationship with the Third World for the first time in a CDU programme, although this demand had been found in papal teaching for a long time. The programme included now the Catholic idea of *subsidiarity* as well, although not specifically mentioning the term. The role of the state should be to establish the goals for public activities and rule on the basis of the principles of freedom and justice. However, private enterprise and voluntary organisations were to be responsible for providing social services to meet citizens' demand (CDU 1995 (1975)).

The full development of Christian democratic ideology and language: 1978

In 1978, the CDU approved a platform, a *Grundsatzprogramm*, for the first time. The title *Freedom, Solidarity, Justice* signalled a strong interest in values and ideology. Although it was a Christian democratic party, the CDU now rejected the idea that a specific political programme could be derived from Christian belief. Christian understanding of man might, however, constitute an ethical foundation for responsible politics. This ethical foundation is constituted by the basic values introduced in the programme three years before and now included in the title of the programme.

The concept of the *person*[5] and the importance of the family as a cornerstone of society were emphasised. Solidarity means to stand up for one another, because both the individual and society have only each other. Thus, solidarity is characterised by the reciprocal relationship between community and the individual. An individual has a right to assistance and solidarity from others, but at the same time is obliged to stand up for the community and make a personal contribution. Solidarity and subsidiarity belong together. Government should support personal initiative and responsible self-help (CDU 1978).

The platform of 1978 marks the full development of Christian democratic ideology and language in the CDU. All key ideas and concepts of Catholic social teaching were included the platform, and nothing has been added in this respect since. The fact that the Protestant Richard von Weizsäcker headed the programme committee illustrates to what extent Catholic social teaching had become a common ideological basis in the interconfessional CDU. The emphasis on personalism, freedom, justice, solidarity and subsidiarity meant that the CDU had now adopted all the key concepts of Catholic social ethics, more than fifty years after Pius XI issued *Quadragesimo Anno*.

It is somewhat surprising that the full version of Catholic social ethics was included in CDU programmes at a time when the influence of Catholicism and religion in general was decreasing in German society, and when bonds between the CDU and the Catholic Church were

---

[5] See the difference between individual and person in Chapter 3.

weakening. In the 1950s, the SPD established a better relationship with the Catholic Church. In 1958, SPD representatives and Catholics met at a conference to discuss religion and socialism. As mentioned in Chapter 4, this resulted in a new formulation of the Christian religion in the Bad Godesberg programme of 1959. The CDU showed some concern at this development, as an important demarcation line between the two parties was now about to be blurred (Buchaas 1981).

Since the late 1960s the relationship between the CDU and the Catholic Church had become more problematic. Continuing secularisation made religious affiliation less important in political life (Lönne 1996). The CDU had grown into a real 'people's party' with a more balanced participation of Protestants. At the same time, more Catholics voted SPD. The CDU *Grundsatzprogramm* of 1978 may be seen as a response to this development. The CDU needed to define its ideological position more clearly at the same time as it had to present itself as a 'people's party'.

The new ideological climate and the increasing popularity of neo-liberal ideas represented in principle an alternative option. However, the historical heritage of the party blocked blatant neo-liberalism as an option. In this situation Catholic social ethics were defined as an alternative both to social democracy and neo-liberalism. This choice illustrates the profound scepticism regarding exaggerated individualism in German Christian democracy. However, the formula *social market economy, freedom, solidarity and subsidiarity* in the years to come should demonstrate its flexibility by making possible a drift to the right while at the same time preserving ideological continuity.

The new ideological climate may be observed in the programme of 1981, *With the Youth – Our Country Needs a New Start*. Here, the accent is somewhat shifted from *solidarity* to *subsidiarity*, and freedom, individual autonomy, is more strongly emphasised than before (CDU 1981). When the CDU returned to power with Helmut Kohl in 1982, this took place under the slogan *Die Wende* (The Turn), even if this turn represented only a modest change to the right in economic policy. Kohl now launched what was coined a *subsidiarity offensive*. Kohl's governmental declaration contained formulations directly from *Quadragesimo Anno*, stating that self-help and assistance based on love of one's neighbour should be preferred to assistance from public authorities. The social responsibility of the family and extended family for sick or disabled family members was emphasised (Plaschke 1984). The subsidiarity offensive illustrates how the combination of subsidiarity and solidarity makes it possible to drift between the one and the other according to the ideological climate or to what is deemed politically expedient.

Later programmes have brought little that is new in terms of solidaristic ideology. The CDU approved a new platform or basic programme in 1994 that represented a continuation of the 1978 platform. 'A false individualism that implies freedom at the sacrifice of others should be rejected', the programme said (CDU 1995 (1994)). Solidarity and subsidiarity were carefully balanced against each other.

Solidarity in the SPD and CDU

What then is the difference between the CDU concept of solidarity and that of the German social democratic party? The key concept in the discourse that includes solidarity is quite similar in the two parties – as both parties consider *freedom*, *justice* and *solidarity* as basic values. There are also other similarities, such as the emphasis on the equal worth of human beings. Neither is the conception of the individual and the relationship between the individual and the group or community very different. Both the SPD and the CDU stress that the individual has to relate to other human beings in order to develop, and that the freedom of the individual is confined by the freedom of others.

There are, however, differences in at least two aspects. First, the social democratic idea of solidarity is not balanced against subsidiarity as in CDU programmes. The SPD platform of 1998 did not signal the same restrictions on the willingness to apply state authority and interventions as did the CDU platform in 1994. Second, also related to solidarity, the SPD programme clearly stated that the social democratic concept of justice also includes redistribution of income, property and power, whereas the CDU platforms did not say anything in this respect. On the contrary, almost, CDU ideology emphasises that personal effort and contribution should be recognised, and that justice means that 'unequal should be treated as unequal' (CDU 1994). Thus, two slightly different conceptions of solidarity are associated with two slightly different conceptions of justice in the two parties.

It has been argued that the CDU is more a party for winning power and staying in office than for implementing a defined ideology, and that values stated in programmes do not add up to more than general statements and an indisputable set of precepts (Broughton 1994). As has been demonstrated here, this is clearly an exaggeration. Throughout its existence the CDU has tried to combine traditional ideas about religion and social values with the appreciation of a strong and productive economy. This has made it possible to address conservatives and business people, the middle class and Catholic workers. The ambition to integrate and reconcile social groups in conflict has given the CDU a pragmatic profile. Nevertheless, some characteristics of CDU ideology can be delineated. The last thirty years represent a strong continuity in terms of key ideological concepts. Freedom, justice and solidarity seem to be as well entrenched in CDU ideology as in SPD ideology. At the same time, the idea of subsidiarity gives the CDU concept of solidarity a distinct profile and allows for political flexibility and reinterpretation of the idea of solidarity when necessary.

What is most surprising – at least for a Scandinavian observer – is the continuity of the Christian profile of the CDU. In a period of strong secularisation and increasing individualism, CDU programme ideology and language has preserved a strong continuity in stating its character as a Christian party. In spite of this, the party has managed to stay on as a large and influential party. This must be due to skilful political strategy and tactics. The flexibility offered by Christian democratic ideology, however, may also have been conducive to this.

Italy: Christian democracy from birth to hegemony to dissolution

Although there was nothing in Catholicism to prevent Catholics from taking an active part in politics, the Catholic path to politics in modern Italy was troublesome and painful. For more than a thousand years the Vatican had been not only a religious authority, but also a secular power and had already participated in politics for centuries when Cavour united Italy in 1861. The Pope had now lost the important provinces of Umbria and Marche, and in 1870 he also lost the city of Rome and now controlled only the restricted Vatican area. This meant a humiliating defeat of the papal state and was the start of a troublesome relationship between religion and politics in the new Italy.

The Church struggled intransigently against what it saw as two sides of the same coin: the Italian state and Liberalism. Succeeding popes refused to accept the new Italian state until the agreement with Mussolini in 1929, and for a long time the Catholics boycotted political participation. The papal encyclicals *Quanta Cura* and the *Sillabo* in 1864 condemned liberal principles and rejected modern civil culture, provoking increased anti-clericalism and new conflicts with the politicians of the new state. In 1874 the Pope declared that Catholics should not vote at elections. Although many Catholics continued to disobey this in the years to come, many practising Catholics were set apart from the rest of the nation and were without the exercise of rights and entitlements as full citizens (Smith 1997). The 'Roman Question', the status of the Vatican, continued to block full Catholic participation in political life until after World War I.

Early Christian politics: Don Sturzo and the Partito Popolare Italiano

Compared to Germany, a Catholic political movement developed slowly and hesitantly in Italy. Before and after the turn of the century, conflicts between the Vatican and the Italian state became gradually less antagonistic. Pope Leo XIII issued in 1888 the encyclical *De Libertate Humana* (*On Human Freedom*), in which he revised the profound anti-liberalism of the *Sillabo*. Leo's *Rerum Novarum* three years later meant a further step towards recognition of politics. The economic crisis of the 1890s pushed social issues more into focus and made the 'Roman Question' gradually somewhat less relevant. The economic crisis, the increased support of the left, and the need for a defence of 'order' made Catholic electoral participation more tempting (Webster 1961). At the same time, as groups of Christian democrats were established, more Catholics had to admit that the boycott of Italian politics was not effective.

The priest Don Sturzo was the key activist and protagonist in the struggle to establish a Christian party and to integrate Catholics into politics. He argued that a Christian party could serve as an instrument in the difficult task of opening a dialogue between Catholics and the modern world. Political participation was a moral obligation, an extension of the moral involvement of the individual and an instrument to promote Christian ethical values, he stated. The exercise of individual rights should develop into collective solidarity in the form of a political party. The individual was fundamentally a social being and could not develop his abilities without association with others, he argued. He denounced class oppression and economic exploitation of classes and argued that social classes should be pacified. Democracy built on equality and social justice would contribute to this. Like Leo XIII in *Rerum Novarum*, he argued that the institutions of civil society, the family, local and professional organisations, were essential parts of a pluralistic free society that should not be subordinate to the state (Hamel 1989).

Don Sturzo's speech in Caltagirone in 1905 was a key event in the process of formulating a specific Christian democratic position in Italian politics and pointed to the establishment of the PPI in 1919. Sturzo described here his ambition to establish a party that was independent of the Church and accepted the nation as the basis for politics inspired by Christian principles. The programme should be democratic and pragmatic and distinguish itself from socialism, conservatism and liberalism (Sturzo 1983 (1905)). Thus, a Christian democratic party had to be a centre party.

The war and a new social situation finally made possible the establishment of a new Catholic party. Catholics loyally took part on the side of
the Italian state in World War I. This removed the last obstacle to full
participation in national politics (Molony 1977; Pollard 1996). After the
war, the Catholic middle class, and others, experienced problems finan-
cially and socially, and this was the final impetus for the establishment of
a Catholic party. Pope Benedict XV was still reluctant, but accepted the
fact when in 1919 Don Sturzo succeeded in uniting different Catholic
groups into a moderate Christian democratic party: *Il Partito Popolare
Italiano* (PPI). The Pope now revoked the ban on political participation.
However, the relationship between the Vatican and political Catholicism
continued to be complicated. The Pope was anxious not to lose control
of the Catholic masses, and the Vatican looked with suspicion on the PPI
throughout its brief history. On the other hand, the party had to be careful
not to be considered as the long arm of the Vatican (Molony 1977).

The PPI was an immediate success and achieved 20 per cent of the vote
at the election in 1919 (Smith 1997). The PPI was a cross-class party,
supported both by the petty bourgeoisie, rural workers and landowners.
Although some workers as well voted for the PPI, working-class support
was not strong. Like the German *Zentrum*, the PPI came to play a key role
in parliamentary politics. It took part in all governments from 1919 to
1922 as neither socialists nor liberals alone were able to muster a majority
in Parliament (Pollard 1996).

Don Sturzo was eager to emphasise that the PPI was not a Catholic
party (Molony 1977). The party should stick to Christian basic principles, but not label itself 'Christian'. The first appeal to the nation and the
first programme in 1919 made freedom and social justice key values (PPI
1919a; 1919b). On the one hand, the PPI argued for social reforms, the
right to employment, restriction of working hours and social insurance
against disability, unemployment and old age. On the other hand, government should decentralise authority and responsibility and not restrict
the role of the family, classes and local communities, but respect individual freedom and private initiative. It denounced class struggle and called
for social collaboration. In the years to come, the PPI developed a radical view on the social question and was concerned with the relationship
between the individual and the social group, particularly the family, class
and local community (Scoppola 1976; Kersbergen 1995). Contrary to
the German Zentrum, however, emphasis on social integration was not
yet accompanied by the introduction of a concept of solidarity.

The PPI established informal links to other parties in Europe that had
mass support among Catholics. In 1921, Don Sturzo met with the leaders

of the German Zentrum – among them Konrad Adenauer, who at the time was mayor of Cologne (Molony 1977). However, the life of the PPI was to be short. The party supported Mussolini's government and was disbanded in 1927 after conflicts with the Vatican about its attitude to fascism, internal strife and fascist oppression.

The establishment and experience of the PPI, however, had cleared the way for full Catholic participation in political life. The PPI had also succeeded in working out an ideology of integration. It argued for community across class boundaries and made *social justice* and *freedom* core values.

De Gasperi and the establishment of Democrazia Cristiana

In 1942, a number of leaders of the old PPI and a group of Christian anti-fascists founded *Democrazia Cristiana* (Christian Democracy) (Ginsborg 1989). The DC became the dominant party of Italian politics for fifty years, being in government alone or in coalition permanently from 1945 until it was dissolved in 1992 as a consequence of the corruption scandals of *Tangentopoli* (Bribetown). From 1945 to 1981 all the prime ministers were Christian democrats.

We cannot discuss the programme ideology and language of the DC without describing the special characteristics of the party and its exercise of government power. First, the DC was supported by a cross-class alliance consisting of the rural and urban middle class, workers who were concerned about social integration, and liberal groups associated with big business (Murphy 1978). Thus, the party cut across class boundaries. Although the middle class was closest to the heart, *class mediation* was a distinguishing mark. Second, a strong anti-communism served to unite DC voters and factions. Facing the largest communist party in Western Europe, it made *freedom* a key value and slogan in the political struggle. Third, the DC was for most of its history ridden by factionalism. From 1964, the role of factions was even officially recognised in the party (Donovan 1994). Factions were built on different economic ideologies, geography, personal loyalties, etc. Horse-trading and pragmatism became more important than ideas and principles. Fourth, this made the relationship between programmes and political practice problematic. Factionalism made it difficult to formulate a coherent ideology in party programmes. The exercise of government power was not primarily about realising a programme, but about the sharing and distribution of spoils and positions in the *sottogoverno* – the large network of public institutions that was used both to reward political loyalty and to distribute advantages to clients who had provided electoral support. Fifth, the DC was Catholic, but was not the political arm of the Vatican. It enjoyed a close relationship with the Church, but was nevertheless eager to maintain a distance from the Vatican. Thus, we should not take for granted that papal views on society and solidarity automatically were reflected in DC programmes. Finally, the DC was first and foremost a party of mediation. It mediated between classes, between different factions in its own ranks, between Catholics and lay groups in society, and between different parts of the nation that were fragmented geographically, socially or politically (Follini 2000).

The protagonist in the development of DC ideology and programmes was Alcide De Gasperi, who also had been the last chairman of the PPI. Whereas Don Sturzo came from Southern Italy, De Gasperi came from Trentino in the North and was influenced both by the experiences of German Catholicism and his own experiences from the Parliament in Vienna when the north of Italy was part of the Austro-Hungarian Empire. De Gasperi's contribution was to establish continuity with the pre-war PPI and to anchor the new Christian democratic party in a liberal conception of politics. Like Don Sturzo, he argued strongly that Christian democracy should represent a clear alternative to both economic liberalism and collective socialism. In 1945, he became the first Catholic Prime Minister in Italy.

De Gasperi's speeches demonstrate that he was strongly entrenched in Catholic social teaching. He emphasised the need for mediation and integration and argued that the party should address the whole of Italian society and mediate between all classes and social categories. Social solidarity should make both employers and employees feel responsible for production (De Gasperi 1956a (1947)). The principles of *human dignity, freedom, rights of the person* and of *intermediate organisms* and *fraternity* should permeate the state, he declared. He referred to *Quadragesimo Anno* and argued for a more just distribution of wealth (De Gasperi 1956b (1949)). The historical preconditions and ideas of Christian democracy make *personal freedom* and *social justice* the common foundation of our work, he proclaimed (De Gasperi 1956c (1949)). Thus, he was concerned with the idea of solidarity, but both personal freedom and social justice ranked higher in the hierarchy of ideological concepts in his speeches in the postwar years. However, both the idea and the term *solidarity* were part of his political ideology. Solidarity was closely linked to the key value, social justice. Human solidarity and social justice meant fraternity between human beings, and these concepts should work in mind and conscience, and what we need is neither capitalism nor socialism, he maintained, but a people's 'solidarism' in which labour and capital are interwoven and the prevalence of labour is increasing (De Gasperi 1956d (1954)).

In 1942, De Gasperi and a group of collaborators presented *Idee ricostruttive della Democrazia Italiana* (Reconstructing Ideas of Christian Democracy). This was a provisional programme for a new Christian party and represented a clear thematic continuation from PPI programmes, with political freedom and social justice as important values. The new democracy should be inspired by the 'spirit of fraternity that is the fermentation of Christian society'. The importance of small and medium enterprises was reemphasised, but also the need to 'de-proletarianise' workers by providing housing and opportunities for education for their children (DC 1983 (1943)), and the idea of 'de-proletarianisation' was repeated in later programmes. The Catholic idea of the person and his/her freedom was introduced, as well as the integrity of the family. The integrative ideology of the PPI was continued under the label *fraternity*. On the one hand, the programme denounced class struggle, on the other it declared that ethics and the public interest should confine economic freedom. Only the spirit of fraternity nourished by the Bible, it said, could save the people from catastrophes brought about by totalitarianism. However, we now find the term *solidarity* also applied to social policies for workers (De Gasperi 1969 (1943)).

The ideas and themes of the *Idee ricostruttive* were repeated and elaborated upon in DC programmes and key documents in the succeeding years. Family values, ethical values, moral conscience, agricultural reform, defence of small property and business, and social justice were established anew as Christian democratic ideology. Christian *fraternity* was emphasised once again as the social cement of society – directed against unfettered egoism and individualism as well as against socialism and collectivism.

In 1943 and the first years after the war, the term *solidarity* rapidly and increasingly was used in place of equivalent terms such as *fraternity*. The DC declared solidarity with all peoples of the world and wanted solidarity to rule between the peoples of the old Europe (DC 1943). It appealed for a political armistice, social peace and solidarity between all citizens (DC 1947a), and argued for reforms of social security that confirmed the 'principle of solidarity to all subordinated and autonomous workers' (DC 1947b). Thus, a broad concept of solidarity was now established. As we have seen in previous chapters, social democratic parties at this time had not started to apply solidarity to refer to the relationship with the poor peoples of the world. Nor did they did use this concept to describe the relationship between the peoples of Europe, as the DC frequently came to do in the following years.

The new constitution approved in 1946 declared that achieving solidarity should be an absolute obligation for the new republic. The same paragraph (§2) referred to the individual and 'the social relations in which the personality is developed'. This is a formulation originating from Catholic social teaching and indicated that the concept of solidarity applied was closer to the Christian democratic than to the socialist or communist version. This is supported by the fact that at this time De Gasperi had integrated the term *solidarity* firmly in his language, whereas his communist opponent Togliatti referred only sporadically to *solidarity* (see Chapter 8).[6]

Although De Gasperi became recognised more as a pragmatist than as an ideologue and theorist, his congress speeches clearly reflect that he was more preoccupied with ideas and values than his successors. The speeches of succeeding Christian democratic leaders such as Amintore Fanfani, Aldo Moro and Mariano Rumohr do not reflect social Catholicism as coherently. Recurrent themes in their speeches are freedom, social justice and peace, but their references to solidarity were only brief, and they utilised the concept more occasionally and in a less integrated manner than De Gasperi (DC 1976b). The continuity in terms of freedom and *social justice* reflects two basic characteristics of what came to be DC strategy in the decades to come. The strong insistence on *freedom* expressed a firm and honest rejection of fascism, communism and totalitarianism in general. On the other hand, it simultaneously served as a convenient weapon against the PCI and was part of the party's anti-communist stance. However, this lack of continuity in terms of coherent exposition of ideology, basic values and the concept of solidarity was mirrored in succeeding election programmes as well.

The Vatican's strong anti-communism had been a key factor in the impressive victory of the DC in 1948 and initiated a long period of renewed Catholic influence in Italian politics and culture. At the same time, it had complicated the role of the DC as an independent political party, as the Vatican wanted to see the DC as its long arm in politics (Riccardi 2003). Conflicts with the Vatican contributed to the fall of De Gasperi, and in the early 1950s De Gasperi's successor, Amintore Fanfani, wanted the DC to be no longer 'the servant but the leader of the [Italian] Catholic world' (Lönne 1996; White 2003).

---

[6] De Gasperi and the DC threw communists and socialists out of the coalition government in 1947. The national election the next year took place in a heated political atmosphere with anti-communism as a DC weapon. In an appeal to the nation, the DC said that the voters now could save or destroy freedom. The choice was between 'an inhuman totalitarianism' on the one hand and a 'human conception of political life, in which citizens, associations, and parties collaborate in free competition in pursuit of the common good'. The party emphasised social justice and praised itself for having secured for Italy peaceful collaboration and for having 'secured the Italian working classes the advantages of international economic solidarity' – referring to the Marshall aid (DC 1969 (1948)).

Although the DC was by far the largest political party, it neverthe-less needed allies to secure a stable majority in Parliament. As we have seen in Chapter 4, the Socialist Party, PSI, was in a process of reori-enting itself away from the alliance with the PCI. An alliance between the DC and the PSI was still not possible because of the position of the Catholic Church, but this road was opened after the death of Pius XII in 1958.

The new pope, John XXIII, was determined to disengage the Church from strong involvement in Italian politics, and the DC interpreted his encyclical *Pacem in Terris* as an opening for a governmental alliance with parties on the left. The Second Vatican Council (1960–66) brought about a further dissolution of the strong ties between the Catholic Church and the DC. The emphasis on freedom and individual conscience in the discussions and documents of the Second Vatican stimulated more pluralism.

In 1962 the first centre–left coalition was established between DC, the social democratic party and the republicans (Ginsborg 1989). The DC programme of 1963 explicitly declared for the first time that the party 'moved within the area of the Christian conception of man and the world and the social doctrine of the Church'. Freedom, justice and solidarity were again emphasised as main values. The 'principles of solidarity of the social doctrine (of the Church)' that should protect against the risks that create imbalance between needs and individual income were also added (DC 1963).

The great structural transformation of the Italian economy and society in the 1950s and 1960s brought millions of people from the south to the north and from the rural areas to the cities. Population growth and increased wealth meant secularisation, consumerism and reduced adher-ence to the activities of the Church. The political unrest and the student revolt during the last part of the 1960s radicalised many Catholics, par-ticularly the youth. All this reduced the role of religion in Italian politics.

The effects of the student revolt were a fundamental change in parts of Italian culture. The secularisation that had followed the period of eco-nomic growth and internal migration to the cities and the north was further reinforced. The emancipation of women and sexual liberation contributed to new gender roles as well as to increased individualism. The defeat of the Church and the DC in the referendums on divorce in 1974 demonstrated that many Catholics did not now pay much attention to the messages of the Church and the DC.

The election programme in 1976 noted that individualism had increased and resulted in a certain degree of hedonism. The party denounced 'anarchic individualism' and asserted values based on the economic, cultural and spiritual needs of people and a freedom that only can be realised in a 'correct and articulate social organisation' (DC 1976a). However, in spite of such worries, the emphasis on solidarity was reduced in party programmes in the 1970s and 1980s.

The years 1976 to 1979 were the years of the government of 'national solidarity' – the DC governed with passive support from the PCI. The 1976 programme reflected this concept, but did not elaborate on the idea of solidarity. Echoing corruption scandals, the programme also emphasised that the DC had always demanded that politics and administration should be founded on strict moral values and that public services should be inspired by firm principles of moral honesty in a spirit of service and dedication to the country. The new election three years later did not add much that was new in terms of values and principles (DC 1979).

The programmes of the 1980s reflected the ideological climate of the period. The programme of 1983 was preoccupied with the central position of man and his freedom, and referred to the Christian and interclass character of the party. The paragraphs on morals did not refer to solidarity, but only to the social character of man (DC 1983). Nor did the 1987 programme say much about values, but again emphasised freedom and justice. However, it expressed a growing concern with corruption and the wide practice of *lottizzazione* – the sharing of positions in public and semi-public institutions by the parties. The private should be more private, and the public more public. Society should not be based on *lottizzazione*, but on honour, responsibility and solidarity. A culture of solidarity was necessary, the programme declared (DC 1987).

The end of Democrazia Cristiania

The programmes of the DC had during the 1980s only cautiously reflected the increasing problems of clientelism and corruption. After 1989, communism could no longer be described as a dangerous threat to democracy and religion, and the electoral basis of the DC eroded. Although the corruption scandals primarily destroyed Craxi and the PSI, a general apprehension arose that the leadership of the DC was involved as well (Giovagnoli 1996). The election programme in 1992 was partially influenced by the special situation that corruption scandals had created and indicated that the DC had no ability or will to clean up. Other formulations about values and ideology were also few and brief. In terms of solidarity, the programme did not elaborate on the concept or bring anything new.

The political corruption scandals brought an end to the DC and the old Christian democratic political elite. The DC had finally lost its political and moral credibility. The parliamentary election in 1992 meant a setback of 3 per cent, whereas the *Lega*, the populist anti-Rome group of the north, achieved more than 9 per cent. At the local elections the following year, the DC ended with 20 per cent, losing almost half of its vote, and was split into five small groups in conflict with one another. Later the same year, the DC was dissolved.

Catholic social teaching had influenced all DC leaders. They had administered the country for half a century and used appeals for solidarity to mediate between different classes, between Catholics and lay groups, and between the south and the north. They had led Italy into the European Community according to their idea of solidarity. The increasing individualism of the 1980s reduced the authority of Catholic social teaching. DC leaders no longer had the authority to refer to traditional Catholic values, and party programmes had ceased to mirror the doctrines in a coherent way, except for emphasising the role of voluntary organisations more strongly.

Peculiarities of DC solidarity

Some have argued that the social doctrine of the Vatican did not influence DC programmes in a distinct manner, except that emphasis on family values and strong anti-communism came to be a common platform for the papacy and the DC (Pollard 1996). As shown here, this is certainly not the case in terms of programme language and ideology. The social teachings of the Catholic Church and the ideology in DC programmes share many themes and values; an emphasis on the human person, freedom and social justice, the front against egoist individualism and collectivism, solidarity as integration across class boundaries, the continuous emphasis on private property and business etc. Thus, many key themes in papal teaching have been reflected in DC programmes, particularly in the first period after World War II. In terms of solidarity we have seen here that although papal teaching had emphasised the value of social integration before the DC was established, the DC introduced *solidarity* in programme language earlier than was the case in papal social teaching.

The basic values in DC programmes throughout its history have been freedom, justice and peace. Solidarity has been found in most programmes as well, but not as frequently and well integrated as freedom and justice. The DC idea of solidarity has consistently been the Catholic interclass concept that expresses concern with social integration, as it has been in the German CDU. For both parties this concept has served to bridge the gap between the different classes and social categories to which they appealed. However, we may note a difference between DC discourse on solidarity and that of the German CDU: the CDU has given solidarity a more prominent place in programme language than the DC. From 1975 until today CDU has seen solidarity as a basic value, together with freedom and justice, later with *subsidiarity* as well, whereas DC discourse on values in the programmes has been more fragmented, brief and shallow. Surprisingly, CDU programme language reflects the social teaching of the Vatican more strongly than DC programmes did – or, as has been emphasised above, papal teaching largely reflects the values developed in German Catholicism.

DC programmes seem to reflect another trend in terms of ideology, language and values than that of the German CDU. Early post-war programmes mirrored more completely and coherently Catholic social teaching than did later programmes. In the two last decades of its existence DC programmes represented continuity in terms of values such as freedom and social justice, but not in respect of solidarity. Whereas the ideology in CDU programmes was initially fragmented, but developed into a coherent whole in the 1970s, the DC developed in the opposite direction. The early programmes coherently reflected the ideology and language of Catholic social teaching, but this was gradually dissolved as the DC approached moral bankruptcy and organisational dissolution.

This is certainly a paradox. We might have expected that the closer relationship of the DC and the Church, and the greater influence of the Vatican in Italian politics would have produced the opposite result. There are a number of possible explanations for this. First, this situation may reflect the general demoralisation of the DC, its clientelism and the political corruption that pervaded many levels of the party. This might have made it more awkward to write and talk about morality, solidarity and community. Second, the strong factionalism may have prevented coherence in programme ideology. Third, German thoroughness may have made CDU programmes more elaborate and consistent.

To emphasise the existence of ideological values in DC programmes does not mean denying the pragmatism of DC politics. Many factors contributed to this pragmatism – the need for compromise between the many factions in the party, the need to compromise with other parties and the increasing clientelism and corruption. In the DC, the ideas of Catholic social ethics found in papal encyclicals were increasingly relegated to parliamentary and conference language. In none of the parties studied here has the distance between values and political practice been greater than between the DC language on the one hand and the practice of clientelism and corruption on the other.

Political Catholicism after the DC

After the dissolution of the DC several political groups claimed to represent the true Christian democratic tradition. The largest and most important was the PPI, who took the name of the old party of Don Sturzo. Two other groups, the CCD and the CDU,[7] were later established to challenge the PPI. In 2002, these two small parties united and established the UDC (The Union of Christian Democrats and Centre Democrats).

In their programmes the PPI, CCD and CDU and the new UDC all claimed to represent the Christian democratic tradition from Don Sturzo and to be based on Catholic values such as the primacy of the person, the right to life, scepticism towards modern biotechnology, and the centrality of the family and family life. All mention solidarity briefly in their programmes, although without further elaboration. However, there are some nuances in the contexts in which the concept of solidarity is applied. The PPI emphasised solidarity as a value associated with sustainable growth, subsidiarity, equal representation of men and women, freedom and justice, and international relations. Before the election in 1994, it joined the Centre-Left Olive Alliance. The UDC maintained that all ideologies that sought to let politics absorb ethics failed, but that this does not apply to Christian democracy and social Catholicism. It declares its ambition to create a synthesis of Christian social teaching and liberal-democratic ideology. The principle of subsidiarity should help reconcile the strong demands for (individual) freedom with the Christian democratic tradition of solidarity. It dissociates itself from 'exaggerated Liberalism' and argues for solidarity with vulnerable social groups and the most underprivileged part of the country – southern Italy – but places itself in the centre-right coalition – Casa delle Libertá (UDC, 2003).

However, these small Christian democratic parties did not succeed in filling the political vacuum after the DC. Silvio Berlusconi used his enormous financial resources and business organisation to establish *Forza Italia*, which was the great winner at the national election in 1994 when it achieved more than 20 per cent of the vote and broke definitively the long Christian democratic hegemony in Italian politics. The self-declared heirs of Christian democracy, the PPI and the CCD/CDU achieved respectively 6.8 and 5.8 per cent of the vote.

In the first years of the new century, the fate of political Catholicism in Italy seems to be uncertain. In the future, Christian democratic ideology will probably not be expressed through a single political party. The DC was always a political coalition of orthodox, moderate and left-wing social

---

[7] *Partito Popolare Italiano, Centro Christiano Democratico* and *Christiani Democratici Uniti.*

Catholicism. The general secularisation of society has reduced the role of religion in politics, and what is left of these currents has been channelled into different political parties. The PPI has decided to merge with other centre-left parties and groups in a new party – *Margherita* – under the leadership of Francesco Rutelli who was the Olive Alliance's candidate for prime minister at the election in 2001. The UDC is a junior partner in the alliance *Casa delle Libertá* dominated by Berlusconi's party *Forza Italia*. Thus, today, no strong political party channels the influence of Catholic social teaching and the Catholic idea of solidarity.

As Berlusconi's *Forza Italia* is the dominant partner in this alliance, we must pay special attention to this party. According to the statutes, *Forza Italia* defines itself as a political movement and an association of citizens who feel they belong to 'the traditions of liberal democracy, liberal Catholicism, lay traditions, and the tradition of European reformism'. 'It is', the programme says, 'to be inspired by universal values of freedom, justice, and solidarity in defence of the person.' The party wants 'a modern market economy and a correct application of the principle of subsidiarity' (FI, 1997). Thus, the ambition of *Forza Italia* is not to be the successor to the DC, but to incorporate DC supporters and traditions in a wider political organisation. Typical Catholic catchwords such as solidarity, subsidiarity and justice are included. The *Forza Italia* combines an ambition to introduce more market mechanisms, privatise public property, make the labour market more flexible and decrease taxes – all typical liberalist, right-wing politics – with a conservative value-based policy in terms of culture and families, although the last issue has been somewhat controversial in the party. Thus, *Forza Italia* has no clear ideological identity – it is neither Christian democratic nor clearly liberalist.[8]

The election programme of the alliance in which *Forza Italia* is the dominant party – *Casa delle Libertá* – does not pay any attention to solidarity. Priority is given to tax reduction, deregulation, liberalisation and privatisation. The chapter on social policy stresses the principle of subsidiarity, but subsidiarity is not balanced against solidarity as has been common in Catholic social policy. The main proposals are about reduction of taxes for the family, support to the third sector, the need to encourage the elderly to work longer, and a change in the pension system (CdL 2001). Thus, the conclusion must be that the centre-right alliance *Casa delle Libertá* has not integrated the tradition of social Catholicism in its political ideology and language. It has included only those aspects of Catholic social thinking that have been easy to combine with the liberalism of *Forza Italia*,

---

[8] For a discussion about Berlusconi and his politics in recent years, see Ginsborg (2003).

such as the concept of subsidiarity, the importance of the family and the third sector. These are issues and values that liberal conservatism has no difficulty in integrating with traditional right-wing policies like tax reduction, privatisation and a more flexible labour market. This development is particularly interesting, as the social democratic party – *Democratici di Sinistra* – with its historical roots in the Marxist–Leninist tradition now presents itself with concepts that in some ways are closer to the tradition of social Catholicism. The DS also refers to 'social Christianity' and subsidarity.

The Italian paradox in terms of Christian democratic solidarity is that the strong political institutionalisation of the concept through a dominant political party has ended. On the other hand, the language of this ideology is still alive. We find different versions of this in small Christian democratic parties, and in the larger social democratic DS that was once the strong rival of Christian democracy, but that today has mixed it with social democratic solidarity, as we shall see in Chapter 8.

Norway: Christian politics from pietism to Christian democracy

In Scandinavia, Lutheranism has been the dominating religion since the Reformation in the sixteenth century. In 1900, 99 per cent were Protestants and, in 1995, 87 per cent of the population still regarded themselves as Protestants in Denmark, Sweden and Norway (Lane and Ersson 1999).

A Christian democratic party of some size and influence developed only in Norway. Whereas Christian parties in Denmark and Sweden failed to achieve even 3 per cent at the parliamentary elections until the end of the 1980s, the Norwegian *Kristelig Folkeparti* (Christian People's Party), *KrF*, has achieved between 8 per cent and 14 per cent of the vote at most parliamentary elections. This has made the KrF a member of coalition governments in several periods during the last forty years: even with the prime minister on three different occasions. However, compared to the German CDU and the Italian DC, the KrF represents a special case as it has had to coexist with a larger conservative party that was firmly established in Norwegian politics when the KrF was founded, and it was this party that represented the alliance between business and large segments of the middle class.

Chapter 3 has described the complex relationship between Protestant belief and politics. Protestantism was born out of a reaction to Catholic entanglement in worldly affairs. Lutherans were convinced that Christians should return to the Church and leave the affairs of this world to the government and the state. In Norway, however, Luther's teaching about the two kingdoms was never important. Under absolutism the king emphasised that he was the master of both spheres, and the king was even called the superior bishop – *summus episcopus*.

Contrary to Catholics and popes, the Protestants in Norway did not regard the state as an institution hostile to the claims of the Church. Einar Molland, an important Norwegian theologian of the last century, described mainstream Protestant theology in Norway in this way: both the gospel and the law derive from God and are the word of God. The Lutheran state should be a Christian state with responsibility for both the material and spiritual welfare of its subjects. On the other hand, the Church should not be preoccupied with the solution of the problems of human society, but should concentrate on preaching consolation and forgiveness and on preparing believers for eternal life (Madeley 1982).

However, this conception of the relationship between religion and politics was undermined from below. In the nineteenth century, the upper echelons of the clergy of the state Church were socially and politically associated with the conservative establishment, while grassroots pietism had a stronghold in the south and west. Farmers, fishermen, merchants and artisans constituted the class basis of pietism. They organised voluntary organisations, held their own sermons and developed gradually as a popular opposition of the periphery against the bourgeoisie, the state Church clergy and the conservative political establishment in the capital and the few large cities. They integrated their religious pietism with teetotalism and the struggle for a more pure and traditional Norwegian language than that influenced by Danish in the capital. Thus, a counterculture was formed, and within the Church a large network of voluntary organisations was seen as an alternative to the official Church.

The birth of a Christian party

This popular movement gradually became involved in politics. In the first part of the nineteenth century, Hans Nielsen Hauge and his supporters presented an egalitarian message with a clear ideological front against priests and state civil servants, businessmen and farmers. Money should be earned for the Lord and to create employment and abolish poverty. Hauge's egalitarian ideals influenced many Christians and were probably an important factor in the development of egalitarian ideology in Norway (Furre 1995; Gilje 1995). The religious popular movement sided with the democratic left against the conservatives in the constitutional struggle over the introduction of a parliamentary system in the last part of the century, and supported the liberal left party – *Venstre*. This party was soon split because of cultural conflicts between pietists and liberals – mainly confirming the geographical cleavage between the periphery in the south and west on the one hand, and the cities on the other. In an atmosphere of cultural conflict and threats of secularisation in the 1930s, a group of Christians in the west established a Christian people's party in 1933 – the *KrF*. The party gained two seats in the Parliament in 1936 (Bjørklund 1983).

The religious lay movement in western Norway had now acquired an organised political expression, and the barrier between Protestantism and political engagement in the mundane world had definitely been removed. Those who founded the new party were probably not very well informed about the Lutheran teaching of the two kingdoms. The ambition to promote Christian belief by political means indicates that they were more influenced by reformed theology than by orthodox Lutheran theology (Skipevåg 1990). However, the Lutheran idea of the two kingdoms made many Christians sceptical about the establishment of a Christian party, and contrary to what had happened in Germany and Italy, the KrF never succeeded in achieving major support among Christians and acquiring status as a political representative of the Church. Lay Christians, the clergy and even bishops continued to disperse their votes over a range of parties.

Social democratic theorists and programmes at this time had made the concept and the term *solidarity* a theme. Beginning in the late 1930s, the Norwegian labour party, the DNA, launched social reforms and, after the war, the outlines of a welfare state could be discerned. The influential bishop, Eivind Berggrav, who played an important role in the World Federation of Lutherans as well, regarded this institutionalisation of solidarity with strong scepticism and argued that the role and power of government should be restricted. The family, the school and the Church should be more active in the spheres of care and upbringing. The state should support these institutions, but not govern them (Tønnesen 2000). This represented a parallel to the Catholic idea of subsidiarity and a clear front against the social democratic emphasis on public responsibility for solidaristic welfare.

The first KrF platform reflected Berggrav's views in this respect. It declared that the present situation in society made autonomous Christian activity in politics necessary. The main cause of the crisis of the time was spiritual, and it did not suffice to struggle against de-Christianisation, it was also necessary to promote a clear Christian *Weltanschauung* (a view of the world) as a foundation for growth in society. The KrF's ideal should be neither unlimited competition nor organisation by coercion. Private initiative should be protected in so far as it did not conflict with the general interest. Government should have the right to interfere and smooth out conflicts that could be harmful to society and social life. The party should struggle for social justice on a Christian basis. On the one hand, solidarity was necessary because private initiative was not sufficient, and, on the other hand, solidarity should be expressed through voluntary support, the programme proclaimed (KrF 1936). Thus, these ideas were close to ideas in Catholic social teaching and the predecessors of Christian democratic parties such as the German *Zentrum* and the Italian PPI. Contrary to Liberalism, solidarity was included, and contrary to social democratic solidarity, voluntary activities were preferred to public interventions and institutions.

With the 1936 platform, the KrF had formulated key themes that were to come to define its position in Norwegian politics. As with the Zentrum and the PPI, it defined its position by denouncing both liberalism and socialism, and social democracy. Whereas markets and competition were accepted in principle, the government should interfere if the market resulted in strong social conflicts and unjust distribution of wealth and welfare. The state should be entrusted with the authority and power to harmonise and integrate. Social solidarity should be expressed primarily by voluntary activity.

The breakthrough

During World War II, the state Church demonstrated firm resistance to fascism and the German occupation. In 1942 a large number of priests formulated an appeal, *The Foundation of the Church*, in which they denounced the totalitarian Nazi concept of the state, as German Protestants had done in the Barmen declaration in 1934 (see Chapter 3). This meant a rejection of a strict separation between the two regimes of God and of this world, and a refusal of an obligation to unconditional obedience to the authorities of this world.

After the war, the KrF enjoyed a spotless national reputation, and the election in 1945 made KrF a national party with 8 per cent of the voters. Now the KrF had become a real cross-class party supported by a broad network of Christian organisations that considered the party to be the spokesman for their values and ideology.

During the 1950s and 1960s recurring themes in programmes were community of the people, harmonising conflicts, concepts such as 'the whole people', and the need to unite forces in constructive effort. The social democratic party was in what seemed to be an enduring government position and was not interested in collaboration with other parties. Thus, the KrF chose to ally with the Conservative Party and the Farmer's Party, although it was closer to social democracy in terms of economic and social policy. In 1963 it took part in a centre-right coalition government for a brief period. Later, the KrF has taken part in several centre or centre-right coalition governments. The prime minister was recruited from the party in the periods 1972–73, 1997–2000 and again from 2001.

Christian concern about the Third World

Although the idea of, and the term *solidarity*, had been briefly mentioned in the 1936 programme, it did not appear again in the party programme until more than forty years later. When it was found again in 1977, it was not associated with the idea of social integration and cross-class solidarity, as was the case in Catholic social teaching, but with concern about the Third World.

Foreign policy had never been an important theme in the KrF, but, after the war, the party became concerned about hunger and misery in the Third World (Botnen 1983). Unlike other political parties in Norway, KrF members had personal experience as missionaries in Africa and China. From 1961 concern about the poor world emerged as a theme in programmes, and assistance to developing nations became a recurrent theme. It is contrary to the Christian commandment to love one's neighbour to accept increasing differences between rich and poor nations, the KrF argued (KrF 1965). Assistance should be channelled through UN and Christian missionary organisations. However, this concern about the poor peoples of the Third World was not formulated as a question of solidarity during the next couple of decades.

It is conspicuous how KrF programmes in this period avoid all other burning issues associated with the Third Word. Colonial wars in Asia, France's war in Algeria, the struggle for independence in Africa and the war in Vietnam – none of these issues are mentioned in the programmes. A clear attitude to a Third World conflict – the apartheid system in South Africa – is first found in the 1985 programme. Since then, the party has been continuously preoccupied with Africa and particularly South Africa in party programmes.

The concept of solidarity was not applied again in a programme until some years after the student revolt in 1968. The World Council of Churches' conference in Uppsala in 1968 had now radicalised many theologians and young Christians. A new generation of young Christians, headed by Kjell Magne Bondevik, had achieved influence in the party.[9] Bondevik was strongly concerned with Third World issues

---

[9] Bondevik was elected deputy chairman of the KrF youth organisation in 1968, and later became parliamentary secretary and secretary to the prime minister in 1972. He was elected deputy chairman of the party in 1975. He was later to be chairman for a long period (1983–95) and prime minister (1997–2000).

and argued for support for national liberation movements (Rimehaug 1997). In the campaign against Norwegian membership of the European Union in 1972, the party was allied with left-wing trade unionists and socialists. When the concept of solidarity was finally introduced into the programme in 1977 (KrF 1977), referring to the administration of scarce resources, this was influenced by the personal contributions of Bondevik and his generation. Besides, the campaign against the EU had radicalised the general political climate in the party, and the KrF had to compete with a new left-wing party in recruiting young Christians. All this was conducive to making solidarity an acceptable part of party language.

'Man in society'

As a student of theology Bondevik had been influenced by the theologian Tor Aukrust who had published an extensive study of social ethics, *Man in Society*, in 1965 (Rimehaug 1997). Aukrust defined social ethics as 'ethics about social institutions and how human beings relate to these as persons and community'and argued that the Ten Commandments were not sufficient to guide Christian ethical behaviour in modern society (Aukrust 1965). They might be guiding criteria, but had to be supplemented by more positive criteria, such as *freedom, equality, justice* and *love*. *Freedom* could not be reserved for man's inner being, but should embrace the total of a human being, and freedom is an illusion in a society where citizens are treated as the property of the state or dominated by an overpowering apparatus of production. Thus, the Christian idea of freedom makes claims on the institutions of society. On the other hand, freedom is restricted by obedience to God and love for fellow beings, Aukrust argued. *Equality* stems from the belief that all human beings have been created in the image of God. However, Luther had argued that equality before God did not mean that human beings should be equal in society. Aukrust was somewhat ambivalent on the concept of equality and argued that although men are equal before God, human beings are born different from one another. What is important is not abstract equality, but a spiritual unity of individual persons, and the fact that all human beings have a right to develop their inherent potential. For Aukrust, *justice* was identical to charity and a feeling of solidarity with another human being and means that one can identify with the distress and misery of others. Finally, justice is associated with love. All other criteria of Christian ethics are subordinate to the criteria of love. Freedom, equality and justice are right only to the extent that they express solidarity, responsibility and consideration for one's neighbour, he argued.

Aukrust's analysis and development of Protestant social ethics continued the revision of Lutheran teaching about the two kingdoms. Society
and the state were included in his discourse on freedom, equality, justice
and love and assigned responsibility for the realisation of those values.
Aukrust included the concept of solidarity as well, although he took this
concept for granted and did not discuss it as an ethical concept, as he did
with his other key concepts. We note, for instance, that charity and solidarity were mentioned in the same breath, without any discussion about
the important distinction between the two. However, what is important
is that Aukrust came to influence a new generation of Christians in the
KrF and to change the attitude of the social democratic party towards
religion (see Chapter 4 and (Slagstad 1998)).

The new KrF platform in 1979 described the ideological foundation
of the party more extensively. The interclass character was emphasised.
The party should cut across all traditional lines of conflict in recruitment and policy. Although not mentioning the term solidarity in this
context, the basis for Christian solidarity was spelled out. Man is created in the image of God and is the object of the love of God in Jesus
Christ. Thus, every individual has an infinite value. All human beings
irrespective of race, gender, age, culture and religion have the same
human worth. In a world of want and injustice Christians must acknowledge the global consequences of the basic value that all human beings
have equal worth. In paragraphs about international relations and about
welfare policy, *solidarity* was again made an important concept (KrF
1979).

The integration of solidarity in programme language

Since 1979 both the idea of and the term solidarity have definitely been
integrated in KrF programme language, together with freedom, equality and justice. Two years later, the programme adopted the concept of
Christian democratic values. It was not until the platform of 1991, however, that these concepts were woven together into a systematic whole
and a complete language of solidarity was presented. Now the platform
declared that the struggle for human worth is a struggle for all these
values – freedom, justice, equality and solidarity (KrF 1991).

The European association of Christian parties, the *European People's
Party* approved a new platform in 1992 where the core elements of
Christian democratic ideology and values were described. All these elements were included in the 1994 CDU programme. This is the case for
the KrF programme of 1996 as well. Here, a whole chapter described

what constitutes Christian democratic ideology: first, the *family* is central, not only as an expression of the interest of the individual, but also for the whole structure of society. Second, both *nearness* and *solidarity* are unconditional. Nearness implies that decisions should be made close to the person concerned. The ability of individuals and small communities to make decisions is emphasised as a core value of Christian democratic ideology. Although the term was not mentioned, this is the Catholic idea of subsidiarity. Nearness must be balanced against respect for the equal worth of all individuals of a community. Society is not a range of disconnected institutions with responsibility only for themselves. Institutions – being individuals, families, nations, have responsibility for one another. This is the principle of solidarity, the programme claimed (KrF 1996).

We may note two lines of development in the KrF concept of solidarity. First, when the concept emerged again in programmes in the late 1970s, the student revolt had revived and broadened the concept of solidarity, directing it towards the Third World on the one hand, and towards national social welfare on the other. As the concept was now integrated into programme language, the ground had been prepared by a continuous concern with the harmonising of social conflicts, justice and social integration.

Second, in the past two decades the further development of the concept of solidarity has been part of a broader process of 'Christian democratisation' of the party. Whereas KrF supporters generally have been profoundly sceptical towards Catholicism, the KrF has gradually adopted a programme language that is similar to Christian democratic parties on the Continent, particularly the German CDU. The concept *Christian democrat* was, as mentioned earlier, first applied in a KrF programme in 1981. In 1996, the party published the pamphlet *Christian Democratic Thought*, where all the elements of German Christian democratic ideology are included – freedom, the dignity and equal worth of human beings, responsibility, subsidiarity, the idea of the person and solidarity (Lunde 1996).

In the same year, the programme included all elements in Catholic social teaching and Christian democratic ideology. The present ideology in platforms and programmes is very similar to that of the German CDU, although the political practice of the KrF is to the left of CDU in most aspects. Like the CDU, KrF claims solidarity on the basis of human worth and all human beings being created in the image of God and having the same worth. Both parties accept the market, but emphasise individual responsibility and the family, solidarity and subsidiarity.

The idea of solidarity in the KrF and the DNA

What then, is the difference between the KrF's concept of solidarity and that of Norwegian social democracy, the DNA? Bondevik, who is a Protestant theologian and, in 2004, prime minister, has argued that it is the difference between love of one's neighbour and social democratic solidarity. Although there is a similarity between the two, love of one's neighbour is inclusive, whereas social democratic solidarity is based on working-class struggle for its material self-interests, he argued (Bondevik 2000). A comparison of recent programmes of the KrF and the DNA does not lend support to Bondevik's assertion. There is nothing in recent DNA programmes that indicates that social democratic solidarity is based on class struggle. Social democratic solidarity of today is based on the concept of equal human worth, as is Christian democratic solidarity (DNA 2000; KrF 2001). The Christian idea of equal human worth is founded on all human beings being created in the image of God, whereas the social democratic idea of equal worth is based on general humanist principles of tolerance – certainly also influenced by Christian ideology.

Both the KrF and the DNA share the idea that the market has to be balanced by solidarity, and that this solidarity must find an institutional expression through public responsibility for social welfare and assistance to Third World nations. Both concepts of solidarity are integrated in a complete political language with related key concepts such as freedom, justice and distribution. We saw above that in Germany the social democratic idea of justice is somewhat different from the Christian democratic viewpoint, as the second relates justice to both contribution and distribution. This difference is not found between Norwegian social democracy and Christian democracy. Although the DNA mentions the concept of justice more frequently in programmes, links it more clearly to *equal distribution* and adds the adjective *social* to justice more often than the KrF, *justice* is a key concept in Norwegian Christian democracy as well. Contrary to the German CDU, the KrF applies the concept of distribution numerous times in the present programme, emphasising the relationship between justice and distribution – between rich and poor nations, women and men and the generations. This is close to how *distribution* is applied in the latest DNA programme.

However, there are some differences between the two. Whereas the KrF is concerned with balancing solidarity, particularly institutionalised solidarity, against the principle of nearness or subsidiarity and the family, the DNA is troubled by the relationship between collective solidarity on the one hand, and individual freedom and the right of the individual to chose on the other. Such programmatic formulations indicate that in practical politics the KrF is more inclined to support voluntary organisations whereas the DNA has somewhat more confidence in public responsibility and institutions. Whereas the KrF emphasises *equal worth*, the DNA is more concerned with *equality*, indicating that the DNA is prepared to accept stronger public measures when it comes to distribution of resources and taxation. In some issues, the position in KrF programmes is somewhat to the left of the DNA as it is more committed to development cooperation with Third World countries, and emphasises more strongly that solidarity should mean responsibility for the environment and coming generations.

Conclusion: Christian democratic *vs.* social democratic solidarity

The Catholic and Christian democratic tradition presented here is but one of many rivals that have challenged the concept of solidarity in the labour movement tradition. However, Christian democracy has proved to be the most persistent of those challengers and has succeeded in developing an alternative ideology in which solidarity is interwoven with other ideological concepts into a coherent whole.

Papal Catholic social teaching gradually integrated the idea of solidarity during the 1960s. This idea was explicitly an interclass concept and emphasised social integration, as does the Durkheimian concept. Besides, it included a strong accent on the relationship with the Third World. Protestantism began to express the idea of solidarity at least from the later 1960s, with the World Council of Churches conference in Uppsala being an inspirational event in this respect. The new Protestant idea of solidarity was more exclusively about the relationship between the rich and the poor world. Thus, it did not have the Durkheimian accent on social integration that was so prominent in the Catholic idea.

We have seen above that Catholic or Catholic-dominated parties introduced the Catholic concept of solidarity at different points of time and to different degrees. The German Zentrum introduced the concept in a party programme in 1909. Pesch's *Christlicher Solidarismus* and the later works of the protagonist of German Catholic social theory, von Nell-Breuning, elevated solidarity to become a key concept in German Catholic social theory decades before papal teaching was ready to include it. However, after the war the German CDU did not reflect the key ideas of Catholic social teaching until 1971, and the approval of the platform of 1978 ended the process towards full integration of the values and concepts of Catholic social teaching. The difference between the ideas of solidarity in the Zentrum and the German *solidarismus* on the one hand,

and that of the CDU on the other is primarily that it was associated with corporatism in the Zentrum and part of a more consequent liberal democratic language in the CDU. In spite of the interconfessional character of the CDU, CDU programmes reflect completely modern Catholic social teaching and the significance of the concept of solidarity in this doctrine.

The Italian DC represents another line of development. Due to the influence of De Gasperi, early DC programmes came to mirror key characteristics of papal teaching more clearly than early CDU programmes. Already at the end of World War II, DC programmes emphasised social integration across party lines and introduced both the idea of and the term *solidarity*. However, from the late 1960s DC programmes became less ideologically coherent and the idea of solidarity became less pronounced – foreshadowing the moral and political dissolution in process.

For the Protestant KrF in Norway, the road to *solidarity* was somewhat more complicated. The new radicalised political atmosphere from the late 1960s and the appearance of a new generation of well-educated Christians contributed to bridge the gap between the concepts of charity and solidarity. Concern about the Third World and increased exchange of ideas within the EPP were the most important factors conducive to this. The result has been that the Protestant KrF today has also adopted all core elements of Catholic social teaching in its programmes.

Comparative aspects of Christian democratic solidarity

The analysis of the programmes of the three Christian democratic parties here has demonstrated that the concept of Christian democratic solidarity is not standardised to the same degree as the social democratic concept. CDU programmes reflect the Catholic concept of solidarity most completely, and the DC in the most fragmented and casual way. On the other hand, the Christian democratic concept exhibits more stability in some aspects. First, Christian democratic parties have exhibited more stability than social democracy in terms of what they have seen as the basis of solidarity. Their religion and the command to love one's neighbour, and equality before God, have been a stable foundation, although not always mentioned in programmes. Second, the emphasis on integration and collaboration across class lines has always made the Christian democratic concept inclusive. The explicit intention was not only to build a bridge between the middle strata and the working class, but also to encompass all classes.

To what extent have these parties broadened their idea of solidarity to include other aspects that generally are seen as problematic issues in modern society? Table 6.1 demonstrates the stage at which different issues were made a theme in terms of solidarity in party programmes. Again,

Table 6.1 *Different themes regarded as a question of solidarity in Christian democratic programmes*

		Third World	Welfare state	Gender emancipation	Relationship between generations	Nature, ecology	Ethnical minorities
Germany	CDU	1971	1971	1985	1981		
Italy	DC	1943/63	1979				
Norway	KrF	1979	2001			1977	1981

I must warn: this is not about when these themes were introduced, but when they were explicitly discussed as an aspect of solidarity. Naturally, there might be some element of chance here. Nevertheless, Table 6.1 indicates some interesting differences.

The DC was the first to argue that the relationship to the Third World should be seen as a question of solidarity. Although the concept of the Third World was not invented at that time, the *Idee ricostruttive* of 1943 argued for a reconstruction of the international order based on the right to independence for all nations and solidarity between all peoples. However, self-determination for 'coloured peoples' should only be a goal, and for the time being, colonies should be transferred to the international community under UN jurisdiction. In 1954, De Gasperi argued for solidarity with poor nations (De Gasperi 1956d (1954)), and in 1963 the DC argued that the relationship with the poor nations should be viewed as a question of solidarity. The CDU followed suit in 1971 and the KrF in 1979, even if the KrF had started as early as 1961 to argue for assistance to poor nations.

The welfare state was described as an aspect of solidarity by the CDU in the programme of 1971, by the DC in 1979 and the KrF in 2001. This does not mean that the CDU has been more engaged in public welfare policy than the KrF, although that might be said in relation to the DC. The failure to broaden the concept of solidarity in the DC programmes confirms the general lack of ideological consistence in the DC because of the ideological decay of the party after De Gasperi, and reflects also the fact that the DC never succeeded in developing a comprehensive system of social protection to the degree that the CDU did.

Finally, we should direct attention to the fact that Christian democratic parties more frequently included the European dimension as a question of solidarity than did social democratic parties. The Pope saw nationalism and war between European nations as a defeat of the universal ambition of the Church. After World War II, Christian democratic parties and leaders were pioneers in developing European collaboration

Table 6.2 *The Christian democratic concept of solidarity*

Foundation	Objective	Inclusiveness	Collective orientation
Man created in the image of God Ethics inspired by Christian understanding of man Human dignity Interdependence Individual responsibility to participate and contribute to God's work	Social integration Social harmony Justice	Broad Cross-class	Weaker: the idea of the person and the idea of subsidiarity balance the collective aspects of solidarity

and the establishment of the European Community. Their idea of European unity and solidarity was based on three fundamental values – the Christian religion, peace and democracy. These values were combined with the perceived threat of communism.

The present Christian democratic concept of solidarity has been summarised in Table 6.2 on the basis of the present basic programmes of the CDU, the KrF and the EPP. The foundation of solidarity is formulated somewhat differently in party programmes and the EPP *Basic Programme* of 1992, particularly in terms of how strongly the religious aspect is emphasised. This aspect is more strongly emphasised in the programmes of the CDU and the KrF than in the EPP *Basic Programme*. This is probably due to the fact that the EPP comprises parties with different emphases on their Christian foundation. Even so, we may say that Christian democratic solidarity is founded on several elements that are woven together: men and women are created in the image of God, and ethics inspired by the Christian understanding of man imply giving value to the dignity of people. Solidarity with the poor and weak will make it possible for every human being to live in dignity. Interdependence between all human beings gives every individual a duty to participate in society and work for the common good, and to realise God's will. The goal of solidarity is a society with social integration and social harmony between individuals and groups. This is also a society where justice prevails. Finally, the degree of collective orientation is weaker than in the social democratic concept. It is modified by the emphasis on both the person and on subsidiarity.

The ineliminable core in the Christian democratic concept of solidarity is first and foremost found in the formulation regarding the foundation of solidarity: the idea that all human beings are created in the image of God, and from that it follows that all human beings have the same worth and dignity. As we have seen, this is contrary to the social democratic idea, which may be founded on different aspects: empathy, compassion, human rights and still sometimes even self-interest. However, the implications of this difference are not easy to discern. Also, the Christian democratic concept has as components of an ineliminable core a sympathetic attitude towards the poor and oppressed, and a positive attitude to organise social welfare collectively, and redistribute resources. These issues may be ranked somewhat differently in the political practice of Christian democratic and social democratic parties, and it is possible that the illocutionary force of statements about them are different, but it is not easy to detect this in the programmes. In this regard, the differences within the parties in each of the two political families are as large as the differences between the two political families.

Differences and convergence

The development of the concept of solidarity in the Christian democratic programmes is characterised by two distinguishing aspects – the reflection of papal teaching and the convergence of Christian democratic programmes. First, the two Catholic parties analysed here institutionalised and integrated the concept of solidarity earlier than the Protestant KrF. How could these differences between different national versions of Christian democratic solidarity be explained? We saw in the previous chapter that a mixture of structural, political and ideological variables could explain the early predominance of social democratic solidarity. These were the degree of homogeneity of the class structure, electoral support, and closeness to power and ideological tradition. Because the concept of solidarity was established as institutionalised ideology in both German and Italian Christian democracy before the Norwegian KrF, these variables must be discussed in another context. The strong and early foundation of solidarity in German Christian democracy obviously cannot be explained by homogeneity, as both the Italian PPI, the Zentrum and the CDU existed in heterogeneous societies. In Germany, religious cleavages made the class structure fragmented and heterogeneous. The Catholic Zentrum represented a confessional minority and tried to appeal to a heterogeneous electorate of farmers, the middle class and workers. The same was the case for Italian Christian democracy. The Norwegian KrF, however, could not aim to unite these classes, as social democracy had already succeeded in uniting workers and large segments of the rural population. Thus, the KrF's potential electorate was probably less heterogeneous than the potential electorate of both the German and Italian parties. Because a conservative party already existed in Norway when the KrF was established, the challenge for the KrF was not to mediate between business and the middle classes as was the case in Germany and Italy. Also, although the voters of the KrF constituted a socially hetero-geneous group, the need for an interclass concept of solidarity was not as strong in the two other countries. In Germany and Italy, the heterogene-ity of the class structure made necessary an ideology that could unite and mediate between middle-class Catholics and Catholics in the working class. The concept of solidarity became part of this ideology.

This was also the case for both the German and the Italian parties after World War II when modern Christian democracy was born. Besides, both parties were now in government and in this position an integrating ideology was needed even more because they found themselves responsi-ble for national and social integration. At the ideological level a Catholic ideology of social integration had influenced party leaders and ideologists and was the most credible alternative to both socialist and liberal ideology. The weaker integration of solidaristic ideology in DC party programmes than in the CDU is best explained by the less integrated character and the increasing and gradual moral corruption of the DC. The Protestant character of the KrF is the variable that best explains the late establish-ment of the concept of solidarity in KrF programmes. Besides, we could speculate on whether the need to develop a concept of class mediation was felt less urgently because the probability of attracting voters from the industrial working class was not strong.

The second characteristic of the development described here is the increasing convergence of Christian democratic programmes across confessional lines. This convergence demonstrates that the difference between Catholic and Protestant parties' conceptions of the relationship between religion and politics has been erased. Catholic social teaching and vocabulary has been completely integrated in the Protestant party included in this analysis.

The common adherence to the European People's Party has probably contributed to this increasing similarity in programme ideology. At the congress in Athens in 1992, the EPP approved a new platform that spelled out Christian democratic values. Here we find core values in Catholic social teaching – personalism, freedom and responsibility, equality, jus-tice, subsidiarity and solidarity (EPP 1992). These values are said to be interdependent, equally important and universally applicable. Freedom, the programme declares, is the basis for justice and solidarity, which are indissolubly linked to each other.

7 The languages of modern social democratic and Christian democratic solidarity

The analysis so far has demonstrated that the two most important concepts of solidarity in politics in Europe exhibit both similarities and differences. Although the main tendency has been for the two concepts to become increasingly similar, they have not converged completely. The four aspects of solidarity (its basis, goal, inclusiveness and collective orientation) are configured in different ways in the two concepts. These configurations vary between different times and occasions, and this make them both flexible and applicable in party programmes and political debates. Moreover, the flexibility and ambiguity is enhanced because the two different concepts are located in two different conceptual contexts or political languages. These languages are constituted by the existence of other key concepts, many of which are as flexible and ambiguous as the concept of solidarity. As a consequence, the meaning of solidarity changes not only according to how the different aspects of solidarity are combined, but also through the different meanings of these other key concepts and how these are related to the different meanings of the concept of solidarity. Consequently, it is necessary to identify the other key concepts in the social democratic and Christian democratic language and to discuss how these are related to solidarity. This is the task in this chapter. I shall conclude with a discussion about the role and the advantages of the modern language and concept of solidarity for social democratic and Christian democratic parties.

The modern social democratic and Christian democratic languages

We have in previous chapters seen that the ineliminable core of the concept of social democratic solidarity is loosely defined and allows for great flexibility in terms of its practical political implications. Michael Freeden has noted that political ideologies are characterised by a structure, or morphology, that contains core, adjacent and peripheral concepts (Freeden 1996), and the way these concepts are bound together constitutes the language through which the ideology is expressed. Core, or as preferred here, *basic* concepts may move from the core to the periphery and have a less prominent role in the ideology of a party. I have preferred in this book to narrow the perspective and have consequently reserved the term *language* for how the limited number of basic political concepts are associated and structured in a stable way in party programmes and have not discussed systematically adjacent and peripheral concepts. The task now is to throw light on adjacent concepts.

The modern ideological language found in the programmes of social democratic parties at the transition to the twenty-first century is characterised by the relationship between a few of what are said to be *basic* values or concepts.[1] These are most often *freedom, equality, justice* and *solidarity*. With the possible exception of *equality*, these concepts are not specific for social democracy: most are also to be found in Christian democratic programmes as well. All these concepts are ambiguous, and it is how they are interpreted and the way they are related to the other concepts that constitutes the ideology and language of modern social democracy.

First, we note again that the British Labour Party stands out. In recent Labour programmes, neither a concept of solidarity nor any other values are declared to be basic. *Equality* is mentioned occasionally and in the liberal meaning of *equal opportunities*. The word *justice* is found a few times, but most often when referring to the legal system.

All the other parties have adopted a common language with the key concepts mentioned above. *Freedom*, the SPD argues, is not only the freedom of the individual to realise him- or herself, but requires also that the individual is liberated from dependency, want and fear and given the opportunity to participate in society and politics. The DNA argues that freedom presupposes a *just* distribution of resources and cannot exist if economic and social differences are great. Solidarity implies the will to distribute resources to guarantee freedom and security, the DNA programme states. Therefore, the social democratic concept of solidarity is linked to a concept of freedom that is somewhat different from a traditional liberal concept of freedom. It not only refers to individual political rights, but directs attention to the material basis for freedom as well.

---

[1] Table 7.1 is based on recent programmes and statutes of the parties included – the SPD platform of 1998; PS statutes of 2000; the Labour Party programme of 2001; the PSOE programme of 2000; the SAP programme of 2001; the DNA programme of 2000; and the platform of the Danish Social Democratic Party of 1992. The PSOE election programme does not explicitly state that these are *basic* values or concepts, but the programme emphasises them sufficiently to conclude that the party joins the mainstream of European social democracy in this respect.

Table 7.1 *Basic concepts in the political language of modern social democracy and Christian democracy*

	Freedom	Justice	Equality	Solidarity	Subsidiarity	The person	Responsibility	Other basic values
Social democracy:								
SPD (Germany)	x	x		x				
PS (France)	x		x	x			x	Human rights Human dignity
(Labour Party) UK								
PSOE (Spain)	x	x	x	x				
DS (Italy)	x	x	x	x	x			Federalism
SAP (Sweden)	x		x	x				
DNA (Norway)	x		x	x				
Socialdemo- kratiet (Denmark)	x		x	x				
Christian democracy:								
CDU (Germany)	x	x		x	x	(x)	(x)	
KrF (Norway)		x		x	x	x	x	
EPP	x	x		x	x	x	x	

Second, *equality* has traditionally been a core concept in social democratic language. It is a distinguishing mark of social democratic programme ideology and language today as well, even if the concept is now frequently only mentioned briefly and is poorly defined. The Swedish SAP is most explicit and states that freedom requires *equality* and that human beings, in spite of different points of departure, are given the same opportunity to form their lives. Other social democratic parties are rather brief in their definition of equality. The DNA argues for reduced social differences and the French PS for a social transformation of society. The Danish Social Democratic Party seems to have a formal concept of equality that refers to equal rights. The SPD does not include equality among its basic values, but declares that justice implies a more equal distribution of income, property and power. All in all, equality is still a key value in social democratic programmes, but seems to have a weaker position than in the first decades after World War II. The difference between a concept of equality that means changes in the distribution of resources and a concept that refers primarily to equal opportunities has become less clear in most social democratic programmes. In addition to the four basic concepts of freedom, justice, equality and solidarity, the French PS mentions human rights, human dignity and responsibility as fundamental values. The Italian DS emphasises subsidiarity and federalism. As we shall see in Chapter 8, this reflects specific DS experiences in the Italian context.

The meaning of the social democratic concept of solidarity is not primarily defined by the loose ineliminable core that was specified in Chapter 7: a positive attitude to organise social welfare collectively, redistribute resources, and a sympathetic attitude towards the poor and oppressed. The relationship with and the definition of these other basic concepts are more important in defining what solidarity should mean. To what extent is *freedom* given a prominent place in programmes, and does *freedom* refer to the freedom to keep one's income away from the tax authorities and increased opportunity to choose in the market, or the freedom that follows from the abolition of poverty and discrimination? What is the conception of justice – does it mean redistribution according to need or that personal contribution is rewarded? Consequently, the meaning of social democratic solidarity changes according to the meaning of the other basic concepts with which solidarity is associated.

The Christian democratic language

The political language of Christian democracy shares freedom, justice and solidarity as basic values with the political language of social democracy.[2] The meanings of these concepts are established through the introduction of other concepts. First, contrary to the social democratic programme language, three other basic values are included: subsidiarity, the person and responsibility. These serve to define and specify the meaning of solidarity.[3]

The concepts of the person, responsibility and subsidiarity serve to modify both the individualist aspects of *freedom* and the collective aspects of solidarity. The Catholic idea of the *person* accentuates the fact that the individual may realise him/herself only through social relationships and community with others, the CDU argues. Accordingly, the concept of the *person* emphasises the role of the individual at the same time as it modifies individualism. This double character is found in the concept of *responsibility* as well. On the one hand, it directs attention to the individual's responsibility for his/her own life and fate in society. On the other, it stresses the individual's responsibility to be aware of the needs of others and the obligation to help those in need. The idea of subsidiarity is posed against solidarity, directs attention away from giving priority to public solutions and gives the family, the voluntary sector and the local community an important role in social policy. Thus, the Christian democratic ideology contains a more complex view of the relationship between the collective and the individual than social democratic ideology.

Freedom is associated with social justice and the right to private property. Whereas freedom and justice are connected also in social democratic language, this is not the case with freedom and the right to private property. For Christian democratic parties, the existence of personal property enhances individual freedom, but at the same time they emphasise that it is necessary to abolish need if freedom is to be real. Justice requires both that individual performance is appreciated and that social differences are reduced. What is equal must be treated as equal; and what is different as different. Again we see the characteristic double character of Christian democratic concepts. Christian democratic justice means at the same time to accept and honour differences and to reduce them. Consequently, the meaning of *solidarity* in Christian democratic programmes changes according to which aspects of justice and freedom are emphasised.

The relationship between solidarity and other key concepts in Christian democratic language, particularly the person and subsidiarity, makes the Christian democratic concept of solidarity even more flexible than the social democratic concept. This flexibility and ambiguity make Christian

---

[2] *Freedom* and *justice* are absent in the most recent KrF programme, but this seems to be an exception as these concepts have generally been found in KrF programmes as well.

[3] The CDU seems to regard these concepts as somewhat subordinate, whereas the KrF and the EPP assign them a position as basic values.

democratic ideology more open to adopt impulses and concepts from liberal and liberalist ideology and politics.

Competing languages?

The perlocutionary effect, the effects on the reader, of a language of solidarity is determined not only by the relationship between solidarity and other concepts, but also by the existence or non-existence of conflicting or competing languages in programmes. Therefore, it is not sufficient only to study the language of solidarity in order to understand the function or role of the concept of solidarity in programme ideology, it is also necessary to compare the language of solidarity with other languages that are found in programmes.

Gerassimos Moschonas maintains that social democratic programmes are formulated around *three* themes. The first is the more or less classic social democratic theme which has been discussed in previous chapters. The second is a post-materialist theme sceptical about economic growth, and the third is a theme inspired by neo-liberalism with issues such as competitiveness, reduction of taxes, privatisation, deregulation and commercialisation of public activities. This neo-liberal option is gradually and systematically gaining ground, he argues (Moschonas 2002). It is certainly the case that social democracy has developed a more positive view on the introduction of market mechanisms in new areas, but an analysis of recent party programmes does not indicate that a neo-liberal language has been introduced to any particular extent. We certainly note concepts such as *competition, initiative, innovation* and a few others from neo-liberal language, but concepts such as *privatisation, de-regulation and commercialisation* are generally not found. Thus, although Moschonas may be right in terms of practical politics, he seems to exaggerate when it comes to programme language.[4] A neo-liberal language does not as yet seem to constitute an alternative to the language of solidarity. As Moschonas himself notes, the discourse of solidarity and social cohesion is still at the heart of social democratic programmes.

Christian democratic programmes represent a somewhat mixed picture. A competing language is certainly found in the 1994 CDU platform. Here, we find a remarkable difference between the language in the chapter on fundamental values and the chapter on economic policy. The second is characterised by a language of economic liberalism with terms

---

[4] I do not agree with his contention that social democratic parties of today express a sceptical attitude to growth in their programmes. On the contrary, they are definitely in favour of growth, but argue that growth should be combined with a more active environmental policy and considerations of the problems this creates.

and concepts such as *private initiative, individual performance, competitive power, risk-taking, deregulation, privatisation, flexibility in the labour market, reduction of bureaucratic impediments, reduction of subsidies and restructuring of the welfare state.* This language clearly contrasts with the language in the most recent KrF programme. Here, we find no language that competes with the language of solidarity. The formulations about economic policy and the market are cautious and emphasise that the market must be responsible and regulated. The competitive power of the economy is mentioned, but carefully balanced against the need for protecting the environment and the welfare state. This difference is also found in the actual practical policies of the two Christian democratic parties. The CDU is politically more to the right than the KrF, and this reflects the different social bases of the two parties; in Germany, the CDU represents a class alliance between business and the middle class, whereas in Norway the Conservative Party represents business, and the KrF represents only a tiny alliance of Christians from different social strata.

We may conclude that the Christian democratic concept of solidarity is even more flexible than the social democratic concept. It is specified and moderated not only through other key Christian democratic concepts such as the person, responsibility and subsidiarity, but also by its openness to a competing language – that of the market. This language not only specifies, but may also counteract the ideology of solidarity in Christian democratic parties.

Convergence, but still differences

We have witnessed an increased convergence between social democratic and Christian democratic parties in terms of programme language and the conception of solidarity. In Germany, both the CDU and the SPD emphasise solidarity, freedom, and justice in programme discourse, and this is the case for the KrF and the DNA in Norway as well. In Italy, the heirs of *Democrazia Cristiana* embrace the concept of solidarity, and the social democratic DS has adopted the concept of subsidiarity. *Solidarity* refers in all cases to a general identification with the weak in society, the whole of society, with poor nations of the Third World, nature and the generations to come, etc.

As a result, social democratic and Christian democratic discourse on solidarity of today share many similarities. Both have class mediation as a core function. Class mediation has always been a basic idea in Catholicism, referring mainly to mediation between the rural and the urban middle class, the working class and business. For social democracy the point of departure was working-class solidarity, but social democracy needed a broad concept that could mediate between the working class and first, peasants, and later, the middle class, to win new voters. The transformation of the old working-class idea of solidarity into a broader concept made this mediation possible.

Yet, there are still some differences. Some social democratic parties, such as the DNA, add equality to the list of fundamental values and emphasise somewhat more strongly that equality must be founded on a material basis and a more even distribution of resources. Christian democratic parties combine solidarity with the concepts of the person and of subsidiarity, and prioritise the choice to be made by non-governmental institutions and individual freedom. Besides, Christian democratic parties conceive difference as an aspect of justice. On the other hand, we have seen to an increasing degree that social democratic parties are preoccupied with the individual. The Italian DS includes subsidiarity as a basic value (see Chapter 8). Thus, the lines are blurred, and the different ideas of solidarity seem to become more similar. Even so, the nuances still found indicate that social democratic parties are more inclined to find public solutions to social problems, whereas Christian democracy prefers to turn to civil society, in particular, the voluntary sector. Besides, Christian democratic parties, as exemplified by the CDU, are more inclined to adopt a competing language in their programmes.

Consequently, even if the Christian democratic and social democratic ideology of solidarity have become increasingly similar, this does not mean that all differences between the two concepts of solidarity have disappeared. Another issue is the practical implications of these differences in concrete politics, but this has to be addressed through other types of material and research methods than have been used here.

The advantages of a language of solidarity

Why has the concept of solidarity become increasingly popular? Chapter 5 discussed some structural and ideological variables that explain the differences between the labour movement parties in this respect. Now, it is time to adopt a more hermeneutic perspective. How could *solidarity* be an answer to the challenges with which these parties were confronted in the period in which the new political language was developed? Three types of explanation may be suggested – explanations that are alternative, but also complementary to each other: the political challenge raised by changes in the class structure and the need for electoral alliances; the cultural change after 1968 and 1973; and the nature of political symbols and programmes.

First, the change from a classic Marxist class-based concept of solidarity to a broader and modern concept can be considered as a result of the need for a wider electoral basis for social democratic parties. In the first decades of the twentieth century, social democratic parties gradually had to acknowledge that they could not become majority parties and have access to government power without electoral support outside the industrial working class. In that period, farmers and smallholders were the most probable candidates for an alliance, particularly in Scandinavia. Later, the new middle class became a more important potential reservoir of voters. To continue insisting on a class-based concept of solidarity would not have been conducive to new alliances with the more meritocratic middle class. Although the labour movement parties were late to include other than workers in the concept, the transformation of solidarity from a class-specific to an inter-class concept was an answer to this dilemma.

In the 1970s, social democratic leaders faced new challenges. They had, some in government positions and some in opposition, participated as protagonists in developing the welfare state, backed by extensive support in the industrial working class. From the second part of the 1970s industrial employment no longer continued to grow. The need to broaden the social basis for voter support had long been a theme, and this issue now became even more urgent. Unemployment made the financial foundation of the welfare state more insecure, and the new ideological climate after Thatcher's victory in the UK in 1979 represented a challenge to collective arrangements and the welfare state. In this situation, social democratic leaders could see several advantages in making solidarity a key concept.

First, they were witnessing a fragmentation of class structure. The traditional working class was no longer increasing whereas new social strata in the middle class were developing rapidly. For social democracy, the idea of solidarity could be an answer to this challenge as it could be used to forge an alliance between the industrial working class and the increasing number of white-collar employees. Second, it could be used as a defence against radical change of the existing welfare institutions and the welfare state that they had built or struggled to achieve. Third, it could at the same time be used to appeal to the core of the industrial working class to exhibit wage restraint in the name of reduced inflation and solidarity with the unemployed. Thus, solidarity should no longer be a weapon in workers' struggle, but a mechanism that made workers more moderate, made them set aside demands for wage increases, and identify with the whole of society. This meant a step towards a Durkheimian concept of solidarity.

For Christian democracy, the situation was different. Christian democracy had no historical concept of solidarity upon which a new concept could be developed. However, Christian democracy had the Christian idea of love, the concept of charity and concern for social integration. When the predecessors of Christian democratic parties were established in the second part of the nineteenth century and the first decades of the twentieth, it had long been evident that Christian *love* and *charity* could not serve as key political concepts for parties that wanted to expand their electoral support among voters searching for political solutions to improve their situation. In this situation, it was convenient to transform these concepts into a more modern concept, that of solidarity, and this early Catholic concept of solidarity represented a political concept that could glue together different social classes that otherwise could be posed against each other in class struggle.

As mentioned in Chapter 5, a second phenomenon that made the concept of solidarity more popular was that the student revolt of 1968 changed the climate of both politics and language. The concept of solidarity became a key concept in the radical language of the student movement as a moral and altruistic concept meaning solidarity with the Third World and the oppressed or discriminated against groups in Western society. It moved from the student movement into the language of left-wing and social democratic parties and influenced the language of Christian social ethics as well. The oil crisis in 1973 resulted in an economic setback, and in succeeding years rising unemployment and welfare retrenchment was on the agenda, making social cohesion and solidarity more precarious. Moreover, many social democratic parties, particularly the Scandinavian parties that had administered society during the 1950s and 1960s, were in need of revitalisation, and these could now integrate the new concept in this project. In this period, Christian democratic parties could adopt a concept of solidarity that had become increasingly popular after 1968 and that at the same time had been drained of its radical content. It could be used in competition with social democracy regarding voters, and it established a front and an identity against the liberal and conservative parties. The Christian democratic language with its emphasis on subsidiarity and the person constituted on the other hand a demarcation line between it and social democracy.

For social democracy, the use of *solidarity* in programmes became even more popular when the ideological climate and the political tide changed in the early 1980s. In the next decade social democracy was on the defensive in many countries. The new climate of individualism and market ideology, and dissolution of collective attitudes, had created a need for an ideological language that could meet these new challenges from the right. Here, *solidarity* could serve as a weapon in an ideological counter-offensive against the paradigm of free-market liberalism. The strong flexibility of Christian democratic language made the reigning values in this period less challenging for those parties. They could adjust more easily to the new climate by shifting the emphasis to subsidiarity and personal responsibility. At the same time *solidarity* could still be used to mark the difference between Christian democracy and Liberalism and Conservatism.

The third type of explanation might be sought in the nature of political symbols and programmes. In party programmes, ideological concepts are important in many ways and may serve several functions. First, they serve to give identity to the party and to distinguish the party from its adversaries. Second, ideological concepts will serve to arouse positive connotations both in the electorate and among party activists. Third, they flag the issues and politics of the party, with a precision that is instrumental in that respect. Fourth, good political concepts are concepts that are flexible and may be given new interpretations according to changes in the political environment. Hence, political concepts should not be *too* precise and concrete. For political leaders and ideologues, it is not easy to find concepts that combine these four functions.

Generally, the more heterogeneous the social structure and ideological preferences of the environment, the more complicated it is to find ideological concepts that combine all four functions. When the class structure is heterogeneous and different groups have different ideologies, an ideological concept that provides identity can simultaneously constitute a barrier between the party and certain social groups for whom the concept does not arouse positive connotations. Therefore, ideological concepts which have a too precise instrumental meaning are problematic because they arouse conflicts among voters, at the same time as they may be too binding for party leadership. Finally, the parties of the labour movement may face a dilemma in finding concepts that appeal to both party activists and the electorate. Usually, party activists are more entrenched in party traditions and party ideology, whereas voters are more exposed to the shifting winds and moods of media society.

The increasing popularity of *solidarity* in social democratic language can be understood from these perspectives. The increased heterogeneity of the class structure, the reduction in the traditional working class and the growth of new educated social strata made it extremely difficult to find concepts that had positive connotations for the different groups of voters and which were associated with social democracy's collective project. In a situation where old concepts such as *class struggle*, *exploitation* and *working class* had to be abandoned, parties in the socialist tradition were in need of a new expressive language. The concept of solidarity could be part of such a language. As a result, the conceptual context was changed from one where the emphasis was on *struggle* to one where general concepts such as *freedom, democracy, equality* and *(social) justice* were found side by side with *solidarity*. These came to be the four dominating and most utilised ideological concepts in social democratic language in the last decades of the twentieth century.

Freedom is a value common to social democracy and Christian democracy. In early socialist and classical social democratic language *freedom* referred both to individual political rights and to the collective freedom and the possibility to realise collective interests. However, in modern political language *freedom* more frequently refers to the former and to the freedom of the individual to choose and realise personal interests. Whereas *freedom* and *democracy* could distinguish social democracy from Marxist–Leninist parties, it was of little use in electoral competition with conservative, liberal and Christian democratic parties. On the contrary, socialist and social democratic parties can never win against such parties by offering more opportunities for individual freedom to choose in a society which is dominated by the market. *Justice* has been well integrated and frequently utilised by social democratic parties, but there are some problems with this concept. It is generally accepted and has a broad appeal. No one will argue *against* justice and *for* injustice. Bailey has argued that it pays to use broad and common denominators and hortatory symbols in a language situation where the political audience is large and heterogeneous (Bailey 1981), but this is only partially true. If the symbol is not specific to a party, but shared with political adversaries, it cannot provide identity. Neither are shared and common symbols very useful in this respect. This is the problem with *justice*: does it mean that everybody should have the same? – that everybody should have what she deserves? – what she needs? – what is reasonable according to status, or what she is entitled to according to law? (Bergsdorf 1983). Thus, people and parties are free to define *justice* as they prefer, and social democrats, socialists, Christian democrats, liberals and conservatives are free to establish their own definitions. As a result, *justice* fails to provide identity for both social democracy and Christian democracy.

Even though *equality* is not very precise, it is perhaps *too* precise to appeal to a society in which the industrial working class is decreasing and middle-class values with individualistic and meritocratic attitudes prevail. However, *solidarity* had many advantages. It gave identity, since liberalists seldom utilised it. It confirmed the old values of the labour movements for party activists at the same time as it aroused positive connotations among new groups of voters – particularly those working in the public sector in education, health and the social services. Moreover, it was extremely difficult to find concepts that were rooted in the working class and socialist traditions, yet at the same time appealed to segments of the middle class. But *solidarity* was seen as such a concept. It is not very precise, arouses connotations of collaboration and common efforts to establish public solutions in welfare and the social services, providing aid to poor nations and showing compassion to people in need. At the same time, the personal contribution and sacrifices required are not precisely defined. Thus, the objectives associated with the use of *solidarity* in party documents appeal both to the heart and the head, as good political concepts should do (Bailey 1981). *Solidarity* is more precise than *justice* and less precise than *equality*. It is a concept that can appeal to many different groups at the same time as drawing a line between left and right – conservative parties being inherently averse to the collective connotations of solidarity.

Finally, a discourse about *solidarity*, *freedom*, and *justice* and *equality* as well can be understood in the light of the character of party politics in the period discussed here. In Scandinavia, Germany, France and Spain, *solidarity* acquired the status of a basic value at a time when the political differences and conflicts between social democracy and parties to the right were reduced. Conflicts over concrete issues were no longer so sharp, and credibility and communication skills gradually became more important for electoral mobilisation. In this situation, emphasis on values and ethics could compensate for the absence of controversial issues.

Summing up, the advantages of *solidarity* are the vagueness, the flexibility and the positive connotations of the concept. The vagueness is associated not only with the term and the concept, but is also determined by the language in which *solidarity* is located and the relationship with other key concepts such as *freedom*, *justice* and *equality*. When the accent is shifted from one concept to another, for instance from *solidarity* to *freedom*, or from *freedom* to *equality*, the meaning and political implications of solidarity are changed. It is the many alternative ways of combining or shifting emphases that constitute both the vagueness and the flexibility of the concept. This makes it difficult to define and to interpret what political actions should be deduced from the concept.

Some problems

Thus, both the modern concepts of social democratic and Christian democratic solidarity are problematic. For social democracy, the first dilemma is the relationship between solidarity and individualism.

Modern social democratic programmes struggle with the relationship between solidarity and collective orientation on the one hand and individualism on the other. They reflect the increasing individualism and values of self-realisation of our time. From the late 1980s many programmes have tried to reconcile solidarity and community with formulations that recognise the need for the freedom of individuals to pursue their interests and values, as explicitly stated in the SPD programmes of 1989 and 1998. 'Solidarity', the 1989 programme said, 'is necessary to enhance individual possibilities for development.' 'The goal of the welfare state', the 1998 programme said, 'is to stimulate personal responsibility and individuality, not guardianship.' Thus, 'we must continuously determine the relationship between solidarity and individuality', the programme insists (SPD 1998). Naturally, such statements do nothing other than state that modern social democracy is confronted with challenges in an era of individualisation. This essential point is only raised and not elaborated upon, let alone resolved. Increasing individualism is perhaps the greatest challenge to collective solidarity, and if social democracy wants to have electoral success, it must find some ways to reconcile those two key concepts.

Second, when it comes to the basis for solidarity, the emphasis has shifted from self-interest to ethics, empathy, compassion or another kind of altruism, even if *self-interest* emerges now and then in programmes. The relationship between self-interest and altruism is formulated, as in the 1998 SPD programme, but only in general ways that do not offer any solutions. The idea of *informed* or *restrained* self-interest is mentioned, but how restrained can self-interest be before solidarity is no longer based on self-interest, but on altruism? Therefore, to use the label *enlightened* about self-interest does not solve the problem. The concept of informed self-interest is based on the idea that a well-educated and well-informed person should understand that it is in her self-interest to show solidarity with others, for instance with people in the Third World or with future generations. Even if it is probably in the long-term self-interest of the rich world to establish a more just world economic order, this does not necessarily mean that it is in the short-term interest of individuals in the rich world. In any case, solidaristic behaviour presupposes a long-term view and identification with the interests of the next generation. Consequently, it is more fruitful to view solidarity as an expression of altruism than of self-interest.

A third problem concerns the relationship between the old classic concept of solidarity as community in action, struggling against employers or other adversaries, and solidarity defined as a contribution to production and economic growth in collaboration with others. At the same time the second form of solidarity implies acting in the interests of employers and owners, something which may frequently be in direct conflict with the old labour movement meaning of *solidarity*. Both those definitions of solidarity are reflected in modern social democratic programmes, but without being discussed. Still, some social democratic parties have preserved remnants of class solidarity in programmes, but most often this idea has been left behind. In most respects the concept of solidarity in modern social democratic language represents a return to Fourier's view of solidarity as a concept with a plural meaning and an imprecisely defined content that is well suited to arouse positive emotional connotations.

A fourth aspect is the reluctance to utilise the concept of *solidarity* in contexts that may provoke resistance among voters. The belated and rare use of *solidarity* concerning the relationship between the majority population and ethnic minorities is conspicuous. The same can be said about the late introduction of *solidarity* in the context of gender issues. Here also, the vagueness demonstrated in formulations is conspicuous. The reluctance to utilise *solidarity* regarding controversial and unpopular issues may raise doubt about the willingness to exercise solidarity in practice in the same areas. This reluctance is probably due to electoral considerations, as minorities that most need solidarity in modern societies are often stigmatised and unpopular among the majority population.

For Christian democracy, the main problem lies exactly where we find the great advantage of the Christian democratic language compared to social democratic language: the strong flexibility of the language allows for a continuously stronger emphasis on subsidiarity and personal responsibility and a weaker role for solidarity. The danger of making solidarity a concept devoid of any meaning is further increased by the introduction of a completely different and competing political language.

Social democratic and Christian democratic solidarity in the twenty-first century

Historically, the social democratic and the Christian democratic language of solidarity have been addressed to different audiences. Social democratic parties have tried to communicate with organised labour in industry and white-collar areas, whereas Christian democracy aimed to embrace all classes from business to industrial workers. Both parties have been protagonists in developing generous welfare states, and, as demonstrated by Huber and Stephens, these different social bases have been reflected in institutional differences in the welfare states where social democracy, and respectively Christian democracy, have had a strong influence (Huber and Stephens 2001). As we have seen here, these differences are mirrored in the different concepts and languages of solidarity as well.

The ambition of both social democracy and Christian democracy to win the middle class compels them both to avoid issues that may alienate these social strata. Their ideological traditions, with a somewhat different conception of solidarity, may serve to compensate for the lack of political conflicts and to appeal to general values in society. In a situation where the differences between the parties are not clear, the profiling of basic values and ethics can be convenient. 'When nothing else succeeds ethics will always pass', as one commentator has observed (Herzinger 2002). The insistence on *solidarity, justice* and *equality* may serve simultaneously to demonstrate historical continuity and to build a bridge between the individualism of the presence and the collective orientation of the past.

The social democratic and the Christian democratic ideas of solidarity are important only to the extent that these parties are influential. Generally, the political influence and significance of political parties has been reduced from the 1960s (Webb 2000) or 1970s (Montero and Guenther). Voters' identification with parties has weakened, trust in parties has been reduced, and membership declined. Parties have lost some of their capacity to mobilise mass participation, to articulate political interests and integrate the interests of different classes and groups, something which also applies to social democracy and Christian democracy. New media and information technology have created alternative channels for political communication, and new social movements have succeeded in political mobilisation for solidarity and other issues (see Chapter 10). Social democracy is confronted with a new situation, both because of the numerical reduction in the industrial working class and also because the erosion of *class* as an influential factor for voting has made workers disperse their votes over many parties. For Christian democracy, secularisation has reduced the significance of religion in politics, and increasing individualism makes religion become a home-made mixture of elements created by the individual.[5] The result is that believers disperse their votes over more parties than before.

Moreover, the key role of solidarity in social democratic and Christian democratic programmes is only partially founded upon and reflected in

---

[5] A report from a group of social scientists demonstrates that only a small minority, 4.6 per cent, of Italians is of the opinion that religion should influence politics, whereas 62.7 per cent say that it should have no influence at all (Conti 2003). See also the analysis of sociologist Ilvo Diamante (2003).

the attitudes of those who vote for these parties. My own analysis of comparative survey data indicates that social democratic and Christian voters generally express attitudes of solidarity somewhat more strongly than do voters who are more to the right, although it varies among countries, but such differences are not very strong (Stjernø and Johannessen 2004).[6] The idea of equality is more pronounced among social democratic voters than among both Christian democratic voters and those more to the right, but even among social democratic voters, the preference for equality is not very strong. Christian democratic voters, on the other hand, are not more inclined to support issues that indicate the idea of subsidiarity. Generally, as we have seen in party programmes, differences between ideologies among voters are not very strong, and ideological confines are blurring. As Michael Freeden maintains, ideologies not only overlap one another, but in many cases components of their conceptual repertory percolate into other ideologies (Freeden 2001).

In the first decade of the new millennium both social democracy and Christian democracy are confronted with great challenges. In 2001 and 2002, social democratic parties were ousted from government in Italy, Portugal, Denmark and Norway. Parties relying on support from populist anti-immigration parties assumed governmental power, and social democratic parties are bewildered about what strategy to pursue. British New Labour has abandoned much of traditional social democratic ideology and politics and developed a new mixture of social democratic, liberal and communitarian ideology. The French PS was defeated at the national election in 2002, and the SPD has lost much support because of its ambition to reform the welfare state, even if still in government together with the Green Party. On the other hand, Swedish social democracy has stayed on as a government party and enjoys an electoral support that is looked upon with envy by most other social democratic parties. With the notable exception of the SAP, social democratic parties are torn everywhere between the collectivism of traditional working-class solidarity and the modern middle-class mixture of individualism and welfare orientation. To compete with conservative or Christian democratic parties, social democracy has moved to the right, and books abound with accusations that social democracy and politics in general has left solidarity behind (see for instance (Padgett and Paterson 1991; Thomson 2000; Moschonas 2002)).

Nor is the prospect for Christian democratic solidarity, as we knew it, convincing. As mentioned, European politics and society have been

---

[6] Data from Eurobarometer 1993. Whereas there are no significant differences in such attitudes between those of social democratic and Christian democratic voters in Italy and Norway, significant differences were found between SPD and CDU/CSU voters.

secularised. Contrary to what we have witnessed in the USA and other parts of the world, religion has lost much of its ability to influence the political behaviour of citizens and voters. Moreover, both Catholic and Protestant believers have today spread their loyalty across the political spectrum, and Christian democracy no longer has the monopoly of representing those who regard themselves as Christians. Finally, Christian democratic parties are not in a position to transform religious values into practical politics. The German CDU was defeated at the elections in 2002 and in 2003. The Catholic *Arbeitnehmer-Flügel* (employee wing) has lost both members and influence in the party, and the party leader – the Protestant Angela Merkel – represents individualism more than the collective aspects of Catholic social teaching in her ambition to outshine the SPD in cutting welfare benefits. In Italy, Christian democracy is represented only by a small party that is part of the Berlusconi government – a government with a prime minister who declares that his models are Margaret Thatcher and Ronald Reagan.[7] On the centre-left, remnants of Christian democracy are in the process of being integrated into a liberal-radical party in the Olive Alliance. In Norway, a Christian democratic Protestant party is part of a coalition which is dominated by a conservative party and dependent on the parliamentary support of a right-wing populist party, and this coalition has cost the KrF dear. In most other European countries, conservative parties are more influential than Christian democratic parties. Besides, many Christian democratic parties have moved to the right and today prioritise personal responsibility and subsidiarity above solidarity. Thus, we should not expect the Christian democratic ideology of solidarity to be influential in European politics in the years to come. In this respect, Martin Convey may be right when he asserts that the age of Christian democracy in Europe has ended (Conway 2003).

Both social democracy and Christian democracy are confronted with a new type of challenge. In France, Italy, Denmark and Norway, right-wing populist parties have achieved considerable electoral support in the traditional working class and eroded the social basis of social democracy. Although there are differences between these parties, the formulation of Le Pen *socially left, economically right, but above all French* is aptly chosen to characterise those parties. They do not preach the individualism of traditional liberalism, but a new mix of individualism and collective orientation. They struggle for more individual autonomy, against

---

[7] Cf. Silvio Berlusconi's speech in the mass media on the day of the general strike against reform of the labour law, 14 April 2002.

bureaucracy and regulations, at the same time as they express consumer interests in publicly financed social and health services, but argue that such services can be operated, organised or owned privately. To the degree that these parties are concerned with solidarity, the basis for the solidarity is the nation. Their idea of solidarity is directed against those who are considered strangers and as 'others'. This new ideological mix represents a strong challenge to both social democracy and Christian democracy.

Social democratic parties are challenged from the left as well. Radical socialist or green parties compete for votes: *Die Grünen* in Germany, VPK in Sweden, SF in Denmark, SV in Norway, *la gauche plurielle* in France, *Rifondazione Comunista* in Italy. These parties have their electoral stronghold in the new educated middle classes, but seek to combine emphases on ecology, gender emancipation and Third World issues with defence of traditional working-class values and Keynesian-oriented solidarity. Still, these parties have not been able to challenge the hegemony of social democratic parties in the working class and their electoral support varies from election to election and country to country, between 4 per cent and 15 per cent. Although their electoral basis is unstable, public employees with higher education seem to constitute the electoral core of these parties, and these parties have not been able to prevent working-class voters from seeking right-wing populism. Even so, they have brought the issues of the new left onto the political agenda and made it necessary for social democratic parties to adapt to this. Most left-wing parties have moved somewhat to the right and become less critical of the system, and their function seems to be a warning to social democracy that it cannot move too far to the right without losing electoral support on the left. At this time, it is unlikely that these parties will be influential carriers of a radical new solidarity in society.

The precarious state of the social democratic and Christian democratic politics of solidarity does not mean that these parties will necessarily cease to be protagonists in European politics. The changed character of voting behaviour has in some ways made politics more like a market, and voter preferences may change swiftly if voters are not satisfied with the present government politics. This does not mean that social democracy and Christian democracy will not survive as parties. The point to be made here is that the concept and the language of solidarity that these parties have institutionalised in their programmes probably will not be concretised to a high degree in practical politics according to their traditional concepts of solidarity. However, these concepts were developed under specific historic circumstances and constructed socially at a time when the class structure, the political constellations and the prevailing ideologies were different. As Freeden remarks, ideological concepts have no intrinsic meaning (Freeden 1996). They change, are redefined and given a new meaning, or meanings, through struggle and rivalry about what should be their proper content. This will certainly be the case for the concepts of social democratic and Christian democratic solidarity as well.

8   Two excursions: Marxist–Leninist and fascist solidarity

Between the two world wars both social democratic and Catholic solidarity were confronted with two rival conceptions of solidarity. The Russian revolution resulted in the establishment of communist parties and the development of the Marxist–Leninist ideology which continued the Marxist tradition and saw class as a foundation for solidarity. From the right, fascism formulated an idea of solidarity that erased the dividing lines between classes that Marxism saw as antagonistic, and established the nation and the race as the basis for solidarity. These alternative ways of defining solidarity were anchored in two different political languages, although a common characteristic was that they both excluded some of the key ideas in social democracy and Christian democracy, like *freedom*, *democracy* and *individual rights*.

Marxist–Leninist solidarity

In Chapter 2, we saw that Lenin evaded ideas that entailed feelings and ethics and that this also applied to the concept of solidarity, even if the concept of unity represented an equivalent in his political language. Nonetheless, Lenin's disciple, Georg Lukács, formulated a consistent concept of solidarity that was characterised by a strong collective orientation: solidarity should mean that the individual subordinated himself to the collective will of the communist party. Since freedom in a capitalist society was illusionary, individual freedom could be postponed to the new society after the revolution. In the Leninist tradition, Antonio Gramsci sketched a third idea of solidarity: worker consciousness should transcend the immediate interest of one's own corporate group and express the interests of allied classes and groups at the same time as it was also to entail values and cultural aspects. The question to be discussed in this chapter is to what extent Marxist–Leninist parties adopted either Lenin's weak language of solidarity, Lukács' concept with the strong collective and authoritarian accent or Gramsci's broader concept. Programmes, theses and texts from the Third International and from the two largest communist parties in Europe, the French PCF and the Italian PCI, will throw light on this.

The Third International

The communist parties that were established in most European countries in the years after World War I re-established the Marxist tradition and added the specific flavour of Leninism. Lenin and the Russian communists considered the attitude of the socialist parties as a betrayal of international worker solidarity, and founded the Third International in 1919 as a reaction to this. The platform of the new International stated that the goal of the proletariat was to break capitalist rule and to 'transform the whole world into a community where all work for the common good, and realise the freedom and brotherhood of all peoples' (Third International 1919–22). This was the only reference to the idea of solidarity. When a second world congress gathered in Moscow the next year, the statutes, theses and resolutions that were approved were devoid of any references to solidarity or equivalent concepts, and this applied to Lenin's speeches as well. Lenin did not refer to the idea of solidarity once, not even when talking about themes that gave many opportunities for so doing, such as the national, colonial and agrarian questions. Considering the conflict about war and political strategy and the deplorable fate of working-class solidarity, this is not surprising.

However, the Leninists and the Third International were ahead of their time in one important area: they raised the issue of colonialism with great vigour and consequence time and again during the 1920s. The *Theses on the National and Colonial Questions* from the second congress stated that:

the entire policy of the Communist International must be based primarily on uniting the proletarians and toiling masses of all nations and countries in common revolutionary struggle to overthrow landowners and bourgeoisie . . . Both within as well as outside it, the Communist parties must incessantly expose in their entire propaganda and agitation the continually repeated violations of the equality of nations and guaranteed rights of all minorities. (Third International 1920)

The Third International referred repeatedly to the relationship between the working class in Europe and the working masses in the 'underdeveloped' world, but the term solidarity was not utilised in such contexts. The preoccupation with national sovereignty for the colonies should bring the communist parties into the front line in the struggle for international solidarity, particularly with the peoples of the Third World. However, because the new Soviet state had a clear interest in establishing a front against the capitalist states in their own colonies, it is not easy to distinguish between loyalty to the Soviet Union and international solidarity in this context.

In other contexts, Lenin, Trotsky, Zinoviev and other Russian communists appealed occasionally for *unity* within the party and in the working class, but this was most often associated with *discipline* in a way that reminded one more of the language of military strategy than about an idea of solidarity that involved affective attitudes, comprehension and reciprocal sympathy. In documents from the congresses of the Third International in the following years the concept of solidarity is found only sporadically, even if it sometimes appeared in speeches and greetings from foreign guests. Generally, the absence of solidarity from most key documents and resolutions in those years is conspicuous.

This demonstrates that Lenin's political language prevailed also after his death in 1924. Moreover, the sectarian policy pursued by the Third International may also have contributed to this. The manifesto adopted at the sixth congress in 1928 condemned social democrats with harsh words, branded the right wing of social democracy as traitors and bourgeois agents, and accused the left wing of social democracy for executing 'subtle manoeuvres to deceive the working class' (Third International 1971a). The theses of the eleventh plenum in 1931 declared social democracy to be 'the chief social pillar of the bourgeoisie' (Third International, 1971b). In a situation where the majority of workers in most European countries supported social democratic parties, communists may have felt it difficult to write or talk about working-class solidarity.

The birth of southern communism – the PCF and the PCI

The new communist parties became strong rivals of social democracy only in France and Italy. In France, the socialist party was split when the majority decided to join the Third International in 1920, and the *Parti Communiste Français* (PCF) was established. Also in Italy the socialist party was split, and the minority established the *Partito Comunista Italiano* (PCI) in 1921 with Gramsci as one of the founding fathers (Smith 1997). The documents of both parties reflect the scant interest in solidarity in the Third International. Neither the idea of nor the term solidarity was expressed in the PCF programmes approved at the congress in 1926 (PCF 1927), nor did the brief declaration of the PCI include an appeal for solidarity (PCI 1921). However, a *Manifesto to the workers of Italy* concluded with an 'enthusiastic cry of solidarity of Italian proletarians and communists to the Communist International of Moscow, the invisible stronghold of world revolution' (PCI 1921). Thus, already from its establishment the term *solidarity* was applied to express loyalty to the CPSU.

Interesting differences between French and Italian communism were soon to emerge. Whereas the PCF soon subordinated itself to instructions from Moscow and pursued the sectarian policy of the Third International in this period, the PCI started to develop the idea of a class alliance between the working class, the peasants, the middle class and the petty bourgeoisie.

In Italy, the shadow of growing fascist violence and influence were more imminent than in France. After Mussolini came to power in 1922, ordinary political activity became increasingly difficult and many liberals and socialists went into exile. The PCI congress in 1926 in Lyons consolidated the PCI on a Marxist–Leninist platform authored by Gramsci. The *Theses of Lyons* is an extensive 120-page document that represents the first Marxist analysis of Italy written by an Italian. Gramsci's analysis was that fascism could not be defeated with a sectarian and maximalist strategy. Worker solidarity was necessary, but not sufficient. In addition, a class alliance between the working class, the peasantry and the lower middle class was needed. The *Theses of Lyons* contains several references to the idea of solidarity, described with concepts in conventional Leninist language, such as *proletarian internationalism* (PCI 1990a). The Marxist idea of solidarity had now been established as party ideology and language expressed, as in other parties, by a range of different terms. Nonetheless, the PCI was now immersed in the sectarian strategy of the Third International and was not able to transform the language of unity and solidarity into political practice (Grand 1989). Until World War II, the PCI, unlike the French PCF, remained isolated and enjoyed little support outside the most militant parts of the working class (Galli 1993).

Unity against fascism

When Hitler came to power in Germany in 1933 and began to crush the labour movement, the threats of fascism became even clearer, resulting in a change of communist strategy and tactics. In 1935, Dimitrov convinced the Comintern congress that communist strategy so far had been sectarian, and a new policy of unity against fascism and a united front with social democracy was approved. Now the PCF changed position and supported the socialist Blum government. At the same time, the idea of solidarity, if not the term, appeared in PCF language. The party called for *unity* and *fraternity* in the struggle against the enemies of peace (PCF 1936). Even if this represented a broadening of the idea of solidarity, the reorientation of tactics did not yet make PCF adopt a broader concept of solidarity. However, the change of policy came too late. In Germany, Italy and on the Iberian Peninsula fascism had prevailed. In Northern Europe, social democracy became hegemonic in the labour movement. The sectarian policy pursued by the communist parties, their subordination to Moscow and the continuous deradicalisation of social democracy made it impossible to re-build a new solidarity in the working class and between the political parties of the labour movement.

Although the Marxist–Leninist tradition brought further the classic Marxist idea of international worker unity, official Marxism–Leninism appears to have been cautious not to use the term *solidarity*. Neither did Marxism–Leninism develop a new discourse on solidarity before World War II. The Marxist concept of solidarity was taken for granted, but formulated in other terms. When *solidarity* now and then appeared, it referred mainly to unity in action, the will to support brothers in need or in the struggle for national sovereignty for the colonies. Lukács' blunt argument that solidarity should mean the elimination of individual freedom and subordination to the party was not reflected in key documents. Neither did the communist parties before World War II transcend a working-class concept of solidarity and broaden the concept to also include other groups, although the idea of a class alliance was in the process of developing.

Marxism–Leninism after the war

The Marxist–Leninist parties still demonstrated ambivalence towards the concept of solidarity after World War II. In the 1950s also, the PCF idea of solidarity was expressed most frequently with the term *worker unity*, used about cohesion in the working class. Yet, Marxist–Leninists began to use the term *solidarity* more during the 1950s and 1960s, although not yet in platforms and electoral programmes and other key documents. When the PCF now argued for an alliance between the working class, farmers and the petty bourgeoisie, this was formulated as *unity of the national and democratic forces*, but it was not clear what this unity should imply (PCF 1954; 1956). This formulation was another concept in the instrumental Leninist tradition and can hardly be viewed as a step towards a broader concept of solidarity. Contrary to the SFIO position on Algeria, the PCF gave early support to the struggle for national independence for Arabic nations, but this also was not formulated as a question of international *solidarity*.

The PCF loyally continued to support the Communist Party of the Soviet Union (CPSU), and when the term *solidarity* appeared, it was about the relationship between parties building on Marxism–Leninism, for instance when in 1956 the PCF emphasised the close unity and solidarity between the PCF and the CPSU and the 'deep democratic nature' of the CPSU (PCF 1956). The PCF took a dogmatic position on Khrushchev's revelations about Stalin and the Hungarian uprising in 1956. Many communists were demoralised, and an electoral defeat in 1958 made the party more positive to an electoral alliance with the socialists. Gradually, the concept of unity was extended to include the middle class, as stated in the 1961 programme (PCF 1961). In 1964, *solidarity* appeared for the first time in congress theses when the party called for struggle against racial prejudice, for the principles of *freedom*, *equality*, *independence for all peoples* and *solidarity* between the French working class and 'all peoples oppressed by imperialism' (PCF 1964). Still, this was combined with the idea of solidarity with the Soviet Union and proletarian internationalism.

The PCF did not as did the Italian communists unequivocally condemn the Soviet invasion of Czechoslovakia in 1968. However, the congress in 1976 toned down the pro-Soviet language, abandoned the idea of the dictatorship of the proletariat and approached the PCI's *euro-communism*, but the party returned to dogmatic pro-Soviet positions already at the next congress two years later. As was the case for many other parties, the PCF language was influenced by the vocabulary of the student revolt, and in the years after 1968 the term solidarity was found more frequently in PCF documents. Now, *solidarity* referred to a broader idea than *worker unity*, and was used in particular about support for national liberation movements in the Third World and for immigrant workers (PCF 1970, 1974). The PCF is one of the few parties analysed here that early and frequently called for solidarity between the national working class and immigrant workers, as it had already in 1974 when the programme declared that it was necessary to 'develop solidarity because the establishment and reactionary forces try to divide workers from immigrants' (PCF 1974).

Togliatti and the national way to socialism

The active role of the communists in the Italian resistance during World War II made the PCI a mass party (Sassoon 1981). The early post-war years also marked the beginning of a long and painful march for the PCI towards social democratic positions[1] and the gradual adoption of a

---

[1] For a more detailed description of the change of PCI positions and a discussion about at what points in time the PCI may be considered not a communist, but a social democratic party, see Sassoon (2003).

more social democratic language in which *solidarity* was to have a more prominent position. The idea of solidarity was gradually transformed from the restricted *worker unity* into a broader concept, and the *term* solidarity was increasingly used to express this idea.

The protagonist in the political transformation of the PCI was Palmiro Togliatti who had returned from Moscow as leader of the party in 1944. He had formulated the new communist strategy against fascism together with Dimitrov at the Comintern congress in 1935, and after the war Togliatti pursued this strategy to build a broad anti-capitalist alliance (Sassoon 1981; 2003). Now, the goal should be not socialism but a 'progressive democracy', and the party should forge an alliance between the working class, farmers and the middle strata in the cities to establish this democracy. For Togliatti, this strategy was founded on an analysis of the national and international situation and was a question of strategic necessity and not a question of solidarity. Yet, Togliatti and his supporters gradually developed a political theory that was different from standard Marxism–Leninism as taught in Moscow. Key concepts in this strategy were the *Italian road to socialism, social and political alliances, structural reforms* and *democracy*. Moreover, Togliatti directed the attention of the party to the role of Catholicism in Italy and the strategic importance of the Catholic masses (Gruppi 1974). The new PCI statutes declared that everybody now could be accepted as a member, independent of religious and philosophical conviction, but reconfirmed that the official doctrine of the party was based on Marxism–Leninism (Galli 1993). As we have seen in Chapter 4, some social democratic parties had at this time adopted a more open attitude to religion. The PCI now followed the same track, took a first step towards the Catholics and distinguished itself from the more pronounced anti-clerical attitudes of the PSI. Nevertheless, many of the party activists believed that Togliatti's course was not a strategy but a convenient tactic, and believed that revolutionary perspectives would be brought out into daylight when the time was ripe. This was labelled *la doppiezza*, the 'duplicity', and it harmed the democratic credibility of the party (Loretro 1991).

Although this way of reasoning had much in common with Scandinavian social democracy's concern about the need for alliances, it differed in one respect: the idea of and the language of solidarity were not important in Togliatti's strategy and language. He insisted that the PCI now defended the interests of the nation (Galli 1993), but continued to identify these with the interests of the workers and to argue that his strategy was in accordance with Leninism. Neither the relationship between communist and socialist workers on the one hand and Catholic workers on the other, nor the relationship between the working class and other classes or social groups, were formulated in a language of solidarity. Continuing the Leninist tradition, Togliatti argued for the need for *unity* or *unity of action*. In addition, he did not describe this unity as the result of a feeling of community, but as something that should be negotiated by PCI and DC leaders (Togliatti 1944). Whereas the social democratic parties of the North had already succeeded in the decades before the war in fusing together the idea of solidarity and the nation by broadening the idea of solidarity to include groups outside the working class, Togliatti still insisted that the interests of the working class and the nation were identical (Togliatti 1969b (1944)).

Nevertheless, Togliatti gradually began to use the concept of solidarity in a broader sense and, hesitatingly, to use the term *solidarity*. In a speech to the Assembly that discussed the new constitution in 1947 he noted that the PCI and Christian democracy represented two large currents that were now meeting each other:

From our side a human and social solidarism, excuse the barbarian term, and from the other side a solidarism that is inspired by another ideology with other origins . . . that arrives at results which are analogous to ours. This is the case with the acknowledgement of labour legislation, the so-called social rights, the new conception of the economic world which is neither individualistic nor atomistic, but founded on the principle of solidarity . . . (Togliatti 1974 (1947)).

In the years to come Togliatti continued to utilise the concept of unity, but he now and then referred to *solidarity* as well. This was the case, for instance, in his important speech to the party congress in 1956 when he formulated 'the Italian way to socialism' and delineated a view on democracy, political freedom and structural reforms that distinguished the PCI from both the CPSU and the PCF.

The PCI also hesitatingly developed a more independent attitude to the Soviet Union. Khrushchev's criticism of Stalin in 1956 and the brutal crushing of the popular revolt in Hungary the same year made the PCI more critical of the CPSU, weakened dogmatic Marxist–Leninist positions and resulted in a more open cultural climate in the party (Ginsborg 1989). In 1956, Togliatti resolutely criticised members who believed that the official strategy was not sincerely meant and denounced the *duplicity* of the party (Loretro 1991). The steady increase in electoral support in the 1960s and a clear victory for the right wing of the party at the congress in 1966 resulted also in a weakening of Marxism–Leninism and in more prudent political language.

It seems to be the mid-sixties that definitely brought the term *solidarity* into PCI language, but it was still mainly used about attitudes in the struggle against imperialism and oppression in other countries, and it was yet not elevated to the status of programme language. That would first happen a couple of decades later.

The increasing irrelevance of PCF ideology

Although the PCF in the 1980s still used several terms to express the idea of solidarity, and alternated between solidarity and fraternity, it was nonetheless in the process of adopting a discourse about solidarity more similar to social democracy (PCF 1985). The 1982 platform frequently mentioned solidarity in the same vein as justice, freedom and dignity (PCF 1982). Solidarity was now integrated into programme language, but not explicitly elevated to a basic value. Equality, justice and peace were still more important concepts than solidarity in PCF language. Not until 2001 was solidarity declared to be both an end and a mean.

What distinguishes the PCF concept of solidarity from all other parties studied here is that the PCF has preserved one aspect of the classic Marxist concept – that solidarity is unity in struggle. For instance, in 1990 solidarity was linked to 'all the progressive forces in the world: the working classes and their trade unions, the movements that struggle for human rights, for democracy, national liberation, anti-racism, equality for women, the entitlements of the young, respect for ecological balance', the programme said (PCF 1990). This reflects the fact that the PCF stuck longer to Marxism and Marxism–Leninism than the PCI.

The 1990s witnessed a continuous electoral decline for the PCF. The party did not seriously try to renew its profile and language as the Italian PCI did from 1989. The national elections in 2002 reduced the PCF vote to less than 4 per cent and probably signalled the definite end of PCF influence in French politics.

The PCI in the years of historical compromise

In the 1960s and the 1970s the PCI continued to try to break out of political isolation and it revised old positions: new positions on the issues of the EEC and NATO also gradually emerged. At the same time, the PCI demonstrated more clearly an independent position in relation to the CPSU. The term *Eurocommunism* came to denote a syndrome of positions based on a liberal conception of democracy: the acceptance of personal freedom, political pluralism, and autonomy for trade unions, religion and science (Sassoon 1981).

The 1968 student revolt in Italy was probably broader, more radical and looked upon with more sympathy by the younger segments of the working class than in most other countries in Europe (Ginsborg 1989).

It was at the same time anti-PCI and regarded the party as part of the establishment. Togliatti's successor, Luigi Longo, criticised his own party for not being able to acknowledge that the party had become too bureaucratic, and was unable to understand the wider implications of the student unrest (Sassoon 1996). Nonetheless, the radical language of the student movement did not influence the programme language of the PCI to a large extent, or pave the way for the development of a new concept of solidarity, as happened in many social democratic parties.

The military coup in Chile in 1973 resulted in a new look at PCI strategy. Enrico Berlinguer, PCI leader from 1972, saw the events in Chile as an indication that a socialist government would not be in a position to carry out a radical programme without a broad alliance and an electoral support that represented much more than 50 per cent of the voters. The PCI congress in 1972 declared that a political alliance with the Catholic masses was necessary, and that this could not be accomplished without a new relationship with the DC, through *a historic compromise*, as it was called. In 1974 Berlinguer elaborated on the new strategy and the need for an understanding between 'the great popular forces' in an important speech to the central committee (Berlinguer 1975). Now, he alternated in an almost imperceptible way between the traditional Leninist term *unity* and a new and broader concept of *solidarity* to describe the relationship between different segments of the popular masses. He referred to Togliatti and argued that 'the broadest popular, democratic and national solidarity was necessary – a solidarity that excluded only the most reactionary and narrow-minded groups'. The problem was, however, that Berlinguer still insisted on the 'exercise of the hegemony of proletarian politics' (Berlinguer 1975). This kind of solidarity was probably not very attractive to the other classes to whom he wanted to appeal.

A recession in 1974–75, high inflation, public deficits and scandals in the DC resulted in increased electoral support for the PCI, with a record of 34.4 per cent at the parliamentary elections in 1976 (Ginsborg 1989). The economic situation and terrorism and political violence in those years made the DC more inclined to reach an understanding with the PCI. In 1976 Giulio Andreotti established a minority Christian democratic government on the basis of an agreement that the PCI and the PSI should refrain from a vote of no confidence. The DC governments in the next three years were to be known as the *governments of national solidarity*, but for the PCI the results were not pleasing. The PCI was seen as partly responsible for the politics of the DC government, and in 1979 the PCI was defeated at the parliamentary elections and returned to opposition in the same year.

*From PCI to DS and the introduction of modern social
democratic solidarity*

In the early 1980s, the political system seemed to be blocked because of the alliance between the DC and the PSI, and the PCI was in an awkward position (Ginsborg 1989). The PCI was excluded from government positions, but was at the same time the dominating force in local politics in the central regions of Emilia Romagna, Tuscany and Umbria. PCI militants were integrated into municipal administration and developed local services with great ability and the party had in many respects become a social democratic party, but it was still concerned with establishing instrumental alliances between the working class and other classes and groups. Piero Fassino, the present DS leader, criticises the PCI for not having acknowledged the need for modernisation in Italy and for the PSI (Fassino 2003). Reluctance to adopt a new concept of solidarity was part of this difficulty in modernising. Even if party resolutions and party leaders now utilised the term solidarity occasionally and in a more generic sense than the classic Marxist concept, *solidarity* was not made an important term in programme language. Although Berlinguer was preoccupied with the ethical aspects of socialism in other contexts, he did not extend this interest to the concept of solidarity or adopt a concept that was founded on ethics and the language of solidarity that at this time was spreading among social democratic parties elsewhere.

Berlinguer had declared that the events in Poland demonstrated that the October Revolution was no longer an inspiration, and in Italy, as elsewhere, the atmosphere of political radicalism had disappeared, and an increasing number of PCI members were considering how to bring about a more profound renewal of the party. In 1983 *solidarity* is found for the first time in a PCI election manifesto, and in 1985, the party Congress approved a programme that represented a decisive step towards the language of solidarity in mainstream European social democracy. Solidarity was firmly placed among the values of socialism, and the concept was used in a way similar to that in social democratic parties, which now referred to social solidarity, solidarity with the Third World and the environment (PCI 1986a).

In 1989, the PCI declared that it was time to break with the Leninist tradition and establish a new socialist party. Two years later, the name of the party was changed to *Partito Democratico della Sinistra*, later renamed *Democratici di Sinistra* (DS) in a not very successful attempt to broaden its appeal by including former members of the PSI, social Christians and liberals. In 1992, the long process of social democratisation was concluded when the DS became a member of the social democratic family and was accepted as a member of the Socialist International.

Today, the DS has adopted statutes and programmes with a language close to that of the French PS. The statutes approved in 2000 declared that the DS represents a confluence of different cultural and political tendencies with the same democratic and anti-fascist values that constituted the basis for the second Italian republic after World War II. These tendencies were defined as representing the tradition of the PCI, the PSI, non-believers, liberals and social Christianity. The 'DS shares the values of freedom and equality, justice and safety, work, social solidarity and peace', the statutes say. There are frequent references to *solidarity*, used in a wide sense as in other social democratic party programmes, for instance, solidarity between generations (DS 2000).

However, the integration of the modern social democratic solidarity discourse in programmes conceals the fact that two different ideas of solidarity are at work in the party. On the one hand, a majority wants to redistribute resources in the social security system to have a system that protects all groups in more or less the same way. On the other hand, a strong minority does not want to accept redistribution that reduces the social protection that well-organised sections of the working class have acquired through struggle and negotiation. The former argues using a modern social democratic concept of solidarity, whereas the latter seems to have an idea of solidarity that represents a mixture of the Marxist concept and the modern social democratic concept.[2] The outcome of this conflict could eventually mean a split in the party.

The DS is the only social democratic party among those studied here that has adopted the concept of subsidiarity in its programme and declares that DS politics are based on this principle (see Chapters 3 and 6 regarding subsidiarity). The DS does not draw any explicit line of demarcation between its concept of subsidiarity and the Christian democratic concept of subsidiarity. At first glance, the central accent of traditional communist ideology makes this surprising. However, the acceptance of the concept

[2] To understand this conflict it is necessary to understand the special characteristics of the Italian welfare state. The Italian welfare state is strongly dualistic. Private white-collar employees, employees in the public sector and the well-organised industrial working class enjoy an extensive pension system and unemployment benefits, whereas less protected groups and youth are poorly, or not at all, sheltered against social risk. Thus, one position in the DS is to reform the pension system by reducing benefits for those who are best protected to introduce unemployment benefits, and increase pensions, etc. for those who today do not enjoy social protection. The other position is to struggle to preserve the rights of the best-organised part of the working class and to try to introduce reforms to improve the situation of those who today are left without protection. The problem then is to find the resources for such a solution. See for instance Fargion (1997) and Rhodes (1997).

of subsidiarity may be a result of what Valeria Fargion has called the *cross-fertilisation* in Italian politics. The PCI accepted early the role of voluntary organisations, whereas Christian democracy accepted an element of state planning (Fargion 1997). Because municipalities were not entitled to impose taxes and were dependent on government grants, the PCI had to rely on local resources, and among these was a well-developed network of organisations and groups. This combination of local power and responsibility on the one hand, and denial of access to government power on the other hand, made the PCI more inclined to view decentralisation and voluntary organisations in a more positive way than has been usual in the communist tradition.

At the same time, the notion of the *individual, individual freedom* and *individual difference* are emphasised several times in the statutes. As in other social democratic parties, the DS recognises the problem of reconciling solidarity and individualism. Also, as most other social democratic parties, the DS includes *equality* in its discourse. Thus, the political trajectory of the DS is clear: it has developed into a normal social democratic party both in terms of general content and in terms of its concept of solidarity.

The DS has modernised its programme language and ideology, but the problem has been to modernise without losing support in the working class. So far, the DS has not succeeded in developing a social and political alliance that unites the traditional industrial working-class electorate with the new middle class. It took part in the government of the Olive Alliance from 1996 to 2001, but the national elections in 2001 reduced its electoral support to about 20 per cent. The establishment of the new party *Margherita*,[3] which is both a competitor and a partner in the Olive Alliance, in 2002, will probably make it even harder for it to become a social democratic party with the same political clout as those of the 'normal' European type. In 2003, the party was ridden with internal discussions about its identity. Should it be a left-wing social democratic party with a working-class and left-wing identity, or should it merge with other groups in the Olive Alliance and develop this into a broad democratic party, or a mixture between a party and a federation?

Conclusion

For a long time Marxist–Leninist parties stuck to the classic Marxist idea of solidarity, but after the change of political strategy in 1935 it was no

---

[3] Established by a merger of the Catholic PPI and the supporters of former Prime Minister Romano Prodi.

longer convenient to emphasise the Leninist idea of solidarity. When the goal was to establish a class alliance, the idea of working-class solidarity had to be toned down. Moreover, Lukács version of this idea was probably too blunt in its emphasis on the abolition of personal freedom and was not adopted in the institutionalised language of Marxist–Leninism. Neither did these parties adopt the concept of solidarity that Gramsci developed. Communist parties were ambivalent towards the term *solidarity*, and *solidarity* was adopted in the programme language of the Leninist tradition much later than in the social democratic tradition. The bellicose, conflict-oriented and cynical approach of the founding father of this tradition, Lenin, may have prevented the inclusion of a softer and more emotive word such as *solidarity* in theoretical texts and programme language. His disgust with general human ethics contributed to the same.

As was the case for social democracy, the increasing frequency of *solidarity* in the programmes took place in a context of a general deradicalisation of political language. The difference between the Italian PCI/DS and the French PCF illustrates this. When the PCF stuck more stubbornly to a restricted concept of solidarity, this was part of its general reluctance to abandon Marxist–Leninist ideology. Consequently, it did not replace the old concept of solidarity with a modern concept in time to avoid losing the confidence of the working class when the Berlin Wall fell and a populist party on the right achieved support in the working class. The PCI/DS went through a more profound process of deradicalisation that entailed adopting a modern concept of solidarity, and it succeeded in surviving, not as a communist, but as a social democratic party.

Fascism: solidarity with the nation – against other nationalities and ethnic groups

The 1920s and 1930s witnessed the emergence of an ideology that presented itself as an alternative to Marxism and social and Christian democracy, as well as to Liberalism. *Fascism* rejected both the liberal preoccupation with individual autonomy and freedom, and the Marxist idea of class solidarity and struggle between antagonistic classes. It accused liberal democracy of conceiving of society as an aggregate of individuals without common beliefs and emotional solidarity and argued that those who speak the same language and share common values in a national community are closer to each other than to anyone else (Sternhell 2001). The nation was not a collection of citizens, but a deeper community, an organism, and therefore, the *nation* should be the basis for solidarity. However, the national organism consisted of healthy and unhealthy parts, and the unhealthy parts should be cured, or eliminated.

Many authors have directed attention to the intellectual paucity of fascism. Contrary to Marxist and social democratic parties, there was no substantial group of intellectuals who could develop fascist theories and ideology (Smith 1997; Eatwell 1999). The fascist concept of solidarity was not located in a discourse where solidarity was integrated with other key concepts. Fascism appealed to many people, not because of its ideological coherence, but because of its emotional and instinctive appeals. Fascism supplemented its lack of a coherent political language with a strong emphasis on other forms of communication – mass rallies, films and other non-verbal means of communication (Freeden 2001).

In Italy, after having been expelled from the Socialist Party, Mussolini returned from the war as an opponent of socialism, established his *sfasci di combattimento* and gained power in 1922. In Germany, Hitler was appointed *Reichskanzler* in 1933. Both presented an ideology that appealed to anti-socialist sentiments among the farmers and the middle class, argued for national unity and national self-assertion, an active welfare policy and a conception of solidarity opposed to that of the labour movement. Although there are important differences between Italian fascism and German Nazism, both are discussed here under the common denomination of fascism.

Even if Italian fascism was not based on biological racism and was not as brutal and totalitarian as German Nazism, both presented themselves as alternatives to Marxism and Liberalism, rejected working-class collectivism and class struggle on the one hand and individualism on the other, and argued for a new solidarity across social classes. Unlike Marxism, fascism did not see the state as an instrument of the ruling class, nor Liberalism as a potential threat to personal initiative and economic development. For both Mussolini and Hitler, solidarity was first and foremost *national* solidarity – a sense of community that forges citizens together in opposition to other nations. Thus, we shall concentrate on the two protagonists, Mussolini and Hitler.

Mussolini: the state creates solidarity

The term *solidarity* does not appear frequently in Mussolini's speeches and texts. After having been appointed prime minister in 1922, he was more preoccupied with *discipline* than with solidarity, and in his main speeches he utilised, as Lenin did, the concept of *discipline* more frequently than the term solidarity. Yet, there is a fascist concept of solidarity which appeared now and then. The foundation for fascist solidarity is the nation, and for Mussolini, solidarity always referred to *national* solidarity.[4] His programme on labour issues, *Carta del lavoro* of 1927, declared that the goal was to develop solidarity between different groups in production by smoothing out contradictory interests between wage earners and employers, in such a way that these 'obsolete interests were subordinated to the interest of production as such' (Mussolini 1927). Thus, this idea had a faint resemblance to the *productivist* concept of solidarity which social democrats in Norway and Denmark presented some years later.

Mussolini developed this idea further in his theoretical work on *The Corporate State*, published in 1935. Here he outlined ideas about the role of the state in creating solidarity in a way that recalls Hegel's idea about the state as representing the general interest of society. The fascist conception of life is anti-individualist and 'stresses the importance of the state and accepts the individual only in so far as his interests coincide with those of the state, which stands for the conscience and the universal will of man as historic entity', he maintained. The role of the state is to create solidarity: 'The state educates the citizen to civism, makes them aware of their mission, urges them to unity: its justice harmonizes their divergent interests; it transmits to future generations the conquests of the mind in the fields of science, art, law, human solidarity' (Mussolini 1938).

The fascist idea of the state as the universal expression of the interest of society was translated into an active labour market and social welfare policy. The relationship between labour market actors was regulated, and strikes and lockouts were forbidden. The law determined wages, working hours and vacations. New initiatives in social security protection were undertaken and partially implemented, concerning pensions, accidents at work, and unemployment and family policy (see Sørensen 1991; Smith 1997). The nation should be united in the struggle for colonisation and expansion in Africa.

Hitler: solidarity built on racism

The German national socialist conception of solidarity paralleled this in most respects. In national socialist ideology, the idea of society as a *Volkskörper*, a *nation-body*, was the point of departure for the idea of solidarity. Some of the parts of this body were healthy and should be cultivated, others were sick and inferior and should be removed (Otto and Sünker 1989). This idea was supplemented by the idea of a *Volksgemeinschaft*, a community of the people. In this community each individual should maximise his/her contribution for the good of the whole

---

[4] See his speeches published in Severino (1923).

community instead of maximising his/her individual self-interest, and should not demand individual rights and entitlements from society. Each individual should be prepared to make great sacrifices for the good of the nation and the community, and the idea of individual rights had no place in this ideology (Rimlinger 1987).

Hitler did not elaborate on his theories as extensively as did Mussolini in *The Corporate State*. If Mussolini was no great theorist, this was even truer about Hitler. In his speech on culture at the NSDAP congress in 1936, he elaborated on the relationships between community (*Gemeinschaft*), individual freedom and democracy. He condemned individualism and democracy because both result in anarchy. Democracy is the mental pre-condition for anarchy, he maintained. If individual freedom is unlimited, community cannot develop. The interest of the totality, the public interest, requires that burdens and duties are imposed on the individual, and restrictions on individual freedom tie the individuals together in a union, strengthen community and the state. The state represents a higher form of community, but must be founded on authoritarian principles to avoid anarchy. However, each higher form of community, such as the state, is only sensible and tolerable when those who rule are of the blood of their own community, he declared (Hitler 1936a). Here, we find a number of core elements in Nazism: the preoccupation with *Gemeinschaft*, community, the disparagement of individualism and individual freedom; the lack of distinction between community and the state; and the obsession with ethnic origin as the basis of solidarity.

Hitler's concept of community is illustrated by the metaphor of community as an organism. In *Mein Kampf*, Hitler declared that the state was 'a national organism and not an economic organisation' (Hitler 1925–27). First, he sought to redefine the Marxist concept of *worker* by including white-collar employees in the concept and by introducing concepts which did not have Marxist connotations, such as *Arbeitertum* and *Arbeitnehmerschaft – workforce* and *employees* (Kele 1975). Second, workers and employers should leave disagreement behind and unite as Germans if Germany was to prosper economically and regain its position as a world power. Consequently, there was no room for internal conflict, particularly not the Marxist idea of conflict between employees and employers, which are irrelevant concepts, he professed. There exist no employer and no employee above the highest interests of the nation, but only representatives of the work of the whole people (Hitler 1936b). The term solidarity was not frequently utilised to express the idea of community, but he wrote mockingly about socialists, who were 'plundered in solidarity with the rest of the world'. Moreover, he criticised those who told lies 'about an internal brotherhood between Negroes, Germans, and Chinese'

Table 8.1 *The fascist concept of solidarity*

Foundation	Objective	Inclusiveness	Collective orientation
The nation	National strength	Wider/more restricted: the nation, not the class	Very strong: no individual freedom
The race	A new kind of human being	Minorities excluded	The individual subordinated or integrated in the collective

(Hitler 1925). Germans should not seek solidarity with people in other countries or with people of other races, but only with the German nation. This national socialist idea of solidarity may be distinguished from Italian fascism by the more aggressive exclusion of those who are, or ought to be, outside national community. Whereas Italian fascism defined the nation in terms of culture, German fascism defined the nation in terms of biology and race (Eatwell 1999).

The German national socialists had, as the Italian fascists had, ambitious plans for an active labour market and social policy. The government should control business and economic life, plan the economy and decide on wages and prices. Class struggle and class solidarity were to disappear and be supplanted by a broad societal solidarity; *volksgemeinschaftlicher Solidarität* (Sørensen 1991). The right to holidays was introduced, child benefits were discussed and extensive plans for improvements in pensions were made, but these initiatives and plans were controversial in the national socialist party, and Hitler decided to let the matter rest until after the war.

Conclusion: the fascist concepts

Summing up, the fascist concept of solidarity represents a concept that was not spelled out among the eight models presented in Chapter 3. The foundation of fascist solidarity is not a class, but the nation. The objective was most often stated to be increasing the strength of the nation, sometimes also as creating a new kind of human being. Fascist solidarity was at the same time wider and more restricted than classic Marxist solidarity, as it cut across class boundaries and entailed (almost) the whole nation. It included all classes, but excluded a range of minorities. What is more important is the kind of exclusion and the brutality with which it was implemented. Fascist solidarity was far more aggressive in defining who were to be left out than other concepts of solidarity. Whereas Marxist solidarity was somewhat silent in the main, or ambiguous about this aspect (solidarity with women, immigrants, poor people of the Third World), fascist solidarity was clear and crisp. This applies primarily to German fascism. Minorities like Jews, Gypsies, gays, the disabled, the mentally ill and black people, were not only to be left out, but actively discriminated against and eliminated, even though there was a difference between German and Italian fascism in this respect. Finally, fascist solidarity, as Leninist solidarity, meant a strong degree of collective orientation. The individual was subordinated to the collective interest of the nation, and the value of individual freedom was rejected. Fortunately, neither the fascist nor Leninist idea of solidarity prevailed in politics in Western Europe.

Part III

The present precariousness of solidarity

9 Solidarity in modern social philosophy and Christian ethics

In previous chapters we have seen that there are several ideas of solidarity in politics in Europe. These ideas grew out of different historical and ideological traditions; Marxism, socialist revisionism, Catholic social teachings, nationalist ideas about the nation and the race. At the beginning of the twenty-first century, two of these traditions are particularly influential in European politics: social democracy and Christian democracy. During the latter part of the previous century both types of party have developed a political language in which the concept of solidarity is firmly integrated and bound together with other key values that are generally highly valued. From the other traditions, Marxism and fascism, only remnants remain. The price of success of the concept of solidarity, however, is that it has lost, if it ever possessed it, a clear meaning. The problem is not only that it is difficult to identify an 'ineliminable' core of the concept, but also that the meaning varies according to how it is related to the other key values of social democratic and Christian democratic values.

The fluidity and looseness of the concepts of solidarity in party politics give rise to intellectual dissatisfaction. Consequently, we must seek the most outstanding thinkers of our time and investigate to see if they may be able to assist us in clarifying the concept and understanding of what solidarity is all about. In this chapter I return to the three traditions discussed in the first part of this book and discuss the present status of the idea of solidarity in modern social theory, socialist and social democratic theory and Catholic and Protestant social ethics. How do the brightest minds in these areas view solidarity, its foundation, objective, inclusiveness, and the relationship between individuality and the collective?

First, I discuss systems theory, rational choice theory and communitarianism. Next, I comment on Marxist theory and the contributions from social theorists who consider themselves, or generally are viewed, as belonging to the political left in a broad sense. These are Ulrich Beck, Anthony Giddens, Jürgen Habermas' communicative theory, Hauke Brunkhorst's argumentation for a global institutionalisation of solidarity, and Richard Rorty's arguments for solidarity from his post-modern position.[1] Finally, I shall discuss the contributions to social ethics from two Christians, the Catholic Hans Küng and the Protestant Jürgen Moltmann.

Modern social theory

Normative theories of solidarity are concerned with the social integration of modern societies and how solidarity may bring about such integration, and see the key to solidarity in the obligation to comply with group norms. Such theories are found in the tradition from classic sociology to Parsons. Talcott Parsons and Niklas Luhmann picked up the thread from earlier theories about interaction, socialisation and social integration, although with quite different conclusions in terms of solidarity. Michael Hechter has proposed a paradigm for seeing solidarity as a result of individual rational pursuit of self-interest. Finally, Alastair MacIntyre has directed a strong attack on the foundation of rational choice theory, asserting that all values are context-bound. American communitarians such as Amitai Etzioni, Richard Bellah and others have built on his contribution.

System theory: Parsons and Luhmann

Max Weber's passages about solidarity in *Economy and Society* in 1922 represent the last important contribution from classic sociology to the reflection on solidarity. Three decades were now to pass until modern sociology again found the concept of solidarity interesting. The protagonist of modern sociology and the bridge between classic and modern sociology, Talcott Parsons, took up the theme again after World War II. After Parsons, another couple of decades were to pass before solidarity again aroused the interest of social theorists. After 1973 the long period of strong economic growth came to a halt; in the 1980s individualism and globalisation increased and the concept of solidarity came onto the political agenda. At the end of the twentieth and the beginning of the twenty-first centuries, social theorists have again directed their interest to the concept of solidarity.

---

[1] This classification is somewhat misleading as Giddens, Habermas, Brunkhorst and Rorty also contribute to modern social theory. It may also be argued that Giddens, Habermas and Rorty must be considered as social liberals and not as social democrats, but I have grouped these theorists together because of their intentions to be part of a left-wing discourse. I could also have included here *structural theories* about solidarity. Structural approaches have most often been inspired by Marxism, and find the source of solidarity in the common situation of individuals and specify the conditions that transform individual interest into group or class solidarity, cf. the discussion of the class foundation of solidarity in the final chapter.

Parsons was influenced by German idealism and in particular, Max Weber, and he asked anew, as had Durkheim and Simmel: How is society possible? Whereas Durkheim saw a combination of increased division of work and common values as the basis for solidarity, Parsons suggested that harmony in society rests on the agreement about basic values and rules that are constitutive for society (Turner and Rojek 2001), and was less optimistic about the effects of increased social differentiation in modern society. Agreement about basic values is the result of internalisation of norms through education, training and culture, Parsons argued. His main concern was social integration, and he did not elaborate extensively on the role of solidarity in constituting integration and social order. In *The Social System,* he referred briefly to solidarity as 'the institutionalised integration of ego with alter' (Parsons 1951). Whereas the concept of *loyalty* refers to motivation to act in accordance with 'the other's' interests and expectation beyond obligation, *solidarity* is an institutionalised role-expectation and means-orientation towards the collective, he maintained. This orientation makes the ego act in accordance with the expectations of others. Not to do so would mean he or she might incur sanctions from the collective. As most individuals are members of many systems of interaction and have several roles to perform, the individual will feel a varying degree of obligation to act according to the expectations and norms of the collective. So, for Parsons, solidarity is linked to the system of interaction.

Twenty years after Parsons published *The Social System,* he returned to social integration and solidarity in *The System of Modern Societies* and *Politics and the Social Structure.* Now, his concern about social integration and solidarity is even more pronounced. Society is a social system with several subsystems, he maintained. The *integrative* subsystem, *societal community,* constitutes the core of society (Parsons 1971). Societal community articulates norms that generate unity and cohesiveness, defines loyalty and preparedness to respond to appeals from the collective, the public interest or the public need. However, social differentiation and the increasing pluralisation of roles in modern society represent a problem for the societal community and the integration of social systems. In modern societies there are many groups with a 'partial' solidarity, and partial solidarity within a group, race or religion is often attained at the expense of a wider solidarity. Where many partial solidarities exist, these must be integrated in a system that minimises internal conflicts and reinforces complementary interest structures. Parsons does not distinguish clearly between social integration and solidarity, but solidarity seems to refer to the attitudes of individuals, whereas social integration is the result of all integrative mechanisms (Parsons 1969). He diagnosed a crisis in the societal community, located in the motivational bases for social solidarity: society had become large scale and highly pluralistic, and old type *Gemeinschaft society* could no longer be institutionalised. This would probably lead to 'a great deal of conflict', he warned (Parsons 1971).

Parsons also picked up another idea from Durkheim, the integrative function of law, which Luhmann and Habermas came to discuss more extensively in the years to come. Inspired by Marshall's concept of citizenship (see below), he argued that the common status of citizenship provides a sufficient foundation for national solidarity because it accepts diversity in terms of religion, ethnicity and territoriality (Parsons 1971).

After Parsons, social integration has continued to preoccupy sociologists, but there are few contributions to the analysis of the relationship between social integration and solidarity. What is common for this tradition is that *interaction* constitutes an important precondition for the constitution of solidarity. This is the case for Niklas Luhmann, the leading exponent of German and European system theory, as well. Luhmann develops Parsons' concern about the disintegrating effects of social differentiation in modern society and argues that differentiation into many autonomous subsystems means that there is no unified structure of value orientations. Social systems are defined by the relationships between social actions that refer to each other, and not by certain patterns of values and structure. Whereas Parsons worried that differentiation might constitute a threat to social integration, Luhmann thought that differentiation and conflict contribute to the renewal and survival of the system. Mutual uncertainty and unpredictability cause individuals to become part of a system (Østerberg 1988). Moreover, Luhmann sees the legal system (*das Recht*) as a foundation for social integration because it creates stable reciprocal expectations, and legitimate decisions that relieve citizens of the need to decide on moral norms and sanctions against free-riders (Luhmann 1993).

Nonetheless, Luhmann is full of contempt for the concept of solidarity and rhetoric in the tradition of the French Revolution and has delivered perhaps the sharpest critique of the concept of solidarity in modern sociological and political discourse (Luhmann 1984). As with Parsons, Luhmann links solidarity to the system of interaction and argues that the system of interaction and the system of society (*Gesellschaftsystem*) have been separated from each other. Systems of interaction presuppose presence and are established when human beings observe the presence of one another and start to communicate. Presence is both the possibility and the limit of the system, and without presence, there is no interaction and no system, and consequently no solidarity, he argues.

For Luhmann, societies are extensive systems of communication. When the means of communication are developed societies are extended to include more human beings, and interaction is no longer possible in society as a whole. The reciprocal control that existed in the old society is made impossible, and the conditions for solidarity no longer exist. The development of the concept of solidarity from the nineteenth century until today is an ideological reaction against the social development of capitalism and a manifestation of a longing for a society that no longer exists: 'solidarity is the wish of individuals who are not content with individualism' (Luhmann 1984). He remarks ironically that the concept has been elevated to a general basic value which we 'may hear about on TV', 'if not, we would not have known about it'. However the task of sociologists is not to take part in the production of ideology, but to enlighten society regarding its own complexity, he maintained.

Although Luhmann's critique is scathing, it is based on a postulate with which we are free to disagree, that solidarity is dependent upon interaction and may not stretch beyond the boundaries of the social system. If this is so, solidarity might never stretch beyond the immediate network, local community or workplace of the individual. However, this argument can be contested. First, it is contrary to what can be observed empirically. Many identify with the suffering of people with whom they do not interact, and support their struggle. Second, this is a problematic postulate in a world where media and communication technology blur the lines between interaction and non-interaction.

Solidarity as rational choice

Durkheim, and later Parsons, asserted that shared values and internalisation of norms constitute the basis for social order and solidarity. The problem with these theories is that they do not account for the fact that groups belonging to the same culture or society may exhibit different degrees of solidarity. This is the starting point for Michael Hechter, who in *Principles of group solidarity* sets out to develop a theory of solidarity based on the theory of rational choice in the tradition of Mancur Olson and James Coleman (Hechter 1987). The literature on collective action, rational choice and its limitations is abundant. It is not the task of this book to discuss this theme in general here, but to concentrate on authors who have contributed to theories about solidarity (see for instance (Elster 1983)).

Rational choice may be considered either a methodological principle from which hypotheses may be generated, or as an assumption about individual behaviour. In both cases individuals are seen as bearers of sets of given, discrete and clear preferences. When faced with a choice between alternatives, individuals choose the alternative they believe will maximise their utility. So, individuals are assumed to be rational, coherent and purposefully realising their maximal interests.[2] In *The Logic of Collective Action*, Mancur Olson contested the conventional assumption that groups of individuals with common interests can be expected to act on behalf of their common interests in the same way as individuals act on their personal interests (Olson 1965). Olson argued that rational individuals in large groups will *not* act to realise collective group interests without being forced to do so or motivated by strong incentives, because a rational individual will see her or his personal interest best served by being passive and expect the others to realise the common goal. Accordingly, Olson is not preoccupied with solidarity, but with the opposite, the problem of free-riders.

The American sociologist, Michael Hechter, is concerned not with free-riders, but with solidarity. For Hechter, solidarity is the preparedness of individuals to use private resources for collective ends and to follow up such preparedness by action. Therefore, solidarity means both certain attitudes and a certain behaviour that is consistent with those attitudes. Why do individuals constitute groups in which group members are solidaristic with one another? Hechter argues that individuals may have common interests in pursuing a common goal, for instance in jointly producing goods that they desire but cannot provide at all, or as efficiently, alone. The incentives may be cost-sharing, as it is less expensive to produce goods collectively, and some goods cannot be produced by individuals themselves. Such goods may be safety, material goods or, we may add, social welfare institutions. To avoid free-riders, the group must develop rules for how group members are to be coordinated and how resources are to be allocated.

Why should group members choose to adhere to such rules? According to Hechter, one possibility is to *enforce* adherence. Another solution is to produce only goods that can be restricted only to those who contribute. Some kinds of social insurance systems are built more or less on such principles, but these mechanisms are not sufficient to prevent individuals trying to be free-riders. The group must develop a monitoring system with persons specialised in control functions, but for large groups this may be costly and bring about bureaucratisation of the

---

[2] It is not the place here to discuss these assumptions, which have been contested a number of times by authors such as Herbert Simon (1947) and Jon Elster (1989a; 1989b).

group and alienation of group members. As a consequence, there are limits to what extent group solidarity may depend on a formal control system.

The group's capacity to control depends also upon the degree to which the contribution of the individual can be measured, and the visibility of individual behaviour. In groups where members are not able to see or understand the contribution of others, suspicion about free-riding may erode group solidarity. For Hechter then, the key condition for solidarity is that group members can monitor and sanction each other and prevent free-riding. Consequently, solidarity depends on communication. Small groups can generate solidarity more easily because all members can observe the behaviour of the others. In large groups, solidarity becomes more difficult, and usually depends upon the existence of formal control systems.

As Hechter himself notes, when rational choice theory is regarded as an assumption about individual behaviour, it is confronted with the problem that it is evident that people frequently do not behave according to the theory. Individuals show love and altruism, give support to people who are oppressed, and die for causes in which they have no egoistic interest. The pioneers of the labour movement engaged in struggle and invested their lives in activities for which they might not rationally expect to be rewarded personally. Hechter tries to solve this problem by introducing behavioural learning theory. Individuals adhere to group norms and adopt pro-social behaviour not only because of the fear of sanctions, but because they learn when they observe that pro-social behaviour is rewarded. In this way, Hechter reintroduces socialisation through the back door. With regret, he has to admit that he is 'forced to conclude that while it is possible for *small* groups to survive on the basis of informal control, it is not possible for *large* groups to do so' (Hechter 1987). This admission is problematic. The prediction that solidarity is strongest when the group is small, densely interacting and closed against the environment, and when members closely monitor each other and exchange rewards, introduces variables that are found also in the theory of solidarity in the Durkheimian tradition (Collins 1994). In more recent works, Jon Elster, a central contributor to rational choice theory and theories of collective action, has expressed what he himself characterises as 'a certain disillusionment with instrumental rationality' (Elster 1989b), and demonstrated a new interest in social norms as the cement of society. In politics, the idea of justice provides an alternative motivational factor for collective action, social reforms and the development of the welfare state, he argues (Elster 1989a; 1989b).

These problems do not deprive Hechter's contribution of the virtue of having reintroduced important issues in the debate on the role of solidarity in the modern welfare state.[3] A fruitful theory about the modern welfare state must account for the rational interest that individuals, groups or classes have in extensive public systems of social insurance, welfare and health services. The modern welfare state exists in a highly complicated society where many of Hechter's prerequisites for solidarity are not present. Modern society is heterogeneous, with low interaction and communication between different groups. For individuals it is often not easy to see and recognise how their fellow citizens contribute to the production and maintenance of public goods. Formal control is not sufficient to ensure that everybody contributes through their taxes, as witnessed by the scope of the black or underground economy. Thus, suspicions about free-riding can easily arise. Even if we do not need to accept rational choice theory as a paradigm, it is necessary to analyse and explain what combinations of individual rationalism and altruistic motivation are present today and are necessary in the future to secure a stable basis for the welfare state.

The historian, Peter Baldwin, has integrated elements of rational choice theory in his comparative study, *The Politics of Social Solidarity* (Baldwin 1990). The difference between Hecther and Baldwin is that the former makes rational choice theory a point of departure, whereas Baldwin claims that his theory is a result of his empirical studies. His historical study is about the social and political forces underlying the welfare states of Scandinavia, France, the United Kingdom and Germany, but it is also a contribution to social theory about mechanisms that bring about solidarity.

Without some sense of collective identity, of community or 'sameness', even a shared predicament is unlikely to prompt mutual aid. Nevertheless, a willingness to pay attention to the needs of others that goes beyond the tenuous one-sidedness of charity or altruism and yet is not the fruit of some form of interest-based, bilaterally advantageous reciprocity seems hard to envisage . . . Only when those who, in different circumstances, would have regarded themselves as self-reliant change their minds, only when sufficiently many see themselves as potentially at risk is a distribution according to need acceptable, is solidarity possible. (Baldwin 1990)

Thus, Baldwin applies rational choice theory, but transcends it at the same time. The rational pursuit of personal interest is integrated into a

---

[3] Hechter's pioneering contribution to the sociological study of solidarity has been followed by the attempts of colleagues in mathematical sociology to construct theoretical models about how obligations develop in a collective and why people comply in groups of different size and character, see Doreian and Fararo (1998).

broader frame where, interdependence, collective identity and normative elements are included as well.

The communitarians: a return to social integration

American communitarianism represents a critique of liberal positions from a sociological and social-philosophical point of view. Communitarian social theorists challenged liberal individualism as expressed by John Rawls (1971; 1985), and have at the same time inspired contributors to social democratic theory and politics (see below for Giddens, and Chapter 4 for Blair).

In *After Virtue*, the founder of modern communitarianism, Alastair MacIntyre, sets out to describe the lost morality of the past and to reject three positions on morality, *individual rationalism*, *emotivism* (the position that moral judgements are nothing but expression of preferences, attitudes and feelings), and *Marxism* (MacIntyre 2000 (1982)). These three positions on morality could only have been formulated with the language that was developed in specific historical situations and contexts, he argues. His investigation of moral virtues from Homer and Aristotle until today concludes that social identities and virtues cannot be understood without understanding the social community in which these identities and values were developed. We inherit from the past of our family, city, tribe and nation a variety of debts, inheritances, rightful expectations and obligations, and we have to learn to understand how others respond to us and how we should relate to them. The meaning of principles such as equality and justice, and we can here add, solidarity, is contextually bound and has no given universal validity. Morality, practice and community are indissolubly woven together, he maintains. He looks back to Comte's idea about historical debt as a basis for solidarity and revives a Durkheimian idea of community. What matters at this stage, he argues apocalyptically, is the construction of local forms of community within which civility and intellectual and moral life can be sustained through the 'new dark ages that are already upon us' (MacIntyre 2000 (1982)). So, MacIntyre ends up by looking to *community* for rescue.

Although communitarians make community a core concept, this concept is not at all clear. MacIntyre does not elaborate on the concept, and neither he nor his successors are clear and coherent about what community is, and the relationship between community and the concept of solidarity. The fundamental criterion for communitarians seems to be geographical closeness and interaction. Some communitarians argue that common values and history might constitute community as well (Bellah *et al.* 1996). Most communitarians do not use the term solidarity, but stick to *community*. In the key document, *The Responsive Communitarian Platform: Rights and Responsibilities*, social justice is based on reciprocity: 'each member of the community owes something to all the rest, and the community owes something to each of its members. Justice requires responsible individuals in a responsive community' (Etzioni 1993).

This insistence on justice is also found in other communitarian texts. Amitai Etzioni, the protagonist of American communitarianism and the main author of the platform, asserts that social justice is the key goal of solidarity, but a left-wing communitarian like Robert Bellah attributes this position to solidarity, emphasising that 'democratic communitarism confirms the central value of solidarity' (Bellah 1998). Nevertheless, the distinction between community and feelings of solidarity remains unclear.

A core idea of the communitarian project is to restore a balance between rights and responsibilities. Individual rights must be balanced against the obligation of personal responsibility and the duty to give something back to the community. First, the individual must feel a responsibility to take care of him/herself. Second, she must be responsible for the welfare of her closest family. Third, societies must feel a responsibility for communities when these are not able to secure welfare for their own members, Etzioni argues. This way of reasoning is close to the Catholic conception of subsidiarity.

Among communitarians, there are different conceptions of the basis for feelings of responsibility. Etzioni identifies three sources for a responsible community. Values are, or must be, inculcated through socialisation in the family and at school. Moral claims and the expectations of society are essential: 'Civil society requires we be each others' keepers', he says. Finally, participation, moral commitment and common values create community and what he calls a 'thick' society (Etzioni 1993; 1996; 2001). Bellah refers to social relations and views reciprocity, loyalty and a shared commitment to the common good as the mark of a full human life, whereas Alan Wolfe argues that social practice and personal experience in living together with others create moral commitment (Wolfe 1989). Consequently, the common denominator in communitarian thinking is that social relationships and social commitment are developed through interaction. This is close to the Durkheimian concept of solidarity.

The preoccupation with interaction and participation makes some communitarians sceptical of institutionalised social policy. Etzioni argues that voluntary organisations and networks must have a vital role in welfare policy and that reduced public responsibility and more 'lean government' will strengthen community. Wolfe asserts that both markets and the state weaken social practices and decrease time and space for moral ties and actions. The more we rely on the market and the state, the less opportunity there is for social relations to grow and develop. There is a need for 'a civil society – families, local networks of friends, solidaristic work places, voluntary organisations, spontaneous groups and movements . . . Every response to a social problem does not need to be an institutional response' (Wolfe 1989). In civil society, there must be space for personal practice based on ethical commitments.

Contrary to this concern about these potentially harmful effects of public social policy, and illustrating the plurality of communitarianism, in his study of American middle-class values, *Habits of the Heart*, Bellah is worried that individualism has become cancerous and undermines the values and institutions of neo-capitalist society (Bellah *et al.* 1996). Bellah utilises the concept of solidarity, but refers to solidarity and community as synonyms, as a 'sense of interconnection, shared fate, mutual responsibility, community'. Community must embrace all human beings, including those of other nations and cannot be restricted to friends, neighbourhood and local community, he maintains. However, when 'sameness', interaction and communication is rejected as the basis for solidarity, what should then constitute this basis? Here, Bellah, as MacIntyre, suggests *conversion*. Those who are privileged should convert to the understanding that human beings are interdependent, reject individualism and accept that massive resources should be used to reduce inequality and to improve conditions for the underclass (Bellah *et al.* 1996).

In addition to this belief in conversion, the communitarian approach raises a number of questions. First, a moral philosophy presupposes a sociology, MacIntyre argues, but he has few words about the sociology of modern society and the world in which his modern virtues will thrive and develop. This is conspicuous, as his revival of community – according to his own words – should save us from the 'new dark ages which are already upon us' (MacIntyre 2000 (1982)). Today, in a world with geographical and social mobility, ethnic plurality, cultural diversity and globalisation communication and interaction is perhaps based more on occupational and professional life than on local community. Accordingly, the question is: is it possible to return to a society and a world where communication and interaction is based upon local community, and what is the probability that MacIntyre's idea of community can save us from the 'new dark ages'?

Second, as mentioned above, the concept of community is not at all clear and coherent. The fundamental dilemma is whether the concept is reserved for communities based on geography and physical closeness, or if it includes also community that is build upon agreement on values when there is no interaction. If community depends on interaction and communication, how far can it extend and how broad can it be? The unclear conception of community leads to an unclear view about how inclusive solidarity can be. Moreover, Etzioni's insistence on common values and his emphasis on interaction and participation naturally raise the question regarding those who do not share common values and do not interact or participate in the way communitarians prescribe. Although he acknowledges this problem and argues that the common values he asks for must be non-discriminatory and possibly generalised, this does not solve the problem.

Third, communitarians disagree strongly about the relationship between solidarity and the welfare state. Some, such as Robert Bellah, argue that public responsibility is an expression of solidarity and the state must be active in social policy in order to reduce social differences. Others, like Alan Wolfe, argue that a strong public involvement in social policy undermines the normative predisposition of individuals to exercise solidarity and reduces solidaristic or other morally founded forms of involvement. Therefore, the state should withdraw and create a larger space for civil society and civic engagement. We may inquire: from what should the state withdraw? Here, Wolfe is most concerned with care and social services – kindergartens, childcare, care for the elderly. As Wolfe admits, we have no guarantee that government withdrawal from those areas would increase moral commitment among citizens. The result might just as likely be that public withdrawal would be replaced by market mechanisms or by nothing at all, and those who have an ability to pay for market-based services would seek instead private- and market-based solutions, while others would be left without any solution.

Fourthly, communitarians underestimate the normative function of the welfare state. The welfare state creates big apparatuses and educates thousands of persons to work in social welfare and health institutions, and it also develops norms and ideology. Those who are employed in health and social services have been trained to feel empathy with their clients and patients, defend their dignity and argue for solidarity with them. In Scandinavia, attitudes to the mentally retarded, gay people, fathers' obligations toward their children, changed *after* the introduction of social reforms that improved the situation of these groups. Thus, it may be premature to say goodbye to Titmuss, who argued that a universal welfare system in itself fosters solidarity and inclusion (Titmuss 1968).

Finally, in Europe there already exists an ideological tradition with a strong emphasis on the need to strengthen civil society: the Christian democratic tradition. The idea of subsidiarity emphasises that government should not interfere in civil society in a way that undermines or destroys the capacity of the individual, the family and the voluntary organisations to take social responsibility. One can hardly argue that societies where Christian democratic parties have been influential are more integrated or more strongly characterised by solidarity or community than societies where social democratic parties with their positive attitudes to public institutions and responsibility have been predominant. Anyway, communitarians should feel obliged to explain the ways in which their ideology differs from European Christian democracy.

Socialist, left-wing and critical theory

We left the theories of solidarity in the socialist tradition in Chapter 2 with the conclusion that the classic Marxist tradition and the Leninist tradition did not integrate a concept of solidarity in their political theories. Besides, revisionists like Bernstein and Wigforss were the first to introduce ethics into the concept of solidarity. What distinguished leading Marxist theorists from Marx to Gramsci was that they were both theorists *and* political practitioners. They developed their theories from the political struggle and *for* the struggle, and their theories influenced the practice of the labour movement and the socialist parties. At least from the 1930s this situation was fundamentally changed. Marxist theorists and political leaders were separated into two different roles, and Marxist theory did not influence the political practice of the dominant parties of the labour movement to any great extent, although it continued to influence the programmes of many parties. Theoretical Marxism now moved into the universities and into philosophy, where Marxists concentrated their work on art, epistemology, and – after some time – on the re-reading of *Capital* as well (Anderson 1977). In the last part of the 1970s, in his analysis of the relationship between Marxist theory and practice, Perry Anderson expressed his hope that the militant upswing after 1968 would bridge this gap.

However, Anderson's expectation was met only to a modest degree. In the past decades, some Marxists have again approached political theory and analysis. Key contributions have been Nicos Poulantzas' *Political power and social classes* (1978), inspired by the theories of the French communist and philosopher Louis Althusser; André Gorz's analysis of the working class in modern capitalism (1981); Ralph Miliband's contributions on the state and class struggle (1973; 1989); and the works of the Russian political scientist Boris Kagarlitsky (1999; 2000). These authors discuss the problem of the stagnation of the working class, the transformation of the structure of the working class and the growth of groups in the middle class. Even if they sometimes mention the challenges this development raises in terms of solidarity (Miliband 1989), this is always done briefly and superficially. They do not discuss the idea of solidarity systematically and elaborate on what a Marxist concept of solidarity should mean today: what is the role of self-interest, class-interest, altruism and empathy?; what is, and should be, the relationship between collective solidarity and individual freedom in a modern liberal democracy? Consequently, modern Marxist theory does not contribute much to a theoretical understanding and development of the idea of solidarity. This does not mean that Marxists are not preoccupied with, or not concerned about, solidarity. They are, and they use the concept frequently, but they take the concept for granted and are more preoccupied with the practical and political task of arguing for solidarity than with analysing and refining the concept. As mentioned in Chapter 2, early Marxists were reluctant or ambivalent about including ethics and compassion in their theories, and this appears to be the case today as well.

The British activist and contributor to research on globalisation, Peter Waterman, is an exception in this respect. Waterman is concerned about *global* solidarity and proposes a distinction between five aspects or components of solidarity; *identity, substitution, reciprocity, affinity* and *complementarity*. Identity, or 'sameness', is the traditional basis for socialist solidarity, but has become problematic today (on self-interest, see below). Substitution means standing up for those weaker and poorer than ourselves, but without taking a paternalistic role, and speaking and acting on their behalf. Reciprocity means interchange and support. Affinity suggests mutual appreciation or attraction. Finally, complementarity means the exchange of desired qualities (Waterman 2000). However, as we shall see below, his attempt to formulate a consistent concept of solidarity with these aspects is problematic and not without weaknesses.

Thus, we must look to theorists who understand the idea of solidarity as part of a more general project of human liberation and emancipation, and identify with the left in a broader and more generic sense.

Giddens, reflexivity and the Third Way

Anthony Giddens' theories about individualisation and reflexive modernisation do not mean that individuals become increasingly more egoistic. Individualisation refers to the increased autonomy of the individual, although according to Giddens, autonomy is not the same as egoism, but implies reciprocity and interdependence (Giddens 1994). Reflexive modernisation refers to the expansion of social reflexivity and means that to an increasing extent the individual must reflect upon the relationship and interdependence with others. Reconstructing social solidarity should therefore not be seen as protecting social cohesion around the edges of an egoistic marketplace, as might be said about some communitarians, Giddens maintains. The challenge is to reconcile individual autonomy and interdependence in the various spheres of social and economic life. The task is not to restore traditional community based on 'sameness', because this means conformism and exclusion and would not lead to emancipation, which has always been the project of the left, he argues. Thus, Giddens explicitly rejects the communitarian idea of civil society and community.

Giddens suggests some principles for a Third Way policy. First, damaged solidarity must be repaired, but individual autonomy and interdependence must be reconciled in a new way that is adapted to modern society. Solidarity in a modern society depends on *active trust*, the commitment to others and a renewal of personal and social responsibility for others. Traditional social democratic concern about life chances should be supplemented by *generative* politics which means that the role of public policy is not to arrange the lives of the citizens, but to make citizens themselves arrange their lives and their responsible relationship with others. In the spirit of Habermas, Giddens wants a *dialogic democracy*. Democracy is not only about interest representation, but about creating public arenas for controversial issues to be discussed and handled. Self-help groups and social movements might mobilise for this. According to Giddens, neo-liberal critique has identified major problematic aspects of the welfare state, and the welfare state has failed, as poverty has not been abolished, he argues. Individual rights and personal responsibility and obligations must be more balanced. The welfare state should not primarily distribute cash, but empower families and the civic culture (Giddens 1994).

Giddens' concept of solidarity represents a bridge between the communitarian idea and that of Habermas. Like most communitarians, he is sceptical towards the present welfare state as a vehicle of solidarity. But his critique of the welfare state is not concrete and not of much relevance when he argues that the welfare state has not abolished poverty because this failure is most conspicuous in a weak welfare state such as the British one, which is Giddens' reference, whereas the universal and more state-oriented Scandinavian welfare states have succeeded in reducing poverty far more efficiently than the British. Similarly to the communitarians, he argues that the family and non-state institutions such as voluntary organisations must have an important role to play in developing community. Finally, Giddens' concept of solidarity is, like the communitarian concept, a Durkheimian concept, although it is more nuanced than the communitarian because he takes Durkheim's reflections on the relationship between individual autonomy and interdependence a step further.

Giddens differs from the communitarians when it comes to community. His concept of solidarity has no nostalgic and no idyllic accent, and he is aware of the potential conformity and exclusion associated with the communitarian concept of solidarity. His idea of dialogic democracy echoes Habermas' emphasis on deliberation and communication, but he is less clear than Habermas in terms of what constitutes solidarity. He refers to active trust, but is not clear about what constitutes trust. The trust mechanism depends on the recognition of personal integrity, he argues, but this does not bring us much further because it is as difficult to develop trust and recognition of personal integrity as solidarity. As we shall see below, Habermas is more explicit in this respect.

Jürgen Habermas: solidarity through discourse

Perhaps the most important contribution to the debate about solidarity in modern society is found in the discourse ethics of Jürgen Habermas.[4] Habermas' ambition is to integrate several theoretical schools of thought. Of interest here is, in particular, his attempt to bridge the gap between concern with individual autonomy and justice in the Kantian tradition, and concern with the good society and community in the Aristotelian tradition and among the modern communitarians. The objective of his discourse ethics is to develop a moral philosophy with universal validity where *justice* and *solidarity* are key concepts. Habermas argues that these concepts represent two sides of the coin, where solidarity is the other side of justice (1984; 1995d). Justice means that all individuals are equally free and autonomous to make their own decisions. Each participant may reject norms that do not do justice to his or her self-understanding. On the other hand, norms are valid only in so far as all those who are affected by norms accept them in a free discourse. Solidarity is an ethical principle that means reciprocal concern for one another: it is about the welfare of others and is part of an inter-subjective and common way of life (*Lebensform*). This reciprocity distinguishes solidarity from charity, he asserts.

Habermas places his discourse ethics in the Kantian tradition that seeks to establish a universal ethic that is binding for all individuals. His idea of solidarity has the theories of G. H. Mead and Lawrence Kohlberg as points of departure. Mead developed the concept of role-taking and the generalised other, which is the capacity of the individual to take the point

---

[4] It is hardly possible to do justice to the extensive, voluminous and complicated works of Habermas, who has continuously integrated new aspects and objections from other authors into his theoretical system. Good introductions are Rehg (1994) and Eriksen and Weigård (2003).

of view of the other, while Kohlberg developed a theory about different levels of moral consciousness where the highest level is reached when an individual has the capacity to recognise abstract principles of behaviour and applies universal principles that one wants all human beings to follow (Eriksen and Weigård 2003). When an individual faces a situation where there are conflicting interests, she or he should transcend their concrete context and particular community and adopt the perspective of *all* those who might be affected by the decision. Each participant ought to look at things from the perspective of all other participants, and the issue at stake must be discussed in an inclusive, non-coercive and public discourse among free and equal partners (Habermas 1995). Thus, all participants can see whether it is possible to make their own position a general rule for all other participants. The result will be increased solidarity among autonomous and free individuals, and justice and solidarity will be reconciled.

Such solidarity is contingent on two characteristics of participating individuals. First, the individual must possess the cognitive capacity for abstractive reflection and conceptualisation of general principles. Second, if individual role-taking of others is to be effective, the individual must have *empathy*. Consensus and universal validity is not possible without a capacity for empathy and for imagining the situation of others. Empathy is developed through socialisation, Habermas states, and everyone who has been socialised through positive social relationships has a capacity for empathy:

anyone that has grown up in a reasonably functional family, who has formed his identity in relations of mutual recognition, who maintains himself in the network of reciprocal expectations and perspectives built into the pragmatics of the speech situation and communicative action, cannot fail to have acquired moral intuition . . . The maxim asserts the reciprocal dependence of socialisation and individuation, the interrelationships between personal autonomy and social solidarity, that is part of the implicit knowledge of all communicative active subjects . . . (Habermas 1995b)

As part of a universal moral, solidarity for Habermas has not a confined and particular meaning and does not mean that one is forced to make sacrifices for a collective which pursues its own interests. He acknowledges that by itself such a normative orientation will not extend beyond the family, the tribe, the town or the nation. Only ever-broader discourses may dissolve such boundaries and make solidarity more encompassing so that in principle it includes all human beings in a universal community of communication. He maintains that no one must be excluded from such a universal solidarity – 'neither underprivileged classes nor exploited nations, neither domesticated women nor marginalised minorities' (Habermas 1995a).

In *Between Facts and Norms*, Habermas discusses the relationship between communicative action, law and democracy in modern society and seeks to bridge the gap between his normative philosophy and the empirical picture that research has drawn of the actual functioning of politics in modern society (Habermas 1996). In modern societies there are three forces of macro-social integration, he maintains: the economic system, the administrative system and solidarity. Law is not only based on the possibility of sanctions by the state but is also founded on the solidarity that grows out of communicative action and deliberation in civil society. On the one hand, the public process of making laws contributes to increased solidarity in society. On the other hand, when law is accepted following a public discourse, this is an expression of solidarity and strengthens societal integration, he argues. In this way, democratic law is both a cause and, if only indirectly, an effect of solidarity. It stabilises expectations about the behaviour of others, secures symmetrical relationships between individuals, and make individuals recognise the individual rights of others.

However, there are some unsolved problems in Habermas' well-developed theory of the role of solidarity and discourse ethics. First, his concept of solidarity is very broad. Solidarity rightly means a moral commitment that goes beyond the question of justice and basic rights, but when solidarity is defined as the general feeling of community that is developed and expressed by the democratic process of establishing law, the concept might lose its political substance.[5] Law, also when introduced through a democratic process, can express and result in *less* solidarity. Not only, or primarily, is the process important, but also what the law is all about. Under some circumstances, democratic processes will result in welfare retrenchment, reduction in development cooperation and restrictive measures against those fleeing from oppression and hunger. Therefore, the content of laws are often more important in terms of solidarity than the process of making law. In a more recent essay, Habermas recognises that it is necessary to distinguish between the solidarity that is established in the law-making process and the extent to which the contents of law articulate solidarity (Habermas 2001a), but this is not yet

---

[5] Thus, I agree with Wildt (1998), who argues that the concept of solidarity has not much to do with the impartial activities of courts of justice. However, I do not agree with his contention that unequal treatment cannot express solidarity. This is dependent on the context and the intention of the lawmaker. In some situations positive unequal treatment might improve the situation of the weak and compensate for previous discrimination and oppression.

integrated into his theoretical system. He now argues that citizens must be able to identify their interests in the contents and the result of the process of making laws as well (Habermas 2001b). We saw above that Hechter had to let *socialisation* into his rational choice approach through the back door, and Habermas has had to reintroduce *self-interest*, even if he offers no real discussion about the relationship between self-interest and discourse.

Secondly, his two conditions for the development of ever-wider discourses among individuals who are affected by political decisions are problematic. One problem is that it is not obvious that the necessary capacity for cognitive reflection is well developed enough among a sufficient number of citizens to make solidarity effective in society and in the international community. Another problem is his emphasis on empathy. Even if we accept that most individuals grow up under circumstances that may be conducive to empathy, we may doubt that this is sufficient for the *application* of empathy in an ever-wider discourse. Is it not possible that individual personal interests reduce the preparedness to show empathy when those interests are at stake?

Besides, Habermas is not clear about the relationship between the emotional and the cognitive aspects of solidarity. Clearly, some cognitive capacity is a prerequisite for the abstract universalisation that is necessary for solidarity, but what about emotions and empathy? Is empathy only a necessary step at lower levels of reasoning, as Habermas may be understood, but not necessary at the highest level as well? Arne Johan Vetlesen discusses the relationship between emotional and cognitive aspects in the adoption of an abstract-universal perspective and argues that emotions and empathy and not only cognition play a role on the highest level of moral development (Vetlesen 1994). Solidarity necessarily invokes in us the recollection of experiences that are more emotional than cognitive-intellectual. In a person incapable of feeling affection for others, identification and empathy would not convince us that she/he had solidarity with another person or group, Vetlesen argues. Although this seems to be a reasonable position, I am not sure that it is an adequate criticism of Habermas, as he is quite explicit in *Justice and Solidarity* that empathy is a prerequisite for discourse and for reaching consensus.

A third problem is Habermas' optimism, or exaggerated idea, about the role and the effectiveness of discourse. As he directs attention to, in *Between Facts and Norms*, many political issues do not find their solutions according to principles of free discourse, but on the basis of power, influence, voting, negotiations and compromises, and he is well aware of the role of strategic action, bargaining and compromise. He argues that discourses must be institutionalised and directs attention to the voluntary organisations and social movements and civil society as mediums for communicative actions and social mobilisation (Habermas 1996). Nevertheless, when political conflicts reflect real differences of interest between groups and/or classes, this *struggle* develops a *particularistic* solidarity and not the universal solidarity that should be the result of reciprocal role-taking and discourse (Slagstad 2001). Besides, it is hard to find systematic reflection on adversaries and opponents in Habermas' social philosophy. In a world where not autonomous individuals, but collective and corporate actors, make important decisions, free discourse has necessarily a limited effect. Despite his aim of confronting normative theory with actual politics, his idea of discourse stylises one aspect of politics, that of dialogue and argumentation and does not give sufficient attention to the other aspects of politics (Slagstad 2001). He does not succeed in bridging the gap between his normative theory and the sad empirical descriptions of the actual functioning of political processes in modern society and seems to play down the practical and organisational problems of institutionalising discourse in politics.

Finally, when Habermas ties solidarity, discourse and interaction together, a third problem arises. As mentioned above, Parsons and Luhmann also linked solidarity to interaction. For Luhmann this meant that solidarity was no longer a fruitful concept because the system of interaction and the system of society have been split from one another. Habermas' answer is that solidarity is made possible through ever-wider discourses where all individuals take the perspective of all others. But if discourses are conditional upon interaction and communication, what about those individuals who need the solidarity of others with whom they never interact or communicate and consequently are not included in relevant discourses? Although Habermas insists that nobody should be excluded from universal solidarity, it is not easy to see how solidarity could be extended to those who are not part of discourses. As Vetlesen remarks, solidarity concerns others, abstract and absent, rather than those who are concrete and present. Solidarity is put to the test, not so much when we are participants of interaction as when we are not. Solidarity addresses a 'them' rather than an 'us'. Hence, solidarity often means to be called upon to take a step towards interaction rather than being a part of the interaction in advance. The relationship between empathy and solidarity is that whereas empathy is rooted in feelings of close interaction, solidarity is the ability of the individual to imagine or mentally abstract from personal empathic experience and extend one's empathy to unknown and non-experienced others. In this way, despite his universalising ambition, Habermas' concept of solidarity is too narrow, as Vetlesen maintains (1994).

In any case, Habermas' discourse ethics represent the most developed approach to solidarity in modern social and political theory. His concept of solidarity is universal and liberal and not restricted as in the Marxist tradition. He insists that a solidarity that allows the individual to submit him/herself to a collective is a false solidarity (Habermas 1995). Habermas' solidarity is ethical more than political, although it obviously has political implications.

The political and legal institutionalisation of solidarity

In a modern society there can be no real solidarity, either in a socialist, social democratic or Christian democratic version, if solidarity is not institutionalised. This means that solidarity in modern societies must be embedded in public economic, social and educational policies and in international trade and foreign policy. There can be no solidarity without accepting the right to political participation and expression of opinion, legal rights to protection against the hazards of life and terms of trade, and foreign aid that embodies the aim to share resources and improve the situation of peoples in other parts of the world. In his classic essay, *Citizenship and Social Class*, T. H. Marshall directed our attention to how the concept of citizenship expanded from including first, civil rights in the eighteenth century to political rights in the nineteenth century, and finally, social rights in the twentieth century (Marshall 1965). Without using the term solidarity, his emphasis on the concept of citizenship makes clear that the concept of citizenship is a condition for solidarity in modern society.

This theme has been taken up by Steven Lukes in the essay *Solidarity and Citizenship* (Lukes 1998) and by the German sociologist Hauke Brunkhorst in his *Solidarität* (Brunkhorst 2002). Both bring the relationship between citizenship and solidarity into focus. Lukes notes that today Marshall's arguments seem somewhat optimistic, as the number of marginalised and excluded persons has increased, and migration across national borders has anew made inclusion and citizenship burning issues. Today, he argues, the system of social rights must be improved and be made more inclusive so that also those who have been left outside can enjoy social citizenship. He suggests that Marshall's list should be complemented by a fourth type of citizenship, *cultural* citizenship. All individuals within a territory should enjoy the right to develop their own culture and have resources to do so. Accordingly, for Lukes, solidarity means accepting diversity and differences (Lukes 1998).

Hauke Brunkhorst develops Luhmann's theory about social systems and functional differentiation in modern society, but does not share

Luhmann's opinion that *solidarity* is not a fruitful concept. Together with Habermas, Brunkhorst shares a concern about democratic deliberations, social justice and the normative aspects of society in a globalised world. Brunkhorst's *Solidarität. Von der Bürgerfreundschaft zur globalen Rechtsgenossenschaft (Solidarity. From friendship among Burghers to a Global Community of Law)* represents a bold ambition to establish a new normative concept of solidarity and re-think the relationship between democracy, law and rights, solidarity and globalisation (Brunkhorst 2002).

Brunkhort's historical analysis of the idea of solidarity differs somewhat from the one given in this book. He argues that the modern idea of solidarity has three main roots, Jewish-Christian universalism, the idea of friendship in Aristotle and among burghers in the Middle Ages, and the idea of human rights from the French revolution in 1789. As has been made clear in this book, my disagreement here is with the second issue, and I have emphasised the labour movement tradition more strongly. Yet, this disagreement is of little interest here, because my interest is in the logic in Brunkhorst's analysis of the preconditions for an idea of solidarity that can meet the challenges we face today.

Brunkhorst's point of departure is the two problems of inclusion in modern society. The first is that individualisation entails a desocialisation of individuals. Historically, the process of individualisation raises the problem of the social order and how the individual should be reintegrated. Hobbes' answer to this problem was through a state under the rule of law, and the answer of the French revolution was a *democratic* state under the rule of law. Democracy, Brunkhorst maintains, is the only practical answer to the process of individualisation that has accompanied the functional differentiation in society. Without democracy it is not possible to integrate the productive potential of the individualisation process in society and institutionalise individuality permanently.

The second problem is the 'social issue'. The social misery and problems following industrialisation raised the problem of the inclusion of the new working class. Wherever a democratic state based on universal suffrage and the rule of law had been established, social rights were legally established and institutionalised. This provided a solution to the problem of social inclusion and integration of new social strata, but this 'egalitarian mass democracy' was confined to Europe and the USA and bound to the nation-state, Brunkhorst maintains. In a completely globalised world every culture has to live with individualisation, labour markets and educational systems that exclude a large number of people from society. The question now is if there is a potential of solidarity that can meet the challenges on a global level, as it once was on a national or regional level.

Brunkhorst's contention is that there will be no solution without a globalisation of democratic solidarity.

Globalisation has made it necessary to put the old issue of inclusion on the agenda again because it makes national solidarity collapse and welfare states come under siege. On a world scale both the two old forms of exclusion are found, absence of political inclusion in a democratic community of law and absence of social rights. The new slogan should be *No liberalisation without representation,* Brunkhorst argues. Today, the normative challenge for the citizen of the nation-state is to see him/herself as a citizen of the world. The old idea of solidarity between citizens and the love of one's neighbour must be developed into a practical project of creating an egalitarian and self-determined solidarity among strangers. Public law should be developed at the international level, but if international law is to be legitimate, this presupposes that nobody is excluded. The universal ambition of the democratic concept of human rights is a normative solution of the challenge to globalise egalitarian solidarity, Brunkhorst concludes. This is a sympathetic line of argument, but with weaknesses to which I shall return in the final chapter.

A post-modern view on solidarity

Like Habermas, Richard Rorty is part of the liberal tradition, but unlike Habermas, he has been considered a post-modernist as well, although he does not feel comfortable with that label. The point of departure for Rorty's reflections on solidarity in *Contingency, Irony and Solidarity* is the assumption that those who stood up for the Jews during World War II did this not because they saw Jews as their fellow human beings but because they identified with Jews as neighbours or compatriots (Rorty 1989). Consequently, solidarity is founded on feelings of compassion with people who are 'like us' and not on reason or a theory about what is common to *all* human beings, as a general conception of human worth or human dignity. This 'us' is something less and more local than humankind, and the feeling of solidarity is necessarily founded on the similarities and dissimilarities that constitute 'us' and 'them', The constitution of 'us', according to Rorty, is made through language and vocabularies contingent on history. Solidarity is something we may attain by becoming sensitive to the concrete pain and humiliation that our fellow human beings are experiencing. The public responsibility of the ironic[6] liberal is

---

[6] Rorty defines as ironic a person with a 'radical and continuous doubt about his own vocabulary, who understands that he can not resolve his doubts through his own vocabulary and who does not believe that his own narrative is more close to reality than others' (Rorty 1989).

to make the conception of 'we' more inclusive so that it includes those whom we earlier defined as 'they', and such an imaginative empathy may develop solidarity. Poets, authors, journalists and anthropologists can best contribute to this through 'thick' narratives, which develop understanding for the pain and humiliation that other human beings may experience.

Rorty's point of departure is that there are no truths or inherent universal human characteristics that are not contingent on history or institutions. Consequently, he does not share with Habermas the aim of establishing universal validity for solidarity. Rorty's vision of a utopian liberal society is a society where individuals understand that the language in which they formulate their morals, their consciences and the way they view community is historically and institutionally contingent, at the same time as they commit themselves morally. This understanding makes it impossible to claim that one's own attitudes and morals have universal validity, and this recognition should make for acceptance of differences and different life-styles. For Rorty, moral progress means more human solidarity and an increased capacity to recognise that differences associated with ethnicity, religion and ways of life are unimportant. What counts are the similarities when it comes to pain and humiliation and our capacity to include human beings who are unlike 'us'.

Rorty accepts that an individual who is exposed to a post-modern and ironic approach may experience this as cruel. He postulates that to be cruel is the worst a liberal human being can be,[7] but solves the dilemma that this poses for a liberal by postulating a sharp distinction between private and public. In the private sphere, the liberal may cultivate self-realisation, creativity and irony, but, in the public sphere, he must take responsibility for the solidarity that is necessary to develop liberal democracy.

The advantage of Rorty's approach compared to that of Habermas is that it highlights and more directly discusses the increasing pluralisation of modern society, as solidarity today requires acceptance of differences. Rorty's position seems somewhat more 'realistic' than Habermas' sympathetic goal of universal validity. Nonetheless, Rorty has left several questions unanswered. First, Norman Geras and other authors have severely criticised the argument that a universal notion of human beings and human dignity does not provide a forceful basis for solidarity (Geras 1995; Elshtain 2003). Geras demonstrates that research has documented

---

[7] To be reasonable, this must be understood not as a description but normatively. One may not assert that liberals have been more concerned about the suffering of others – particularly when it comes to suffering and oppression in the Third World liberals have not been in the front expressing solidarity.

that exactly such a concern was the basis for many of those who assisted Jews in escaping from fascism and the Holocaust. Consequently, Rorty's argument that there is no such thing as a common human nature, but that culturally contingent socialisation and context vocabularies are all there is, does not convince. He may be right that many people are more concerned about human suffering and humiliation among those who are close to themselves, but he does not provide an answer to why this *ought to be* so from a normative point of view. Moreover, his own preoccupation with human suffering and humiliation brings him in fact close to the universal idea of human dignity.

Rorty is not clear about what he sees as the foundation of the solidarity he calls for. Why should people take responsibility in the public sphere for the solidarity that is necessary to develop liberal democracy? It would not suffice here to say that solidarity is dependent on the historical context and the sharing of a vocabulary. Besides, he refers to *feelings* of solidarity, which might indicate that he thinks that solidarity is based more on feelings than on (historically contingent) reasoning (Dean 1996). He is also unclear about how the transition from 'they' to 'us' can best be brought about. Further, a sharp distinction between the private and public sphere is neither possible nor desirable and does not take into account the insight that feminism has given us (Fraser 1990). Finally, Rorty's reference to the special responsibility and task of poets and journalists in creating empathic descriptions that contribute to increased solidarity is not particularly convincing. Although poets, journalists and others may contribute, they generally do not possess more empathy or knowledge than most other people.

Modern Catholic and Protestant theology on solidarity

Chapter 3 demonstrated how two somewhat different concepts of solidarity developed in Catholicism and in Lutheran Protestantism. Now it is the time to see how modern contributors to Catholic and Protestant social ethics have made the concept of solidarity a part of their message. I shall concentrate on two theologians who have both formulated a radical reinterpretation of the relationship between religion and politics. These authors are not usually considered mainstream, but both have brought the concept of solidarity into the focus of Catholic and Protestant social teaching as professors of theology. The Catholic Hans Küng has in many respects been regarded as an outsider by those within the Catholic Church. The reformed Protestant Jürgen Moltmann has inspired radical Protestants and influenced the reorientation of the World Council of Churches.

A Catholic outsider: Hans Küng

The Swiss theologian Hans Küng[8] has been a major contributor to modern Catholic theology, although he is controversial and on the margins of official Catholic teaching. For Küng, the Second Vatican Council (see Chapter 3) represented a breach with the medieval character of the Church, but a breach that was not radical enough. The Church preserved outdated positions on contraceptives and the celibate, and the process of democratisation and modernisation was stopped (Küng 2003). The fundamental premise for Küng's theology is that the Church today is confronted with problems that can be addressed only from the standpoint of a modern worldview (Pitchers 1997). Modern individuals must see the Church and Christ as relevant for them, and the Church cannot meet society with an outmoded language and ideology. Küng wants to contribute to the modernisation of Catholic social ethics by redefining Jesus, and stripping him of historically defined characteristics such as God's miracles and his interventions in the laws of nature. For Küng, the core message of Jesus is the coming kingdom where God sides with the sinners. The challenge is to investigate the implication of forgiveness and service to one's neighbour in the modern world.

The point of departure for Küng's reflection on solidarity is that being a Christian means to live as a socially committed human being with Christ as a reference. 'To be a Christian means to live, act, and suffer as a real human being in succession to Jesus Christ in the modern world. It means to be responsible to God and to be of help to other human beings', he says in *Being a Christian* (Küng 1977). Because God wants what is good for human beings, Jesus, who generally lives according to the law, does not flinch from acting contrary to the law when this is necessary to contribute to the good. He states that the law is made for people and not for the religious and political system, and he argues that dogmatism and legalism should be replaced by a more humane system. This is a fundamentally different position to that of both Catholic scholastics as well as conventional Lutheran teaching on the two kingdoms and *sola scripture*. Because love should rule Christian behaviour, Christians should serve, renounce and forgive. To the indignation of the pious, Jesus exercises solidarity with all poor, wretched and miserable persons, with the excluded and neglected, the weak, the branded and the immoral, Küng says.

---

[8] Küng became professor of theology in Tübingen in Germany in 1960 and served as adviser to the Second Vatican Council (1962–65). He has time and again criticised papal authority and was the first major Catholic theologian to reject the doctrine of the infallibility of the Pope. In 1979, he lost his right to teach as a Catholic theologian. He is considered the most renowned Catholic theologian of dissent.

Whereas *Being a Christian* represents a radical theological interpretation of the need for solidarity, *A Global Ethic for Global Politics and Economics* more than twenty years later presents more general ethical and political arguments for solidarity (Küng 1997). Küng's point of departure in reflecting on ethics in politics is a study of interest and ethics in the writings of European and American politicians, from Richelieu to Kissinger. He wants to introduce ethics in international politics and economic activity and asserts that it is possible to reconcile the pursuit of national and economic interests with ethical responsibility. Increasing interdependence makes a new post-modern paradigm of politics develop, although slowly, he argues. This paradigm represents a middle way between real and ideal politics. On the one hand, political ethics should be realistic and not mean inflexible doctrinaire points of view that do not allow for compromise. On the other hand, politics must be governed by an ethic of responsibility, which means that conscience must be applied in concrete situations.

Küng wants believers of different religions and believers and non-believers to seek to establish an ethical consensus. Referring to the communitarian Michael Walzer, Küng argues that a universal ethical consensus should include a 'core morality' or 'moral minimalism': the right to life, to just treatment, physical and mental integrity. It is possible to establish a minimalist consensus that can be the basis for a global ethic which unites different nations, cultures and religions, he argues. A commitment to a culture of solidarity and a just economic order should be part of the core of such a consensus. Other values are the humane treatment of every human being, non-violence, tolerance, truth, equal rights and partnership between men and women. Modern society cannot be held together by fundamentalism, moralism or arbitrary pluralism, he maintains, but only by such a binding and common ethic.

In the rich world, solidarity means that individuals claim less for themselves. Thus, self-restraint is necessary. Self-restraint and solidarity cannot be expected for only part of the population, but must be required of all, employees and employers, rulers and ruled, and primarily those who have the greatest possibility to practice it. Insight into the need for self-restraint must be an element of a common global ethic. Moreover, because self-realisation and self-fulfilment are important aspects of modernity, this consensus should combine autonomous self-realisation and responsibility in solidarity he argues (Küng 1997), echoing Giddens.

In some respects, Küng continues the tradition of the German *solidarismus* (see Chapter 6) and maintains that solidarity implies a rejection of both economic liberalism and socialism. Similar to the tradition of Pesch and Nell-Breuning, he argues for a policy of order (*Ordnungspolitik*), which means that the relationship between the market, the state and social institutions like the family and the voluntary sector must be organised and structured: a social market economy combined with individual freedom and social justice. Solidarity and subsidiarity must be balanced against each other, as mainstream Catholic social teaching professes. Moreover, his concept of solidarity has the same cross-class character. In other respects, he differs strongly from official Catholic social teaching. He rejects any suggestion of a unity based on ideas about a Christian or Catholic restoration in Europe and asserts that the Church has to come to terms with the main characteristics of modernity: individualisation, pluralism, gender equality, contraceptives and birth control.

Küng represents an attempt to formulate a Catholic position for a modern world. We see a clear development in the reasoning about solidarity based on the understanding of Jesus in *Being a Christian*, in 1977, and in his more recent texts. In the first, solidarity is deduced from the role of Jesus, and is integrated into a language with other key terms of Catholic social teaching. In more recent texts, such as *Yes to a Global Ethic* (1995) and *A Global Ethic for Global Politics and Economics* (1997), solidarity is based on the interdependence of human beings in the modern world and anchored in an understanding that can be shared across religious cleavages. These texts mirror Küng's ecumenical engagement: 'Peace among religions is the prerequisite for peace among nations', he says in *Theology for the Third Millennium* (1988). In recent texts, his concept of solidarity reflects his commitment to develop an ethical basis for solidarity across religions and religious paradigms. This concept is more concrete than that formulated in papal encyclicals. It has not the problematic dualistic character of the papal concept, which on the one hand means identification with the poor and on the other preaches a policy of condemnation and passivity towards the prevention of HIV/AIDS and overpopulation. Time and time again Küng has forcefully attacked the dualism of John Paul II and criticised him for betraying the modernisation that was initiated with the Second Vatican Council and for making the Church into 'a medieval jail' (Küng 2003b).

Küng tries to build a bridge between Catholicism and other religions and between Catholicism and humanists' struggle for human rights. The differences between religions and cultures make it questionable whether a really binding ethic can be established globally, and consequently rational consensus cannot develop from human community and argumentation, he declares.

The ecumenical declaration, *The Principles of a Global Ethic*, adopted by the Parliament of the World's religions held in Chicago in 1993 invites all, believers and non-believers, to adopt this ethic and live in accordance with it, he declares. In *Declaration towards a Global Ethic*, four irrevocable directives are formulated: commitment to a culture of non-violence and respect for life; to a culture of solidarity and a just economic order; to a culture of tolerance and a life of truthfulness; and to a culture of equal rights and partnership between men and women (Küng 1995). In this way, Küng's ambition to modernise Catholic social ethics leads him to detach the concept of solidarity from the specific language of papal teaching and make it a more universal idea and a concept that non-Catholics also may endorse.

Protestant political theology: Jürgen Moltmann

Among Protestants, Jürgen Moltmann has further developed Karl Barth's criticism of the interpretation of the doctrine of the two kingdoms in traditional German Protestantism. Moltmann was inspired by the Marxist philosophy of Ernst Bloch and his *Das Prinzip Hoffnung* and also by Theodor Adorno and the Frankfurt school (Moltmann 1984b). In *Politische Theologie, Politische Ethik*, Moltmann presented what he labelled as *political theology*, *political hermeneutics* and a *theology of hope*. As with Küng, he tries to modernise the Church by developing a theology and social ethics that are more relevant for social practice in the modern world.

The teaching about the two kingdoms places the mundane realm under the law, but it remains unclear what exactly this law is, Moltmann maintains. Is it natural law, Israel's law or the law of any society? Most often, Lutherans interpret this in a positivist way as the existing law and rarely find criteria in natural law for what is just and what is not. Therefore, the teaching about the two kingdoms offers no criteria for Christian ethics. It brings realism into Christian teaching but does not give hope of a better world. The central dichotomy is not between the kingdom of God and that of the world, but between *regnum dei* and *regnum diaboli*, the Kingdom of God and the Kingdom of Evil (Devil). Luther intended that the two kingdoms specified by God should fight the power of the devil, he argues (Moltmann 1984b).

Moltmann refers to Marx's famous thesis of Feuerbach and emphasises that the goal of political theology is not only to understand the world, but also that it aims at contributing to a process of change that opens a future for the Kingdom of God. Political theology does not represent a new dogma, but aims at raising the political consciousness of the Church and Christians about the political function of the Church. Moltmann declares Christians should read the Bible with the eyes of the poor and oppressed and understand their predicament and let this guide their political behaviour. Human liberation is liberation to community, and human community is community in freedom. Societies and nations that recognise that their citizens should enjoy human rights, must acknowledge that *all* humankind should enjoy the same rights. Collective egoism threatens human rights as much as individual egoism, he asserts, and international solidarity in the struggle against hunger and military crises has priority over loyalty to one's own people, class, race or nation (Moltmann 1989). With this interpretation of Protestantism, Moltmann integrated Protestant social ethics into politics and challenged modern Protestantism to encounter the misery and poverty in the Third World and economic injustice in the First.

The key concepts in Moltmann's political theology are *peace, justice* and *freedom*. God creates peace and justice, and the Church and Christians are the instruments of God in this world. Consequently, the Church must be aware of its social and political context. The Church must struggle for a 'life in anticipation' and prepare for a life in peace and justice, and community and solidarity are instruments in this struggle. Together, in solidarity we are strong enough to shape our destiny, he maintains in *Creating a Just Future* (Moltmann 1989). In *The Cross and Civil Religion*, Moltmann claimed that political theology should bring Christians 'to the point of solidarity, to the place where Christ awaits them. In the suffering and the outcasts of this earth, Christ awaits his own' (1970). In *Religion, Revolution, and the Future*, he argued further that 'Christians must side with the humanity of the oppressed in the struggle for freedom and justice.' There can be 'no humanity without the end of need' and 'no humanity without solidarity', and Christians must show 'solidarity in suffering and struggling against evil', he says (Moltmann 1969).

Although there are numerous references like these to solidarity in Moltmann's texts, we do not find such a coherent and developed set of concepts as in Catholic social teaching. Whereas the Catholic concept of solidarity is defined in relation to subsidiarity, Moltmann does not elaborate on the relationship between solidarity and other concepts to the same extent. However, his idea of solidarity is similar to the Catholic concept, associated with the concept of justice which refers to the poor and oppressed both in the Third World and in the rich nations. For him, solidarity seems to have both an intrinsic value as an expression of human community and an instrumental value as a means of creating strength in the struggle for justice. In associating solidarity and justice, Moltmann can be seen as a bridge to Habermas who, as we saw above, regards justice and solidarity as two sides of the same coin. We note also that Moltmann's concept of solidarity is not explicitly a cross-class concept comprising both wage earners and employers, as is the Catholic concept.

Moltmann's political theology represents an attempt to develop a socially relevant theology for both Catholic and Protestant theologians. His theology has a cross-confessional character and is ecumenical because he is of the opinion that all Churches face the same problem of the increasing irrelevance of Christian teaching for modern life and the problems of modernity (Moltmann 1984b). Although Moltmann is too radical to be considered a representative spokesman of Protestant theology, his role has been to make many Protestants aware of the imperative of solidarity with the needy.

Both Küng and Moltmann are outsiders in their theology. They were both professor of theology in Tübingen, Bavaria, and are well acquainted with the contributions of the other. Both tried to modernise theology and the understanding of Christ in order to make theology more relevant to modern human beings and modern society. Both bring religion closer to politics, and both develop an ecumenical theology and emphasise community and cooperation between *all* Christians, and between Christians and adherents to other religions and non-believers. What should be particularly emphasised here is that their contributions bring Christian approaches to solidarity closer to the concept of solidarity found in politics. They express the same concern that Christian social ethics should be relevant to the social and political problems and challenges of the world. As we have seen in Chapter 3, they are in this respect part of a general trend in both official Catholic social teaching and the messages from the Lutheran World Federation, and the World Council of Churches. However, both formulate their ideas of solidarity in a more radical way than respectively papal teaching and most Protestants.

Despite these similarities, Küng's and Moltmann's preoccupation with solidarity reflects the different traditions of social ethics in Catholicism and Protestantism. Küng has elaborated more on the concept of solidarity and integrated this concept into a more complete language of solidarity, whereas Moltmann takes the concept of solidarity more for granted, and this mirrors what we saw in Chapter 3. Moreover, Küng aims to establish a position that is both realistic and ethically founded, and this makes his conclusions sometimes less radical politically than Moltmann's – particularly in his early texts.

Conclusion

Compared to the different ideas of solidarity in classic sociology and Marxist and socialist theories, the modern theories presented in this chapter are more refined and complex. These theories have been stylised in Table 9.1. First, the conception of what constitutes the basis for

Table 9.1 *Aspects of solidarity in modern social theory*

	Foundation	Objective/function	Inclusiveness	Collective orientation
Parsons	Interaction Socialisation Agreement about basic values	Social integration	?	?
Luhmann	Interaction Communication	Social integration	Restricted	?
Hechter	Interest Interaction	Maximise interests	Restricted	Medium Reflected view on the relationship between the individual and the collective
Baldwin	'Sameness' Collective identity Interest	Risk avoidance Redistribution of risk	Restricted	Medium: as above
Communitarianism (McIntyre, Etzioni, Bellah, Wolfe)	Social relations Social practice Participation Common values Moral commitment	Social integration	Unclear/varying	Medium: as above
Giddens	Interdependence Active trust	Justice	Broad	Weak
Habermas	Socialisation in the family Cognitive capacity Empathy Reciprocal role-taking	The welfare of others Universal ethical validity	Ever broader	Medium: as above
Rorty	'Sameness'/'Us' Sensitivity to the pain and suffering of others Feelings	Broaden the idea of 'us'	Ever broader	Medium: as above
Küng	Jesus Christ as model: Interdependence	Justice	Broad: all human beings	Medium
Moltmann	Jesus Christ as model: Identification with the poor	Justice?	The poor and oppressed	Unclear

solidarity varies. As seen in Chapter 1, Comte and Durkheim drew attention to *interdependence* as constitutive for solidarity. Comte emphasised the interdependence created by continuity and time whereas Durkheim's concept of organic solidarity was constituted by complementarity in the division of work. Interdependence is the crucial factor in Giddens' contribution to social democratic theory and in Küng's contribution to a modern and radical Catholic interpretation of social ethics. Rorty's emphasis on sensitivity towards the suffering of others represents a bridge between Habermas' *empathy* and Moltmann's identification with the poor as bases for solidarity. Parsons's and Luhmann's system theory is the link between the classic sociologists and the communitarians because of the insistence on interaction as the basis of solidarity. Communitarians emphasise social practice as well. Apart from modern Marxists, who use the concept of solidarity frequently but do not elaborate on it, Hechter and Baldwin are representatives for those who consider *common interests* as the basis for solidarity. Baldwin is the one who most strongly emphasises 'sameness' or similarity as a necessary foundation for solidarity, although Parsons' stress on agreement about basic values probably can be seen as presupposing a certain degree of homogeneity. The communitarian emphasis on local community and interaction probably means some sort of 'sameness' as well. Habermas and Rorty locate the basis of solidarity in the mental habitus of the individual, and Habermas regards both cognitive capacity and empathy as basic.

As we see in Table 9.1, most authors have a broad conception of solidarity. Only those who operate with a restricted concept of interaction as the basis for solidarity, such as Luhmann, and those who see *interest* as constitutive, have a restricted idea about what should be included.

The authors who have been discussed above do not always make explicit what they see as the goal or the function of solidarity. Again, there is a line from systems theory to communitarianism where social integration is emphasised. Giddens, Küng and Moltmann see solidarity as instrumental in terms of creating justice, whereas maximising interest and the redistribution of risk is the goal of solidarity in Hechter and Baldwin respectively.

Finally, we note that most authors do not argue for a strong collective orientation in terms of solidarity. They reflect on the relationship between solidarity on the one hand and the individual and his or her need for autonomy or freedom of choice on the other, but they do not discuss this extensively and in depth. Those who are particularly preoccupied with the individual such as Giddens, do not linger much on solidarity, and those who are more preoccupied with solidarity do not go deeper into a discussion about the implications for individual and personal choice, like Habermas.

In previous chapters we have seen that there is no such thing as *a* concept of solidarity in politics, but several competing and conflicting concepts that are located in somewhat differing political languages. We must conclude in this chapter that modern social and political theory and Christian social ethics also present a wide range of ideas of solidarity, and that these concepts vary in terms of foundation, objectives, inclusiveness and collective orientation. The main trend is towards a broad and inclusive idea of solidarity that has justice or social integration as main objectives. Modern theories vary most probably when it comes to the foundation of solidarity. Is this empathy, ethics, religion, interaction, social practice or interests?

What remains? Attempt at a definition

What then, is the validity of the theories and concepts of solidarity that have been presented here? Comte's idea about interdependence created through time and continuity still has some validity. Individuals are born into a context, a society and an economic situation that they have not created, and individual success and wealth depend on history, economic cycles and public policy as much as on the behaviour of the individual. Similarly, no individual is able to create wealth without some sort of social relation to others. Durkheim's idea of interdependence developed by the increasing division of work is valid, but the unresolved question in Durkheim's conception of organic solidarity has still not been solved. How is the factual interdependence created by the division of work and increasing individualism related to the growth of personal consciousness and translated into a subjective feeling of community with other human beings? Is it not possible that increasing individualism may be stronger than factual interdependence and create social conflicts and disintegration, as also Durkheim feared? [9] Because Comte's and Durkheim's concepts of solidarity were sociological more than political, it is necessary

[9] Durkheim seems to postulate the relation between increasing division of work and solidarity. He maintains that 'there exists a social solidarity arising from the division of labour. This is a self-evident truth, since in them [modern societies] the division of labour is highly developed and engenders solidarity' (see Durkheim 1963 (1897). Lewis Coser notes in his introduction to the British translation of *De la division de travail* that Durkheim is ambiguous on this point. He appears to return to his concept of common consciousness and he emphasises that common consciousness is still needed to assure the overall coordination and integration of society as a whole. Mckinney and Loomis (1957) call attention to the fact that Durkheim in his later work on suicide modifies his conception of the relation between common and personal consciousness: the change from mechanical to organic solidarity does not automatically result in common consciousness being reduced. However, it changes form. In this way, common consciousness may be the foundation for either an egoistic or an altruistic social order.

to transform these ideas into ethical and political concepts. Although well founded, sociological observations about continuity and interdependence are primarily valid as arguments for the restraint of individualism, but one cannot logically argue that these ideas must be extended to imply collective solidarity.

Solidarity in Europe cannot be founded on 'sameness' and homogeneity. Increasing pluralisation and individualisation of society due to changes in the labour market, family structure, life-styles and cultural identity call for solidarity based on the acceptance of diversity. What is needed is that the majority exercise solidarity with a minority – the poor, the unemployed, ethnic, religious and sexual minorities. In addition, the majority in the rich world constitutes only a minority and should be expected to show solidarity with the poor in the Third World. Nancy Fraser suggests that *recognition of differences* should be a key value (Fraser 1995). Yet, this cannot replace the concept of solidarity, only supplement it because solidarity is a stronger and more encompassing concept than recognition. Solidarity means recognition, not vice versa. If, as Baldwin argues (1997), the solidarity of the post-war European welfare states was based on the premise that their populations were stable and homogeneous, the increasingly multicultural character of European societies makes recognition of difference as well as solidarity more precarious and more difficult.

Although solidarity certainly is most effectively and solidly based on the combination of rational self-interest and collective interest, a narrow conception of self-interest in the tradition of rational choice theory may not be the primary basis of solidarity in Europe today. It is still in the interest of underprivileged groups or discriminated-against minorities to stand together in solidarity, but for large segments of the population increasing wealth and levels of consumption have solved urgent material problems. Moreover, environmental problems set limits to increased personal consumption, and consequently, demands for improved standards of living are legitimate only for segments of the population in Europe – the poor and unemployed, those outside the labour market, low-wage categories of the working and lower middle classes. In a welfare state, solidarity presupposes preparedness to sacrifice individual advantages for the benefit of others or for society as a whole and, to some extent, to renounce the freedom to pursue one's own self-interests (Hagen 1999). This problem of combining individual self-interest with collective solidarity represents the most threatening challenge to solidarity.

The welfare state represents a special challenge in an era of individualism. Can a welfare state based on collective solidarity survive in a society with a high degree of individualism? That probably depends on what is

Table 9.2 *Solidaristic attitudes and institutions*

	Solidaristic institutions	Not-solidaristic institutions
Solidaristic individuals	1. Classic social democracy Universalism	2. Pre-social democratic?
Not-solidaristic individuals	3. Equivalence/insurance based (Christian democratic)	4. Liberalist Basic minimum Selective or universal

meant by 'collective solidarity' which refers generally to institutions with a high degree of universalism and fair degree of redistribution. We can imagine four ideal-type situations. First, both individual attitudes and welfare institutions may be marked by a high degree of solidarity. This represents classic social democratic society as existed in Scandinavia until the late 1970s. Second, we may have a situation with solidaristic attitudes but where welfare institutions either are lacking, are inadequate, or do not redistribute resources to any significant extent. This represents the pre-social democratic welfare state or a liberal welfare state which does not correspond to attitudes of citizens. The third case represents a situation when there is a well-developed welfare state, but individuals support this because of their own personal interest and the feeling of solidarity is low. The fourth case is when neither individual attitudes nor welfare institutions are characterised by solidarity. This is a situation where the majority does not care for the minority; welfare institutions reflect this and are characterised neither by universalism nor by redistribution.

Most nations in Western Europe have probably moved towards a situation where there are universal welfare institutions, but where individual attitudes have become more marked by individualism (see Table 9.2). As has been demonstrated again and again in recent research, this individualism is so far combined with a general support for the welfare state (Svallfors and Taylor-Goobye 1999; Gelissen 2002), and such attitudes may endure as long as the majority or the most influential social strata believe that they are better protected against the risks of modern society by collective social protection and social services. Consequently, the survival of the welfare state in Europe depends upon the recognition of members of the middle class that it is more in their personal interest to organise social protection publicly than individually. As public social security institutions generally are less expensive and offer more security than private ones, rational individuals may continue to defend a welfare state based on a combination of self-interest and solidarity. The remaining problem is that individuals marked by a high degree of individualism and emphasis on self-interest can be expected to accept redistribution and equality only to a limited extent. In a situation where individualist values prevail we must expect pressure from the well-to-do to reduce redistribution and to introduce insurance principles in social security institutions, which means stronger links between individual contributions and benefits. This situation does not necessarily threaten the welfare state *per se*, but can challenge the redistributive aspects of social security institutions. Universalism may survive, but the welfare state can become more like a collective insurance company. Some researchers argue that the welfare states in advanced industrial societies are undergoing major transformations in this direction. They are not dismantled, but restructured. Universalism and social rights are weakened, and individual responsibility, labour force participation and private delivery of services are strengthened (Gilbert 2002). This would be contrary to the traditional social democratic idea of solidarity, but not to Christian democratic solidarity ideology. Another problem is naturally that this kind of rationality based on self-interest cannot be the basis for solidarity with the Third World or marginal minorities in the rich world.

Of course, one could argue for another conception of self-interest; that self-interest must be *informed* or *enlightened*, i.e. based on knowledge about society and insight into the long-term effects of personal choice. Thus, everyone has a personal interest in paying taxes to finance policies that reduce unemployment and secure a welfare state without poverty because this prevents crime, which again makes society safer also for the well-to-do. Or one could say that it is in the rational self-interest of citizens in the rich world to increase development cooperation with the Third World, because this probably results in a more peaceful world. However, this is to stretch the concept of self-interest and deny that most people are capable of defining their self-interests even when they do not want to take into account long-term effects of personal choice. Middle-class and middle-aged persons in modern society can very well understand the long-term effects of personal choice, but still prefer to base their choices on short-term considerations because they do not expect to experience the consequences in the long run. People who define their self-interest as preserving their income in their own pockets, fighting taxation and living in protected areas should not be dismissed as uninformed or 'unenlightened', only as individualistic and egoistic.

If solidarity cannot be founded on identity, sameness and self-interest, the problem of reciprocity, affinity and complementarity arises (see above). The challenge is to define solidarity in a way that draws a clear demarcation between charity and paternalistic welfare. When individuals in affluent nations are called upon to exercise solidarity with the weak, poor or oppressed, it is hard to see the relationship between the acting person and the recipient as one of reciprocity and symmetry. Most often relationships that require solidarity are not symmetrical. One part, the well-to-do citizen in Europe, is in a privileged situation and *the other* is not. What do we expect the poor or oppressed, in our nation or in the Third World, to give back when we argue that economic and social policy or development cooperation should be founded on solidarity? Clearly, we must not expect gratitude because this constitutes a relationship charac- terised more by charity than by solidarity. This problem is even more acute in situations where we see no collective subject in active strug- gle. Thus, we must tone down the emphasis on reciprocity but perhaps emphasise the existence of a struggling subject. I have much sympathy for this idea, but this also creates difficulties for concepts of solidarity that have been described in previous chapters. If we require a struggling subject, then we cannot talk about solidarity with nature or coming gen- erations, and hardly when we see groups in need that do not constitute themselves as *struggling* individuals or groups, such as immigrants and the poor, and in some cases Third World nations. If, on the other hand, we abandon criteria of reciprocity and struggle, the distinction between solidarity and compassion becomes blurred.

A conclusion has to be that in modern society solidarity must be based on altruism for large segments of the population. As mentioned above, self-interest may still be the basis for the collective actions of underpriv- ileged and discriminated-against groups, but for the well-to-do and the middle class solidarity must be based on a minimum of insight and com- passion for the plight of others. This should not be mixed up with *pater- nalistic* altruism; solidarity should be based on a *political* altruism. This means that solidarity must be exercised collectively, be directed at social change or change of power relations and not based on the individual inter- ests of the persons involved (Passy 2001). Both empathy and cognition are needed, but the relationship between the two is highly complicated and cannot be postulated theoretically. If people do not have any empathy at all, cognition will most probably not be conducive to altruistic soli- darity. On the other hand, empathy without knowledge and insight may lead to a solidarity with unforeseen and unwanted consequences. The more political altruism is combined with a broad conception of inter- est, the stronger will be solidarity. As self-interest is socially constructed, new experiences, social and political events and political activities may change the extent to which people see their interest as strictly economic; or as a wider interest in developing a better world for their children and successors. Nonetheless, in this way the narrow concept of self-interest in rational choice theory is transcended by an element of empathy or identification with others.

The concept of political altruism is no panacea and gives no hope for the construction of a strong solidarity that includes a broad segment of the population, the poor and excluded, the working class and parts of the middle strata, even if this must be the goal. Its weaknesses are obvious. It is anchored neither within a strong individual self-interest nor in a strong class interest, although supporters of this idea should seek both types of anchoring. Nevertheless, it is the most adequate and realistic idea of solidarity in present-day society. Solidarity will not grow automatically out of the social structure of modern individualised society. It never did, not even during the rise of industrial society. Solidarity has to be constructed socially and politically through the practice of individuals, groups, professional and political organisations, churches, and networks nationally and internationally.

This raises the complex issues of education, mass media and communication technology. In Europe, increasing levels of education and the role of mass media create a basis for a public with greater knowledge and more information than ever before in history. Higher education improves the ability to understand and to reflect on the state of society and the world, even if higher education is standardised and the mass media are often biased and subjected to markets and competition for viewers. Even if the mass media are largely in the hands of monopolies, they bring the suffering of others directly into our homes and create both cognitive and affective preparedness for solidarity. Information technology has an enormous democratising effect. Solidarity movements create national and worldwide networks and may much more easily than before mobilise members and sympathisers to engage in solidaristic politics. Zygmunt Bauman complains about the 'carnival aspects' of explosive communities in modern society (Bauman 2000). Here, he points to feelings of community that are volatile, transient and 'single-aspect' or 'single-purpose'. Thus, in media society, we may experience short outbursts of solidarity and mobilisation around an issue of current interest, but after a while this issue might be shoved into the background and rapidly supplanted by another issue.

Solidarity must include a state of readiness for *collective action* – either by staying together with others in the struggle for a defined objective, or by sharing resources with them. The preparedness for sharing cannot be solely about a private and individual decision to give to individuals or groups that have less. It must include willingness to act collectively and to redistribute through other arenas than the private one. In modern society this means to use politics as an arena and to be willing to use taxes and governmental institutions to share and redistribute. As Brunkhorst argues, solidarity must be expressed in democratic institutions and anchored in a legal system of rights (Brunkhorst 2002). The distinction between the public and private arenas constitutes the difference between solidarity and charity. Nonetheless, communitarians are probably right that institutionalised solidarity may be perverted if it is not maintained through some kind of social or political practice, but this is a dilemma with which modern solidarity has to live.

Habermas is right that ever-widening discourses may be conducive to solidarity, but he underestimates the problem of those who are never included in such discourses. In addition, what are needed are also social and political confrontations that do not follow the principles of discourse, but which change the relations of power and hegemony in society. In this way, a new basis for discourse may develop; a discourse with other premises and rules for communication. Both social democratic and Christian democratic parties are bound by electoral considerations to aggregate voters spread over a range of interests and ideologies. Trade unions and social movements that represent those who are underprivileged or discriminated against, churches and left-wing parties are probably more important actors in this respect. Political involvement at this level may influence the internal balance in social democracy and Christian democracy, tilting it against those who are more preoccupied with solidarity than those who are more concerned with individualism and subsidiarity.

Finally, we have arrived at a proposal for a definition of the concept of solidarity in modern society: for most people in modern society solidarity must mean standing up for those who are less privileged and different from oneself. For the underprivileged, it still means to stand together with those who are in the same situation and for other underprivileged groups. For the majority, it is based not on personal interest, but on political altruism: it is founded on empathy and cognition, and the balance between the two may vary. Solidarity is developed through communicative action and the ability to take the role of the 'other(s)'. It means the preparedness to share resources with others, through personal contributions to those who are struggling and through taxation and redistribution organised by the state. Thus, solidarity means a readiness for collective action and a will to institutionalise it through the establishment of rights and citizenship. It is normally expressed through relating to others who are engaged in struggle. If it is not possible to fulfil this criterion, one should at least be prepared to support underprivileged groups when they initiate such struggle.

10 Epilogue: hope and challenges – individualisation, consumerism and globalisation

This exposition of the development of the *concept* of solidarity cannot be concluded without some remarks about the prospects of the *phenomenon* of solidarity in the first decade of the twenty-first century. This final chapter discusses the prospects for solidarity defined in the way proposed in Chapter 9 – a broad and inclusive solidarity, not built upon sameness or homogeneity, but on the acceptance of difference, on political altruism and empathy. What are the challenges that confront this kind of solidarity? Four types of challenges will be discussed: the erosion of the class foundation of solidarity, increasing individualism and consumerism, worries that the welfare state undermines solidarity, and the effects of what is often referred to as globalisation.

First concern: the class foundation of solidarity

As emphasised in Chapter 2, the labour movement idea of solidarity was necessary in order to overcome working-class fragmentation. Chapter 5 concluded with the assertion that the concept of solidarity emerged and was most strongly developed in nations where the working class was homogeneous and where different religious and ethnic loyalties did not create cleavages. Neither the idea nor the phenomenon of solidarity reflects social structure in a mechanistic way, but some social structures favour both while others counteract them. Today, social scientists frequently express their concerns about the changes in the social and class-related foundations for solidarity. Claus Offe has described the key figure of a male wage earner, without property, but employed full-time for most of his adult life, who provides for his family with a steady stream of predictable income. These male wage earners shared some cultural patterns, such as work discipline, the perception of being involved in a social conflict with employers, the ability to rationally engage in collective action when their labour unions made a decision to do so, and a sense of solidarity (Offe 1987). At least from the 1970s, this key figure has gradually lost much of its significance.

The numerical reduction of the industrial working class in most western nations has reduced the social basis for working-class trade unionism and for the influence of an ideology that maintains working-class solidarity as a pivotal element. This is neither the time nor the place to contribute to the time-honoured debate about who belongs to the working class, a discussion that has continued unabated since the days of Kautsky. Erik Olin Wright has done so by contributing extensive analyses of classes in modern society and he has suggested that ownership of the means of production should be supplemented with skill and expertise (education) as criteria for defining classes (Wright 2000). He did so himself and with data from the 1980s concluded that the working class at that time still constituted a majority. Even if this were the case today, the problem would remain that the structure of the class has changed. The number of industrial workers is still decreasing and the number of people employed in private and public services is increasing, and only a minority of people living in Western European societies believe that they belong to the working class (see below).

Working life has become more fragmented and plural and there are a variety of contracts that recognise all sorts of variations within full- or part-time employment. Women have increased their labour market participation and in some countries constitute a large segment of the public sector as well as within low-paid employment. Immigrants have occupied other segments in the work world and have made the labour market and society far more heterogeneous. Higher levels of education and increased employment in personal and social services and in business and information-related work have expanded the possibilities for individual careers. As a consequence, the increased heterogeneity and diversity of the workforce has made the class structure more opaque. Ownership and control of the means of production is more distant, more impersonal and more diffuse, and increased competition in a more globalised world has made it more difficult for wage earners to identify a common adversary.

As Eric Hobsbawm has noted, these and related developments have encouraged 'a growing division of workers into sections and groups, each pursuing its own economic interest irrespective of the rest'. Everywhere, solidarity in political consciousness has given way to the 'values of consumer-society individualism and the search for private and personal satisfaction above all else' (Hobsbawm 1981). Offe describes these processes as a *destructuration of collectivities* and he concluded, in the late 1980s that the prospects for the welfare state were rather glum (Offe 1987).

Although the description above seems to be rather conventional and gloomy, foreshadowing the demise of class solidarity in modern

Table 10.1 *Subjective class identification. Percent saying that they belong to different social classes*

	Working class	Lower middle class	Middle class	Upper middle class and upper class	N = 100%
France	26	9	47	13	924
Germany	24	14	45	14	132
Great Britain	50	13	27	3	943
Denmark	22	8	58	11	971
Norway	33	12	43	10	947
Italy	18	10	59	15	975
Spain	26	18	45	5	920

Source: Eurobarometer 1993

post-industrial societies, it is not undisputed. Marshall *et al.* conclude their extensive analysis of classes in modern Britain by insisting that 'class is still the most common source of social identity and retains its salience, as such, [and] there is no obvious lack of class awareness among the population of modern Britain as a whole' (Marshall *et al.* 1988). Similarly, Svallfors, arguing on the basis of Swedish data, has pointed out that class is still the single factor that best explains patterns of attitudes towards the welfare state in Sweden (Svallfors 1996). My own comparative study of attitudes relating to the welfare states in Germany, Norway and the UK demonstrated that the influence of class was much stronger in Norway and the UK than in Germany (Stjernø 1995). Thus, the social and political significance of class varies among the nations of Western Europe. Variations are also found in subjective class identification and these are indicated in Table 10.1.

In the UK, 50 per cent and in Norway, 35 per cent reported that they belong to the working class. In all the other countries listed in this table, those who identify themselves as belonging to the working class constitute a minority of 20–26 per cent of the population. Although there are no data referring to the stability of class identification, it is very difficult not to draw the conclusion that working-class identity in this day and age is a more precarious basis for the phenomenon of solidarity in society than before. Besides that, subjective class identification is generally *not* associated with solidarity these days. Only some aspects of solidarity are associated with subjective class identification, in particular, attitudes towards equality (Stjernø and Johannessen 2004).

Another key issue related to the social structure is the increased significance of the middle class for social and political solidarity in modern society. As Table 10.1 shows, in most Western European countries today many more persons believe that they belong to the middle class than to the working class. In the countries included in this study, 40–60 per cent report that they belong to the middle class and another 10–20 per cent report that they belong to the 'lower middle class'. The increasing size and significance of the middle class raises a question about the consequences for the idea and for the phenomenon of solidarity in modern society. Generally speaking, the growth and development of the middle class, the increased level of educational attainment, and the spread of individualism are characteristics of contemporary society that are tightly knit and linked together. Social differentiation and increased opportunities for social mobility and for higher education have resulted in more individualistic patterns of thinking and different expectations in the working class.

The working class was heterogeneous when the idea of solidarity was developed in the labour movement. Heterogeneity is also a quality of the contemporary middle class. The middle class can be divided into at least three main categories: those employed in the private sector, those employed in the public sector and the self-employed who work as consultants, experts, lawyers, architects, salesmen, etc. All three groups can then be further differentiated, by income and by the level of educational attainment, by the type of work performed, and by place and function in the hierarchy of the workplace. Some segments of the middle class are close to the working class, while other segments have a high degree of autonomy and/or function as employers in the work world. The resulting configurations make it difficult to identify the borders between the working class and the different segments of the middle class.

Can this highly differentiated hodgepodge constitute the social foundation for the phenomenon of solidarity in our own day, eventually in an alliance with the working class?

In the 1960s, Stein Rokkan directed attention to the ideological profile of a middle class that was growing in number and influence. He pointed out that the middle class wanted a differentiated wage system that would compensate for the time and effort and costs of higher education, and social security within collective pension systems (Rokkan 1966). The meritocratic aspects were in conflict with the egalitarian ideology of the labour movement, the collective aspects were contrary to the liberal and individualist ideology of conservatives. The increasing electoral significance of the educated middle class forced social democrats and conservatives to pursue a policy that might attract middle-class voters. Social democrats accepted a social security system with some achievement-oriented principles, and the conservatives accepted the development of a public welfare system.

Bo Rothstein has noted that from a strictly economic and rational point of view, the middle class *may* or *may not* support solidarity within a welfare state that has a high degree of redistribution. If the middle class is prepared to pay high taxes to finance redistribution, this is not because it is the prime beneficiary of redistribution, since the working class and the less-well-to-do benefit most of all from such a system. Nonetheless, the middle class may be willing to support solidarity within a welfare state under very specific conditions. The first condition is that the middle class must consider averting risk to be an important quality; the other alternatives to solidarity within a welfare state must appear to offer it less security. The second condition is that government needs to be seen as being reliable and efficient in providing social security and social services. The third condition is that the political behaviour of the middle class must be influenced by the ideological conviction and the moral view that politics should be based upon solidarity (Rothstein 2000). As I have shown in an earlier study, middle-class attitudes concerning collective welfare arrangements are more positive in Norway than in the UK and Germany (Stjernø 1995). In Norway, those who vote for parties of the political centre and on the right more clearly support solidarity within a welfare state than the same groups in the two other countries. Consequently, it may be argued that the individualism of the middle class does not *per se* erode institutionalised solidarity. The crucial issue appears to be the extent to which a common political platform and an alliance are developed between the working class and the middle class in order to pursue policies that are based upon solidarity.

An answer may be incorporated into the development of the occupational structure of modern information and service societies. The hodgepodge heterogeneity of the middle class will probably mean that political loyalty will be dispersed throughout the political spectrum. Self-employed people may be more disposed to vote for liberal and conservative parties, but the middle class within the private sector may split according to type of work, income level, the political agenda and the ideological currents of the day. The financial and information sectors provide few hopes for the development of a social basis for solidarity. Here, workplaces are smaller, specialisation is high and wages are even higher, and they are often decided upon individually. Union membership is low. Conditions for the development of solidarity in these sectors can increase if opportunities for individual mobility are reduced and if the occupational structure stabilises. There are few indications of a development in that direction, and even if this were to change, it is still not likely that these sectors of the middle class would develop into a force supporting solidarity in political parties.

The most probable candidates for supporting politics based upon traditional social democratic solidarity are those people who make up the lower segments of the middle class. Here, the boundaries with the working class are unclear and subjective class identity might change in accordance with changes in the social, political and economic conditions within society. Other candidates are those segments of the middle class that are employed within the welfare state itself, the institutions that are meant to be the most concrete expressions of collective solidarity. Occupations and professions in health care, in education and in social services, have wage earners who are employed in large workplaces, with hospitals and educational institutions as an inner core that can constitute a new social basis for solidarity.

This kind of class analysis suffers from several weaknesses. First of all, it certainly underestimates the complexities of the social structure and it excludes all others outside of the labour market. Second, Herbert Kitschelt argues that not only class, but a range of factors influence political identity. These include whether the source of income is located in the private or the public sector, whether the source of income is in the domestic or the internationally competitive part of the economy, or in consumer experiences (Kitschelt 1993). Since class membership no longer determines voting behaviour, or does so to a much lesser degree, the same can probably be said about the key ideological value of solidarity that was so strongly integrated into the working class. Third, Pierre Bourdieu argues that the kind of class analysis used above builds too restrictively upon the conception of class, and he extended class analysis to include cultural characteristics in a more integrated way (Bourdieu 1984). In addition to production, economy and exploitation, a class analysis must include *cultural* capital (education), *social* capital (social relationships) and *symbolic* capital (prestige). It is the sum and similarity in the configuration of all of these characteristics that constitute today's classes, according to Bourdieu.

The discussion about a class-based foundation for solidarity is most relevant when material self-interest is the core element in the conceptualisation of solidarity. It is less relevant for an idea of solidarity that is based upon the acceptance of difference, empathy and political altruism. This constellation in the conceptualisation of solidarity must entail reflection and concern regarding the precarious conditions of our global environment and the great imbalance in the relationship between rich and poor nations. Bordieu's approach may be more suitable to an analysis of this conception of solidarity which can no longer be understood as being simply a function of characteristics of the economy, the labour market and the workplace. As Gramsci wrote, the struggle for cultural and symbolic definitions and power becomes more and more important for the constitution of solidarity in Western societies.

Cultural capital includes education. Increased education has certainly fuelled the process of individualisation. Education has created opportunities for increased social mobility for the individual and has made self-realisation and the prospects of a career a more important aspect of middle-class ideology. But higher education also promotes a better understanding of how our society functions and of the relationship between Western postindustrial societies and the rest of the world in a globalised day and age. The historian Paul Ginsborg has characterised the young and educated within the middle class as being the *reflexive strata*, referring to their ability to sustain a critical view of modern development (Ginsborg 2002). If he is right, then teachers, social workers and other professionally educated groups, together with public employees and others, are carriers of social and political capital. This leads one to hope that higher education can be conducive to the universal discourse about solidarity that is called for by Habermas and others. However, the evidence concerning the effects of education on solidarity is inconclusive. A recent study on popular support for welfare schemes concludes that people who have attained a higher educational level tend to 'endorse income solidarity more strongly, and have greater trust in others and a stronger sense of solidarity' (Oorschot 2001). Another study concludes the opposite, and finds that individuals who have attained a higher educational level are less in favour of solidarity in society than those with lower educational achievements (Arts and Gelissen 2001). At this point, the relationship between education and solidarity is very ambiguous.

All in all, even if we broaden our conception of class, the changes in the employment structure we have witnessed in Western Europe can hardly be said to be conducive to the development of solidarity in society.

Second concern: individualism

The second challenge is individualisation. As we noted in Chapter 1, Durkheim saw increasing individualism as a part of the historical process. The increase in personal consciousness occurs at the expense of shared consciousness and creates more room for individual dissent. In one area, Durkheim believed that shared consciousness had grown stronger, in the conception of the individual. The individual had become some kind of religion, he wrote. 'We carry on the worship of the dignity of the human person, which like all strong acts of worship, has already acquired its superstition' (Durkheim 1984 (1893)).

Durkheim shared his concern about the detrimental consequences of increased individualism for social integration and solidarity in society with other sociologists in the nineteenth century, and this concern has continued to be important in sociology. In our day, two important contributors to the analysis of individualism are Ulrich Beck and Anthony Giddens. Beck and Giddens developed their theories about individualisation and reflexive modernity from very different points of departure, but reached quite similar conclusions.[1]

Beck's three-stage periods of social change, premodernity, modernity and reflexive modernity, are built upon two key concepts – *risk* and *individualisation*. Modernity and industrial society are closely associated. They are both structured by social classes and characterised by a concern with the distribution of goods, and by their domination by instrumental science. Reflexive modernity is somewhat different. It is more individualised and characterised by its concern about risk. There are three aspects in the process leading to reflexive modernity. First, one aspect also emphasised by Giddens, is that the historically prescribed social forms of dominance and of living together are *dis*-embedded – they are no longer anchored in the local community or in the social structure as firmly as they once were. Second, traditional knowledge, faith and social norms lose their stability and safety. Finally, a re-embedding process takes place and a new type of social commitment develops. This re-embedding has new forms of social control or new ways to reintegrate individuals into the social fabric (Beck 1992).

In reflexive modernity there are great changes in the labour market and in family structure including more flexible working hours, the decentralisation of the work site, the reduced dependency of women, and the erosion of existing value systems, all of which result in increased individualism. The family no longer integrates different generations or the sexes. Individuals become the agents of their own livelihoods, mediated by the market, and become responsible for the planning and organisation of their own social life and development.

While social and biographical situations are differentiated, the market, money, law, mobility and education, are standardised. There is a two-pronged process of individualisation and standardisation. The dual character of the situation that Beck discerns and describes calls for

---

[1] Beck's *Risikogesellschaft* (*Risk Society*) was first published in Germany in 1986, and is a major contribution to the discussion on the character of modern society. Giddens' *Modernity and Self-Identity* was published five years later – see Beck (1992) and Giddens (1991).

individualised decision-making, but this autonomy is dependent upon the institutions of society. When individuals are dependent upon the labour market they are also dependent upon education, consumption, the welfare state, fashions in medical, psychological and pedagogical counselling and care. Thus, increased individualisation translates into increased market dependency, and this, in turn, means greater dependency upon new social institutions within the welfare state (Beck 1992).

Giddens, too, emphasises this peculiar contradiction between the rule of markets and individualism. From the very beginning, markets promoted individualism in the sense that they stressed individual rights and responsibilities. Modernity opens up the project of the self, but under conditions that are strongly influenced by the standardising effects of commodity capitalism. In this context, the designation of individual wants became central for the further development of markets. 'To a greater or lesser degree, the project of the self becomes translated into one of the possession of desired goods and the pursuit of artificially framed lives' (Giddens 1991).

For Giddens, the consequence of *disembedding* social relations and rapid social change in modern and global capitalism is that the self has to be explored and constructed in a reflexive process that connects and integrates personal and social change. An important aspect of modernity is that the self is seen as being a reflexive project for which the individual is responsible. 'We are what we make of ourselves.' Because social life has become more open, we can choose to become active in a range of differing social contexts. People must choose among a plurality of life-styles, and the choice of life-style is increasingly important in the constitution of one's self-identity. A fundamental component of daily life has to do with the increasing need to choose. The individual has a wide range of opportunities and a myriad of choices in order to actualise the fundamental value of self-realisation. When morality is based upon self-realisation, i.e. when 'being true to oneself' is seen as being most important of all, universal moral criteria lose their significance, and references to other people are only significant within the sphere of intimate relationships.

As we noted in Chapter 9, Giddens does not assert that increased individualism diminishes all forms of solidarity. He only claims that it changes the conditions of solidarity. However, we may deduce that increased individualism, disembedding and the stronger commitments to the values of self-realisation and autonomy must necessarily work together to make individuals less inclined to subordinate themselves to a collective for the sake of the common good. Decisions of that kind are seen as being contingent upon individual reflection, and this represents a serious challenge to the collective foundations of solidarity in modern society. In short, solidarity can no longer be founded upon tradition, inherited loyalties or class identifications. Consequently, solidarity must increasingly be founded on ethics, empathy and cognition.

However, we should emphasise that individualisation does not necessarily and solely mean an increase in egoism. Another side to individualisation is the acknowledgement that *if I am to be valued as unique and utterly irreplaceable, then other individuals must be seen as being equally unique and irreplaceable.* The general acceptance of the universality of human dignity and human rights in Western Europe is strongly associated with individualisation and modernity. In a manner of speaking, universalism and individualism are two faces of the same coin. As we have seen, modern social democratic and Christian democratic ideologies combine an emphasis upon human dignity and human rights with solidarity. The idea that increasing individualism and egoism erodes solidarity must be supplemented with the understanding that individualism and ideas about universal human dignity are inextricably woven together. In contemporary society, we find a new mixture of solidarity, individual autonomy and self-realisation. The balance between these values and goals vary, in social classes, in individuals, and in different contexts and over time. Today's modernity is *liquid*, as Zygmunt Bauman maintains (Bauman 2000).

If modern solidarity is individualistic, reflexive and liquid, this represents a challenge for social democratic and for Catholic solidarity. Social democratic parties can no longer count upon mass support anchored in the industrial working class, but must address individuals for whom the idea of solidarity is not a clearly given or clearly defined value. These individuals sometimes do, and sometimes do not, construct their own definitions of solidarity, which they may or may not integrate in the practice of their own individual life projects. The Catholic Church and the Christian democratic parties are challenged because religion no longer has the same authority to instruct believers about what solidarity should mean. Catholics and Protestants construct their own versions of Christian ethics, choose those commandments which they see as being relevant for them, and adhere to some of the teachings of the Church and neglect others. The Church is still a point of reference and it still contributes to the individual's personal identity, but each individual constructs this point of reference in a personal way.

Third concern: consumerism

Although the development of individualism has roots going back to the Renaissance, the increased individualism of the last decades is certainly associated with the growth of the middle class. In addition to the growth of the middle class and individualism, there has been a marked increase in *consumerism*, and it is the combination of all three that probably constitutes the most important threat to solidarity in our time.

Traditional class solidarity grew out of the common experiences of poverty and insecurity in the industrial workforce. Scarcity was tackled by collaboration, the exchange of services and by the practice of reciprocal loyalty. However, the enormous economic growth that took place in most countries in Western Europe from the 1930s and particularly after World War II almost eradicated mass poverty. In Norway, for example, the GNP measured in fixed prices increased sevenfold from 1935 to 1990, and fourfold from 1950 to 1990. This made the expansion of the welfare state and the strong growth in private consumption possible. For most people, the hazards of life were very much reduced, and the opportunities for personal choice in the consumption of material goods and in the selection of a life-style grew vastly. A basis for increased individual autonomy was created, and the pressing need for collective solidarity seemed to dwindle for the vast majority.

In a reflexive and liquid modern society social identity is increasingly associated with being a consumer. By and large, many people spend less time in the workplace and more time engaged in costly leisure time pursuits, and a greater share of the population lives on public or private transfers. The balance between the role of production and the role of consumption in creating social identities has tipped (Bauman 1997). As income and purchasing power increase the possibilities to choose commodities and services in the marketplace, the individual develops a stronger sense of self-sufficiency. The recognition that every individual human being is dependent upon others is reduced and support for collective arrangements may erode.

Consumerist attitudes have developed in relation to public welfare policy, too. Collective welfare arrangements are more often than not viewed as being consumer services that should be adapted to the individual preferences of the consumer (Lorentzen 2003). The existence of a money surplus makes the consumer more inclined to demand the *right* to be allowed to buy social and medical services in the private market whenever public services cannot meet their demands and preferences. In this way, consumerism has stimulated the development of a new concept of individual freedom. This new concept insists upon the freedom to choose how one's own money should be used, without regard for what is in the collective interest of society or in the interest of those who do not have the opportunity to pay for private services. The dilemma between collective solidarity and individual freedom is constantly being made visible, and in an acute way, by consumers who are tipping the scales more in favour of individual freedom.

The ideology of consumerism has become part of the dominating ideology propagated by leaders of public services under the title *New Public Management*. NPM stresses economic efficiency and orients itself to the rational production of services for consumers. The dilemma in health and social service provision is that the relationship between efficiency and quality is a problematic one. More resources do not necessarily improve quality or increase service provision, and neither do they necessarily lead to the greater satisfaction of the public. When politicians are under financial pressure they may tend to restrict funds for public services, but this will often prevent the provision of high quality services. This is a critical matter for any potential alliance between the employees of the welfare state and the consumers of welfare state services. They have a common interest in defending public services only so long as the welfare state delivers efficiently quality services which consumers do not find elsewhere. In our day and age, many consumers have great purchasing power, and they will not shy away from purchasing higher quality health and social services in the marketplace, when public services do not provide the services they want.

The problem with the NPM ideology is not that it is orientated towards meeting the demands and needs of consumers in a rational and efficient manner. The problem is that consumer orientation directs attention away from the political context. The bright light that is made to shine upon the *consumer* castes a gloomy shadow upon the *citizen* and the broader social consequences of personal choice remain undisclosed in those very same shadows. Consumerism and the preoccupation with private well-being are inextricably linked together, but this attitude and solidarity do not go well together. Moreover, the great emphasis given to a consumer orientation may result in the increased disposition to accept or actively further competition, market principles and the privatisation of health and welfare services. The results can lead to arrangements that were formerly based upon solidarity *being replaced* by arrangements that are based upon individual purchasing power.

Fourth concern: does the welfare state undermine solidarity?

What is the relationship between solidarity and the welfare state? Today, the welfare state is regarded as an expression of institutionalised solidarity, and many theorists worry that individualism and consumerism will erode solidarity. As mentioned above, Claus Offe wrote in the last part of the 1980s that the prospects for the welfare state were not good. At the present time, there is considerable evidence that does not support Offe's pessimistic predictions. Despite retrenchment and cuts, the welfare state has survived, and the crisis of the welfare state is no longer a fashionable research theme.[2] Social research very often concludes that popular support for the welfare state continues to be firm, and surveys that chart the attitudes of citizens in many countries, attest to the continuing legitimacy of the welfare state (Svallfors 1999; Gelissen 2002). However, this persistent support for welfare measures does not suffice to set at rest worries that increased individualism may, one day, erode institutionalised solidarity. The general tendency of welfare state change since the 1970s seems to be the weakening of arrangements that are anchored in citizenship, in universalism and in equality. The principles of selectivity, private delivery, personal responsibility and labour force participation have all been strengthened (Gilbert 2002). Besides that, public opinion is often somewhat contradictory and equality is not a predominant value in most Western European countries (Svallfors 1997; Gelissen 2002; Stjernø and Johannessen 2004).

A more fundamental question can be asked. To what extent does the welfare state foster or erode solidarity? Two different views answering this question are often pitted against one another – that of Richard Titmuss and that of the communitarians (see Chapter 9). Whereas Titmuss maintained that a well-developed universal welfare state creates community, the communitarians criticise the welfare state for undermining the sense of common responsibility that is a precondition for community and solidarity, and say that public responsibility for economic redistribution and the provision of social services relieves civil society of the moral responsibility to take care of needy members of the community. Arrangements that were originally based upon solidarity function in a manner that undermines the moral foundations upon which these collective arrangements are built. The German philosopher Kurt Bayertz presents a similar argument. The dialectic of *Verstaatlichung* (making something a public responsibility) transforms behaviour based upon moral involvement and solidarity into institutionalised *quasi-solidarity*. Personal involvement in the situation of the *other(s)* loses its moral character and changes into the bureaucratic act of paying taxes, he argues (Bayertz 1996).

This may be true to some extent. If solidarity is best anchored in the social practice of civil society, as communitarians claim, then the extent

---

[2] While this is true of most Western countries, this does not apply to the UK and perhaps to the Netherlands, where welfare state reforms have been more radical.

to which public arrangements aim to reduce the need for this solidarity in the social practices of civil society may be contrary to the interests of solidarity and community. As we have seen in Chapter 9, social theorists have different opinions about the extent to which social practice is a necessary condition for solidarity, and Habermas, for one, argues that cognition and empathy are more important. Although Bayertz's arguments appeal to common sense and seem pertinent, they do not undermine the argument that cognition and empathy can be the foundation for institutionalised solidarity. For many people, acceptance of being a tax-payer is *not* based upon the risk of being punished if caught cheating. On the contrary, their acceptance is based upon the recognition that tax-paying is the most rational and effective way to pay for the common tasks that are required to keep society functioning in an orderly and responsible manner.

Moreover, communitarians do not seem to fully take into account the fact that the welfare state has already changed the social structure in a way that provides for an alternative basis for solidarity. There are at least two features of the new social structure that have helped the welfare state to survive – notwithstanding the many claims that it is in crisis, the diagnoses that describe its ailments and one prognosis after another predicting its decline and death. The welfare state has already created a large number of occupational groups that serve it, and these consist of professionals, more often than not, with higher education and with the ability to speak out and influence politics. In many countries, these groups have become strong defenders of the welfare state.

Secondly, an increasing number of people are provided for by the welfare state, either as social security beneficiaries or as consumers of health and social services. As long as pensioners, patients within the health services, families dependent upon kindergartens and social services do not believe that these benefits and services can be better provided by private firms, they share an interest in defending the public and collective arrangements of the welfare state.

In the struggle over welfare arrangements, strong alliances may develop between occupational groups and professionals serving the welfare state and the consumers of its services and the recipients of its transfers. On both sides of this possible alliance, women will often be overrepresented. Even if there is no *a priori* reason to believe that this alliance will be weaker than the alliance that developed in the late 1930s between the industrial working class and smallholders, farmers and fishermen in Scandinavia, it probably will. This possible new alliance is more difficult to stabilise and more vulnerable to internal disagreement. The professionals who serve the welfare state and its consumers *are* characterised by a high degree of fragmentation, organisationally and politically. They are not bound together by reciprocal feelings of empathy. They do not share a common vision of society. They do not experience a common adversary that can serve to unite them. As we have seen, these were important characteristics of the ideology of the labour movement in the heyday of working-class solidarity in Scandinavia.

Perhaps the greatest challenge for the maintenance of such an alliance is the fact that it can only exist as long as the welfare state and those employed within it actually provide arrangements and services that consumers prefer. When these are not provided to the satisfaction of consumers with purchasing power, alternatives will be sought in the private market; and the fiscal pressure on public budgets and the ambition of governments to increase productivity can prevent welfare state professionals from providing high quality services.

The point being made here is that pure self-interest may be insufficient for the producers and the consumers of welfare services to successfully defend existing welfare arrangements. Welfare state service professionals and the consumers of welfare state services may have a common interest in defending the welfare state based upon individual self-interest, but this common stance does not necessarily include the normative aspects of solidarity. Alliances that are built primarily upon a conception of self-interest and which are not supported by reciprocal empathy or by a common normative understanding are very vulnerable, as Durkheim has already emphasised.

The discussion conducted here demonstrates that the relationship between solidarity and the welfare state is a complicated one. The modern welfare state rests upon the preparedness of its citizens to share risks and resources. Increasing individualisation, consumerism and enhanced possibilities for personal savings do not necessarily represent threats to the welfare state as such, since citizens can consider the welfare state to be a large insurance company. However, the more this view prevails, the more likely it is that universalism, redistribution and solidarity will be undermined.

An alliance between the working class and segments of the middle class may be able to constitute a strong defence for solidarity and related values, but at the moment it seems more likely that increasing pluralisation and heterogeneity in the employment structure and concomitant changes in the cultural and the ideological foundations of society will reduce the level of solidarity within the welfare state. Assuming that an alliance between the working class and segments of the middle class can defend solidarity in the welfare state, we should not further assume that this alliance will defend solidarity with the Third World and immigrants, and with oppressed and discriminated-against groups in its own and in other countries.

Fifth concern: the ambiguous phenomenon of globalisation

It has been argued above that the combined effects of the reduction in the industrial working class, class destructuration, individualisation and consumerism represent the main challenges to solidarity in present-day society. However, this discussion cannot be concluded without some remarks about the dual character of *globalisation* in this respect. It is impossible for me to discuss the phenomenon of globalisation fully, within the limits of these concluding remarks. For a better introduction, I refer the reader to the extensive literature on globalisation.[3]

The outbreak of World War I represented a defeat for the idea of international worker solidarity that the socialist parties had propagated and for the universal ambitions of the Catholic Church. After World War I, the *nation* became the frame of reference for solidarity, and after World War II, the national welfare state was established and gradually legitimised by a language of solidarity. In the next decades, the discourse of solidarity was founded upon the idea that the nation-state controlled its own territory and was able to conduct an economic policy with some sort of redistribution and an employment policy with the aid of national instruments and decision-making. The central question today is to what extent these ideas are still valid in an era of globalisation.

The idea of solidarity has always expressed concern about the expansion of the market, either as a conservative and defensive response to the dissolution of the social bonds that accompanied this expansion, or as a radical and offensive mobilisation for a new and better society. As globalisation means that national barriers are removed or reduced, and as this allows for the free international flow of capital, investment, goods and services, globalisation implies a further expansion of the market and constitutes a threat to the idea of solidarity. Multinational or transnational corporations have become key actors with an enormous capacity to influence national governments and international institutions. The strategic position of trade unions and employees has been weakened and the position of owners of capital and investors has been strengthened, because those who own or control capital are more free to move their assets from one place or nation to another when their demands are not met. In each Western European nation, democratically

---

[3] In addition to those works already referred to in this text, see Beck (1999), Beynon and Dunkerley (2000), Dower and Williams (2002) and Singer (2002). Among the many network links that can be recommended are www.cepr.net, www.globalresearch.ca, www.polity.co.uk/global.

elected representatives have to take this new reality into account whenever corporate taxation is discussed, and this may pressure governments to decrease taxes, to reduce welfare expenditures and to make social policy arrangements more in conformity with the market. Workers in nations with higher wages are poised against workers from low wage countries which are interested in attracting investments, and solidarity across borders is made more difficult. From this point of view, there is little doubt that globalisation constitutes a serious threat to traditional forms of solidarity.

Another aspect is that not only the economy, but also social problems are globalised. The global warming of the atmosphere and air pollution do not respect national borders. War and natural disasters are responsible for the flight of millions across borders and continents and affect the safety, labour markets, culture and identities of other nations. Terrorism can occur anywhere. Genetically modified food can be easily spread to every corner of the world. Increased travel spreads infection and disease from one country to another. We should not underestimate the resilience of the nation-state, but the effects of globalisation can be translated into the conclusion that the nation-state, on its own, cannot guarantee the safety or the welfare of its citizens (Held and McGrew 2002).

A third aspect of globalisation is the growth of international and transnational organisations and networks. From 1976 to 1995, 1,600 multilateral treaties were ratified, 100 of which created new international organisations. At the beginning of the twenty-first century, there are more than 4000 international congresses or conferences held each year (Held and McGrew 2002). Modern international organisations and conferences have an ambiguous character. Many of the most important and influential international organisations are dominated by the wealthy nations of the world, and particularly by the USA, including the World Bank, The International Monetary Fund (IMF) and The World Trade Organisation (WTO). These institutions can hardly be said to represent international solidarity. Nevertheless, these organisations are arenas – or potential arenas – for political struggle and for public discourse, and they do create possibilities for the development of new alliances.

A fourth aspect of globalisation is closely associated with the growing complexity of international organisations – the increase in international laws and regulations. International laws and treaties regulate trade, transport and communication, and require the recognition of universal human rights. This constitutes a net of legal regulations, at a regional level, as in Europe, and at the global level. David Held characterises this as an 'emerging framework of cosmopolitan law', whereas Hauke Brunkhorst argues that a world legal system has already developed (see Chapter 9).

The nation-state is no longer the protagonist in law-making. Law is developed by the establishment of international organisations, by negotiations, treaties, judgments and decisions of regional or international courts of justice (Held and McGrew 2002; Brunkhorst 2002). A third position is that the principal characteristic of international law is *not* that it represents a new and positive international order; on the contrary, it is an expression of US hegemony and the USA will respect international law only to the extent that it serves US interests (see below).

Parties or social movements as carriers of solidarity?

Another aspect of globalisation is the growth of international voluntary organisations, networks and cooperation between trade unions, churches, campaigns and action groups. The social democratic and Christian democratic parties that are studied in this book developed from popular social movements in the early days of industrial society, from the labour and trade union movement and from religious lay movements. Their concept of solidarity represented the search for an answer to the problems that accompanied the growth of markets and industrial capitalism. From the 1960s, and particularly in the wake of the student revolt in 1968, a second wave of new social movements entered the political scene in Western Europe (Eley 2002; Kjeldstadli 2002). These movements developed as a response to the challenges that the established political parties did *not* meet. They entailed the direct grass-roots participation of thousands, mostly young people who rejected or harshly criticised the established parties. The most important issues were nuclear disarmament, combating threats to the environment, opposition to discrimination against sexual and ethnic minorities and gender concerns. In recent years, challenges associated with globalisation have triggered another new wave of collective and social mobilisation, again by groups that are for the most part outside social democratic and Christian democratic parties.

The development of these new channels for solidarity is to a large extent due to the changed role and function of the established political parties. The 'catch-all' character of social democratic and Christian democratic parties makes it necessary for these parties to aggregate demands and to make compromises among a wide range of groups and interests in order to win elections. These political parties have participated in Western European governments for so long that they are generally perceived as being a part of the political establishment that is bound up with the state. They are universally expected to be *responsible* and that means having an eye for the realism of any reform, for the consequences for public finances, for the dangers of inflation and for the impact upon national competitive power. As mentioned in Chapter 7, voter identification with political parties has weakened since the 1960s, trust in political parties has been reduced, membership has declined, and parties have lost some of their capacity to mobilise mass participation (Webb 2002). Political parties try to develop coherent ideologies in order to integrate different segments of the electorate and to create political identity, but this ideology must be able to address different classes and groups. Party ideology needs to be flexible and should not have too many hard edges or too many provocative opinions. Focusing upon new and controversial issues, struggling for the interests of oppressed minorities, or for solidarity with those who are struggling in other countries and who are not even voters, can jeopardise the chance of winning a majority of votes. When new issues arise and when it does not seem likely that these issues can be used to mobilise broadly, political parties will not be the first ones to openly commit themselves. To be sure, political parties have not lost their function of articulating social interests and they are still indispensable for democracy and for representative government to function. Many parties have shown a great capacity for renewal and adaptation (Montero and Guenther 2002), but the articulating function has been weakened and the political scene has opened itself up to other actors. When the practice of social democratic and Christian democratic solidarity has been weakened or lost, a crucial question must be raised. To what extent can solidarity be anchored in the social movements of the first wave (trade unions and churches), of the second wave (diverse movements of the 1960s and 1970s), or of the third wave (concerns about globalisation and about US hegemony since the 1990s)?

The trade union movement has become increasingly aware that globalisation represents a very severe threat to the labour movement. The International Confederation of Free Trade Unions (ICFTU) discussed globalisation and the need for concerted action on an international level, a main issue at its world conference in 1996 (Munck 2002). At the regional level, trade unions are beginning to establish joint strategies against multinational corporations, and many trade unions were present in the demonstration against the WTO summit in Seattle in 1999. Although the involvement of trade unions does not as yet have the character of a social mass movement, this might still be the early beginnings of a new form of international solidarity within the trade union movement. When it comes to religion, we have seen in previous chapters that the Catholic Church and the Lutheran World Federation are actively involved in the work for international solidarity and peace, and the same is true for the World Council of Churches. These organisations seem to be more

strongly committed to solidarity than most national Christian democratic parties. Pope John Paul II has shown concern about Third World
issues and about the immorality of waging pre-emptive war, referring
to the US and British war in Iraq. The Lutheran World Federation has
called for global solidarity as a response to the globalisation of the world
economy.[4]

What about the second wave social movements – the identity movements that were established after 1968? Scholars of social movements
Sidney Tarrow and Ann Gamson, regard these social movements as being
a new foundation for the development of a common identity and solidarity (Gamson 1997; Tarrow 1998). These movements usually emerge
when participants identify a common interest that is based either upon
self-interest or upon the individual's personal involvement. The first is
the case when participants share one or more common characteristics,
such as being a woman, belonging to a stigmatised sexual minority or
being disabled. The second is the case when people only share a common
subjective interest in an issue or a problem, such as the environment or
international solidarity. In both cases, these movements develop a more or
less coherent ideology in which many of the elements that were once part
of the traditional working-class ideology are found. They define boundaries between themselves and their environment and identify external
adversaries or enemies, and this in turn helps the participants in the movement to establish a collective identity with a clear distinction between *us*
and *them*.

To what extent can these second-wave movements become stable foundations for solidarity? Undoubtedly, they have had an impact on politics
in general, and social welfare policy, in particular. They have often regis-
tered and brought attention to new needs and have identified social problems long before the established political parties have done so. Political
parties negotiate compromises among different social groups and classes
before they make decisions, but movements function as a vanguard and
put forward the interests of specific groups and bring to the fore new
knowledge and insights about emerging social needs. At the same time,
these movements can unite participants in spite of their political, gender,
ethnic and age differences. In welfare politics, this applies particularly to
feminist movements, which have led the way in many countries in the
struggle for child-care facilities, shorter working hours, leave of absence
from work for families with children, and the establishment of centres for
abused or battered women and victims of incest.

---

[4] See LWF (2003a) and the interview with the general secretary of the LWF, 7 March
2003, see Noko (2003).

As agents for a broader-based solidarity, there are several problems associated with these kinds of movements. Only a few of them can claim to represent the general interests of the entire society, as the labour movement once could in the heyday of working-class solidarity. Some women's movements and certain environmental movements can also make similar claims. Generally speaking, these movements are often dependent upon political trends and ideological fashions, and they rise and fall with the development of the political agenda in the media. The lack of a strong material base and weak organisational structures make these movements dependent upon the involved commitment of participants, and movements often do not survive because they so quickly consume the involved commitment of their participants. As a consequence, the social movements only survive when the movements are institutionalised, co-opted or reduced to interest groups. In Germany, the green movement was institutionalised into a less radical Green party, and in Scandinavia, the women's movement was integrated into the established political parties. The movement may continue to exist, but to a lesser degree, no longer as a large and *vivid* movement, really, more as an unclear current or trend which to some extent succeeds in uniting women across other dividing lines. Even if these social movements are valuable contributors to new forms of solidarity, they are unlikely to be strong enough to become effective carriers of a new *global* solidarity.

What about the more recent third wave? How do the new movements *against* the global problems associated with globalisation fit into this picture? This new wave represents the ambition to establish a new form of solidarity across national borders that differs from the traditional international solidarity of the labour movement. The International Movement for Democratic Control of Financial Markets and their Institutions (ATTAC) was established in France in 1998, and rapidly spread to other countries in Western Europe. The WTO summit in Seattle in 1999 witnessed a mass movement of protesters from the wealthy nations of the world that allied itself with Third World resistance to further liberalisation, and their efforts made the conference a fiasco. The alternative conferences of the World Social Forum in Porto Alegre, Brazil, have during the past few years gathered tens of thousands of participants from all over the world. There is both resistance against globalisation and a globalisation of resistance. The foundation for this resistance is not primarily made up of the working class, but it is a new alliance of peasants in the Third World and groups springing from the middle classes in the wealthy nations of the world. At the moment these movements have still not established an organisational network that is comparable to the early labour movement. The sceptical attitude of many activists towards political parties and organisations has made it very difficult to establish a coherent and broad political alliance.

Even so, the world-wide demonstrations in February 2003 against the US and UK attack upon Iraq have demonstrated the potential international strength of these transnational movements. These demonstrations manifested a broad alliance of first, second and third wave social movements. Trade unions and churches, feminist and environmental groups, Attac and many others, marched together in opposition to the spectre of pre-emptive war. These demonstrations made great use of the web and e-mail, for political purposes, and have created new conditions for the expression of global solidarity. Tarrow's hypothesis that contentious, transnational social movements are able to broker and certify new political identities, and be a new model for future political action by appropriating and using already existing institutions and resources, seems to have been confirmed (Tarrow 2003). A temporary political identity that had never existed before was *brokered*, and these new political actors were recognised or *certified* by the overwhelming coverage they were given by the media on an international scale. New norms and forms for collective action were established, in a way that may become a *model* for later commitment and activities. Affiliated groups *appropriated* the resources of many institutions and organisations to serve the common purpose of the project.

We may have witnessed, in embryo, the beginnings of what might develop into a new form of global solidarity. Parallel to the history of the latter part of the nineteenth century, this solidarity is a response to the expansion of the market into new areas of social life. The impact of this struggle may very well determine the next phase in the development of the world in which we live.

Global citizenship – global ethics?

I argued in Chapter 9 that in a complex world solidarity cannot only be about *attitudes* towards others, but must be institutionalised into the rights and obligations that we all share in order to be effective. Brunkhorst regrets that the growth of international law has not been accompanied by the development of a public arena where those affected by international law and decisions can make their voices heard and exercise some influence upon decision-making. A strong public arena at the global level, where free deliberations and decision-making are woven together is a necessary component for global solidarity. A sovereign parliament is an example of a strong public arena at the nation-state level, where debate and decision-making are interwoven, but there is no concomitant global public arena, because public debate and decision-making power are still unconnected there (Brunkhorst 2002).

The globalisation of solidarity presupposes the globalisation of law and must include the full development of the individual's rights and obligations in the context of global citizenship. These, in turn, presuppose the universality of democratic political practices. Without democracy within, between and beyond the world of the nation-state there can be no true global solidarity. The *real* struggle is to complete the constitutional project of the French revolution of 1789, Brunkhorst maintains. That means the establishment of democratic solidarity on an international scale – by creating a strong public arena where democratic debate and decision making authorities are connected on a global scale. The key issue is whether or not it will be possible to build a global society based upon democracy and law. Brunkhorst is optimistic. Electronic communication and modern means of transportation can facilitate the spread of the idea of human rights and ultimately the development of a global public arena where debate and decision-making are joined. Non-governmental organisations (NGOs), international non-governmental organisations (INGOs), transnational networks, grass-roots movements, women's organisations and churches constitute a growing transnational 'people', he argues (Brunkhorst 2002). Another scholar of globalisation, David Held, argues in a similar vein for the establishment of a *cosmopolitan* democracy. This should mean the impartial administration of law at the international level; greater transparency, accountability and democracy in global governance, with strong and more competent governance at all levels, locally, nationally, regionally and globally. This system should be based upon the cosmopolitan social democratic values or ethics, Held maintains. These are *global social justice, democracy, universal human rights, the rule of law, human security* and *transnational solidarity* (Held and McGrew 2002). His proposition is to globalise the values that are found in social democratic and Christian democratic political parties.[5]

The recognition of the need for a global ethics is increasingly found in the writings of diverse social philosophers. As mentioned in Chapter 9, in *A Global Ethic for Global Politics and Economics*, the Catholic philosopher and theologian, Hans Küng, argues that a global ethics should be the answer to increasing interdependence between human beings and nations in the globalised world (Küng 1997). Nigel Dower argues that those who regard themselves as being global citizens should be clear about their own

---

[5] After the US and UK attack on Iraq in 2003, Held is less optimistic and argues that the war 'is in danger of dragging us back to a pre-legal order and a deeply uncivil international society' (Held 2003), www.polity.co.uk/global/.

moral preferences. He believes that the common core of a global ethics should take responsibility for the global community, and ground itself in the belief that all human beings have equal worth. Global citizens must consciously and carefully balance their loyalties to the nation-state with their loyalties to the global community (Dower 2002).

I am in sympathy with these arguments. In our day and age, solidarity should entail the ambition to build an international order that is based upon democratic participation and the rule of law. Can one seriously doubt the need for an ethics that includes concern for global issues, the recognition of the equal worth of every human being, and the need to ground international relationships on these principles and values?

There are, of course, problems associated with this position. Ethics alone will not be able to constitute a very firm foundation for global solidarity. This was sufficiently discussed in the previous chapter and needs no repetition here. Another problem is that Brunkhorst, and others, too optimistically describe the existing achievements of public global deliberation and the status of the existing international legal system. More areas are regulated by international law and by international agreements, but this is often merely the result of Western economic and bargaining strengths, as Brunkhorst himself admits. The immediate prospects of developing an international system based upon *democratic* law are rather glum, there are still far too many nation-states in the hands of despotic regimes, and the present policy of the US is hardly a reassuring one. As I argued in Chapter 9, law is, in itself, the expression of a *weak* form of solidarity. It is the *content* of law that determines to what extent law expresses a *stronger* form of solidarity. Besides that, modern means of transportation and the extensive use of electronic communication have not yet reached enormous numbers of people and do not as yet constitute a basis for global public deliberation. The technology is too unevenly distributed and large parts of the world are excluded.

A third problem is the complicated relationship between participation and democracy at the nation-state level and democratic participation at the international or global level. The globalisation of economy, law and politics has still not yet reached the point where the governments of Western Europe have lost the will or the capacity to pursue national goals. Duane Swank has studied the relationship between changes from the 1970s to the 1990s in the Scandinavian welfare state, and internationalisation of the economy. He concludes that the evidence indicates that the changes are small and probably not due to internationalisation. Consequently, national development can still be influenced by democratic participation at the nation-state level (Swank 2000). The nation-state still provides for democratic participation in the most effective way, and this historical achievement cannot easily be transferred to a law-making authority at the international level. The fact that there are still despotic regimes at the nation-state level that make a mockery of democratic practices, further complicates the possibilities of moving in the direction of global decision- and law-making by a global body. Even if we all woke up one morning and discovered that US dominance and the despotic regimes had disappeared, the transfer of law-making to global bodies at this point in time would severely reduce the possibilities for democratic participation. Identities are still anchored in the nation-state and in ethnic and linguistic communities within the nation-state, and the increasing distance between citizens and legislative bodies is, in itself, a serious political problem. Transferring decision-making power to more distant bodies is only a solution to the extent that the institutions of the nation-state have lost the right to make independent decisions. It is doubtful that this is true to the degree that Brunkhorst believes.

Finally, a global community that is able to fully express its feelings of solidarity must first build global institutions that reflect democracy and solidarity. Today, the UN is the only global institution that provides even a glimmer of hope for this eventuality. But the reader is reminded that the contemporary UN is far from being such an institution (Imber 2002). While many of the specialist agencies in the field of health and welfare, such as UNICEF and WHO, represent positive examples of global solidarity, this can hardly be claimed in matters that affect the global economy, or for matters affecting peace and security. These areas are dominated by the veto powers of the Security Council and particularly by the US. Although discussions in the Security Council occasionally resemble authentic discourse, in the more important matters, such as the decision on whether or not to go to war in Iraq, sessions are more often characterised by negotiations and bargaining, where offers, pressures and threats lack transparency.

A unipolar world system cannot be reconciled with global solidarity. If the concept and language of solidarity in the programmes of the political parties that have been studied in this book are to be put into practice, then those parties must make a stand against unilateralism. The history and the character of the political parties in question make that kind of decision a great challenge. The third-wave social movements that have so recently emerged onto the world's stage might be able to help social democratic and Christian democratic parties to meet this challenge. Competition with other political parties, those that establish a positive relationship to these new movements, may also help social democratic and Christian democratic parties in Western Europe to rise to the occasion of this challenge.

In Europe, solidarity has been one of the motives that have made Christian democratic and social democratic parties open the European Union to poorer countries in central Europe. However, as time and again has been emphasised in this book, today, those who address the issue of solidarity in modern Western societies must also address the issues of individuality and equality. The previous prime minister and chairman of the Danish social democratic party, Poul Nyrup Rasmussen, has emphasised the need to combine individualism and solidarity in a new way. In an interview after the electoral defeat of the Danish social democrats in 2002, he spoke of how he hoped to reconcile individualism and solidarity as follows:

Now, we shall initiate the real human liberation in which personal talent may be developed in an elegant and intelligent way so that others do not suffer. You may become the most clever and wise irrespective of your own background, and you may become that without throwing others away from the table. We are closer to this dream than we have been before. This new human individualistic community is the social democratic message to the Danish people. (Rasmussen 2001)

So far, however, this message seems to be too optimistic. Neither Rasmussen nor his party has been able to contain or fight the policy of the present Danish government – a policy that is characterised more by individualism and the fear of others than any other government in Scandinavia in modern times. Unfortunately, individualism and the fear of strangers seem to characterise other European nations as well, and this makes it difficult to be optimistic about immediate developments regarding solidarity. On the other hand, we are not at the end of history and history is full of surprises. Projections about the future that are based upon the present are almost always proven wrong.

References

DOCUMENTS

Adler, A. (ed.) 1919–22. *Theses, Resolutions and Manifestoes of the First Four Congresses of the Third International*: Ink Links.

CCD 2000. *Programma*. Rome: Centro Christiano Democratico.

CCD, CDU *et al.* 2000. *Dichiarazione Comune di Intenti. Roma 2.1.2000*. Rome: Centro Christiano Democratico.

CdL 2001. *Casa delle Libertá. Il programma politico 2001*. Rome: Casa delle Libertá.

CDU 1994. *Grundsatzprogramm der CDU Deutschlands: 'Freiheit in Verantwortung'. 5. Parteitag, 21.–23. Februar 1994, Hamburg*. Bonn: Christlich Democratische Union Deutschland.

 1945a. 'Gründungsaufruf der CDU. Berlin, 26. Juni 1945', in Hintze (ed.), 1995.

 1945b. 'Kölner Leitsätze, Vorläufiger Entwurf zu einem Programm der Christlichen Demokraten Kölns im Juni 1945', in Hintze (ed.), 1995.

 1947. 'Ahlener Programm. Zonenausschuss der CDU für die britische Zone, Ahlen/Westfalen 3. Februar 1947', in Hintze (ed.), 1995.

 1949. 'Düsseldorfer Leitsätze. Wirtschaftsausschuss der CDU der britischen Besatzungszone. 15. juli, Düsseldorf', in Hintze (ed.), 1995.

 1953. 'Hamburger Programm. 4. Bundesparteitag, 18.–21. April 1953, Hamburg', in Hintze (ed.), 1995.

 1971. 'Berliner Programm. In der Form der zweiten Fassung vom 18. Bundesparteitag, 25.–27.1, Düsseldorf', in Hintze (ed.), 1995.

 1975. 'Unsere Politik für Deutschland. Mannheimer Erklärung. 23. Bundesparteitag, 23.–25. juni 1975, Mannheim', in Hintze (ed.), 1995.

 1978. 'Grundsatzprogramm. "Freiheit, Solidarität, Gerechtigkeit". 26. Bundesparteitag, 23.–25. Oktober, Ludwigshafen', in Hintze (ed.), 1995.

 1981. 'Mit der Jugend – Unser Land braucht einen neuen Anfang. 30. Bundesparteitag, 2.–5. November 1981, Hamburg', in Hintze (ed.), 1995.

 1994. 'Grundsatzprogramm. "Freiheit in Verantwortung". 5. Parteitag, 21.–23. Februar, Hamburg', in Hintze (ed.), 1995.

CDU 2000. *La garanzia di scelte giuste*. Rome: Christiani Democratici Uniti.

DC 1958. *Programma della D.C. per il quinquennio 1958–63*. Rome: Editori Cinque Lune.

 1968. *Il programma della D.C. Al servizio del paese*. Supplement to *Il Popolo*, 19 April 1968. Rome: Il Popolo.

1943. 'Il Programma di Milano della Democrazia Cristiana. 25 Luglio 1943', in Damilano (ed.), 1969.

1944. 'Il Programma della Democrazia Cristiana. Gennaio 1944', in Damilano (ed.), 1969.

1947a. 'Quattro mozioni del II Congresso Nazionale formulate ed approvate dal Consiglio Nazionale della D.C.' in Damilano (ed.), 1969.

1947b. 'Direzione Centrale della D.C. Messaggio della Direzione ai Comitati Regionali e Provinciali ed alle Sezioni del Partito sulla fedeltá alle istituzoni e metodo della democrazia', in Damilano (ed.), 1969.

1948. 'Appello della Democrazia Cristiana al Paese. "Salvare la libertà"', in Damilano (ed.), 1969.

1958. 'Programma della Democrazia Cristiana per il quinquennio 1958–63', in Damilano (ed.), 1969.

1963. 'Programma elettorale della Democrazia Cristiana per la IV Legislatatura. 28 Marzo 1963', in Damilano (ed.), 1969.

1976a. *Il programma elettorale della DC*. Supplement to *Il Popolo*, no. 123, 1976. Rome: Il Popolo.

1976b. (1954–73). *I congressi della Democrazia Cristiana*. Rome: Edizioni Cinque Lune.

1979. *Il programma elettorale della DC*. Supplement to *Il Popolo*, 17 May 1979. Rome: Il Popolo.

1983. *Programma della Democrazia Cristiania. Un programma per garantire lo sviluppo. Un patto di stabilita e giustizia. Elezioni politiche 1983*. Rome: Democrazia Cristiania.

1943. 'Idee ricostruttive della Democrazia Cristiania. Luglio 1943', in Marcucci (ed.), 1983.

1987. *Un programma per l'Italia. Elezioni politiche 14–15 giugno 1987*. Rome: Democrazia Cristiania.

1992. *Elezioni politiche '92. Il programma elettorale della D.C.* Supplement to *Il Popolo*, 1 April 1992. Rome: Il Popolo.

DNA 1885. 'Programmet for Den socialdemokratiske Forening. Vedtatt den 29.3 1885', in Fjerstad (ed.), 2001.

1887. '1ste landsmøte i Arendal 21. og 22. august 1887', in Fjerstad (ed.), 2001.

1891. '5te landsmøte i Kristiania 1. og 2. august 1891', in Fjerstad (ed.), 2001.

1894. 'Det norske Arbeiderpartis program 1894', in Fjerstad (ed.), 2001.

1909. 'Det principielle program', in Fjerstad (ed.), 2001.

1939. 'Det norske Arbeiderpartis arbeidsprogram', in Fjerstad (ed.), 2001.

1939. 'Det norske Arbeiderparti, 2 dokument 1939', in Fjerstad (ed.), 2001.

1945. 'Arbeid og samvirke. Retningslinjer for Det norske Arbeiderpartis program', in Fjerstad (ed.), 2001.

1949. 'Det norske Arbeiderparti – Prinsipp-program 1949', in Fjerstad (ed.), 2001.

1953. 'Arbeidsprogram 1953–1957. Vedtatt på landsmøtet 1953. Det norske Arbeiderparti', in Fjerstad (ed.), 2001.

1961. 'Nye gode år. Det norske Arbeiderpartis Arbeidsprogram 1962–1965', in Fjerstad (ed.), 2001.

1969a. 'Prinsipper og perspektiver. Vedtatt på landsmøtet 11.–14 mai 1969', in Fjerstad (ed.), 2001.

1969b. 'Vekst – Trygghet – Trivsel. Arbeidsprogram for Det norske Arbeiderparti 1970–1973 vedtatt på landsmøtet 11.–14 mai 1969', in Fjerstad (ed.), 2001.

1973. 'Tryghet for folket. Det norske Arbeiderpartis arbeidsprogram for perioden 1974–77', in Fjerstad (ed.), 2001.

1974. *Arbeiderpartiet og kristendommen. Innstilling fra et utvalg nedsatt 26. november 1973 av Arbeiderpartiets sentralstyre.* Oslo: Tiden Norsk Forlag.

1977. 'Du skal vita kva det gjeld. Solidaritet. Arbeid. Miljø. Arbeidsprogram 1978–81. Arbeiderpartiet', in Fjerstad (ed.), 2001.

1981. 'Det norske Arbeiderparti – Prinsipp-program 1981', in Fjerstad (ed.), 2001.

1985. 'Ny vekst for Norge. Arbeiderpartiet 86–89. Arbeidsprogram', in Fjerstad (ed.), 2001.

1989. 'Krav til innsats for felles framtid. Arbeidsprogram for Det norske Arbeiderparti 1990–1993', in Fjerstad (ed.), 2001.

1992. 'Mer fellesskap – sosialdemokratisk program for 90-åra. Vedtatt på Arbeiderpartiets landsmøte, november 1992', in Fjerstad (ed.), 2001.

1996. 'Samråderett Prinsipp- og arbeidsprogram Det norske Arbeiderparti. Prinsipp- og arbeidsprogram. Vedtatt på landsmøtet i Det norske Arbeiderparti 7.–10. November 2000', in Fjerstad (ed.), 2001.

2000. 'Det norske Arbeiderparti. Program for 2001–2005. Vedtatt på landsmøtet 12. november 2000', in Fjerstad (ed.), 2001.

DS 2000. *Il patto che ci unisce. Statuto dei Democratici di Sinistra.* Rome: Democratici di Sinistra.

EPP 1992. *Basic Programme.* Adopted by the IXth EPP Congress, Athens, November. Brussels: European People's Party.

2001. *A Union of Values.* Adopted in Berlin, 13 January 2001. Brussels: European People's Party.

Forza Italia (FI) 1997. *Statuto di Forza Italia 1998.* Approvato dalla Assemblea Nazionale. Milano, 18 January 1997. Milan: Forza Italia.

First International (ed.) 1934. *Thèses, manifestes et résolutions adoptés par les I'er, II'e, III'e e IV'e Congrès de l'Internationale Communiste (1919–1923). Textes complets.* Rome: Feltrinelli.

ILP 1898. *Independent Labour Party. Reports 1–6, 1893–1898.* London: Labour Literature Society.

KrF 1936. 'Kristelig Folkepartis prinsipp-program 1936', in Fjerstad (ed.), 2001.

1945. 'Kristelig Folkeparti. Program ved Stortingsvalget 8. oktober 1945', in Fjerstad (ed.), 2001.

1957. 'Kristelig Folkeparti. Program ved Stortingsvalget 1957', in Fjerstad (ed.), 2001.

1961. '4 år med Kristelig Folkeparti. Program ved stortingsvalget 11. sept. 1961', in Fjerstad (ed.), 2001.

1965. 'Vegen og målet. Kristelig Folkepartis prinsipielle program 1965', in Fjerstad (ed.), 2001.

1977. 'Program for stortingsperioden 1977–81. Kristelig Folkeparti', in Fjerstad (ed.), 2001.

1979. 'Prinsipp-program for Kristelig Folkeparti. Vedtatt på landsmøtet 1979', in Fjerstad (ed.), 2001.

1985. 'Handlingsprogram for Kristelig folkeparti. Ta vare på livet! For Storingsperioden 1985–89', in Fjerstad (ed.), 2001.

1991. 'Prinsipp-program for Kristelig Folkeparti. Vedtatt på landsmøtet 1991', in Fjerstad (ed.), 2001.

1996. 'Kristelig Folkeparti stortingsperioden 1997–2001', in Fjerstad (ed.), 2001.

2001. 'Program for Kristelig Folkeparti 2001–2005', in Fjerstad (ed.), 2001.

Labour Party 1934. *For Socialism and Peace. The Labour Party's Programme of Action*. London: The Labour Party.

1938. *The Labour Party National Executive Committee*. London: The Labour Party.

Labour 1900. 'Manifesto of the Labour Policy Representation Committee', in Craig (ed.), 1975.

1910. 'Labour Manifesto', in Craig (ed.), 1975.

1923. 'Labour's Appeal to the Nation', in Craig (ed.), 1975.

1924. 'Labour's Appeal to the People', in Craig (ed.), 1975.

1931. 'National Labour Manifesto. An Appeal to the Nation by the Rt. Hon. Ramsay MacDonald, Prime Minister', in Craig (ed.), 1975.

1931. 'Labour's call to action: the nation's opportunity', in Craig (ed.), 1975.

1935. 'The Labour Party's call to power', in Craig (ed.), 1975.

1945. 'Labour Manifesto 1945: Let us face the future. A declaration of Labour policy for the consideration of the nation', in Craig (ed.), 1975.

1950. 'Labour Manifesto 1950. Let us Win Together: A declaration of Labour policy for the consideration of the nation', in Craig (ed.), 1975.

1959. 'Britain Belongs to You: The Labour Party's policy for consideration by the British people', in Craig (ed.), 1975.

1970. 'Labour Manifesto 1970. Now Britain's Strong: Let's make it great to live in', in Craig (ed.), 1975.

1979. *British Labour Party Election Manifesto to 1979 'The Labour Way Is the Better Way'*. London: Labour Party.

1981–83. *Report of the Annual Conference of the Labour Party 1981, 1982, 1983*. London: Labour Party.

1983. *British Labour Party Election Manifesto 1983 'The New Hope for Britain'*. London: Labour Party.

1987. *Labour Party Election Manifesto 1987 'Britain Will Win with Labour'*. London: Labour Party.

1992. *Labour Party Manifesto 1992 'It's Time to Get Britain Working Again'*. London: Labour Party.

1997. *Labour Party Manifesto, General Election 1997 'New Labour because Britain Deserves Better'*. London: Labour Party.

2001. *Ambition for Britain. Labour Manifesto 2001. New Labour. New Britain*. London: Labour Party.

2003. 'About Labour', http://labour.org.uk/aboutlabour/.

Lefranc, G. (ed.) 1977. *Le Mouvement socialiste sous la troisième republique, tome 2 1920–40*. Paris: Petite Biblioteque Payout.

LWF 1948. *Proceedings of the Lutheran World Federation Assembly*. Lund, Sweden, 30 June–6 July 1947, Philadelphia: United Lutheran Publication House.

1957. *Messages of the Third Assembly*. Lutheran World Federation, Minneapolis: Augsburg Publishing House.

1965. *Proceedings of the Fourth Assembly of the Lutheran World Federation*. Helsinki, 30 July–11 August 1963, Berlin and Hamburg: Lutherisches Verlagshaus.

1970. *Kirche vor den Herausforderungen der Zukunft*. Porto-Alegre – Evian-les-Bains, 1970. V. Vollversamlung des Lutherischen Weltbundes, Stuttgart: Kreuz-Verlag.

1977. *Daressalam 1977. Sechste Vollversamlung Lutherischer Weltbund*. Frankfurt: Otto Lembeck.

1990. *I Have Heard the Cry of my People: Proceedings [of] the Eighth Assembly [of the] Lutheran World Federation*, Curitiba, Brazil. 25 January–8 February. Geneva: Lutheran World Federation.

2003a. *The Assembly Study Book. I Have Heard the Cry of my People*. Geneva: Lutheran World Federation.

2003b. *Letter from the Lutheran World Federation European Pre-Assembly Consultation*. 26 February 2003. Geneva: Lutheran World Federation.

NS 1991. 'Orden og rettferd. Program for Nasjonal Samling (NS)', in Sørensen (ed.), 1991.

OSF 1901. *Troisième Congrès General des Organisations Socialistes Françaises*. Lyon, 28 May 1901. Paris: Société Nouvelle de Libraire.

PCE 1975. 'Programa electoral del Partido Comunista 1933', in Artola, 1975, vol. II.

PCF 1927. *Thèse sur la situation nationale et les tâches générales du parti*. V Congrès national du Parti Communiste Français, Lille, 20–26 June 1926. Paris: Bureau D'Editions.

1936. 'Pour le salut du people français! Manifest du VII congrés national du Parti Comuniste (S.F.I.C)', in Thorez (ed.).

1954. *XIIIe Congrès du Parti Communiste Français, Paris 3–7 juin 1954. Projet de thèse sur la situation politique et les tâches du Parti*. Paris: PCF.

1956. *XIV Kongress der Französischen Kommunistischen Partei. Thesen der Französischen Kommunistischen Partei im Kampf für den sozialen Fortschritt, fur den Frieden, fur eine Zukunft nationaler Grösse*. Approved at 44th Congress, Le Havre, 18– 21 July 1956. Paris: PCF.

1961. *XVIe Congrés du Parti Communiste Français*, Saint-Denis, 18–21 May 1961, supplement to *Bulletin de Propagande*, No. 34. Paris: PCF.

1964. *Projet de résolution et projet de statuts. XVII congrès du parti communiste français*. Paris: PCF.

1970. *PCF 19ème congres 4–8 fevrier 1970 Nanterre. Thèses adoptées par le Congrès*. Paris: PCF.

1974. *Union Programme commun Socialism. Le parti communiste propose*. XXIe Congress, Vitry, 24–27 October 1974. Paris: PCF.

1982. *Construire le socialisme en couleurs de la France. 24 Congrès du Parti Communiste Français*, Saint Ouen, 3–7 February. Paris: Editions Sociales.

1985. *PCF Resolutions. 25e Congrès*, Paris 1985. Paris: Province Impression.

1990. *Projet de résolution pour le 27ème congrès soumis par le Comité central a la discussion du Parti*. Paris: PCF.

PCF and PS 1972a. *Das gemeinsame Regierungsprogramm*, Supplement to *L'Humanité d'Alsace et Lorraine*, no. 31, 28 July 1972.

PCI 1921. 'Partito Comunista Italiano. Sezione della Internazionale Comunista. Manifesto ai Lavoratori d'Italia', in PCI (ed.), 1962.

1962. *Resoconto stenografico del XVII Congresso Nazionale del Partito Socialista Italiano. Livorno 15–20 gennaio 1921. Con l'aggiunta dei documenti sulla fondazione del Partito Comunista Italiano*. Milan: Edizioni Avanti!

1986a. 'Elementi per una dichiarazione programmatica del Partito Comunista Italiano', in *L'Unità* (ed.), *If PCI e la Svolta del 1956*. Rome: Rinascita, 1986.

1986b. *Documenti per il Congresso XVI. Progetti di tesi, programma, emendamenti, statuto, criteri e procedure*. Rome: Rinascita.

1987. *Tesi, Programma, Statuto. I Documenti approvati dal XVII Congresso del PCI*. Rome: Rinascita.

1988. 'The political documents of the 18th Congress'. *The Italian Communists*, vol. IV (1988).

1990a. 'Tesi per il congresso. Lioni, January 1926', in Cafagna (ed.), 1990.

1990b. 'Dare vita alla fase costituente di una nuova formazione politica', in PCI (ed.), 1962.

1921. 'Il programma del Pcd'I', in Cortesi (ed.), 1999.

PPI 1919a. 'L'appello al paese del Partito Popolare Italiano. 18 gennaio 1919', in Universitá di Bologna (ed.), 1967.

1919b. 'Il programma', in Universitá di Bologna (ed.), 1967.

1993. *Statuto del Partito Popolare Italiano*. Rome: Partito Popolare.

PS 1906. *Parti Socialistes. 3e Congrès National*. Limoges, 1–4 November 1906. Paris: Au Siege du Conseil National.

1910. *Parti Socialistes. 7e Congrès National*. Paris, 15–16 July 1910. Paris: Au Siege du Conseil National.

1913. *Parti Socialistes. 10e Congrès National*. 1913. Paris: Au Siege du Conseil National.

1925. *Les deux méthods. Conférence par Jean Jaures et Jules Guesde*. Lille, 1900. Paris: Librairie Populaire.

1928. *Pour les Elections Législatives de mai 1928. Le programme du Parti Socialiste*. Paris: Librairie Populaire.

1946. *Le programme d'action du Parti Socialiste*. Paris: Éditions de la Liberté.

1956. *48e Congrés National 28 juin – 1 juillet 1956 Lille*. Paris: Librairie-Papeterie des Municipalités.

1972. 'Le projet de memorandum du parti socialiste sur l'unité organique, 1945', in Quillliot (ed.), 1972.

1978. *Le programme commun de gouvernement de gauche. Propositions socialistes pour l'actualisation*. Paris: Flammarion.

1981. '110 propositions pour la France. Adoptées par le congrès du Creteil, January 2 1981. Parti socialiste', in Mitterand (ed.), 1981.

1999. *Verse un monde plus juste. Contribution du Parti Socialiste au Congrès de l'Internationale Socialiste*, October 1999. Mimeo. Copenhagen: Arbejderbevegelsens arkiv og bibliotek.

2001. *La déclaration de principe du Parti Socialiste*. Paris: Parti Socialiste.

1932. *Elections Législative de 1932. Notre Plate-Forme. Discours de Léon Blum au Congrès extraordinaire tenu a Paris les 30 et 31 Janvier 1932*. Paris: Librairie Populaire du Parti Socialiste.

PSI 1902. *Partito Socialista Italiano. Rendiconto dell'VII Congresso Nazionale*, Imola, 6–9 September 1902. Rome: Libreria Socialista Italiana.

1904. *Partito Socialista Italiano. Rendiconto dell'VIII Congresso Nazionale*, Bologna, 8–11 April 1904. Rome: Luigi Mongini.

1945. *Programma e Azione del Partito. Dichiarazione Programmatica votata nel Congresso clandestino del Agosto 1943*. Rome: Partito Socialista Italiano.

1955. *Statuto del PSI approvato dal 31 Congresso*, 31 Congresso Nazionale del Partito Socialista Italiano. Milan: Edizioni Avanti.

1957. *Proposte per una Dichiarazione programmatica del P.S.I.* Rome: S.E.T.

1960. *Gli operai votano P.S.I.* Rome: S.E.T.

1961. *34. Congresso Nazionale*. Milan 15–20 March. Milan: Edizioni Avanti.

1972. *Tesi per il 39. congresso Nazionale del PSI*. Rome: SET.

1978. *Per il progetto socialista. 40. Congresso. Mozione N. 1.* Supplement to *Il Compagno*, no. 2. Rome: Partito Socialista Italiano.

1981. 'Il Rinnovamento socialista per il rinnovamento dell'Italia. Atti del 42. Congresso del PSI. Palermo 22–26 aprile 1981', in Molaiolo (ed.), 1981.

1892. 'Il Programa di PSI', in Molaiolo (ed.), 1982.

PSOE 1888. 'Manifiesto de los delegados del primer congreso del Partido Socialista Obrero Espanol. Barcelona, 25 de agosto de 1888', in Artola (ed.), 1975, vol. II.

1918. 'Programa del Partido Socialista Obrero', in Artola (ed.), 1975, vol. II.

1931. 'Programa parlamentario del P.S.O.E.' in Artola (ed.), 1975, vol. II.

1934. 'Programa del P.S.O.E.', in Artola (ed.), 1975, vol. II.

1979. *Programa Elecciones 79*. Madrid: PSOE.

1982. *Por el cambio. Programa Electoral Partido Socialista Obrero Espanol*. Madrid: PSOE.

1986. *Programa 1986/1990 Para seguir avanzando por buen camino*. Madrid: PSOE.

1989. *Programa Electoral 1989*. Madrid: PSOE.

1993. *Programa Electoral 1993. El programa de la mayoria*. Madrid: PSOE.

1996. *Espana en positivo. Programa electoral. Elecciones generales 1996*. Madrid: PSOE.

2000. *Elecciones generales 2000*. Madrid: PSOE.

SAP 1915. 'Manifest til Sverges arbetande folk 7. mars 1914', in SAP (ed.), 1915. *Socialdemokratiska partistyrelsens berättelse över år 1914*. Göteborg: Framåt 1915.

1986. *Framtiden i folkets hander. Socialdemokratiskt program for medborgarskap och valfrihet*. Stockholm: Socialdemokraterna.

1998. *Valgmanifest*. Stockholm: Socialdemokraterna.

1897. 'Program för Sverges Socialdemokratiska Arbetareparti antaget på 4:de partikongressen i Stockholm den 4. juli 1897', in Kokk (ed.), 2001.

1911. 'Program för Sverges Socialdemokratiska Arbetareparti. Antaget på åttonde partikongressen i Stockholm 9–16 april 1911', in Kokk (ed.), 2001.

1920. 'Program för Sverges Socialdemokratiska Arbetareparti. Antaget på elfte partikongressen i Stockholm 1920.' in Kokk (ed.), 2001.

1944. 'Program för Sveriges Socialdemokratiska Arbetareparti. (Enligt beslut å sjuttonde kongress 1944)', in Kokk (ed.), 2001.

1960. 'Program för Sveriges Socialdemokratiska Arbetareparti. (Enligt beslut å partiets tjuguförsta kongress 1960)', in Kokk (ed.), 2001.

1975. 'Socialdemokraterna. Program (Fastställd av 1975 års partikongress)', in Kokk (ed.), 2001.

1990. 'Socialdemokraternas partiprogram (Antaget på socialdemokraternas 31: a kongress 1990)', in Kokk (ed.), 2001.

2001. Partiprogram för Socialdemokraterna beslutat av partikongressen i Västerås den 6 november 2001. Stockholm: Socialdemokraterna.

Second International 1889. *Le Congrès Marxiste de 1889*. Le Congrès Possibiliste de 1889. Congrès International Ouvrier Socialiste 14–21 juillet 1889. Paris: Minkoff Reprint.

1975 (1889). *Kongress-Protokolle der Zweiten Internationale Band I*. Paris 1889 – Amsterdam 1904. Glashutten in Taunus: Detlev Auermann KG.

1976. *Kongress-Protokolle der Zweiten Internationale Band II Stuttgart 1907 – Basel 1912*. Glashutten in Taunus: Detlev Auermann KG.

1980. *Die II Internationale 1918/1919 Protokolle, Memoranden, Berichte und Korrespondenten*. Berlin: J. H. W. Dietz Nachf. GMBH.

1986. 'Statut der 2. Internationale', in Siegel (ed.), 1986.

Socialdemokratiet 1876. *Gimleprogrammet*. 'Socialdemokraten' 10. juni 1876, Copenhagen: Arbejderbevegelsens arkiv.

1888. *Program for Det danske Socialdemokrati af 14. juli 1888*, Copenhagen: Arbejderbevegelsens arkiv.

1913. *Program for socialdemokratiet i Danmark*, Copenhagen: Arbejderbevegelsens arkiv.

1934. *Danmark for folket*. Copenhagen: Arbejderbevegelsens arkiv.

1945. *Socialdemokratiets program 1945. Fremtidens Danmark*, Copenhagen: Arbejderbevegelsens arkiv.

1961. *Socialdemokratiets arbejdsprogram 1961. Idé og hverdag*, Copenhagen: Arbejderbevegelsens arkiv.

1969. *Socialdemokratiets arbejdsprogram. Det nye samfund – 70'ernes politik*. Copenhagen: Arbejderbevegelsens arkiv.

1977. *Lighed og Trivsel. Solidaritet*. Principprogram vedtaget på Socialdemokratiets 32. kongress September 1977. Copenhagen: Socialdemokratiet.

1992. *Socialdemokratiets principprogram. Vedtaget på Socialdemokratiets ordinære kongress 1992*. Copenhagen: Socialdemokratiet.

Socialist International 1977. *Resolution about the Political Situation*. 13th Congress of the SI, Geneva, 26–28 November 1976. *Socialist Affairs*, 27(1) 1977.

1979. SI Congress 1978 Vancouver. *Socialist Affairs*, 1.

1990. 'Prinzipienerklärung der Sozialistischen Internationale, beschlossen auf dem 1. Kongress der Sozialistischen Internationale in Frankfurt am Main 1951: Ziele und Aufgaben des Demokratischen Sozialismus', in Dowe and Klotzbach (eds.), 1990.

SPD 1880. *Protokoll des Kongress der Deutschen Sozialdemokratie. Abgehalten auf Schloss Wuden in der Schweiz an 20.–23. August 1880.* Riesbach: Verlag von A. Herter, Industriehalle.

1903. *Protokoll über die Verhandlungen des Parteitages der Sozialdemocratischen Partei Deutschlands, abgehalten zu Dresden vom 13. bis 20. september 1903,* Buchandlung Vorwärts.

1906. *Protokoll über die Verhandlungen des Parteitages der Sozialdemocratischen Partei Deutschlands, abgehalten zu Mannheim vom 23. bis 29. september 1907,* Buchandlung Vorwärts.

1908. *Protokoll über die Verhandlungen des Parteitages der Sozialdemocratischen Partei Deutschlands, abgehalten zu Nürnberg vom 13. bis 19. september 1908,* Buchandlung Vorwärts.

1909. *Protokoll über die Verhandlungen des Parteitages der Sozialdemocratishen Partei Deutsclands, abgehalten zu Leipzig vom 12. bis 18. september 1909,* Buchandlung Vorwärts.

1912. *Protokoll über die Verhandlungen des Parteitages der Sozialdemocratishen Partei Deutsclands, abgehalten in Chemnitz vom 15. bis 21. september 1912,* Buchandlung Vorwärts Paul Singer G.m.b.H.

1875. 'Programm der Sozialdemokratischen Partei Deutschlands, beschlossen auf dem Vereinigungskongress in Gotha 1875', in Dowe and Klotzbach (eds.), 1990.

1921. 'Programm der Sozialdemokratischen Partei Deutschlands, beschlossen auf dem Parteitag in Görlitz 1921', in Dowe and Klotzbach (eds.), 1990.

1925. 'Programm der Sozialdemokratischen Partei Deutschlands, beschlossen auf dem parteitag in Heidelberg 1925', in Dowe and Klotzbach (eds.), 1990.

1975. *Ökonomischer-politischer Orientierungsrahmen für die Jahre 1975–1985. Parteitages der Sozialdemocratishen Partei Deutsclands, vom 11. bis 15. september 1975. Protokoll der Verhandlungen. Anlagen.* Rosengarten Mannheim: Vorstand der SPD.

1976. *Weiter arbeiten um Model Deutscland. Regierungsprogramm 1976–80. Ausserordentliche Parteitages der Sozialdemocratishen Partei Deutsclands, vom 18. und 19. september 1976. Protokoll der Verhandlungen. Anlagen.* Dortmund-Westfalenhalle: Vorstand der SPD.

1875. 'Programm und Organisationsstatuten der Sozialistischen Arbeiderpartei Deutschlands, beschlossen auf dem Vereinigungskongreß in Gotha 1875', in Dowe and Klotzbach (eds.), 1990.

1891. 'Programm der Sozialistischen Arbeiderpartei Deutschlands, beschlossen auf dem Parteitag in Erfurt 1891', in Dowe and Klotzbach (eds.), 1990.

1952/54. 'Aktionsprogramm der Sozialdemokratischen Partei Deutschlands, beschlossen auf dem Parteitatg in Dortmund 1952 under erweitert auf dem Parteitag in Berlin 1954', in Dowe and Klotzbach (eds.), 1990.

1959. 'Grundsatzprogramm der Sozialdemokratischen Partei Deutsclands, beschlossen von Ausserordentlichen Parteitag der Sozialdemokratischen

Parteis Deutschlands in Bad Godesberg vom 13. bis 15. November 1959', in Dowe and Klotzbach (eds.), 1990.

1989. 'Grundsatzprogramm der Sozialdemokratischen Partei Deutschlands, beschlossen vom Programmparteitag in Berlin 1989', in Dowe and Klotzbach (eds.), 1990.

1998a. *Arbeit, Innovation und Gerechtigkeit. SPD-Wahlprogram für die Bundestagswahl 1999.* Bonn: SPD.

1998b. *Grundsatzprogramm der Sozialdemokratischen Partei Deutschlands. Beschlossen vom Programm-parteitag der Sozialdemokatischen Partei Deutschlands am 20. Dezember 1989 in Berlin geändert auf dem Parteitag in Leipzig am 17.04 1998.* Bonn: SPD.

2000. *Grundwerte heute: Solidarität. Dokumentation der Podiumdiskussion vom 8. November 2000 in Berlin.* Berlin: SPD.

2001. 'Kursbestimmung. Sozialdemokratie heute: Sicherheit im Wandel. Bereit für die Zukunft'. Bonn: SPD.

Third International 1919–22. 'Theses, resolutions and manifestoes of the first four congresses of the Third International', in Adler (ed.), 1919–22.

1919–22. 'Statutes', in Adler (ed.), 1919–22.

1920. 'Workers of the World and Oppressed Peoples, Unite! Proceedings and documents of the Communist International', in Riddell (ed.), 1987, 1–2.

1924. *Fifth Congress of the Communist International.* Moscow: Communist Party of Great Britain.

1971a. 'Programme of the Communist International adopted at its sixth congress', in Degras (ed.), 1971, 2–3.

1971b. 'Theses of the eleventh ECCI plenum on the Task of the Comintern sections in connection with the deepening of the economic crisis and the development of the conditions making for a revolutionary crisis in a number of countries', in Degras (ed.), 1971, 2–3.

1919. 'Statutes', in Riddell (ed.), 1987.

UDC 2003. *Chi siamo.* Rome: Unione dei Democratici Cristiani e Democratici di Centro.

Ulivo 2001. *Ulivo. Insieme per l'Italia. Programma elettorale 2001.* Rome: Ulivo.

Vatican 1966. *The Documents of Vatican II.* London: Geoffrey Chapman.

1968. 'Gaudium et Spes. Pastoral constitution on the Church in the world today', in Turner (ed.), 1968.

WCC 1948. *Minutes of the Meetings of the Central Committee of the World Council of Churches.* Amsterdam: World Council of Churches.

1955. *The Evanston Report. The Second Assembly of the World Council of Churches.* London: SCM Press.

1962. *New-Delhi. World Council of Churches.* Stuttgart: Evangelische Missionsverlag.

1966. *World Conference on Church and Society. Official Report. World Council of Churches.* Geneva: World Council of Churches.

1967. *World Conference on Church and Society. Official Report. World Council of Churches.* Geneva: World Council of Churches.

1968. *Uppsala Speaks. Reports of the Sections of WCC. World Council of Churches.* Geneva: Friendship Press.

1968. *The Uppsala Report. World Council of Churches.* Geneva: CBPac.

Zentrum 1924 (1922). 'Richtlinien der Deutschen Zentrumspartei. Beschlossen auf dem 2. Reichsparteitages der Deutschen Zentrumspartei zur Berlin am 10. Januar 1922', in Schreiber (ed.), 1924.

1870. 'Soester Programm, Oktober 1870', in Mommsen (ed.), 1952.

1909. 'Berliner Erklärung, 1909', in Mommsen (ed.), 1952.

1923. 'Richtlinien der Deutschen Zentrumspartei, 1923', in Mommsen (ed.), 1952.

1871. 'Programm der Zentrumsfraktion des Deutschen Reichstages. März 1871', in Heinen (ed.), 1952.

LITERATURE

Adler, M. 1964 (1932). *Die solidarische Gesellschaft. Soziologie des Marxismus 3.* Vienna: Europa Verlag.

Adler, A. (ed.) 1919–22. *Theses, Resolutions and Manifestoes of the First Four Congresses of the Third International.* Ink Links.

Alberigo, G. and A. Riccardi (eds.) 1990. *Chiesa e papato nel mondo contemperaneo.* Rome-Bari: Editori Laterza.

Allum, P. 1990. 'Uniformity Undone: Aspects of Catholic Culture in Postwar Italy', in Baränski and Lumbley (eds.).

Anderson, B. S. and J. P. Zinsser 1989. *A History of Their Own. Women in Europe from Prehistory to the Present.* Vol. II. London: Harper & Row.

Andersen, E. *et al.* (eds.) 1974. *Arbejderkvinder i alle lande. Et Clara Zetkin-utdvalg.* Copenhagen: Tiderne skifter.

Anderson, P. 1977. *Considerations on Western Marxism.* London: NLB.

Artola, M. (ed.) 1975. *Partidos y programmas politicos 1808–1936.* 2 vols. Madrid: Aguilar.

Arts, W. and J. Gelissen 2001. 'Welfare states, solidarity and justice principles: does the type really matter?' *Acta Sociologica* 44.

Aukrust, T. 1965. *Mennesket i samfunnet 1–2.* Oslo: Forlaget Land og Kirke.

Bailey, F. G. 1981. 'Dimensions of rhetoric in conditions of uncertainty', in Paine (ed.).

Bakunin, M. 1992a. 'Speeches at the Basle Congress', in Cutler (ed.).

1992b. 'The policy of the International', in Cutler (ed.).

1992c. 'All-round education', in Cutler (ed.).

1992d. 'Three lectures to the Swiss members of the International', in Cutler (ed.).

Baldwin, P. 1990. *The Politics of Social Solidarity.* New York: Cambridge University Press.

1997. 'State and citizenship in the age of globalisation', in Koslowski and Føllesdal (eds.).

Baränski, Z. and R. Lumbley (eds.) 1990. *Culture and Conflict in Postwar Italy.* New York: St. Martins Press.

Barclay, D. E. and E. D. Weitz (eds.) 1998. *Between Reform and Revolution. German Socialism and Communism from 1840 to 1990.* New York: Berghahn Books.

Baring, A. 1998. *Machtwechsel. Die Ära Brandt-Scheel*. Berlin: Ullstein Buchverlag GmbH & Co.

Bartolini, S. 2000. *The Political Mobilizaton of the European Left 1860–1980. The Class Cleavage*. Cambridge: Cambridge University Press.

Bauer, R. and H. Diessenbacher (eds.) 1984. *Organisierte Nächstenliebe. Wohlfahrtsverbände und Selbsthilfe in der Krise des Sozialstaates*. Opladen: Westdeutscher Verlag.

Baum, G. and R. Ellsberg (eds.) 1989. *The Logic of Solidarity. Commentaries on Pope John Paul II's Encyclical 'On Social Concern'*. New York: Orbis Books.

Bauman, Z. 1997. *Work, Consumerism and the New Poor*. London: Open University Press.

2000. *Liquid Modernity*. Cambridge: Polity Press.

Bayertz, K. (ed.) 1996. *Politik und Ethik*. Stuttgart: Philipp Reclam jun.

1998. *Solidarität. Begriff und Problem*. Frankfurt: Suhrkamp Verlag.

1999. *Solidarity*. Dordrecht/Boston/London: Kluwer Academic Publishers.

Bebel, A. 1879. *Die Frau und der Sozialismus*. Zürich-Hottingen: Verlag der Volksbuchhandlung.

Beck, U. 1992. *Risk Society. Towards a New Modernity*. London: Sage Publications.

1999. *What is Globalization?* Cambridge: Polity Press.

Becker, W. 2003. 'From political Catholicism to Christian Democracy: the development of Christian parties in modern Germany', in Kselman and Buttigieg (eds.).

Beecher, J. and R. Bienvenue (eds.) 1971. *The Utopian Vision of Charles Fourier. Selected Texts on Work, Love, and Passionate Attraction*. Boston: Beacon Press.

Beilharz, P. 1992. *Labour's Utopias. Bolshevism, Fabianism, Social Democracy*. London: Routledge.

Bell, D. S. and B. Criddle 1994. *The French Communist Party in the Fifth Republic*. Oxford: Clarendon Press.

Bellah, R. 1998. 'Communitarism properly understood. A defense of "democratic communitarism"', in Etzioni (ed.).

Bellah, R. *et al.* (eds.) 1996. 'Introduction', in *Habits of the Heart. Individualism and Commitment in American Life*. Berkeley: University of California Press.

Bendix, R. 1960. *Max Weber. An Intellectual Portrait*. New York: Doubleday & Company.

Benum, E. (ed.) 1998. *Overflod og fremtidsfrykt 1970 –. Aschehougs Norges historie*. Oslo: Aschehoug.

Berger, S. (ed.) 1982. *Religion in West European Politics*. London: Frank Cass.

Bergh, T. 1987. *Storhetstid (1945–1965), vol. 5 Arbeiderbevegelsens historie*. Oslo: Tiden Norsk Forlag.

Bergsdorf, W. 1983. *Herrschaft und Sprache. Studie zur politischen Terminologie der Bundesrepublik Deutschland*. Pfullingen: Neske.

Bergström, V. 1989. 'Program och ekonomisk politik 1920–1988', in Misgeld, Molin and Åmark (eds.).

Berkling, A. L. (ed.) 1982. *Från Fram til folkhemmet. Per Albin Hansson som tidningsman och talare*. Stockholm: Metodica Press.

Berlinguer, E. 1975. *La proposta comunista. Relazione al Comitato centrale di controllo del Partito comunista italiano. In preparazione del XIV Congresso. Roma 18–20 ottobre 1976, 10 dicembre 1974*. Turin: Einaudi.

1976. *Il PCI e la Crisi italiana. Rapporto e conclusioni alla riunione plenaria del Comitato centrale e della Commissione centrale di controllo del Partito comunista italiano. Roma 18–20 ottobre 1976.* Rome: Editori Riuniti.

Berman, S. 1998. *The Social Democratic Moment. Ideas and Politics in the Making of Interwar Europe.* Cambridge, MA: Harvard University Press.

Bernstein, E. 1910. *Die Arbeiterbewegung.* Frankfurt am Main: Literarische Anstalt Rütten & Loening.

1973 (1899). *Sosialismens forutsetninger.* Oslo: Pax Forlag.

Bernstein, R. 1990. 'Rorty's liberal Utopia', *Social Research 1.*

Beynon, J. and D. Dunkerley (eds.) 2000. *Globalization: The Reader.* London: Athlone Press.

Bjørklund, T. 1983. 'Fra lokalparti til landsparti', in Garvik (ed.).

Bjørnson, Ø. 1990. *På klassekampens grunn (1900–1920).* Oslo: Tiden Norsk Forlag.

Blair, T. 1997. *New Britain. My Vision of a Young Country.* Boulder, CO: Westview Press.

Blum, L. 1945. *Pour être socialiste.* Paris: Éditions de la liberté.

Bondevik, K. M. 2000. Likheter og ulikheter, Forskjeller mellom nestekjærlighet og solidaritet. *Arbeiderbladet 11.11.* Oslo.

Botnen, B. 1983. 'En verden langt der borte', in Garvik (ed.).

Bottomore, T. and P. Goode (eds.) 1978. *Austro-Marxism.* Oxford: Clarendon Press.

Bourdieu, P. 1984. *Distinction. A Social Critique of the Judgement of Taste.* London: Routledge & Kegan Paul.

Bourgeois, L. 1910. *Solidaritet.* Copenhagen: Gyldendalske Boghandel Nordisk Forlag.

1912. *Solidarité.* Paris: Librairie Armand Colin.

Bourgeois, L. and L. Croiset 1902. *Essai d'une philosophie de la solidarité. Conférences et discussions.* Paris: Félix Alcan.

Bozza, T. (ed.) 1956 (1947). *Alcide De Gasperi. Discorsi politici 1–2.* Rome: Editori Cinque Lune.

Brandt, W. 1974. *Über den Tag hinaus. Eine Zwischenbilanz.* Hamburg: Hoffmann und Campe.

1976. *Begegnungen und Einsichten. Die Jahre 1960–1975.* Hamburg: Hoffmann und Campe.

Branting, H. 1948. 'Demokrati eller diktatur. 28. oktober 1919', in Edberg (ed.).

Brenner, R. 2002. *The Boom and the Bubble. The US in the World Economy.* London: Verso.

Brisbane, A. (ed.) 1876. *General Introduction to Social Science.* New York: C. P. Somerby.

Broughton, D. 1994. 'The CDU–CSU in Germany: Is there any Alternative?' in Hanley (ed.).

Brunkhorst, H. 2002. *Solidarität. Von der Bürgerfreundschaft zur globalen Rechtsgenossenschaft.* Frankfurt: Suhrkamp.

Brunner, O., W. Conze, and R. Koselleck (eds.) 1972. *Geschichtliche Grundbegriffe. Historisches Lexikon zur politisch-sozialen Sprache in Deutschland.* Stuttgart: Klett-Cotta.

Bryld, C. 1992. *Den demokratiske socialismes gennembrudsår. Studier i udformingen af arbejderbevægelsens politiske ideologi i Danmark 1884–1916 på den nationale og internationale baggrund.* Copenhagen: Selskabet til forskning i arbejder-bevægelsens historie.

Buchaas, D. 1981. *Die Volkspartei. Programmatische Entwicklung der CDU 1950–1973.* Düsseldorf: Droste Verlag.

Buchanan, T. and M. Conway (eds.) 1996. *Political Catholicism in Europe, 1918–1965.* Oxford: Clarendon Press.

Budge, I. and H.-D. Klingemann 2001. 'Finally! Comparative over-time mapping of party policy movement', in I. Budge *et al.* (eds.).

Budge, I., D. Robertson and D. Hearl (eds.) 1987. *Ideology, Strategy and Party Change: Spatial Analyses of Post-War Election Programs in 19 Democracies.* Cambridge: Cambridge University Press.

Budge, I. *et al.* (eds.) 2001. *Mapping Policy Preferences. Estimates for Parties, Electors, and Governments 1945–1998.* Oxford: Oxford University Press.

Bull, P. 2000. 'New Labour, New Rhetoric? An analysis of the rhetoric of Tony Blair', in Landtsheer and Feldman (eds.).

Cafagna, L. (ed.) 1990. *Le tesi di Lioni. Riflessioni su Gramsci e la storia d'Italia 1926.* Milan: Franco Angeli.

Carr, W. 1991. *A History of Germany. 1815–1990.* London: Edward Arnold.

Catalan, J. 1999. 'Spain, 1939–96', in Schulze (ed.).

Chevallier, J. *et al.* (eds.) 1992. *La Solidarité: Un Sentiment Républicain?* Paris: Presses universitaire de France.

Christensen, S. 1992. *Nye mål i en ny verden. Socialistisk Internationale 1976–1992.* Copenhagen: Fremad.

Christiansen, N. F. 1997. 'Solidaritetens historie', *Dansk Sociologi* 1.

Christoffersen, S. A. (ed.) 1995. *Hans Nielsen Hauge og det moderne Norge.* Norges forskningsråd.

Cingolani, P. 1992. 'L'idée d'humanité chez Auguste Comte: Solidarité et continuité', in Chevallier *et al.* (eds.).

Classen, J. (ed.) 2001. *What Future for Social Security? Debates and Reforms in National and Cross-national Perspective.* The Hague: Kluwer Law International.

Cohn-Bendit, D. 1975. *Der grosse Basar. Gespräche mit Michel Lévy, Jean-Marc Salon, Maren Sell.* Munich: Trikont-Verlag.

Collins, R. 1994. *Four Sociological Traditions.* New York: Oxford University Press.

Comte, A. 1973 (1852). *System of Positive Polity.* New York: Burt Franklin.

Coninck-Smith, N. D. and M. Thing (eds.) 1997. *Historiens kultur. Fortælling. Kritik. Metode.* Copenhagen: Museum Tusculunams Forlag.

Conti, P. 2003. 'Gli Italiani e il Cattolicesimo', *Corriere della Sera*, 10.10. Milan.

Conway, M. 2003. 'The age of Christian Democracy: the frontiers of success and failure', in Kselman and Buttigieg (eds.).

Cortesi, L. (ed.) 1999. *Le origini del PCI. Studi e interventi sulla storia del comunismo in Italia.* Milan: FrancoAngeli.

Craig, F. W. S. (ed.) 1975 (1950). *British General Election Manifestos 1900–1974.* London: Macmillan.

Crosland, A. 1994 (1956). *The Future of Socialism*. London: William Pickering.
Crow, G. 2002. *Social Solidarities. Theories, Identities and Social Change*. Buckingham, UK: Open University Press.
Cuperus, R. and J. Kandel (eds.) 1998. *Transformation in Progress. European Social Democracy*. Amsterdam: Wiardi Beckman Stiftung/Friedrich Ebert Stiftung.
Cutler, R. (ed.) 1992. *The Basic Bakunin. Writings 1869–1871*. New York: Prometheus Books.
Dahl, E. 1999. Solidaritet og velferd. Grunnlaget for oppslutningen om velferdsstaten. Oslo: Fafo.
Damilano, A. (ed.) 1969 (1943). *Atti e documenti della Democrazia Cristiana 1943–1967*. Rome: Edizioni Cinque Lune.
De Gasperi, A. 1956a (1947). 'Non diserteremo il nostro posto! 18. novembre 1947', in Bozza (ed.).
1956b (1949). 'La Democrazia Cristiana per la libertà e la giustizia. 15. maggio 1949', in Bozza (ed.).
1956c (1949). 'I presupposti storici e ideali della Democrazia Italiana. Fiuggi, 30.7–2.8 1949', in Bozza (ed.).
1956d (1954). 'Nella lotta per la democrazia,' 27.6 1954, in Bozza (ed.).
1969 (1943). 'Idee ricostruttive della Democrazia Cristiana', in Damilano (ed.).
Dean, J. 1996. *Solidarity of Strangers. Feminism after Identity Politics*. Berkeley: University of California Press.
Degras, J. (ed.) 1971. *The Comintern International 1919–1943*. London: Frank Cass.
Diamante, I. 2003. 'Il Dio relativo dei novi credenti'. *La Repubblica*, 22 June.
Donegani, J.-M. 1982. 'The political cultures of French Catholicism', in Berger (ed.).
Donovan, M. 1994. 'Democrazia Cristiana: party of government', in Hanley (ed.).
Doreian, P. and T. Fararo (eds.) 1998. *The Problem of Solidarity. Theories and Models*. Amsterdam: Gordon and Breach Publishers.
Dorr, D. 1983. *Option for the Poor. A Hundred Years of Vatican Social Teaching*. Dublin: Gill and Macmillan.
Dowe, D. and K. Klotzbach (eds.) 1990. *Programmatische Dokumente der Deutschen Sozialdemokratie*. Bonn: J. H. W. Dietz Nachf.
Dower, N. 2002a. 'Global ethics and global citizenship', in Dower and Williams (eds.).
Dower, N. and J. Williams (eds.) 2002b. *Global Citizenship. A Critical Reader*. Edinburgh: Edinburgh University Press.
Driver, S. and L. Martell 1997. 'New Labour's communitarianisms'. *Critical Social Policy*, 17.
Durand, J.-D. 2002. *Storia della Democrazia cristiana in Europa. Dalla Rivoluzione francese al postcomunismo*. Milan: Guerini e Associati.
Durkheim, E. 1984 (1893). *The Division of Labour in Society*. London: Macmillan.
Eatwell, R. 1999. 'Fascism', in Eatwell and Wright (eds.).
Eatwell, R. and A. Wright (eds.) 1999. *Contemporary Political Ideologies*. London: Pinter.

Edberg, R. (ed.) 1948. *Demokratisk linje. Tal og artiklar av Hjalmar Branting och Per Albin Hansson.* Stockholm: Tiden Förlag.

Edelstein, W. and G. Nunner Winklar (eds.) 1984. *Zur Bestimmung der Moral. Philosophische und Sozialwissenschaftliche Beiträge zur Moralforschung.* Frankfurt am Main: Suhrkamp Verlag.

Eley, G. 2002. *Forging Democracy. The History of the Left in Europe, 1850–2000.* Oxford: Oxford University Press.

Elshtain, J. B. 2003. 'Don't be cruel: reflections on Rortyan liberalism', in Guignon and Hiley (eds.).

Elster, J. 1983. *Sour Grapes.* Cambridge: Cambridge University Press.

1989a. *The Cement of Society. A Study of Social Order.* Cambridge: Cambridge University Press.

1989b. *Solomonic Judgements. Studies in the Limitations of Rationality.* Cambridge: Cambridge University Press.

Engels, F. 1998 (1844–45). *The Condition of the Working Class in England.* London: ElecBook.

Eppler, E. 1998. 'Some programmatic remarks about the German SPD', in Cuperus and Kandel (eds.).

Eriksen, E. O. and J. Weigård 2003. *Understanding Habermas.* London: Continuum.

Eriksen, T. L. (ed.) 1987. *Den vanskelige bistanden.* Oslo: Universitetsforlaget.

Esping-Andersen, G. 1985. *Politics Against Markets. The Social Democratic Road to Power.* Princeton: Princeton University Press.

1990. *The Three Worlds of Welfare Capitalism.* Cambridge: Polity Press.

Etzioni, A. 1993. *The Spirit of Community. The Reinvention of American Society.* New York: Simon & Schuster.

1996. *The New Golden Rule. Community and Morality in a Democratic Society.* New York: Basic Books.

2001. *Next. The Road to a Good Society.* New York: Basic Books.

Etzioni, A. (ed.) 1998. *The Essential Communitarism Reader.* New York: Rowman & Littlefield Publishers.

Fairclough, N. 2000. *New Labour: New Language.* London: Routledge.

Fararo, T. and P. Doreian 1998. 'The theory of solidarity: an agenda of problems', in Doreian and Fararo (eds.).

Fargion, V. 1997. 'Social assistance and the North–South cleavage in Italy', in Rhodes (ed.).

1997. *Geografia della cittadinanza sociale in Italia.* Bologna: Il Mulino.

Fassino, P. 2003. *Per Passione.* Milan: Rizzoli.

Ferrera, M. 1993. *Modelli di Solidarità. I destinatari della protezione sociale nei principali modelli del welfare occidentale, le dinamiche evolutive e le radioni della crisi dei tradizionali mecchanismi di retribuzione.* Bologna: Il Mulino.

Feuer, L. (ed.) 1959 (1848). *Basic Writings on Politics and Philosophy. Karl Marx and Friedrich Engels.* New York: Doubleday and Company.

Fielding, S. 2003. *The Labour Party. Continuity and Change in the Making of 'New' Labour.* Basingstoke: Palgrave Macmillan.

Fjerstad, L. I. (ed.) 2001. *Vi vil! Norske partiprogrammer 1884–2001. Et samarbeidsprosjekt mellom NSD og Institutt for samfunnsforskning.* Versjon 1.1. Bergen: Norsk Samfunnsvitenskapelig Datatjeneste/ISF.

Follini, M. 2000. *La DC*. Bologna: IL Mulino.

Førde, E. 1981a. 'Prinsipprogrammet. Foredrag i Oslo Arbeiderpartis representantskap 2. september 1980', in Førde (ed.).

Førde, E. (ed.) 1981b. *Vi er alle sosialdemokratar. Åtte foredrag*. Oslo: Tiden.

Fourier, C. 1822a. *Théorie de l'Unité Universelle. Deuxième Volume*. Paris.

1822b. *Théorie de l'Unité Universelle. Troisième Volume*. Paris.

1876. 'Social destinies', in Brisbane (ed.).

Fraser, N. 1990. 'Solidarity or singularity', in Malachowski (ed.).

1995. 'From redistribution to recognition? Dilemmas of justice in a "postsocialist" age'. *New Left Review*, 212.

Freeden, M. 1996. *Ideologies and Political Theory. A Conceptual Approach*. Oxford: Oxford University Press.

2001a. 'Ideology – balances and projections', in Freeden (ed.).

Freeden, M. (ed.) 2001b. *Reassessing Political Ideologies. The Durability of Dissent*. London: Routledge.

Friis, J. and T. Hegna (eds.) 1974. *Arbeidernes Leksikon*. Oslo: Pax Forlag.

Frostin, P. 1994. *Luther's Two Kingdoms Doctrine. A Critical Study*. Lund: Lund University Press.

Furre, B. 1991. *Vårt hundreår. Norsk historie 1905–1990*. Oslo: Det Norske Samlaget.

1995. *Hans Nielsen Hauge og det nye Norge*. Hans Nielsen Hauge og det moderne Norge. Oslo: Norges Forskningsråd.

Galen, G. von. 1979 (1877). 'Der Antrag Galens 1877', in Heinen (ed.).

Galli, G. 1993. *Storia del Pci. Il Partito comunista italiano: Livorno 1921, Rimini 1991*. Milan: Kaos Edizioni.

Gamble, A. and T. Wright (eds.) 1999. *The New Social Democracy*. Oxford: Blackwell.

Gamson, J. 1997. 'Messages of exclusion: gender, movements, and Symbol boundaries'. *Gender & Society*, 11(2).

Garvik, O. (ed.) 1983. *Kristelig folkeparti mellom tro og makt*. Oslo: J. W. Cappelen.

Gelissen, J. 2002. *Worlds of Welfare, Worlds of Consent? Public Opinion on the Welfare State*. Leiden and Boston: Brill.

Geras, N. 1995. *Solidarity in the Conversations of Mankind*. London: Verso.

Gerth, H. 1872. *The First International. The Minutes of the Hague Congress of 1872*. The Hague: University of Minnesota Press.

Geyer, R. *et al.* (eds.) 2000. *Globalization, Europeanization and the End of Scandinavian Social Democracy?* Houndsmills: Palgrave.

Giddens, A. 1991. *Modernity and Self-Identity. Self and Society in Late Modern Age*. Cambridge: Polity Press.

1994. *Beyond Left and Right. The Future of Radical Politics*. Cambridge: Polity Press.

Giddens, A. (ed.) 2001. *The Global Third Way Debate*. Cambridge: Polity Press.

Gide, C. (ed.) 1901. *Selections from the Works of Fourier*. Perth: Swan and Sonnenschein & Co.

Gilbert, N. 2002. *Transformation of the Welfare State. The Silent Surrender of Public Responsibility*. Oxford: Oxford University Press.

Gilje, N. 1995. 'Hans Nielsen Hauge – en radikal ildsprofet fra Thune', in Christoffersen (ed.).

Ginsborg, P. 1989. *Storia d'Italia dal dopoguerra a oggi. Società e politica 1943–1988.* Turin: Einaudi.

2002. 'Se il ceto medio scende in piazza'. *Repubblica*, 27 February.

2003. *Berlusconi. Ambizioni patrimonali in una democrazia mediatica.* Turin: Einaudi.

Giovagnoli, G. 1996. *Il partito italiano. La Democrazia Cristiana dal 1942 al 1994.* Rome: Editori Laterza.

Giovanni, P. I. 1991. *Lettera Enciclica Centesimus Annus del Sommo Pontefice Giovanni Paolo II nel Centenario della 'Rerum Novarum'.* Rome: The Vatican.

Giugni, M. and F. Passy (eds.) 2001. *Political Altruism? Solidarity Movements in International Perspective.* Lanham: Rowman & Littlefield.

Gorz, A. 1981. *Farvel til proletariatet.* Oslo: 1981.

Goulet, D. 1983. 'Economic systems, middle way theories and Third World realities', in Houck and Williams (eds.).

Gramsci, A. 1973a. 'Bidrag til den politiske teori', in Nielsen (ed.).

1973b (1919). 'Statens erobring', in Nielsen (ed.).

Grand, A. D. 1989. *The Italian Left in the Twentieth Century. A History of the Socialist and Communist Parties.* Bloomington and Indianapolis: Indiana University Press.

Gruppi, L. 1974a. 'Introduzione', in Gruppi (ed.).

Gruppi, L. (ed.) 1974b. *Comunisti, socialisti cattolici Togliatti.* Rome: Editori Riuniti.

Guignon, C. and D. R. Hiley (eds.) 2003. *Richard Rorty.* Cambridge: Cambridge University Press.

Gunther, R. and J. Montero (eds.) 2002. *Political Parties. Old Concepts and New Challenges.* Oxford: Oxford University Press.

Habermas, J. 1984. 'Gerechtigkeit und Solidarität. Eine Stellungnahme zur Diskussion über "Stufe 6" ', in Edelstein and Nunner Winklar (eds.).

1995a. *Justification and Application. Remarks on Discourse Ethics.* Cambridge, MA: MIT Press.

1995b. 'On the pragmatic, the ethical, and the moral employment of practical reason', in Habermas (ed.).

1995c. 'Lawrence Kohlberg and Neo-Aristotelianism', in Habermas (ed.).

1995d. 'Reflections on a Remark of Max Horkheimer', in Habermas (ed.).

1995e. 'Remarks on Discourse Ethics', in Habermas (ed.).

Habermas, J. (ed.) 1995f. *Justification and Application. Remarks on Discourse Ethics.* Cambridge, MA: MIT Press.

1996. *Between Facts and Norms. Contribution to a Discourse Theory of Law and Democracy.* Cambridge, MA: MIT Press.

2001a. 'Learning from Catastrophe? A Look Back at the Short Twentieth Century', in Pensky (ed.).

2001b. 'The Postnational Constellation and the Future of Democracy', in Pensky (ed.).

Hagen, R. 1999. *Rasjonell solidaritet.* Oslo: Universitetsforlaget.

Hamel, P. 1989. *Partecipazione e democrazia in Luigi Sturzo e Alcide De Gasperi.* Caltanissetta and Rome: Salvatore Sciascia Editore.

Hanley, D. (ed.) 1994. *Christian Democracy in Europe. A Comparative Perspective.* London: Pinter.

Hansson, P. A. 1948. 'Folkhemmet, medborgarhemmet. Tal i andrakammarens remissdebatt 1928', in Edberg (ed.).

1982a (1928). 'Folkhemmet, medborgarhemmet. Tal i andrekammarens remissdebatt 1928', in Berkling (ed.).

1982b (1929). 'Folk och klass. Ny Tid 10 september 1929', in Berkling (ed.).

Hansson, S. O. (ed.) 1996 (1960). *PS. Palme själv.* Stockholm: Tidens förlag.

Hayward, J. E. S. 1959. 'Solidarity: the social history of an idea in nineteenth century France'. *International Review of Social History,* 4.

1961. 'The official social philosophy of the French Third Republic: Leon Bourgeois and solidarism'. *International Review of Social History,* 6.

Heath, A. F., R. M. Jowell and J. K. Curtice 2001. *The Rise of New Labour. Party Policies and Voter Choices.* Oxford: Oxford University Press.

Hechter, M. 1987. *Principles of Group Solidarity.* Berkeley: California University Press.

Heinen, E. (ed.) 1979 (1877). *Staatliche Macht und Katholizismus in Deutschland. 2. Band: 1867 bis 1914.* Paderborn: Ferdinand Schöningh.

Held, D. 2003. *Return to the State of Nature*: www.politity.co.uk/global/.

Held, D. and A. McGrew 2002. *Globalization/Anti-Globalization.* Cambridge: Polity.

Herder 1959. *Herders Sozialkatechismus. Band Grundfragen und Grundkräfte des sozialen Lebens.* Freiburg: Herder.

Herzinger, R. 2002. Wenn nichts mehr geht – Ethos geht immer. *Die Zeit* no 8, 14 February.

Heywood, P. (ed.) 1999. *Politics and Policy in Democratic Spain: No Longer Different?* London: Frank Cass.

Hintze, P. 1995a. 'Die CDU als Programmpartei', in P. Hintze (ed.).

Hintze, P. (ed.) 1995b. *Die CDU-Parteiprogramme. Eine Dokumentation der Ziele und Aufgaben.* Bonn: Bouvier Verlag.

Hirst, P. 1997. *Globalisering, demokrati og det civile samfund.* Copenhagen: Hans Reitzels Forlag.

Hitler, A. 1925. *Mein Kampf.* Munich: Franz Eher Nachf.

1936a. 'Die grosse kulturpolitische Rede des Führers', in NSDAP (ed.).

1936b. 'Proklamation des Führers', in NSDAP (ed.).

Hix, S. 2000. *A History of the PES 1957–1994.* Brussels: Party of European Socialists.

Hobsbawm, E. 1981a. 'The forward march of Labour halted?' in Jacques and Multhern (eds.).

1981b 'Observations on the debate', in Jacques and Multhern (eds.).

1994. *Age of Extremes. The Short Twentieth Century 1914–1991.* London: Abacus.

Holtham, G. and R. Hughes 1998. 'The state of social democracy in Britain', in Cuperus and Kandel (eds.).

Houck, J. W. and O. F. Williams (eds.) 1983. *Co-Creation and Capitalism. John Paul II's Laborem Exercens.* Washington: University Press of America.

Huber, E. and J. D. Stephens 2001. *Development and Crisis of the Welfare State. Parties and Policies in Global Markets.* Chicago: University of Chicago Press.

Hudson, W. S. 1970. 'Calvin, a source of resistance theory, and therefore of democracy,' in Kingdon and Linder (eds.).

Imber, M. 2002. 'The UN and global citizenship', in Dower and Williams (eds.).

Jackson, T. P. 1999. *Love Disconsoled. Meditations on Christian Charity.* Cambridge: Cambridge University Press.

Jacques, M. and F. Multhern (eds.) 1981. *The Forward March of Labour Halted?* London: New Left Books.

Jakubinski, L. 1970. 'Uber die Herabstufung des gehobenen Stils bei Lenin', in Schklowski *et al.* (eds.).

Janssen, P. 1985. 'Political thought as traditionary action: the critical response to Skinner and Pocock', *History and Theory*, 24.

Jaurès, J. 1976a (1900). 'Prolétariat et bourgeoisie: certitude de l'antagonisme, possibilité de la cooperation', in Rebérioux (ed.).

1976b. *La classe ouvrière.* Paris: Maspero.

John, P. I. 1989a. 'On human work. Encyclical *Laborem Exercens*', in McGrath (ed.).

1989b. 'On social concern. *Sollecitudo Rei Socialis*', in Baum and Ellsberg (eds.).

John, X. 1964. '*Mater et Magistra.* Encyclical Letter of John XXIII', in Kirwan (ed.).

Johnston, A. 1991. *The Protestant Reformation in Europe.* London: Longman.

Jones, P. D. A. 1968. *The Christian Socialist Revival 1877–1914. Religion, Class, and Social Conscience in Late-Victorian England.* Princeton: Princeton University Press.

Juul, S. 1997. 'Solidaritet og integration i det moderne samfund', *Dansk sociologi*, 1.

Kagarlitsky, B. 1999. *New Realism – New Barbarism. Socialist Theory in the Era of Globalization.* London: Pluto Press.

2000. *The Return of Radicalism. Reshaping the Left Institutions.* London: Pluto Press.

Karvonen, L. 1994. 'Christian parties in Scandinavia: victory over the windmills', in Hanley (ed.).

Kasanski, B. 1970. 'Lenins Sprache', in Schklowski *et al.* (eds.).

Kautsky, K. 1915. *Det socialistiske program.* Oslo: Det Norske Arbeiderpartis Forlag.

1971. *The Class Struggle.* New York: Norton.

Kautto, M. *et al.* (eds.) 1999. *Nordic Social Policy. Changing Welfare States.* London: Routledge.

Kele, M. H. 1975. *Nazi and Workers. National Socialist Appeals to German Labor, 1919–1933.* Chapel Hill: University of North Carolina Press.

Kelley, D. R. 1990. What is happening to the history of ideas? *Journal of the History of Ideas* 51.

Kergoat, J. 1997. *Histoire du parti socialiste.* Paris: Editions la Decouverte.

Kersbergen, K. von 1995. *Social Capitalism. A Study of Christian Democracy and the Welfare State.* London: Routledge.

Ketteler, von 1952 (1864). 'Die Arbeitefrage und das Christentum', in Mommsen (ed.).

1979 (1869). 'Katholische Sozialpolitik. Eine Ansprache, gehalten auf der Liebfrauen-Heide bei Offenbach am 25. Juli 1869', in Heinen (ed.).

Kiersch 1979. 'Die französische Sozialistische Partei (PS)', in Paterson and Schmitz (eds.).

Kildal, N. (ed.) 2000. *Den nya sociala frågan. Om arbete, inkomst och rättvisa.* Göteborg: Daidalos.

Kingdon, R. and R. Linder (eds.) 1970. *Calvin and Calvinism. Sources of Democracy.* Lexington, MA: D.C. Heath and Company.

Kirwan, J. M. (ed.) 1964. *The Social Thought of John XXIII.* Birmingham, UK: Catholic Social Guild.

Kitschelt, H. 1993. 'Class structure and Social Democratic Party strategy', *British Journal of Politics* 3(23).

Kjeldstadli, K. 1997. 'Solidaritet og individualitet', in Coninck-Smith and Thing (eds.).

  2002. Fra Pariserkommunen til Porto Alegre. Hvordan og hvorfor oppstår sosiale bevegelser. Del 1. *Kontur 3.* Oslo.

Kjeldstadli, K. (ed.) 1994. *Et splittet samfunn. 1905–1935.* Aschehougs Norges historie. Oslo: Aschehoug.

Klüber, F. 1963. *Individuum und Gemeinschaft in katholischer Sicht.* Niedersachsen: Niedersächsischen Landeszentrale für Politisches Bildung.

Koht, H. 1977a (1923). 'Kommunisme og nasjonaltanke', in Koht (ed.).

Koht, H. (ed.) 1977b. *Norsk vilje.* Oslo: Noregs boklag.

Kokk, E. (ed.) 2001. *Socialdemokratins program 1897 till 1990.* Stockholm: Arbetarrörelsens arkiv og bibliotek.

Kopp, R. (ed.) 1984. *Solidarität in der Welt der 80er Jahre: Leistungsgesellschaft und Sozialstat.* Basle: Helbing & Lichtenhahn.

Koselleck, R. 1972. 'Einleitung', in Brunner, Conze and Koselleck (eds.).

  1996. 'A response to comments on the *Geschichtliche Grundbegriffe*', in Lehmann and Richter (eds.).

Koselleck, R. (ed.) 1989. *Vergangene Zukunft. Zur Semantik geschicthlicher Zeiten.* Frankfurt: Suhrkamp Taschenbuch Verlag.

Koslowski, P. and A. Føllesdal (eds.) 1997. *Restructuring the Welfare State. Theory of Reform of Social Policy.* London: Springer.

Kselman, T. and J. A. Buttigieg (eds.) 2003. *European Christian Democracy. Historical Legacies and Comparative Perspectives.* Notre Dame, IN: University of Notre Dame Press.

Küng, H. 1977. *20 teser om det 'at være kristen'.* Copenhagen: Niels Steensens Forlag.

  1988. *Theology for the Third Millenium. An Ecumenical View.* Doubleday: New York.

Küng, H. 2003b. 'Solo divieti, la Chiesa sta perdendo il suo popolo'. *Corriere della Sera*, 15 October, Milan.

Küng, H. (ed.) 1995. *Yes to a Global Ethic.* London: SMC Press.

  1997. *A Global Ethic for Global Politics and Economics.* London: SMC Press.

  2003a. *Ansprache. Reden zum Symposion anlässlich des 75. Geburtstag von Prof. Dr. Hans Küng*: http://uni-tuebingen.de/uni/uoi/kuenggeb/akueng.html. 18 December 2003.

Landtsheer, C. D. and O. Feldman (eds.) 2000. *Beyond Public Speech and Symbols. Explorations in the Rhetoric of Politicians and the Media.* Westport, CT: Praeger.

Lane, J.-E. and S. Ersson 1999. *Politics and Society in Western Europe.* London: Sage Publications.

Lange, E. (ed.) 1994. *Samling om felles mål 1935–1970.* Aschehougs Norges historie. Oslo: Aschehoug.

Le Bras-Chopard, A. 1992. 'Methamorphose d'une notion: La solidarité chez Pierre Leroux', in Chevallier *et al.* (eds.).

Lehmann, H. and M. Richter (eds.) 1996. *The Meaning of Historical Terms and Concepts.* Occasional Paper No. 15. Washington, DC: German Historical Institute.

Lenin, V. I. 1964 (1917). 'The state and revolution. The Marxist theory of the state and the tasks of the proletariat in the revolution', in *Collected Works,* vol. XXV. Moscow: Progress Publishers.

    1967 (1902). *What Is To Be Done?* Moscow: Progress Publishers.

Leo, X. 1983 (1891). *Rerum Novarum. Encyclical Letter of Pope Leo XIII on the Condition of the Working Classes.* London: Catholic Truth Society. The Ludo Press.

Leonardi, R. and M. Fedele (eds.) 2003. *Italy: Politics and Policy. Volume Two.* Aldershot: Ashgate.

Leroux, P. 1979 (1859). *La Greve de Samarez. Tome I.* Paris: Editions Klincksieck.

    1985 (1840). *De l'humanité.* Paris: Fayard.

Leung, J. and M. Kau (eds.) 1957. *The Writing of Mao Zedong.* New York: M. E. Sharpe.

Lewin, L. 1992. *Ideologi och strategi. Svensk politik under 100 år.* Stockholm: Norstedts Juridik.

Liedman, S.-E. 1999. *Att se sig själv i andra. Om solidaritet.* Falun: Bonnier Essä.

Lönne, K.-E. 1986. *Politischer Katholizismus im 19. und 20. Jahrhundert.* Frankfurt am Main: Suhrkamp.

    1996. 'Germany', in Buchanan and Conway (eds.).

Lorentzen, H. 2003. *Moderniseringen av sivilsamfunnet.* Oslo: PAX.

Loretro, P. d. 1991. *Togliatti e la 'doppiezza'. Il PCI tra democrazia e insurrezzione (1944–49).* Bologna: Il Mulino.

Lösche, P. 1998. 'Is the SPD still a Labor Party? From 'community of solidarity' to 'loosely coupled anarchy', in Barclay and Weitz (eds.).

Lösche, P. and F. Walter 1992. *Die SPD. Klassenpartei. Volkspartei. Quotenpartei.* Darmstadt: Wissenschaftliche Buchgesellschaft.

Luhmann, N. 1984. 'Die Differenzierung von Interaktion und Gesellschaft – Probleme der sozialen Solidarität', in Kopp (ed.).

    1993. *Das Recht der Gesellschaft.* Frankfurt: Suhrkamp.

Lukács, G. 1971 (1923). *Geschichte und Klassenbewusstsein.* Neuwied: Luchterhand.

Lukes, S. 1985. *Marxism and Morality.* Oxford: Clarendon Press.

    1998. 'Solidärität und Bürgerrecht', in Bayertz (ed.).

Lunde, N. T. (ed.) 1996. *Kristendemokratisk tenkning. En artikkelsamling om ideologi.* Oslo: Kristelig folkepartis studieforbund.

L'Unitá (ed.) 1986. *Il PCI e la Svolta del 1956*. Rome: Rinascita.

Luther, M. 1957 (1520). 'The freedom of a Christian', in Porter (ed.).

Macciotta, G. 1970. 'Rivoluzione e classe operaia negli scritti sull'Ordine Nuovo', in P. Rossi (ed.), *Gramsci e la cultura contemporanea*. Rome: Editori Riuniti.

MacIntyre, A. 2000 (1982). *After Virtue. A study in moral theory*. London: Duckworth.

Madeley, J. 1982. 'Politics and the pulpit: the case of Protestant Europe', in Berger (ed.).

Maier, L. 1979. 'Die Sozialistische Arbeiterparti Spaniens', in Paterson and Schmitz (eds.).

Malachowski, A. (ed.) 1990. *Reading Rorty. Critical Responses to 'Philosophy and the Mirror of Nature' and Beyond*. Cambridge: Basil Blackwell.

Marcucci, G. F. (ed.) 1983. *Documenti programmatici dei democratici cristiani (1899–1943)*. Rome: Edizioni Cinque Lune.

Marklund, S. and A. Nordlund 1999. 'Economic problems, welfare convergence and political instability', in Kautto *et al.* (eds.).

Marsh, D. 1992. *The New Politics of British Trade Unionism. Union Power and the Thatcher Legacy*. Basingstoke: Macmillan.

Marshall, G., H. Newby, D. Rose and C. Vogler 1988. *Social Class in Modern Britain*. London: Hutchinson.

Marshall, T. H. 1965a. 'Citizenship and social class', in Marshall.

Marshall (ed.) 1965b. *Class, Citizenship, and Social Development*. New York: Doubleday & Company.

Marx, K. 1971 (1864). 'Stiftelsesadresse fra den Internasjonale arbeiderassosiasjon', in Marx (ed.), *Karl Marx. Verker i utvalg 4. Politiske skrifter*. Oslo: Pax Forlag.

1998a (1846). *The German Ideology*. London: ElecBook.

1998b (1895). *The Class Struggle in France*. London: ElecBook.

Marx, K. and F. Engels 1959 (1848). 'Manifesto of the Communist Party', in Feuer (ed.).

1976 (1846). *The German Ideology. Collected Works*, vol. V. London: Lawrence and Wishart.

McGrath, E. (ed.) 1989. *The Priority of Labour*. Anand, India: Diaz el Rio.

McKibbin, R. 1990a. 'Why was there no Marxism in Great Britain?' in McKibbin (ed.).

1990b. *The Ideologies of Class. Social Relations in Britain 1880–1950*. Oxford: Clarendon Press.

Mckinney, J. and C. Loomis 1957. 'An application of *Gemeinschaft and Gesellschaft* as related to other typologies', in Tönnies (ed.).

McMillan, J. F. 1996. 'France', in Buchanan and Conway (eds.).

Meadows, D. *et al.* 1972. *The Limits to Growth*. New York: Universe Books.

Mény, Y. 1990. *Government and Politics in Western Europe. Britain, France, Italy, West Germany*. Oxford: Oxford University Press.

Merton, R. 1957. *Social Theory and Social Structure*. New York: The Free Press.

Meyer, T. 2001. 'From Godesberg to the *Neue Mitte*: the new Social Democracy in Germany', in Giddens (ed.).

Michels, R. 1914. *Probleme der Sozialphilosophie*. Leipzig and Berlin: B. G. Teubner.

Midttun, J. 1994. 'Sosialdemokrati og folkekirke. En undersøkelse av bakgrunnen og følgene av forandringen i Arbeiderpartiets offisielle holdning til kirke og kristendom på partilandsmøtet i 1975. Hovedoppgave i kristendom', *Det teologiske fakultet*. Oslo: University of Oslo.

Miliband, R. 1973. *The State in Capitalist Society*. London: Quartet books.

1989. *Divided Societies. Class Struggle in Contemporary Capitalism*. Oxford: Clarendon Press.

Minkin, L. 1991. *The Contentious Alliance. Trade Unions and the Labour Party*. Edinburgh: Edinburgh University Press.

Misgeld, K., K. K. Molin and K. Åmark (eds.) 1989. *Socialdemokratins samhälle. SAP och Sverige under 100 år*. Stockholm: Tiden.

Mitterand, F. 1981. '110 propositions pour la France', in Mitterand (ed.), *Politique 2 1977–1981*. Paris: Fayard.

1992. 'Lettre à tous les Français', in Chevallier *et al.* (eds.).

1995a. 'Discours devant le Bundestag. Bonn, le Jeudi 20 janvier 1983', in Mitterand, 1995d.

1995b. 'Lux du President aux Françaises, Vendredi 31 decembre 1982', in Mitterand, 1995d.

1995c. 'Realiser la nouvelle alliance du socialisme et de la liberté: inaugural speech in 1981', in Mitterand, 1995d.

1995d. *Discours 1981–1995*. Paris: Europolis.

Molaiolo, A. (ed.) 1981. *Il compagno 1. Quaderni di documentazione*. Rome: Partito Socialista Italiano.

1982. *PSI novanta anni di storia. Almanacco socialista. Cronistoria schede commenti documentazione sul socialismo italiano*. Rome.

Molony, J. N. 1977. *The Emergence of Political Catholicism in Italy. Partito Popolare 1919–1926*. London: Croom Helm.

Moltmann, J. 1969. *Religion, Revolution and the Future*. New York: Charles Scribner's Sons.

1970a. 'The Cross and civil religion', in Moltmann *et al.* (eds.).

Moltmann, J. *et al.* 1970b. *Religion and Political Society*. New York: Harper & Row.

1984a. *On Human Dignity. Political Theology and Ethics*. Philadelphia: Fortress Press.

1984b. *Politische Theologie. Politische Ethik*. Munich: Kaiser/Grünewald.

1989. *Creating a Just Future. The Politics of Peace and the Ethics of Creation in a Threatened World*. London: SCM Press.

Mommsen, W. (ed.) 1952. *Deutsche Parteiprogramme. Vom Vormärz bis zur Gegenwart*. Munich: Isar Verlag.

Montero, J. 1999. 'Stabilising the democratic order: electoral behaviour in Spain', in Heywood (ed.).

Montero, J. and R. Guenther 2002. 'Introduction: reviewing and reassessing parties', in Gunther, Montero and Linz (eds.).

Moody, K. 1997. *Workers in a Lean World. Unions in the International Economy*. London: Verso.

Moschonas, G. 2002. *In the Name of Social Democracy. The Great Transformation: 1945 to the Present*. London: Verso.

Mowat, C. L. 1968. *Britain. Between the Wars 1918–1940*. London: Methuen & Co.

Munck, R. 2002. *Globalisation and Labour. The New 'Great Transformation'*. London: Zed Books.

Murphy, D. 1978. 'Italien', in Raschke (ed.).

Mussolini, B. 1927. 'The Labor Charter. Promulgated by the Grand Council of Fascism on April 12, 1927', in Mussolini (ed.), *The Doctrine of Fascism*. New York: Howard Fertig.

1938. *The Corporate State*. Florence: Vallechi Publisher.

Narr, W.-D. 1966. *CDU-SPD. Programm und praxis seit 1945*. Stuttgart: W. Kohlhammer.

Nell-Breuning, O. von and H. Sacher 1954. *Zur Christlichen Gesellschaftslehre*. Freiburg: Herder.

Nielsen, K. Ø. (ed.) 1973. *Antionio Gramsci. Politikk og kultur*. Oslo: Gyldendal Norsk Forlag.

Noko, I. 2003. *Violence Cannot Create Peace, Only Lead to more Violence*, Lutheran World Federation, 7 March.

NSDAP (ed.) 1936. *Der Parteitag der Ehre. Vom 8. bis 14. September 1936. Offizieller Bericht über den Verlauf des Reichsparteitages mit sämtlichen Kongressreden*. Munich: Zentralverlag der NSDAP, Franz Eher Nachf.

Nullmeyer, F. and F. W. Rüb 1993. *Die Transformation der Sozialpolitik. Vom Sozialstaat zum Sicherungsstaat*. Frankfurt: Campus.

Nyhamar, J. 1990. *Nye utfordringer (1965–1990), vol. 6 Arbeiderbevegelsens historie*. Oslo: Tiden Norsk Forlag.

Offe, C. 1987. 'Democracy against the welfare state? Structural foundations of neoconservative political opportunities', *Political Theory* 4(15).

Olsen, E. 2001. *Den røde tråd*. Copenhagen: Socialdemokratiet.

Olson, M. 1965. *The Logic of Collective Action. Public Goods and the Theory of Groups*. Cambridge, MA: Harvard University Press.

Oorschot, W. v. 2001. 'Popular support for social security', in Classen (ed.).

Oorschot, W. v. and A. Komter 1998. 'What is it that ties? Theoretical perspectives on social bond', *Tÿdschrift Sociale Wetenschappen*, 41(3).

Ormières, J.-L. 2002. *Politique et religion en France*. Brussels: Editions Complexe.

Østerberg, D. 1988. *Metasociology. An Inquiry into the Origins and Validity of Social Thought*. Oslo: Norwegian University Press.

Otto, H.-U. and H. Sünker 1989a. 'Nationalsozialismus, Volksgemeinschaftside-ologie und Soziale Arbeit', in Otto and Sünker (eds.).

Otto, H.-U. and H. Sünker (eds.) 1989b. *Soziale Arbeit und Faschismus*. Frankfurt: Suhrkamp Verlag.

Padgett, S. and W. Paterson 1991. *A History of Social Democracy in Postwar Europe*. London: Longman.

Paine, R. (ed.) 1981. *Politically Speaking. Cross-Cultural Studies of Rhetoric*. Philadelphia, PA: ISHI Inc.

Palme, O. 1969. *Politik är att vilja*. Stockholm: Bokförlaget Prisma.

(1960). 'Individen och kollektivet', in Hansson (ed.).

378   List of references

1996a (1968). 'Ungdomsprotesten 1968', in Hansson (ed.).

1996b (1973). 'Et demokratiskt genombrott', in Hansson (ed.).

Paolo IV. 1967. *Lettera Enciclica Populorum Progressio di Sua Santita Paolo VI.* Milan: Vita e Pensiero.

Parsons, T. 1951. *The Social System.* Glencoe: The Free Press of Glencoe.

1969. *Poltics and the Social Structure.* New York/London: The Free Press/Collier-Macmillan.

1971. *The System of Modern Societies.* Englewood Cliffs, NJ: Prentice-Hall.

Passy, F. 2001. 'Political altruism and the solidarity movement', in Giugni and Passy (eds.).

Paterson, W. and K. Schmitz (eds.) 1979. *Sozialdemokratische Parteien in Europa.* Bonn: Neue Gesellschaft GmbH.

PCI 1988. 'The political documents of the 18th Congress. Vol. 4', in *The Italian Communists.*

Peignot, J. 1988. *Pierre Leroux. Inventeur du socialisme.* Paris: Éditions Klincksieck.

Pelling, H. 1966. *The Origins of the Labour Party 1800–1900.* Oxford: Clarendon Press.

Pensky, M. (ed.) 2001. *Jürgen Habermas: The Postnational Constellation. Political Essays.* Cambridge: Polity.

Pesch, H. 1901. *Liberalismus, Socialismus und christliche Gesellschaftsordnung. Erster teil.* Freiburg: Herder'sche Verlagshandlung.

1919. *Christlicher Solidarismus und soziales Arbeitssystem.* Berlin.

1998 (1924). *Heinrich Pesch on Solidarist Economics. Excerpts from the Lehrbuch der Nationalökonomie.* Lanham: University Press of America.

Pharo, H. 1987. 'Indiafondet: Norsk bistand i utviklingshjelpens barndom', in Eriksen (ed.).

Pio XI 1931. *Quadragesimo Anno. Lettera Enciclica di S.S. PiO XI.* Rome: The Vatican.

Pitchers, A. 1997. *The Christology of Hans Küng. A Critical Examination.* Berne: Peter Lang.

Plaschke, J. 1984. 'Subsidiarität und "neue Subsidiarität". Wandel den Aktions-formen gesellschaftlicher Problembewältigung', in Bauer and Diessenbacher (eds.).

Pocock, J. G. A. 1985. *Virtue, Commerce, and History.* New York: Cambridge University Press.

Pollard, J. 1996. 'Italy', in Buchanan and Conway (eds.).

Porter, J. M. (ed.) 1957. *Martin Luther. Selected Political Writings.* Philadelphia, PA: Fortress Press.

Poulantzas, N. 1978. *Political Power and Social Classes.* London: Verso.

Projektgruppe Parteiensystem. 1978. 'Bundesrepublik Deutschland', in Raschke (ed.).

Pryser, T. 1977. *Thranerørsla i norske bygder.* Oslo: Det norske samlaget.

1988. *Klassen og nasjonen (1935–1946), vol. 4 Arbeiderbevegelsens historie.* Oslo: Tiden Norsk Forlag.

Przeworski, A. 1980. 'Social democracy as a historical phenomenon', *New Left Review.*

1985. *Capitalism and Social Democracy.* Cambridge: Cambridge University Press.

Quillliot, R. (ed.) 1972. *La S.F.I.O et l'exercice du pouvoir 1944–1958.* Paris: Fayard.

Raguer, H. 1990. 'La presenza politico-sociale e il confronto con le ideologie', in Alberigo and Riccardi (eds.).

Rallings, C. 1987. 'The influence of election programs: Britain and Canada 1945–1979', in Budge, Robertson and Hearl (eds.).

Ramet, S. 2000. 'Religion and politics in Germany since 1945: the evangelical and Catholic churches', *Journal of Church & State* (Winter).

Raschke, J. (ed.) 1978. *Die politische Parteien in Westeuropa. Geschichte – Programm – Praxis. Ein Handbuch.* Hamburg: Rowohlt.

Rasmussen, P. N. 2001. Jeg svigter ikke. *Berlingske Tidende* 23 December. Copenhagen.

Rawls, J. 1971. *A Theory of Justice.* Cambridge, MA: Belknap Press of Harvard University Press.

1985. 'Justice as fairness: political, not metaphysical', *Philosophy and Public Affairs*, 14.

Rebérioux, M. (ed.) 1976. *La classe ouvrière.* Paris: Maspero.

Rehg, W. 1994. *Insight and Solidarity. A Study in the Discourse Ethics of Jürgen Habermas.* Berkeley: University of California Press.

Rhodes, M. 1997. 'Southern European welfare states: identity, problems and prospects for reform', in Rhodes (ed.), *Southern European Welfare States. Between Crisis and Reform.* London: Frank Cass.

Riccardi, A. 1990. 'Da Giovanni XXIII a Paolo VI', in Alberigo and Riccardi (eds.).

2003. *Pio XXII e Alcide De Gasperi – una storie segreta.* Rome and Bari: Laterza.

Richter, M. 1995. *The History of Political and Social Concepts.* Oxford: Oxford University Press.

Riddell, J. (ed.) 1987a. *The Second Congress of the Communist International, 1920.* Moscow: Pathfinder.

1987b (1919). *Founding the Communist International: proceedings and documents of the First Congress.* New York: Anchor Foundation.

Rimehaug, E. 1997. *Midtbanespilleren: Kjell Magne Bondevik og Kristelig folkeparti.* Oslo: Luther Forlag.

Rokkan, S. 1966. 'Norway: numerical democracy and corporate pluralism', in Dahl (ed.).

Rorty, R. 1989. *Contingency, Irony and Solidarity.* Cambridge: Cambridge University Press.

Rothstein, B. 2000. 'Universell välfärdsstat och medborgarinkomst – en kritisk analys', in Kildal (ed.).

Sabatucci, G. (ed.) 1976. *La crisi italiana del primo dopoguerra: La storia e la critica.* Rome: no publisher.

Sassoon, D. 1981. *The Strategy of the Italian Communist Party.* New York: St. Martin's Press.

1996. *One Hundred Years of Socialism. The West European Left in the Twentieth Century.* London: I.B. Tauris.

380 List of references

1999. 'Premature obsequies: social democracy comes in from the cold', in Gamble and Wright (eds.).

2003. 'Reflections on a death foretold: the life and times of the Italian Communist Party', in Leonardi and Fedele (eds.).

Scheler, M. 1966 (1913–16). *Der Formalismus in der Ethik und die Materiale Wertethik. Neuer Versuch der Grundlegung eines ethischen Personalismus.* Bern: Francke.

Schjørring, J. H., P. Kumari, N. A. Hjelm and V. Mortensen (eds.) 1997. *From Federation to Communion. The History of the Lutheran World Federation.* Minneapolis: Fortress Press.

Schklowski, V. *et al.* (eds.) 1970. *Sprache und Stils Lenins.* Munich: Carl Hanser.

Schmid, H. 1997. 'Den fornuftige solidaritet', *Dansk sociologi.*

Schmidt, U. 1987. *Zentrum oder CDU. Politischer Katholizismus zwischen Tradition und Anpassung.* Opladen: Westdeutscher Verlag.

Schreiber, G. (ed.) 1924. *Grundfragen der Zentrumspolitik. Ein politisches Handbuch in Frage und Antwort.* Berlin: Verlag der Germania A.-G.

Schulze, M.-S. (ed.) 1999. *Western Europe. Economic and Social Change since 1945.* London: Longman.

Schumacher, K. 1973 (1945). 'Politische Richtlinien für die SPD in ihrem Verhältnis zu den anderen politische Faktoren, 1945', in Dowe and Klotzbach (eds.).

Scoppola, P. 1976. 'L'affermazione e crisi del P.P.I.', in Sabatucci (ed.).

Seigel, J. 1987. 'Autonomy and personality in Durkheim: an essay on content and method'. *Journal of the History of Ideas* 5.

Severino, B. Q. d. (ed.) 1923. *Mussolini as Revealed in his Political Speeches (November 1914–August 1923).* London: J.M. Dent & Sons.

Share, D. 1989. *Dilemmas of Social Democracy. The Spanish Socialist Workers Party in the 1980s.* New York: Greenwood Press.

Sigel, R. 1986. *Die Geschichte der Zweiten Internationale 1918–1923.* Frankfurt: Campus.

Simon, H. A. 1947. *Administrative Behavior: a study of decision-making processes in administrative organization.* New York: The Macmillan Company.

Singer, P. 2002. *One World: The ethics of globalization.* New Haven/London: Yale University Press.

Sivertsen, H. 1975. Arbeiderpartiet og kristendommen. *Sosialistisk Perspektiv* 5.

Skinner, Q. 1969. 'Meaning and understanding in the history of ideas', *History and Theory* 8.

1980. *The Foundations of Modern Political Thought,* vols. I–II. Cambridge: Cambridge University Press.

1988. 'A reply to my critics', in Tully (ed.).

Skipevåg, L. M. 1990. 'Ein systematisk, kritisk analyse av Kristeleg Folkeparti si tenking om forholdet mellom kristendom og politikk i 1933 og 1945'. Hovudoppgåve i kristendomskunnskap vårsemestret 1990. Oslo: Det teologiske Menighetsfakultetet.

Slagstad, R. 1998. *De nasjonale strateger.* Oslo: Pax Forlag.

2001. *Rettens ironi.* Oslo: Pax Forlag.

Smith, D. M. 1997. *Storia d'Italia dal 1861 al 1997.* Rome and Bari: Editori Laterzi.

Sonne, H. 1974. *Stauning eller kaos. Socialdemokratiet og krisen i trediverne.* Copenhagen: Hans Reitzel.

Sørensen, Ø. 1991. *Solkors og solidaritet. Høyreautoritær samfunnstenkning i Norge ca. 1930–1945.* Oslo: J. W. Cappelens Forlag A.S.

Steenson, G. P. 1991. *After Marx, Before Lenin. Marxism and Socialist Working-Class Parties in Europe, 1884–1914.* Pittsburgh: University of Pittsburgh Press.

Sternhell, Z. 2001. 'Fascism and the fate of ideas. Reflections on the fate of ideas in twentieth-century history', in Freeden (ed.).

Stjernø, S. 1995. *Mellom kirke og kapital. Tysk velferdspolitikk med sideblikk til engelsk, svensk og norsk.* Oslo: Universitetsforlaget.

Stjernø, S. and A. Johannessen 2004. 'Attitudes of solidarity. A comparative study of eight nations in Western Europe'. Working Paper. Oslo: Oslo University College.

Sturzo, D. L. 1983 (1905). 'Il discorso di Caltagirone (1905)', in Marcucci (ed.).

Svallfors, S. 1996. *Välfärdsstatens moraliska ekonomi.* Umeå: Boréa Bokförlag.

— 1997. 'Worlds of welfare and attitudes to redistribution: a comparison of eight nations', *European Sociological Review* 3(13).

Svallfors, S. and P. Taylor-Goobye (eds.) 1999. *The End of the Welfare State? Responses to State Retrenchment.* London: Routledge.

Svensson, A. 1984. *Anspielung und Stereotyp. Eine linguistische Untersuchung des politischen Sprachgebrauch am Beispiel der SPD.* Opladen: Westdeutscher Verlag.

Svensson, T. 1994. *Socialdemokratins dominans. En studie av den svenska socialdemokratins partistrategi.* Uppsala: Uppsala Universitet.

Swank, D. 2000. 'Social democratic welfare states in a global economy: Scandinavia in comparative perspective', in Geyer *et al.* (eds.).

Tarrow, S. 1998. *Power in Movement. Social Movements and Contentious Politics.* Cambridge: Cambridge University Press.

— 2003. Beyond globalization: why creating transnational social movements is so hard and when is it most likely to happen? www.antenna.nl/~waterman/tarrow.html.

Terrill, R. 1973. *R.H. Tawney and his Times. Socialism as Fellowship.* Cambridge, MA: Harvard University Press.

Therborn, G. 1989. 'Nation och klass, tur och skicklighet', in Misgeld, Molin and Åmark (eds.).

Thomson, S. 2000. *The Social Democratic Dilemma.* London: Macmillan.

Thorez, M. (ed.). 1936. *De la nation française.* Paris: PCF.

Tilly, C. 2001. 'Do unto others', in Giugni and Passy (eds.).

Tilton, T. 1990. *The Political Theory of Swedish Social Democracy. Through the Welfare State to Socialism.* Oxford: Clarendon Press.

Titmuss, R. 1968. *Commitment to Welfare.* New York: Pantheon Books.

Todd, E. 1991. *The Making of Modern France. Ideology, Politics and Culture.* Oxford: Blackwell.

Togliatti, P. 1969a (1944). 'La politica di unitá nazionale dei comunisti. Rapporto ai quadri dell'organizzazione comunista napoletana, 11 aprile 1944', in Togliatti (ed.).

— 1969b (1944). 'Unitá nazionale. Da Rinascita, anno I n. 3, agosto-settembre 1944', in Togliatti (ed.).

Togliatti, P. 1974 (1947). 'Per una Costituzione democratica e progressiva. Dal discorso tenuto all'Assemblea costituente l'11 marzo 1947', in Gruppi (ed.).

Togliatti, P. (ed.) 1969c. *La politica di Salerno*. Rome: Editori Riuniti.

Tombs, D. 2002. *Latin American Liberation Theology*. Boston: Brill Academic Publishers.

Tønnesen, A. 2000. '. . . *et trygt og godt hjem for alle'? Kirkelederes kritikk av velferdsstaten etter 1945*. Trondheim: Tapir Akademisk Forlag.

Tönnies, F. 1957. *Community & Society*. East Lansing: Michigan State University Press.

Tully, J. (ed.) 1988. *Meaning and Context. Quentin Skinner and his Critics*. Cambridge: Polity Press.

Turner, B. and C. Rojek 2001. *Society & Culture. Principles of Scarcity and Solidarity*. London: Sage Publications.

Turner, D. (ed.) 1968. *The Church in the World*. Dublin: Scepter Books.

Tynjanow, J. 1970. 'Das Wörterbuch des Polemikers Lenin', in Schklowski *et al.* (eds.).

Uertz, R. 1981. *Christentum und Sozialismus in der frühen CDU. Grundlagen und Wirkungen der christlich-sozialen Ideen in der Union 1945–1949*. Stuttgart: Deutsche Verlags-Anstalt.

Universita di Bologna (ed.) 1967. *Due documenti per la storia politica dei cattolici italiani. In occasione del Convegno di Studio della Democrazia Cristiana. Lucca 28–30 aprile 1967*. Bologna: Istituto Giuridico, Universita di Bologna.

Valli, B. 2001. Wojtyla e il Concilio – un' Ereditá che divide. *La Repubblica*. Florence: 10–11.

Vandenbroucke, F. 1999. 'European social democracy: convergence, divisions, and shared questions', in Gamble and Wright (eds.).

Vetlesen, A. J. 1994. *Perception, Empathy, and Judgement. An Inquiry into the Preconditions of Moral Performance*. University Park, PA: Pennsylvania University Press.

Vincent, M. 1996. 'Spain', in Buchanan and Conway (eds.).

Waterman, P. 2000. 'Nine theses on a new global solidarity', http://www.antenna.nl/^waterman/Pages/Peters/ninetheses.htm.

Webb, P. 2002. 'Conclusion: political parties and democratic control in advanced industrial societies', in Webb, P., D. Farrel and I. Holliday (eds.) 2002. *Political Parties in Advanced Industrial Democracies*. Oxford: Oxford University Press.

Weber, M. (ed.) 1978 (1922). *Economy and Society. An Outline of Interpretive Sociology*. Berkeley: University of California Press.

Webster, R. A. 1961. *Christian Democracy in Italy. 1860–1960*. London: Hollis & Carter.

Went, R. 2002. *The Enigma of Globalization. A journey to a new stage of capitalism*. London: Routledge.

Wertman, D. 1982. 'The Catholic Church and Italian politics: the impact of secularisation', in Berger (ed.).

White, S. F. 2003. 'Christian democracy and Pacellian populism? Rival forms of postwar Italian populism', in Kselman and Buttigieg (eds.).

Wigforss, E. (ed.) 1941. *Från klasskamp til samverkan*. Stockholm: Tidens Förlag.

Wildt, A. 1998. 'Solidäritet – Begriffsgeschichte und Definition heute', in Bayertz (ed.).

1999. 'Solidarity: its history and contemporary definition', in Bayertz (ed.).

Wilson, D. J. 1987. 'Lovejoy's *The Great Chain of Being* after Fifty Years', *Journal of the History of Ideas* 48.

Wolfe, A. 1989. *Whose Keeper? Social Science and Moral Obligation*. Berkeley: University of California Press.

Wright, A. 1999. 'Social democracy and democratic socialism', in Eatwell and Wright (eds.).

Wright, E. O. 2000. *Class Counts*. Cambridge: Cambridge University Press.

Zedong, M. 1957. 'On correctly handling contradictions among the people', in Leung and Kau (eds.).

Zetkin, C. 1971 (1928). *Zur Geschichte der proletarischen Frauenbwegung Deutschlands*. Frankfurt: Verlag Roter Stern.

1974a (1889). 'Nutidens arbejderkvindespørsmål', in E. Caspersen (ed).

1974b (1896). 'Uden arbejderkvinder ingen sejr for socialismen', in E. Caspersen (ed).

Zoll, R. 2000. *Was ist Solidarität heutu?* Frankfurt: Suhrkamp Verlag.

Index

Printed in Great Britain
by Amazon

78009446R00234